The Invention of a People

Plateaus – New Directions in Deleuze Studies

'It's not a matter of bringing all sorts of things together under a single concept but rather of relating each concept to variables that explain its mutations.'
Gilles Deleuze, *Negotiations*

## Series Editors

Ian Buchanan, University of Wollongong
Claire Colebrook, Penn State University

### Editorial Advisory Board

Keith Ansell Pearson
Ronald Bogue
Constantin V. Boundas
Rosi Braidotti
Eugene Holland
Gregg Lambert
Dorothea Olkowski
Paul Patton
Daniel Smith
James Williams

### Titles available in the series

### Forthcoming volumes:

Visit the Plateaus website at www.euppublishing.com/series/plat

# THE INVENTION OF A PEOPLE
## Heidegger and Deleuze on
## Art and the Political

*Janae Sholtz*

EDINBURGH
University Press

Edinburgh University Press Ltd
13 Infirmary Street, Edinburgh, EH1 1LT

First published in hardback by Edinburgh University Press 2015

www.euppublishing.com

Typeset in Sabon by
Servis Filmsetting Ltd, Stockport, Cheshire

A CIP record for this book is available from the British Library

ISBN 978 0 7486 8535 6 (hardback)
ISBN 978 1 3995 5422 0 (paperback)
ISBN 978 0 7486 8536 3 (webready PDF)
ISBN 978 0 7486 8537 0 (epub)

# Contents

# Acknowledgements

Thanks to my mentors, those who have inspired me, and those who supported my work at conferences or otherwise, Len Lawlor, Robert Bernasconi, Mary Beth Mader, Sarah Clark Miller, Claudia Baracchi, Dorothea Olkowski, Manfred Frank, Berta Nance, Cynthia Marshall, Ellen Armour, Pat Shade, Miguel De Beistegui, Ronald Bogue, Dennis Schmidt, Daniel Smith, Daniella Vallega-Neu, Alejandro Vallega, Drew Hyland, Dale Wilkerson, Jason Wirth, John Drabinski, and for comments, Andy Amato, Mike Ardoline, Jared Bly, Josh Hayes, David Macauley, Magus Magnus, Anish Patel, Louis Ruprecht, Sam Talcott.

Thanks to Alvernia University for support through Faculty Excellence Grants and the Faculty Salon Series, and the intellectual inspiration of my colleagues; Brian Fridge, the Bacon Estate, the Higgins Estate, Rosenthal Gallery and Geoffrey Hendricks for gracious permissions and artwork; Carol Macdonald for promoting my project and Edinburgh Press editorial staff for facilitating its progression; Ian Buchanan and Claire Colebrook for accepting this project into the series.

Thanks and love to Kyle and Julien, for the crazy and amazing path that we have forged together; my entire family for patience and love; my friends, especially Len Lawlor, for guidance, unwavering encouragement, and being a kindred spirit; Cheri Carr, for keeping my spark, intellectual and otherwise, spritely; Sharin Elkholy, for incisive scrutiny and caring friendship, and Ruth Hall McFall, for being my rock, always.

# Abbreviations

## Works by Martin Heidegger

BW    *Basic Writings*, ed. David Farrell Krell (New York: HarperCollins, 1993)

EGT    *Early Greek Thinking*, trans. D. Farrell Krell and F.A. Capuzzi (New York: Harper & Row, 1975)

GA    *Gesamtausgabe* (Frankfurt am Main: Vittorio Klostermann)

GA2    *Sein und Zeit* (1977)
     *Being and Time: A Translation of Sein und Zeit*, trans. Joan Stambaugh (Albany, NY: State University of New York Press, 1997)

GA4    *Erläuterungen zu Holderlins Dichtung* (1981)
     pp. 24–49, 'Homecoming/To Kindred Ones', in *Elucidations of Hölderlin's Poetry*, trans. Keith Hoeller (New York: Humanity Books, 2000)
     pp. 51–65, 'Hölderlin and the Essence of Poetry', in *Elucidations*
     pp. 175–207, 'Hölderlin's Earth and Heaven', in *Elucidations*

GA5    *Holzwege*, 1935–46 (1977)
     pp. 57–72, 'The Age of the World Picture', in *Off the Beaten Track*, ed. and trans. Julian Young and Kenneth Haynes (Cambridge: Cambridge University Press, 2002)

GA6.1   *Nietzsche, 1936–39* (1996)
     pp. 1–220, *Nietzsche, Vol. I, The Will to Power as Art*, trans. David Farrell Krell (San Francisco: HarperSanFrancisco, 1991)
     pp. 1–233, *Nietzsche, Vol. II, The Eternal Recurrence of the Same*, trans. David Farrell Krell (San Francisco: HarperSanFrancisco, 1991)

GA6.2   *Nietzsche, 1939–46* (1997)
     pp. 1–287, *Nietzsche, Vol. 3, The Will to Power as Knowledge and as Metaphysics*, ed. David Farrell Krell (San Francisco: HarperSanFrancisco, 1991)

pp. 1–250, *Nietzsche, Vol. 4, Nihilism*, ed. David Farrell Krell (San Francisco: HarperSanFrancisco, 1991)

GA7   *Vorträge und Aufsätze* (2000)

pp. 1–35, 'The Question Concerning Technology', in *The Question Concerning Technology, and Other Essays*, trans. William Lovitt (New York: Harper & Row, 1977)

GA9   *Wegmarken* (1976)

pp. 136–54, 'On the Essence of Truth', trans. John Sallis, in *Pathmarks*, ed. William McNeill (Cambridge: Cambridge University Press, 1998)

GA11  *Identität und Differenz* (2006)

*Identity and Difference*, trans. Joan Stambaugh (New York: Harper & Row, 1974)

pp. 36–49, 'The Turning', in *The Question Concerning Technology, and Other Essays*, trans. William Lovitt (New York: Harper & Row, 1977)

GA38  *Logik als Frage nach dem Wesen der Sprache* (Summer Semester 1934), (1998)

GA39  *Hölderlins Hymnen 'Germanien' und 'Der Rhein'* (Winter Semester 1934/5), (1980)

GA40  *Einführung in die Metaphysik* (Summer Semester 1935), (1983)
*Introduction to Metaphysics*, trans. G. Fried and R. Polt (New Haven: Yale University Press, 2009)

GA45  *Grundfragen der Philosophie: Ausgewahlte 'Probleme' der 'Logik'* (Winter Semester 1937/8), ed. Friedrich-Wilhelm von Herrman (1984)

GA51  *Grundbegriffe* (Summer Semester 1941) (1981)
*Basic Writings: From Being and Time (1927) to the Task of Thinking (1964)*, trans. David Farrell Krell (New York: Harper & Row Publishers, 1977)

GA53  *Hölderlins Hymne 'Der Ister'* (Summer Semester, 1942), (1984)
*Hölderlin's Hymn 'The Ister'*, trans. William McNeill and Julia Davis (Bloomington: Indiana University Press, 1996)

GA54  *Parmenides* (Winter Semester 1942/3), (1982)
*Parmenides*, trans. Andre Schuwer and Richard Rojcewicz (Bloomington: Indiana University Press, 1998)

GA65  *Beiträge zur Philosophie (Vom Ereignis)*, (1989)
*Contributions to Philosophy (From Enowning)*, trans. Parvis Emad and Kenneth Maly (Indianapolis: Indiana University Press, 1999)

GA89    *Zollikoner Seminaire: Protokolle – Gespräche – Briefe* (1989)
*Zollikon Seminars. Protocols-Conversations-Letters*. ed. M.
Boss, trans. R. Askay and F. Mayr (Evanston: Northwestern
University Press, 2001)

H    *Holzwege*, 5th edn (Frankfurt am Main: Vittorio Klosterman,
1972)
pp. 1–56, 'The Origin of the Work of Art', in *Off the Beaten
Track*, ed. and trans. Julian Young and Kenneth Haynes
(Cambridge: Cambridge University Press, 2002)
pp. 91–142, 'What are Poets For?', in *Poetry, Language,
Thought*, trans. Albert Hofstadter (New York: Harper &
Row, 1971)

NI/    *Nietzsche, Vols. 1 and 2*, trans. David Farrell Krell (San
NII    Francisco: HarperSanFrancisco, 1991)

NIII/    *Nietzsche, Vols. 3 and 4*, ed. David Farrell Krell (San
IV    Francisco: HarperSanFrancisco, 1991)

OBT    *Off the Beaten Track*, trans. Julian Young and Kenneth
Haynes (Cambridge: Cambridge University Press, 2002)

Of    'Of the Origin of the Work of Art (first elaboration)', trans.
Markus Zisselsberger, in *Epoché* 12:2 (2008)

Ofr    *De l'origine de l'oeuvre d'art. Premiére version (1935)*, ed. E.
Martineau (Paris: Authentica, 1987)

OWL    *On the Way to Language*, trans. Peter D. Hertz (New York:
Harper & Row, 1982)

PLT    *Poetry, Language, Thought*, trans. Albert Hofstadter (New
York: Harper & Row, 1971)

R    'Rectoral Address: The Self-Assertion of the German
University', in *The Heidegger Reader*, trans. G. Veith, ed. G.
Figal (Indiana: Indiana University Press, 2000), pp. 108–15

VS    '*Vier Seminare*' (Frankfurt am Main: Klostermann, 1986)
*Four Seminars* (Bloomington: Indiana University Press,
2003)

WHD    *Was Heisst Denken?* (Tübingen: Max Niemeyer, 1997
[1954])
*What is Called Thinking?* trans. J. Glenn Gray (New York:
Harper Perennial, 2004)

Wm    *Wegmarken*, 2nd edn (Frankfurt am Main: Klostermann,
1967)
pp. 213–53, *The Question of Being*, trans. Jean T. Wilde and
William Kluback (New Haven: College and University Press,
1958)

## Works by Gilles Deleuze

B        *Bergsonism*, trans. Hugh Tomlinson and Barbara Habberjam
         (New York: Zone Books, 1988)

CI       *Cinéma I: L'Image-Mouvement* (Paris: Les Éditions de
         Minuit, 1983)
         *Cinema I: The Movement-Image*, trans. Hugh Tomlinson and
         Barbara Habberjam (Minneapolis: University of Minnesota
         Press, 2001)

CII      *Cinema II: The Time-Image*, trans. Hugh Tomlinson
         (Minneapolis: University of Minnesota Press, 2001)

DR       *Différence et Répétition* (Paris: Presses Universitaires de
         France, 11th edn 2003 [1968])
         *Difference and Repetition*, trans. Paul Patton (New York:
         Columbia University Press, 1994)

ECC      *Essays Critical and Clinical*, trans. Dan Smith and
         Michael Greco (Minneapolis: University of Minnesota Press,
         1997)

EPS      *Spinoza et la problème de l'expression* (Paris: Les Éditions de
         Minuit, 1968)
         *Expressionism in Philosophy: Spinoza*, trans. Martin Joughin
         (New York: Zone Books, 1990)

F        *Foucault* (Paris: Les Éditions de Minuit, 1986)
         *Foucault*, trans. Seán Hand (Minneapolis: University of
         Minnesota Press, 1988)

FB       *Francis Bacon: Logique de la sensation* (Paris: Seuil, 1981)
         *Francis Bacon: The Logic of Sensation*, trans. Daniel Smith
         (Minneapolis: University of Minnesota Press, 2004)

ID       *L'île déserte et autre textes. Textes et entretiens 1953–1974*
         (Paris: Les Éditions de Minuit, 2002)
         *Desert Islands and Other Texts 1953–1974*, trans. Michael
         Taormina (New York: Semiotext(e), 2004)

LS       *Logique du sens* (Paris: Les Éditions de Minuit, 1969)
         *The Logic of Sense*, trans. Mark Lester (New York: Columbia
         University Press, 1990)

N        *Negotiations 1972–1990*, trans. Martin Joughin (New York:
         Columbia University Press, 1995)

NP       *Nietzsche et la philosophie* (Paris: Presses Universitaires de
         France, 1994 [1962])
         *Nietzsche and Philosophy*, trans. Hugh Tomlinson (New
         York: Columbia University Press, 1983)

PS    *Proust et les signes* (Paris: Quadrige, Presses Universitaires de France, 1996 [1964])
      *Proust and Signs: The Complete Text*, trans. Richard Howard (Minneapolis: University of Minnesota Press, 2000)

RP    'Reversing Platonism', trans. Heath Massey, in Len Lawlor, *Thinking Through French Philosophy: The Being of the Question* (Bloomington: Indiana University Press, 2003)

TRM   *Two Regimes of Madness Texts and Interviews 1975–1995*, trans. Ames Hodges and Mike Taormina (New York: Semiotext(e), 2006)

## Works by Gilles Deleuze and Félix Guattari

AO    *Capitalisme et schizophrénie. L'anti-œdipe* (Paris: Les Éditions de Minuit, 1972/1973)
      *Anti-Oedipus: Capitalism and Schizophrenia*, trans. Robert Hurley, Mark Seem and Helen R. Lane (New York: The Viking Press, 1983)

MP    *Capitalisme et schizophrénie tome 2. Mille plateaux* (Paris: Les Éditions de Minuit, 1980)
      *A Thousand Plateaus: Capitalism and Schizophrenia*, trans. Brian Massumi (Minneapolis: University of Minnesota Press, 1987)

K     *Kafka. Pour une literature mineure* (Paris: Les Éditions de Minuit, 1975)
      *Kafka: For a Minor Literature*, trans. Dana Polan (Minneapolis: University of Minnesota Press, 1986)

QP    *Qu'est-ce que la philosophie?* (Paris: Les Éditions de Minuit, 1991)
      *What is Philosophy?* trans. Hugh Tomlinson and Graham Burchell (New York: Columbia University Press, 1996)

## Works by Gilles Deleuze and Claire Parnet

D     *Dialogues* (Paris: Flammarion, 1977)
      *Dialogues*, trans. Hugh Tomlinson and Barbara Habberjam (New York: Columbia University Press, 2007)

Where both original and English translation page numbers are given, original first and English second.

# Introduction

## *Inspirations*

Thinking about the conception of this project, I am drawn back to a very particular point in my graduate studies at the New School for Social Research, to a moment which has remained with me as the years have progressed and my philosophical journey has crystallised. That moment was during a lecture given by my professor, Claudia Baracchi, whom I had come to admire for her intellectual elegance, insight, and inspiration concerning Plato's *Ion*. Socrates is questioning Ion, the rhapsode, about the nature of his skill in interpreting poetry and, by extension, the source of the poet's gift – whether it be wisdom or inspiration. Socrates then presents an image of the nature of inspiration:

> It's a divine power that moves you, as a 'Magnetic' stone moves iron rings. (That's what Euripides called it; most people call it 'Heraclian'.) This stone not only pulls those rings, if they're iron, it also puts power in the rings, so that they in turn can do just what the stone does – pull other rings – so that there's sometimes a very long chain of iron pieces and rings hanging from one another. And the power in all of them depends on this stone. In the same way, the Muse makes some people inspired herself, and then through those who are inspired a chain of other enthusiasts is suspended.[1]

Inspiration extends from the divine through the poet to the listener herself, a vibratory chain that reaches to the very core of one's being. Thinking about certain melodies that had haunted me, or words that had moved me, this image seemed to ring true, as an image that encompassed more than just the poetic. I began to think of this as an image of my experience of philosophy. Of course, this dialogue is meant to separate the task of the poet and the philosopher. The poet's poeticising is no art, in the sense of *technē* as knowledge about the nature of that which is spoken, but an affective connection, a channelling of elusive and vertiginous elements and forces. Yet, even

1

maintaining that philosophy is about sober, rational discourse and knowledge, what is it that sets one on the path in the first place, to pick up with one philosopher over another? I experienced this vibratory force when I read Heidegger for the first time, and then, again, with Deleuze. I have never been able to give up either and have found myself constantly reading and thinking them together. I am inspired by both and these connections have very literally served to amplify my own voice, which has resulted in the work that is before you. This book began as a vague intuition – as I read Heidegger and Deleuze, I began to see subtle parallels, linkages that at first seemed subterranean and murky, but I became more and more convinced that the paths of these two monumental thinkers were in fact crossing. Whether this was altogether conscious on Deleuze's part was not so much the issue for me. Of course, I have not been in the majority in this opinion. Few commentators have attempted to link the two in a positive or productive way, Miguel De Beistegui's *Truth and Genesis* being a notable exception.

I became a *bricoleur*, piecing together concepts and lines of thought, following Deleuze's twists of Heideggerian language, seeking out direct and indirect references to Heidegger in Deleuze's texts. One can find a few direct references to Heidegger, most notably in *Difference and Repetition*, where Deleuze offers a six point account of what he judges to be Heidegger's innovations, and, worth noting, expresses a healthy appreciation for his work. My intuition was that Deleuze reads Heidegger as a companion on a particular journey, but one who had just veered off the path too soon, or, as Deleuze says in *What is Philosophy?*, who got lost in the necessarily blinds paths of philosophising into the future (QP, 104/109). In any case, I became more and more convinced that Heidegger was of subterranean important for Deleuze's thought, and that their philosophical rings intersected – as was the ringing in my own ears. So, I attuned my reading of the two to this register. There are points of intersection that go beyond any explicit citation on the part of Deleuze: his privileging of ungrounding and the unthought that are clearly tied to a Heideggerian problematic; their mutual determination to theorise being as event; and the vestige of the generative and irreducible tension between earth and world in the movement of territorialisation and deterritorialisation. In many cases, the extension of this project relies on an imaginative projection on my part. Their mutual fascination with Paul Klee is largely unthematised in their own work, yet I see Klee as providing a unique window into their philosophical worlds, especially in terms of what remains to be thought. I was delighted to discover a short essay on Alfred Jarry where Deleuze suggests that pataphysics opens the way for phenomenology (ID, 105/74) – and even more intrigued to find that Deleuze had once suggested that Jarry was 'the French poet who not only understood but also preceded Heidegger',[2] especially given that Jarry was known for a poetic form constructed as a mélange of languages and even slang. One can imagine my excitement to find that these two shared an intellectual friend, Kostos Axelos, who acted as interpreter and translator for Heidegger and was both a publisher for Deleuze and part of his intimate circle of friends for a time. Metaphorically, what I was discovering was a synaesthesia of the myriad Heideggerian and Deleuzian senses and affects. The final impetus for this project came when reading Deleuze's *What is Philosophy?*, where Deleuze directly addresses Heidegger's philosophical and political legacy, the gist of which is encapsulated in this line: 'He got the wrong people, earth, and blood' (QP, 104/109). It is because of the intuitive engagement, which I have just outlined, that I came to these words perhaps differently than most. For those who read Deleuze as having already dismissed phenomenology and moved past Heidegger (of which there are many), these words are a straightforward indictment and dismissal of the German philosopher. But for me, there was something more. First of all, Deleuze goes on to suggest the features of a people-to-come, indicating that he supports the general task of theorising this relationship: 'It is the double-becoming that constitutes the people to come and the new earth. The philosopher must become nonphilosopher so that nonphilosophy becomes the earth and people of philosophy' (QP, 105/109). So, I thought, it must be a matter of understanding what Deleuze means by 'the wrong people, earth and blood'. Of course, the simple answer is that he is merely reiterating the numerous criticisms of Heidegger's involvement in National Socialism, but, as any reader of Heidegger is aware, these issues are not just ontic considerations, and Deleuze would surely have known this. It has been my claim that the wrong earth and wrong people concern ontology and the political as such. Further, given that Deleuze's considerations of a people-to-come are almost always articulated with respect to the potential of art, there is a direct parallel with Heidegger's triadic gathering of earth, art, and a people that animates Deleuze's work. It is this path that I have begun to trace in this book.

This book is a concrescence of these resounding reverberations between the two thinkers. There are organisational elements within the book that seek to preserve the space of these encounters, zones of proximity which, as a nod to yet another level of affinity in their work, I have called plateaus – these interstices exist between some of the chapters and major sections of the book, revealing the emergence of a place (*milieu*) in between Heidegger and Deleuze that inaugurates new lines of thought (and flight).

> For the poet is a light and winged and holy thing, and there is no invention in him until he becomes inspired and goes out of his mind.[3]

Between Heidegger and Deleuze, for whom philosophy and art are partners in the elucidation of being and becoming, we can think Socrates' words anew, as offering sustenance for the future of thought. Whether from the holy named by the poet or the violent otherness of the dark precursor, we need more inspiration in our philosophising. In order to reinvent philosophy (Heidegger's *anderen Anfang*; Deleuze's *recommencement*), we must heed the forces of non-philosophy (of art and externality) in order that our philosophical sense may become otherwise.

Contemplating the nature of my inspiration, its plural sources, and the particular focus on the question of a people – which for Heidegger and Deleuze engages two levels of inquiry: not only who the 'we' includes but who 'we', as human beings, are – led me to question the presentation of my own discourse and to consider that thinking, which many consider a solitary pursuit, is, on multiple levels, always a communal event. Though Heidegger and Deleuze differ in their understanding of the status of history – as the inevitable unfolding of the destiny of being or as the outcome of contingent encounters which then serve as a non-linear backdrop that can potentially be animated for creative repetitions – each is acutely aware of the inflection of the present with the voices of the past. Thinking is, at least in part, an invocation of the accumulations and transformations of our past – the *we* of history, the *we* of past ideas, language and events. Philosophy has developed around this question of inheritance, in many ways thanks to Heidegger. Yet, if the discussion of inspiration reveals anything, it is also that thinking is more than this as well. François Zourabichvili maintains that Deleuze is both the closest and the farthest away from Heidegger with regard to this issue.[4] Both agree that thinking concerns a possibility rather than a capacity, and it is not a foregone conclusion that we have even begun to think, yet they differ with respect to the guarantee of this possibility: 'Whence the metaphors of the gift are substituted for those of violence' (DR, 188n1/321n11). In one sense, I have outlined a process of selection, of figures and paths that are tangentially related to both figures, and the mere fact of selection introduces the element of randomness into the equation. Yet, inspiration also requires attention to the outside that has always already entered in.

Dramatising the fact that this project is wholly a collective enunciation, writing on Heidegger and Deleuze has been an imaginative process in which I am both a creator and simply a conduit for these generative spaces. This is a situation that Deleuze openly embraces and seeks to generate in his own writing – the writing between himself and others that he conceptualises as free indirect discourse (*discours indirect libre*), as a way of lending his voice to the other which results in being confounded with its inverse.[5] Deleuze quite literally displaces the image of the singularity of authorship, and, by proxy, thinking, by writing with Félix Guattari, but his previous method of writing also engages thinkers as more than mere objects of investigation, developing a discourse which, by borrowing the voice of the other, highlights the anonymity and plurality in thinking itself. It is, quite self-consciously, for all of these reasons that the material henceforth is presented in the voice of *we* rather than *I*.

Consequently, we have simultaneously opened up one of the animating paradoxes of the book: the question of who it is that we let in and how, a question which is both opened and foreclosed by a necessary violation of the space of thinking. The question not only concerns our thinking, but very real decisions concerning politics, where it is linked with the problem of foundational violence with respect to nationhood, peoples and communities. Now, we seek to address the question of the 'we' beyond our own personal commitments, by linking this problematic to the multifaceted fabric of past and present negotiations surrounding the question of the 'we'.

In *The Postmodern Condition*, Lyotard presents the determination of the 'we' as the crucial political issue of our time, as it is connected to the consequent tyrannical solidification of certain types of knowledge and power. Specifically, discourses on the nature of a people serve as tools for the legitimisation of socio-political orders. Lyotard distinguishes modernity, as characteristic of any discourse that justifies itself with reference to a meta-discourse, from postmodernity, with its incredulity toward metanarratives and recognition that the utopian aspirations of high modernism are unrealisable.[6] In other words, the postmodern condition is characterised by a critical awareness of how the language of origin and sameness legitimates power, oft-times eventuating real and horrific practices of exclusion and violence. Though it is uncontroversial to suggest that the majority of postmodern thinkers are attuned to issues of difference and otherness, our entrance into this conversation is specifically geared toward a compendium of thinkers who explicitly thematise forms of sociality that counter these paradigms by offering re-conceptualisations of community. This is a lineage that can be traced from Georges Bataille and includes Jean-Luc Nancy and Maurice Blanchot.[7] Generally, they seek to dispel the rhetoric of inclusion that surrounds 'community' and 'peoples', which has been used as political capital in global capitalist societies as well as communist regimes, and, likewise, has served as the underlying basis for utopian projects of restoring a lost social order or grand politics of solidarity. The suspicion and resistance toward the utopian projects of modernity rests upon the fact that these visions define the parameters of the perfect community from the outset; these parameters bound the community and set up a structure whereby the community is now merely a matter of production of the 'proper' elements and values, a matter of filling in an already determined ideal. Such grand utopian visions were always based on master narratives, and at best were revealed as a thinly veiled pretext for grasping power and control, at worst, when based on a narrative of national and racial purity, as leading to the dystopian reality of genocide.

In the name of establishing a new politics, a counter-politics, these thinkers engage with the problem of undoing social homogeneity, avoiding both fascism and communism, as well as a kind of philosophical totalitarianism stemming from longstanding ontological commitments to the unity of being, the correspondence of being and the human, and the privileging of origin. These political ontologies rely on the underlying distinction between politics (*le politique*), which indicates the conventional, pre-established definitions of political institutions and aims, and the political (*la politique*), which attempts to think the place of the political and the various ways in which communities, or peoples, are established. The ontological turn in political theory is to a large extent indebted to Heidegger, who makes the distinction the foundation of his thinking of the *polis*,[8] an inheritance that is complicated because these thinkers are themselves critical of Heidegger, their work explicitly defined as post-Heideggerian.[9] It is into this discourse that we wish to insert our discussion of Heidegger and Deleuze, and, in what will be a common refrain for this book, we begin in the middle – in this case, in the middle of a debate that has only mythological beginnings and conceivably no end. Given the existential condition of sociality, the question of who we are and how we identify with others is unavoidable, and the persistence of the question is fundamentally philosophical. Though the debate between grand political ideologies may have been dissolved, the resolution of politics in the triumph of democracy and individualism obfuscates one of the primary issues of politics itself – the 'who' of politics, how to think the 'we'.

## Communities and Peoples: The Origins of the Question and the Question of Origins

The assumption of commonality or belonging as the basis of community is generally accepted as a logical outgrowth of the concept. Even contemporary accounts that consider the largesse and virtuality of communities, such as Anderson's 'imagined communities',[10] rely on such notions to provide the consistency and reason for drawing boundaries around peoples. Identification on the basis of commonality and belonging form part of our historical consciousness, often tied to the more primordial notion of autochthony, the view of peoples tied together through common birth or origin. Animating the cultural imagination, autochthony secures itself through myths of origin. For example, in the *Menexenus*, Plato advocates an autochthonous vision of the 'good birth' (*Eugeneia*). True inhabitants are descended from those born from the same earth, a situation that confers the Athenian privilege of citizenship, and those born from immigrants are fated to always be outsiders, or Metics. The language of autochthony undergoes multiple transmutations through the tradition, especially under the aegis of Romanticist nostalgia for the return to lost origins, a classic nineteenth-century problem. Heidegger, though a recipient of the German Romanticist tradition, does not fully accept the romanticist nostalgia for lost origin; he seeks to make of the people a philosophical issue, reading the possibility of becoming a people through his plans to reform philosophy and overcome metaphysics. Moreover, the employment of the language of autochthony in the service of conceptions of nationalism and peoplehood in twentieth-century politics reveals the inherent problems with beginning from such an exclusive demarcation of inclusion, a situation that complicates and renders quite precarious Heidegger's philosophical attempts to define a people.

Inevitably, the philosophical question of what it means to be a people was exacerbated by the tumultuous events of the twentieth century, the clash of burgeoning nations and ideologies, the onslaught of modernity, the rise of the technological age, and, ultimately, the aftermath of the unthinkable events of the Second World War. The turn to political issues, largely those of culpability and responsibility, is an identifying mark of post-war philosophical thinking, marking an event envisaged as philosophy interrupted in the breach of the real. Georges Bataille, Maurice Blanchot and Jean-Luc Nancy, all of whom tacitly take the postmodern critique of meta-narrative as their starting point and are thus engaged in a kind of political ontology, address the problem through a reconsideration of notions of community and by examining the underlying presuppositions that inform consideration of group identification. The fascist insistence on homogeneity, national socialist obsession with purity, communist galvanisation of the proletariat, and capitalist hegemony all bear the marks of assumptions concerning solidarity, identity, and belonging that become the focus of explicit philosophical critique by these thinkers.

As the catalyst for future exchanges between Jean-Luc Nancy and Maurice Blanchot, Georges Bataille's fixation on the problem of community marks the proliferation of multiple exchanges concerning the pitfalls of totalisation and the paradoxical problem of conceiving community beyond commonality.[11] Throughout his life, Bataille made multiple attempts to conceive alternative communities that would be resistant to the homogenising forces of society. He was critical of traditional views of the community as something to be produced or completed, and he devised conceptual apparatuses to dismantle or break apart the enclosure of such understandings. Bataille's reasons for contesting the characteristics of homogeneity and totality were based on several factors: first, such views, enshrined in community, actually work against the possibility of communal life and communication between people. This is because the nature of human finitude, rather than delimiting the individual, opens the individual to its lack of totality and the excessiveness of existence. This excessiveness is also an insufficiency in that it always suggests a remainder and incompleteness, hence the priority of heterogeneity over homogeneity. Bataille developed several concepts to counteract the unifying priorities of homogeneity and totality which seek to control and limit the excessiveness of being, many of which become central to Nancy and Blanchot's reworkings of the issue of community as well. Chief among these were the notions of expenditure, inoperativity (*désoeu-vrement*), and the unavowable (*inavouable*).

Implicit in Bataille's philosophic stance is the idea that there are other possible forms of life; that submitting to social norms and the dominant social order limits our ability to become and transform ourselves and our communities. Bataille experimented with community on three different occasions, with the 'secret' society *Acéphale*, the political group *Contre-Attaque*, and the *Collège de Sociologie*. Bataille's occupation was never merely theoretical, but always situated, an urgent response to the imminent horizon.[12] Bataille responds to the milieu of war and destruction within which he is inextricably bound as witness and participant, as well as the homogenising social forces seeking to shore up these ruptures. With the onset and progression of war, Bataille, evincing a general sense of abandonment,[13] proposes the necessity of thinking 'the community of those who have no community'.[14] This community operates beyond death, confronting finitude in terms of the ecstatic desire for the other. He associates the political disasters of war and decimation with the repression of expenditure and the violent inner passions necessary for maintaining the illusion of homogeneity and social order. Bataille seeks to release the violent inner passions, focusing on the visceral, the erotic, and the relation of society to the primeval. At the heart of his vision is the contestation of the desire for homogeneity. Such a contestation is possible through the experience of the insufficiency of existence. Insufficiency is the realisation of the dispossession of self, the fracture of totality which opens onto an outside and secures the possibility of the impossible community, a community of heterogeneity. Interestingly, though Deleuze initially advocates Bataille's zeal for erotic excess, he eventually comes to criticise Bataille, calling him the French pope of sad passions,[15] while nonetheless remaining passionately possessed by the thought of the outside.

Bataille's commitment to erotic excess does achieve a sense of communion as infinitely deferred and incomplete, but one that may be considered romanticised, intellectualised, and withdrawn from the political. The community of lovers, Bataille's paradigm, cannot be extended because of its ultimate singularity; Bataille even calls the world of lovers the oblivion of the world.[16] In *The Inoperative Community* (1983), Jean-Luc Nancy, focusing on Bataille's notion of inoperativity, develops a conception of community recalcitrant to the economy of production, seeking to reconcile Bataille's commitments with political being. For Nancy the inoperativity of community preserves the essence of infinite communication, the always 'to come' communication of the absent. Nancy develops an account of community that preserves the space necessary for communication through the marriage of the singularity of being and the clinamen, as the tendency of singular being to be inclined outside itself: 'There has to be an inclination or an inclining from one toward the other, of one by the other, or from one to the other.'[17] The singularity of being, '*a* body, *a* voice, *a* death', is derived from its exposure to these external relations; this singularity evades the absolute and resists the fusion that renders community a species of the absolute, or immanence, while its inclination always puts the being in question or puts the being of the question to others. Community is a perpetual, interminable negotiation of singularity and inclination.

Maurice Blanchot, who wrote *The Unavowable Community* in response to Nancy's 1983 article, emphasises the resistance of communicability inherent to Bataille's conception and focuses on instances of impossibility implied in the idea of the unavowable, as what cannot be affirmed or assimiliated. There is always a remainder, or excess, that cannot be assimilated by the social order and an element of transgressiveness within it that necessarily undoes this order.[18] From consideration of unavowability, Blanchot develops a notion of contestation at the heart of the relation between beings. Beings find their own being, as immanent completeness, contested by their encounters, thus opening the space for ex-istence: 'an existence shattered through and through, composing itself only as it decomposes itself constantly, violently and silently'.[19] In each case, what is crucial is the avoidance of immanence, the idea of completion or wholeness of the community. This will to essence/immanence makes community a work of death which utterly rejects movement, otherness and communication,[20] for which Nazism, and the horrors of the concentration camps, serve as the primary example as well as the logical conclusion of this metaphysics of the absolute.

Though often hailed as the product of post-Heideggerian thinkers, much of this work is indebted to the Heideggerian move toward human existence as primordially *mitdasein*, being-with-others. Such is Nancy's view that *Dasein* is always related to and with-others, wherein the individual is 'merely the residue of the experience of the dissolution of community'.[21] Conceiving of human existence as fundamentally *mit-sein*, rather than essentially individual and objectively present, allows us to understand human existence in its connectivity rather than through what separates individuals who will then comprise some sort of after-the-fact aggregate. It is a philosophical issue for Heidegger because it is a matter of transformative thinking and fundamental ontology; these are what will lead to human beings acceding to their essence. Each of these thinkers tries to rethink the we outside of homogeneity and self-identity, while insisting on the ontological primacy of the we, in a truly Heideggerian vein. Ironically, it is also on Heidegger that much of the debate and criticism falls, as his own emphasis on *Volk*, even as a *future* people, comes under fire from this post-war perspective. Criticisms abound: *Mit-sein* as ontological condition falls to the ontic consideration of *the* (German) people; though Heidegger posits *mit-sein*, he does not fully flesh it out (Nancy's view); or Derrida's criticism that Heidegger's philosophy ultimately does not break from the metaphysical privilege of unity, as his predilection for gathering and belonging reveal. In fact, preoccupation with community can be read as an attempt to move away from the conceptually and politically laden *Volk* favoured by Heidegger.

We maintain that Deleuze continues this line of thinking (of being-with), and can be situated within this tradition of attempting to rethink the boundaries of community in the post-war climate. By situating Deleuze in this lineage, we are engaging the debate about the a-political nature of his work and arguing against those who would claim that it has no political efficacy on the grounds of its naive or irresponsible exaltation of creation and desire for its own sake, and that Deleuze is not concerned about real social conditions.[22] On the contrary, Deleuze's political ontology emerges from a refusal to break with (to seek transcendence from) the real conditions of deterritorialised flows of capital and consumption that threaten to close in upon us, eradicating our ability to think otherwise. His micropolitics hinges on the possibility of the 'minor', of formations that elude national boundaries, state hierarchy and identity, racial or otherwise, yet which operate from within, immanent to the system under scrutiny. Significantly, Deleuze maintains Heidegger's language of a 'people' rather than eschewing such language in favour of talk of 'community', which thinkers such as Nancy self-consciously adopt in order to avoid the negative associations with *völkisch* thinking. The question is why?

Granted, these thinkers of community are responding to the failure of communism, and of major ideologies in general, more directly than to the Heideggerian problematic, but this critique was prefigured by a prescient Heidegger, who presented the concern topologically, in terms of a Europe caught between the two pincers of American capitalism and Bolshevism. Since the outgrowth of these two possibilities was the result of technological thinking predicated on a certain trajectory of philosophy and metaphysics, Heidegger looked forward to a recommencement (and alternative political formula) initiated out of philosophy. To be sure, Heidegger saw Germany, philosophically, as the centre of Europe. Thus, from this centre, thought needed to be reborn with a politics to follow. Becoming a people/political entity meant something like becoming historical, which meant, as well, becoming philosophical. All of this is laid out topologically in terms of returning to the earth, *autochthony*.

Here, there are some grounds for comparison. Deleuze revives the image of the pincers, in reference to a double articulation that composes the earth;[23] he also returns to philosophical topology, or geophilosophy. With regard to Heidegger's topology, Deleuze conducts the geological equivalent of Nietzsche's *Genealogy of Morals*,[24] de-centring the German origin, revealing the layers of the earth and its shifting surface as the non-teleo-historical beginnings of multiple conceptual personae. Of course, Deleuze's critique extends well beyond Heidegger, offering a model (in geophilosophy) that represents an alternative to the canonised trajectory of philosophy, the grand narrative and the kind of immanence to which Nancy et al. are opposed. We argue that Deleuze is reluctant to leave Heidegger behind because he recognises that the impasse for thinking requires a particular ontological dispensation, i.e. the issue of a people is essentially connected to the reformulation of immanence, the earth, through an engagement with the essence of art.

This is the hypothesis with which we approach Deleuze's statement that 'Heidegger got the wrong people, the wrong earth, the wrong blood.' In other words, Deleuze's particular understanding and contribution to the political question of the 'we', to which one must attach the language of 'a people-to-come', resides in his particular connection to Heidegger. Given that thinking, poeticising and the coming of a people are clearly united for Heidegger,[25] and that the same can be claimed for Deleuze,[26] such an analysis requires an examination of the convergence of the ontological, the political and the aesthetic (as the components of a people-to-come) within their respective works.

The fact that Deleuze directly critiques Heidegger's problematic linkage of a people and its earth in *What is Philosophy?* complicates matters, necessitating a thorough examination of these interactions. Which leads almost immediately to a rejoinder: what would be the *right* conception of a people, earth, or even blood? This is the paradox: in determining the *right* people, one immediately engages with the critique of foundational violence which has self-consciously become part of the postmodern condition. To replace one vision of a people with another does nothing to address the problematic assumptions involved in carving out a grand narrative that serves to legitimate and concretise certain ways of being at the expense of others. Deleuze is well aware of this difficulty. His philosophy is predicated on the critique of representation and the privilege of identity and sameness, which is reinforced by his ontological commitment to becoming and difference in itself. In the final analysis, Deleuze's vision of a people-to-come provides a solution to this impasse. His emphasis on minor literature and the fluidity of the concept is employed to produce diagrams of a people that resists totalisation, homogeneity and concretisation. Thus, it will be argued that Deleuze's thought is both an avowal and displacement of Heidegger, in the sense that he both extends and radicalises Heideggerian themes such as event, difference, a people, and the aesthetic dimension of life.

Topologically, the space of their interaction is marked by a productive tension, not unlike the Heideggerian *Riss* out of which the *Gestalt* arises. We will investigate what Deleuze's taking up of this Heideggerian language might mean, and how his own philosophical commitments influence or transform it. We examine how it is possible to speak of the relation between thinking, art and a people, a relation which Heidegger's work sets up, beyond the Heideggerian purview while remaining tied to the idea of the essential connections between the three that Heidegger's work reveals. Through the critical evaluation of their respective positions, we will show how Heidegger's concept of a people is insufficiently open to difference, contingency and the future (the Event), and that Deleuze's people-to-come corresponds to a radical reworking of what it means to be human, demanding incessant redefinition and openness toward future unknowns in order to engender new forms of *mit-sein*, which differ from other attempts in the emphasis they give to immanence and an existence that precedes a concern for the particularly human.

## Displacements

Heidegger and Deleuze's proximity inheres within the milieu of their specific divergences. Both are concerned with overcoming Platonism and the metaphysics of presence, and both interpret Nietzsche's reversal of Platonism as a benchmark in this process, though they interpret this moment quite differently – this will be the focus of Part I. Heidegger refuses the overcoming that Nietzsche offers, while Deleuze interprets Nietzsche's eternal return and doctrine of will to power as a crucial and effective overturning of Platonism that points to an entirely new ontological position. In contrast, Heidegger places Nietzsche at the end of metaphysics, which allows him to use Nietzsche's insights as a stepping off point for positing the overcoming of metaphysics.[27]

Heidegger's critique of aesthetics runs parallel to this analysis. Just as the lack of a name for Being allows for the recognition of Western philosophy as the naming of Being and for moving beyond to question the essence of Being itself, so too the fleeing of the gods, as in Nietzsche's abolishing of the supersensuous, is a prerequisite for beginning an inquiry into the essence of art. For Heidegger, the purpose of art must be reset, its greatness restored from the ashes of aesthetics. Heidegger believes that the aestheticisation of art is art's demise. Overcoming aesthetics, for Heidegger, demands an overcoming of art based in sensation or feeling, the final stage of aesthetics which Nietzsche's philosophy represents.

Deleuze rejects Heidegger's interpretation, instead crediting Nietzsche with anticipating an entirely novel ontological system based on immanence, difference, and the power of the simulacrum or, as Deleuze will later call it, the power of the false. Deleuze does not refer to the subjective feelings of individuals as the basis for a logic of sensation, but always to the pre-individual, thus ridding his aesthetics of the spectre of subjectivisation indicative of what Heidegger describes as the history of aesthetics.

Heidegger and Deleuze's positions on Nietzsche will serve merely as a backdrop for our main concerns. In other words, we refrain from any critical evaluation of their respective interpretations of Nietzsche, but rather treat this moment as a productive space of convergence from which to draw insights as to why the two thinkers are committed to certain ontological positions and to explain how their philosophies concerning the function of the artwork differ. The difference between Heidegger and Deleuze's interpretations of the eternal return is extremely salient in that it both reveals an inheritance of the question of Nietzsche's Overman as his vision and directive for a future humanity and offers a touchstone for explaining their differing positions on the subject of 'going beyond', both socially and philosophically.

We illustrate the displacement of Heidegger by Deleuze by comparing a similar structure within their thinking: the figures of the ordered and the unordered, as a productive tension expressed through works of art. Each are characterised as movements, whether as the sway between the unconcealed and the concealed or as the constant movement of deformation and reformation in the infinite process of becoming. Their philosophies are momentarily aligned on this point: Being is not static, it is a movement, an Event.[28] As thinkers of the event, both Heidegger and Deleuze are invested in presenting the conditions under which something new arises and in presenting a form of thinking adequate to these conditions. We must then ask the question of how a transformation in thinking is, or relates to, a transformation of what it means to be human and to become a people. As has been suggested, for both philosophers, artworks provide the possibility of a leap into new modes of life. The irreducible jointure of art and ontology will be the focus of Part II.

For Heidegger, the poem, because of its inherent connection to the richness of language, allows us to reclaim our ability to listen to language and its essential connection to Being. His emphasis on language and remembrance, rooted in a particular land and linked to a particular poet, reflects his commitment to the pre-orientation or destiny of a people and marks a decisive difference from how Deleuze will conceive a people. Deleuze will emphasise the importance of 'minor discourses' – those discourses within a language that are less visible or that go undetected – which brings him very close to Heidegger's thought of retrieving what has been silent within language. Yet language is only one aspect of discourse for Deleuze. He holds that different modes of art such as painting, writing, music, etc., must be taken as singularities that express different things according to their different modes of presentation, material conditions and constellation of problems. The heterogeneity of expressive materials and the a-signifying quality of the artwork are central to its being, allowing Deleuze to connect the human practice of art to counterparts in the natural world.

For Heidegger, we have not yet begun to think, and the task that lies before us is one of remembrance. Through the self-refusing earth, the very essence of Being/Truth is revealed. Acknowledging this concealment opens up a clearing and leads to another relationship to earth and world, another beginning in terms of moving past the presuppositions of metaphysics and *technē* as the dominant experience of Western thought. Radicalising the Heideggerian claim, Deleuze holds that it is what *cannot* be thought, the nonsense within sense, which must be thought.

The question is how we are to accomplish this task: what is it to think the unthought or the nonthinking within thought? Here again Heidegger and Deleuze share a similar problem: how to get beyond a certain type of thinking that occludes that which they would have us think. For Deleuze, we must think the conditions of thinking, and these conditions begin with the being of the sensible, the plane of immanence, which remains an informal element out of which our representations are formed. The move toward the deterritorialised must be understood in terms of an earth tending toward the cosmic,[29] a plane of forces, speeds, intensities and potentialities. Recognition of a deterritorialised plenum ungrounding the earth allows for new and transformative alliances between bodies and the earth that would have been hitherto unthinkable. Thinking is to enter into the process of becoming which occurs by virtue of this molecular level. A general power of works of art is to elevate the moment of ungrounding, or deterritorialisation, thus making visible invisible forces and drawing us toward the plane of immanence.[30]

According to Heidegger, the work is also the means by which a people instantiates itself. The decision of a people to be defined by the work is an instance of its being transposed into its endowment and taking hold of the possibilities that remain latent within it. Since, for Heidegger, art is tied to a particular world and a particular people, he contends that modernity is an artless age: there is no 'people' for the art, or art itself has ceased to be related to or arise out of a people. One must ask the question of if it is possible to speak of 'a people' in the wake of the demise of what Heidegger refers to as great art. For a moment, let us suppose that the essential structure of the relation between a work of art and a people-to-come remains viable. Either we can agree with Heidegger that our time is 'artless' or, remaining within Heidegger's formula, we can ask out of what 'soil' modern art grew? In other words, where are and who are the people and the endowment to which modernity is entitled? This line of questioning may prompt us to re-conceive the notion of a people entirely, and Deleuze offers us just such a re-conceptualisation.

The unthought revealed through the work of art that each philosopher describes has its counterpart in a kind of people. Hence, the final displacement that we address pertains to a people-to-come, the focus of Part III of the book. Instead of conceiving a people as tied to or arising out of a particular location, nation-state, or cultural heritage, Deleuze speaks not of 'a people' but of 'several people, an infinity of peoples, who remain to be united' (CII, 220) and invented. He introduces the notion of a missing people. For Deleuze, a people is never preordained or inscribed by national boundaries. Deleuze's criticism of origin can be seen as an explicit criticism of Heidegger's notion of a people. Even origin as beginning will not be a radical enough departure in so far as it maintains a connection to the past that precludes the possibility of the radically new. Deleuze develops the notion of milieu, which we connect to the amorphous pack, centre-less and perpetually in transformation, to replace the former notion. He also connects historicity with the domination of a particular state apparatus, directly confronting Heidegger's thinking in this criticism, and arguing that there is an arbitrariness involved in every worldview that reflects the general character of the movement of thought and the movement of Being as Becoming. A people is, and must always be, to come. This is the impossible possibility that corresponds to thinking as becoming and creation as opposed to will to truth (QP, 55/54). If Heidegger's people becomes as marked by its being transposed into the truth of its endowment, into its proper place, Deleuze's people becomes by way of the power of the false, by having no place. Thus, Deleuze rejoins our compendium of thinkers of the non-community, the 'beyond-we', and this inquiry rejoins a contemporary and unresolved debate concerning Deleuze's place in the political.[31] Given this context, we must ask, *what is the difference that Deleuze's difference makes?*

Like Deleuze, these thinkers are concerned with re-opening being-with as a question and creating a space for new conceptions of community to arise, rather than giving concrete and normative descriptions of what they should be. Remaining within this open space is itself a kind of formidable and tenacious activity, a form of resistance – to the present, to repetition of the past, and to philosophies of totality. Breaking this homogeneity is imagined through a variety of models and images, each evoking a sense of escape or ecstasis – whether Bataille's erotism and death, Nancy's exposures via the fragility of the nude and the openness of literature, or Blanchot's shattering of lover against lover. The common thread between these thinkers of community beyond community is the disavowal of immanence, as a false desire for totalisation aimed at essence, the violent eradication of otherness, and the closure of the political;[32] it is always a matter of 'getting out', to the Outside (*le Dehors*). Deleuze enters this discussion as one similarly committed to dismantling the forms of thought that mask difference for the sake of sameness, homogeneity, and representation. The difference resides first in Deleuze's understanding of pure immanence, as a positive term rather than a prong of a dichotomous relation of inclusion and exclusion. While still invoking a concept of the Outside, Deleuze differs from these thinkers in that he operates from the inside – in the fissures and the cracks. Pure immanence, rather than the immanence of self or community, is univocal, necessitating that the Outside is within; our lives are a variety of complications and implications of a radical immanence.

With regard to the systematicity of the book itself, we do not approach either thinker from a linear or chronological perspective. In both cases our work begins in the middle, a mark of the particular problematic with which we are dealing. The guiding thread running through our narrative is how each negotiates a recommencement of thinking with respect to art and ontology, in order to illuminate a new formation of the political.

## Notes

1. Plato, 'Ion', in *Complete Works*, ed. John M. Cooper and D.S. Hutchinson (New York: Hackett, 1997), 533d-e, p. 941.
2. François Dosse, *Gilles Deleuze and Félix Guattari: Intersecting Lives*, trans. Deborah Glassman (New York: Columbia University Press, 2011), pp. 95–6.
3. Plato, 'Ion', 534b, p. 942.
4. François Zourabichvili, *Deleuze: Une philosophie de l'événement* (Paris: Presses Universitaires de France, 1994), p. 24.
5. Ibid., p. 6.
6. Jean-François Lyotard, *The Postmodern Condition: A Report on Knowledge*, trans. Geoff Bennington and Brian Massumi (Minneapolis: University of Minnesota Press, 1984). See pp. 27–37.
7. There is a substantial body of literature devoted to the postmodern discourse on community. See, for example: Jean-Pol Maldou, 'The Law, the Heart: Blanchot and the Question of Community', *Yale French Studies* 93 (1998), pp. 60–5; Marie-Claire Ropars-Wuilleumier, 'On *Unworking*: the Image in Writing According to Blanchot,' in *Maurice Blanchot: The Demand of Writing* (New York: Routledge, 1996), pp. 138–53; Michael Strysick, 'The End of Community and the Politics of Grammar', *Cultural Critique* 36 (1997), pp. 195–215; Ginette Michaud, '*In media res*: Interceptions of the Work of Art and the Political in Jean-Luc Nancy', *SubStance* 34:1 (2005), pp. 104–28; Ana

Luszcynska, 'The Opposite of the Concentration Camp: Nancy's Vision of Community', *The New Centennial Review* 5:3 (2005), pp. 167–205; Irving Goh, 'The Question of Community in Deleuze and Guattari (I): Anti-Community', *symploke* 14:1–2 (2006), pp. 216–31; Karim Benammar, 'Absence of Community', in *Who is this 'We'? Absence of Community* (Montréal: Black Rose Books,1994), pp. 31–43.

8. See Heidegger, *Parmenides* (GA 54, Winter Semester 1942/43).
9. See Oliver Marchart, *Post-foundational Political Thought* (Edinburgh: Edinburgh University Press, 2007).
10. Benedict Anderson, *Imagined Communities: Reflections on the Origin and the Spread of Nationalism* (London: Verso, 2006).
11. For a compilation of articles chronicling the exchange opened up through Bataille's problematic, see Andrew Mitchell and Jason Kemp Winfree, eds, *The Obsessions of Georges Bataille: Community and Communication* (Albany: State University of New York Press, 2009).
12. 'What would be at stake is a confrontation of the *situated* character of Bataille's interventions in and on community in the 1930s (urgency of the struggle against fascism, disengagement of Nietzsche from Nazi ideology, proximity to the "'non-conformist'" tendency which will later not be foreign to collaboration, hostility to the union of the left, tensions between the "'mystical'" interests of Bataille and the sociology of Caillois, Leiris . . .), a confrontation of this historical embeddedness with the withdrawal from immediacy and from (en)closure which is a distinctive trait of Bataille's thought.' See Patrick French, 'Friendship, Asymmetry, Sacrifice: Bataille and Blanchot', *Parrhesia* 3 (2007), pp. 32–42 (n2).
13. Georges Bataille's *Le coupable* (*Guilty*) was written between September 1939 and the summer of 1943.
14. See the epigraph to Blanchot's *La Communauté Inavouable* (Paris: Éditions de Minuit, 1983); translated as *The Unavowable Community*, trans. Pierre Joris (New York: Station Hill Press, 1988).
15. According to Deleuze, Bataille's characterisation of the erotic in terms of transgression reintroduces the moral imperative. See 'On the Superiority of American Literature', in *Dialogues*.
16. Blanchot, *The Unavowable Community*, p. 34.
17. Jean-Luc Nancy, *The Inoperative Community* (Minneapolis: University of Minnesota Press, 1991), p. 3.
18. Bataille theorises the relation of taboo and transgression in *L'Erotisme* (Paris: Les Éditions de Minuit, 1957). Taboos are necessary for a community brought into being through or by work to curb the natural violent tendencies that interfere with this common goal. Eroticism, death and sensuality are all instances that reveal this violence, and are thus labelled transgressive. The irony is that transgression is used to

curb these tendencies through either ordered release or through the social disapproval of the transgression even as it is being acted on. Bataille advocates unemployed negativity, which is to say a different sort of transgressiveness that cannot be assimilated by the social order, thus made part of the 'work'.

19. Blanchot, *The Unavowable Community*, p. 6.

20. Nancy, *The Inoperative Community*, p. 12.

21. Ibid., p. 3.

22. See, for instance, Peter Hallward, *Out of this World: Deleuze and the Philosophy of Creation* (London: Verso, 2006), as well as Erin Gilson's review of Hallward in *Continental Philosophy Review* 42 (2009), pp. 429–34, and Alain Badiou's criticism of Deleuzian's who naively celebrate everything as event, surprise and creation in *Deleuze: The Clamor of Being* (Minnesota: University of Minnesota Press, 2000). Irving Goh, while acknowledging that Deleuze is not known for attempting a theory of community, claims that this theme silently animates Deleuze's work. See his 'The Question Of Community in Deleuze and Guattari (I): Anti-Community'.

23. See MP, Ch. 3, beginning with the image of the double-pincered lobster (God).

24. Deleuze's partial titling of chapter 3 of *A Thousand Plateaus* as 'The Geology of Morals' is a clear nod to the excavating process that Nietzsche conducts with regard to morality in *Genealogy of Morals*; the insinuation is that Deleuze is conducting the same sort of critique with regard to an ontology of the earth. Once this becomes clear, it is difficult not to place the critique in proximity to Heidegger, the thinker of the earth.

25. In 'What are Poets for?' Heidegger places the poet and the thinker on the same path, that of reaching into the abyss of the oblivion of Being in order that mortals may come into their own essence. The thinker must ask the question of being in order to recognise the oblivion of being, and the poet must trace the tracks of the fugitive gods, name the sacred, and give direction in this time of need. Couple this with Heidegger's clear linkage of the work of art with the becoming historical of a people in 'The Origin of the Work of Art' (henceforward *Origin*), and there is little room to contest this conjunction.

26. Deleuze establishes a distinction between philosophy and art in *What is Philosophy?*, yet the body of his work suggests a special affinity between philosophy and the arts: 'they share the same shadow' (QP, 206/218); they 'forewarn of the advent of a people' (QP, 105/110), which echoes the sense of preparation for a future people that arises in the final version of *Origin*.

27. Nietzsche's philosophy does not overcome metaphysics because, though he reverses the priority of the supersensuous and the sensuous, he is still

working with the same concept of truth as correctness and adequation. Heidegger's twist free of metaphysics involves a fundamental change in the understanding of truth, as *aletheia* or unconcealedness. It is Heidegger who truly overcomes Platonism and restores the essence of art as related to the essence of truth.

28. Deleuze credits Heidegger with identifying the generative capacity of positive, unmediated difference: 'this difference is not "between" in the ordinary sense . . . it is the Fold, *Zwiefalt*. It is constitutive of Being and of the manner in which Being constitutes being, in the double movement of the "clearing" and "veiling"' (DR, 90/65).

29. At the beginning of Chapter 4 we investigate how Deleuze's use of the cosmic is related to Kostas Axelos' idea of 'planetary thought', which is a direct confrontation with Heidegger's theorising of the separation of world and being and represents a cosmological vision of the unfolding of being, one that transcends the human. Though planetary thinking is also a key concept for Heidegger, his vision of widening the scope of thinking beyond Western metaphysics, even if more inclusive, remains bound to the 'world' as defined by the human. This concept is re-envisioned by Kostas as the larger milieu of unfolding out of which the world (of technology) happens; thus the planetary becomes the vantage from which the Heideggerian is overcome. See Deleuze's 'How Jarry's Pataphysics Opened the Way for Phenomenology' and 'The Fissures of Anaxagoras and the Local Fires of Heraclitus', both in ID. See also Christian Kerslake, *Immanence and the Vertigo of Philosophy: From Kant to Deleuze* (Edinburgh: Edinburgh Press, 2009) for more on this relationship.

30. The artwork is a negotiation of chaos and form that comes to stand in itself, where 'standing' depicts the greatest amount of openness onto the plane of immanence, the infinite, bridled by the most minimal amount of form that it can sustain. The artwork, as characterised by this tension, opens up new degrees of movement, making possible immense amounts of complexity that in its ever-renewing singularity constitutes a provocation to thinking. In this way, art reveals the conditions of the real.

31. See, for instance, Phillip Mengue's *Deleuze et la question de la démocratie* (Paris: L'Harmattan, 2003) and Paul Patton's response in 'Deleuze and Democracy', *Contemporary Political Theory* 4 (2005), pp. 400–13.

32. Nancy specifically refers to 'immanentism' as the desire for a closed community producing its essence and as completely present or identical with itself (Jean Luc Nancy, *Being Singular Plural*, trans. Robert Richardson and Anne O'Byrne (Stanford: Stanford University Press, 2000)). The critique of immanentism can be understood as the desire to move beyond hypostatic ways of understanding community, a concept

which involves three senses: community as substance, community as shared identity, and community as supra-individual. See Gregory Bird, 'Community Beyond Hypostasis: Nancy Responds to Blanchot,' *Angelaki* 13.1 (2008), pp. 3–26.

# PART I

# Divergence, the Point of Nietzsche

# Heidegger's Nietzsche

## *Nietzsche, Metaphysician of the Sensuous*

From the 1930s onward, poetry and art occupy a central position in Heidegger's thought, as they were intimately connected to the question of *aletheia*. The question is: why art in relation to truth? One answer is that Heidegger begins to think of art in response to Nietzsche's claim that 'art is worth more than truth',[1] and as a result of a critical examination of the historical trajectory that has led Nietzsche to this position. Heidegger believes that we can only speak of the beginnings of philosophy through the end: we must 'ponder the former dawn through what is imminent' (EGT, 18). For Nietzsche the reversal of metaphysical truth happens through art, and so, it is art that Heidegger must ponder. Although Heidegger disagrees with Nietzsche's basic position on art, he follows Nietzsche in maintaining art as a possible way out of the destitution into which philosophy has fallen. Heidegger's examination of Nietzsche is essential for understanding the impetus behind his project of re-conceptualising truth and art. Moreover, we find that Heidegger's concern for articulating a new conception of a people-to-come is also prefigured by Nietzsche, for whom the Overman can be viewed not as an individual figure, but as the pure possibility of a future humanity.[2]

Heidegger's analysis of Nietzsche is circumscribed by the question of Being. Accordingly, Nietzsche's two fundamental ideas, the will to power and the eternal return, must be thought together in relation to the question of Being: eternal recurrence as the supreme determination of Being and will to power as the basic character of all beings. Heidegger's articulation of these thoughts in terms of the question of Being indicates his attempt to take Nietzsche seriously as a thinker. The first two volumes of Heidegger's Nietzsche lectures are devoted to explicating these two fundamental thoughts, and they place art at the centre of Nietzsche's thought – as the title of the first volume, *The Will to Power as Art*,[3] suggests. In this first lecture, Heidegger examines Nietzsche's claim that art means more than truth. This claim is integral to Nietzsche's philosophical project: the destruction of Platonism and a return to enhancement of life as the accession of the will to power.

Heidegger and Nietzsche both seek to overcome the metaphysical thinking at the core of Western thought. For Nietzsche, this means overcoming Platonism, which represents the indoctrination of the Idea and metaphysical dualism. According to Nietzsche's critique of Platonism, the Platonic conception of Truth, gauged by correspondence or proximity to the supersensuous realm of the Idea, is misguided. Nietzsche traces the influence of Platonism through history, judging Christianity harshly as a Platonism for the masses, an opiate that promises false security in the face of the trembling and shifting becoming of life. Truth, understood in this fashion, is error, an error whose various instantiations have weakened humanity, destroyed the value of sensuous or physical reality, and led to the historical point of nihilism as a matter of logical course.

Heidegger interprets Nietzsche as announcing a crisis in the meaning of Being prefigured by the path that was set from philosophy's beginnings.[4] That 'God is dead' signifies the collapse of the values that the Western tradition has been founded upon. This collapse progresses under various stages in the development of Western man, notably with the advent of the autonomy of reason: 'The place of God's vanished authority and the Church's profession of teaching has been taken by the authority of conscience and, forcibly, by the authority of reason' (OBT, 165). As a result of valuing the ideal realm of the supersensuous over the earthly physical existence of the sensuous, when these values collapse, we become nihilistic, unable to believe in the absolute but unwilling to embrace life as it is. The nihilistic position retains the prior depreciation of the sensuous and therefore has nothing left to value, resulting in a 'will to nothingness' that denigrates life in general. Yet, paradoxically, nihilism is the saving power that will lift man out of the grip of metaphysics; by this uprooting of the values and worldview that provide the ground for Western thinking, a new space for new values can open up. Though he despises the humanity that fails to acknowledge this demise (the Last Man), Nietzsche views nihilism and its overcoming as a necessary step in the progression of humanity (toward the Overman).[5] We submit that the theme of rescue or renewal precipitated by overcoming one's greatest distress or lowest point, which Heidegger makes foundational in his own philosophy, originates in Nietzsche.

Though Nietzsche sees nihilism as characterising the state of modern Europe, it remains to actually think through this condition. Overturning Platonism requires shattering the pre-eminence of the supersensuous ideal which, at the same time, sanctions an investigation of that which is, true Being, liberated from the supersensuous. The problem is deeply rooted in the human condition: because human beings endure the becoming of the world, the passing of time, and are helpless against this passing, the spirit of revenge develops. Humanity, says Nietzsche, has long suffered from this spirit of revenge, which is the primordial origin of nihilism. What is past is beyond the reach of the will. Rather than endure this thought, the will approaches that which passes, life, with a vengeful persecution, so much so that eventually the will wills its own passing, its own annihilation: the will to nothingness (WHD, 37/93). Nietzsche pronounces that the spirit of revenge has determined all ideas thus far, our desire for stability nourishing the myth of the eternal. Without overcoming the spirit of revenge, man cannot overcome nihilism. Nietzsche would have us become value-producing, replacing eternal ideals with fluid yet precise goals and aims that do not devalue life, as the devaluation of life is humanity's major deterrent to its own progression: 'The major debility of the basic force of *Dasein* consists in the calumnation and degeneration of the fundamental orienting force of "life"' (GA6.1, 161/NI, 159). In order to overcome the spirit of revenge, one must affirm rather than deny 'what is', and 'what is' is physical reality. The counter-movement to nihilism is the return to the sensuous and its rescue from the position of inferiority into which it has fallen. This is why Nietzsche turns to art, as the realm of the sensuous. He opposes art to truth, arguing that sensuous reality is 'more true', in its fleetingness and incessant becoming, than the world of universal, eternal ideas. Truth, traditionally, is the fixation of appearance, while art is the transfiguration of appearance;[6] thus art responds to and corresponds to the ebbs and flows of life better than truth.

According to Heidegger, Nietzsche interprets fine art through the ancient Greek word *technē* as 'bringing forth', then extends this determination of fine art to all of life, locating the drive to bring forth as that which characterises the being of beings itself, as the will to go beyond itself. Life is essentially becoming; the only response that does justice to life is a kind of perspectivism that constantly allows for and accounts for new, creative appearances. As Heidegger interprets it, the essential definition of will to power and beings as a whole is expressed through art rather than truth. At the end of metaphysics, art, for Nietzsche, becomes the stimulus of life. Thereby art is the true activity of life, configured as will to power: *Will to Power as Art*.

In other words, Heidegger asserts, creativity is Nietzsche's new principle for valuation that adheres to the philosophical insights he has made and does not repeat those metaphysical assumptions he critiques. By its nature, will to power is creative: it is the increase of power (GA6.1, 74/NI, 76). More specifically, the will to power is creativity further defined as ordering and value-making, not by any set standard of being, but by giving itself its own rule and order according to its own will to increase and become more.

Nietzsche's contribution to philosophy, and what designates his place at the end of metaphysics, is his integration of being and becoming based on will to power. Ontologically, Heidegger determines that 'the recoining of Becoming as Being is the supreme will to power' (GA6.1, 418/NII, 202). Thus the very reversal that Nietzsche institutes between the sensuous and the supersensuous is the creative effect of will to power.

> Nietzsche's philosophy is the end of metaphysics, inasmuch as it reverts to the very commencement of Greek thought, taking up such thought in a way that is peculiar to Nietzsche's philosophy alone. In this way Nietzsche's philosophy closes the ring that is formed by the very course of inquiry into being as such and as a whole. (GA6.1, 417/NII, 199–200)

The decisive, fundamental positions of the commencement are those of Parmenides, who says that being *is* (*das Seiende ist*), and Heraclitus, who says that being *becomes* (*das Seiende wird*). According to Heidegger, Nietzsche presents us with the proposition that being is both of these: 'being *is* as fixated, as permanent; and that it *is* in perpetual creation (*Schaffen*) and destruction (*Zerstören*)' (GA6.1, 417/NII, 200). Heidegger interprets Nietzsche's claim 'that everything recurs is the closest approximation of a world of Becoming to one of Being' as evidence that Nietzsche, in an attempt to overturn Platonism, has named becoming being but, in the process, has re-calcified the notion of becoming: 'the sense that one must shape Becoming as being in such a way that as becoming it is preserved, has subsistence, in a word, is' (GA6.1, 418/NII, 202). This is the ultimate act of will to power, according to Heidegger. Will to power accomplishes this ultimate willing of becoming as being through the thought of eternal recurrence of the same. 'The will to power, in its essence and according to its inner possibility, is eternal recurrence of the same (*Wiederkehr des Gleichen*)' (GA6.1, 419/NII, 203), that is, metaphysics.

As the gathering of all fundamental positions in Western philosophy, Nietzsche's thought is undoubtedly, for Heidegger, the end of metaphysics, but, because it keeps within the metaphysical purview that it seeks to overcome (i.e. repeats this commencement only in a different form), it does not overcome but offers a 'counterposition (*Gegenstellung*) for our other commencement *(anderen Anfang)*' (GA6.1, 422/NII, 206). This would be Heidegger's project, an unfolding of a more original inquiry into being itself, a questioning that only becomes possible out of this end or completion. The counterposition must adopt a questioning stance to the initial commencement (*ersten Anfang*) (i.e. Parmenides and Heraclitus), returning to the guiding question of philosophy, 'what is being?'

Indeed, Heidegger sees many difficulties with Nietzsche's solution for *overcoming* metaphysics, exposing several instances of Nietzsche's reliance on the same metaphysical system that he is critiquing. He describes Nietzsche's processes of thought as always turning on reversal, which, for Heidegger, is not *overcoming* but merely inversion. Heidegger's sense of true *Destruktion* entails an overcoming of the prior system, where the old ground must be revealed and replaced with something excessive to the prior system. Heidegger explains that, although Nietzsche successfully reveals the inadequacy of Platonic metaphysics and thereby dislodges the security of Truth as *Eidos*, his advocacy of the sensuous relies on the same metaphysical conception of truth as its predecessor.[7] For Nietzsche, the sensuous, semblance and appearance, is more 'in truth' or 'in Being' than truth, but this relation is still gauged by correspondence. Anticipating his own project, Heidegger asserts that Nietzsche does not arrive at the proper question of a discussion of the essence of truth, though this 'oversight' pervades the entire history of Occidental philosophy since Plato and Aristotle.

Another purported example of Nietzsche's complicity with metaphysics is his reliance on and amplification of the subjective activity of value-setting. Heidegger offers his assessment of value-thinking: 'to think in values is to kill radically. It not only strikes down beings as such, in their being-in-themselves (*An-sich-sein*), but it also puts being entirely aside' (OBT, 196). Metaphysical truths reflect a history of value-setting by and through human desires and interests. Nietzsche is one of the first to acknowledge and expose the depth of our humanistic tendency to imprint reality with our own interests and value. That Western metaphysics is characterised by subjectivism is exposed through nihilism, as it first raises the question *of* value by revealing truth *as* a value. 'For Heidegger, because value-thinking is consummate humanism, it decimates everything: relegating not only becoming and fate but Being and even God to the level of values. Value thinking is the height of human-ism because to pose (to depose and to dispose over or of) values is to judge everything that is.'[8] The revaluation of all values according to will to power represents the most extreme form of humanistic value-setting, and, therefore, submergence in the same metaphysical tendencies. The will to will is the highest value for Nietzsche, yet the fact that the will to power posits both the preservation and securing of constancy as well as the enhancement of power brings about a paradoxical situation where certainty as the principle of modern metaphysics is grounded solely in the will to power. As Heidegger interprets Nietzsche, the creative power of enhancement that characterises the will to power is in the service of self-preservation, an increase of power in order to secure constancy. 'In this way [preservation and securing of constancy] Heidegger not only equates the subjectivistic ideal of contemporary modern technological science with Descartes' modern idea of the self-securing, thinking self, but orders Nietzsche's will to power within the same modern Cartesian quest for certainty.'[9] In both instances, value-setting and the will to constancy exemplified by the will to self-preservation, Nietzsche presents traces of humanism, the subjectivist impulse to judge and determine by the standards of man. In fact, our society has been overtaken by the most extreme form of ordering and creating, the ordering of ourselves, whereby human beings become standing reserve for will to power. Heidegger goes as far as to say that all metaphysics that historically preceded the meta-physics of the will to power has been, at least tacitly, metaphysics of the will to power.[10]

One can counter the claim that Nietzsche engages in hyper-subjectivism, especially in the sense of transcendental subjectivity or a subject of Cartesian certainty, by observing that an equally important value posited in the will to power is self-enhancement, interpreted as the impetus to move beyond one's present form or con-dition.[11] One preserves oneself to move beyond oneself. Depending on which value one chooses to emphasise, Nietzsche's commitment to stability and certainty looks very different. At the very least, the Nietzschean subject is not the hypostatised subject of Cartesianism. Nietzsche's subject must possess the 'force of plasticity', that force which 'allows for autonomous, individual growth, which enables one to transform what is past and unfamiliar and make it one's own, to heal wounds, to replace what has been lost, to effect one's own reformation of fragmented forms'.[12] Ultimately, Heidegger interprets Nietzsche as placing self-preservation above self-enhancement as its *raison d'être*, and, thus, Heidegger does re-inscribe Nietzsche back into a subjectivist metaphysics. As we will explain in Chapter 2, this is an interpretative move that Deleuze will problematise by further specifying Nietzschean forces as reactive and active. By adding this further level of analysis, Deleuze offers an alternative understanding of the priority of plasticity in Nietzsche that points beyond the subject altogether.

Nevertheless, with the thought of the will to power as art, Nietzsche thinks that he has found the solution for overcoming metaphysical thinking. As we have seen, Heidegger argues that Nietzsche's philosophy is rather its culmination, taking metaphysical thinking to its most radical extremes. This is the completion that Heidegger sees Nietzsche embodying, and, just as Nietzsche sees nihilism as the entrance into the revaluation of all values, Heidegger understands Nietzsche's philosophy as the threshold to overcoming metaphysics. Nietzsche represents, for Heidegger, a liminal moment in philosophy, both a part and outside of the tradition, the full scope of which can only be understood by embracing the contradictions of Nietzsche, of the will to power, and of the eternal recurrence of the same.

## Revaluating Art on Nietzsche's Body

Heidegger claims that in order to understand what is actually being said by Nietzsche when he names art as a configuration of the will to power we must examine his propositions in light of the question of aesthetics. Similarly to his location of Nietzsche vis-à-vis metaphysics, Heidegger places Nietzsche's views on art at the end of the historical development of aesthetics, which, itself, must be overcome. According to Heidegger, aesthetics is the devolved mode of art that defines our modern epoch. Aesthetics comes to designate a realm in which the art object is gauged by standards of sensuous appreciation or enjoyment, divorced from any standard of truth, and, thus, it cannot be a source of knowledge.[13] Hence, Nietzsche's interpretation of art is, in fact, aesthetics taken to its most extreme degree, physiology.

If Nietzsche's conception of art is beholden to aesthetics and aesthetics is determined by metaphysics, then Nietzsche's thought of the

31

will to power as art is, once again, inextricably linked to metaphysics. But, in being so tied to metaphysics and aesthetics, it represents the completion needed for another beginning. The outcome of this inquiry leads Heidegger to his alternative understanding of art, one that does not leave itself beholden to the history of aesthetics. Importantly, though Heidegger is critical of Nietzsche's conception of art, he does not dispute the position of art at the end of metaphysics: to provide the possibility of transforming thought and moving beyond metaphysical thinking.

Heidegger comprehends great art according to Hegel's standard, as an expression of the historical spirit of humanity. Great art fulfils an absolute need, and it is an expression of truth. Reiterating these ideas, Heidegger claims that great art is great in that it makes manifest and preserves the truth of beings as a whole (GA6.1, 82/NI, 83–4), which opens itself up to man's historical existence. Heidegger also follows Hegel's thesis on the end of art, which informs his scepticism concerning the possibility of great art in his final remarks in 'The Origin of the Work of Art' (henceforward *Origin*).[14] As Spirit reaches its full self-realisation, the need for images and symbols withers away and with it goes the need for any art that uses physical means to express itself. As the aesthetic, art also no longer addresses itself to the absolute, but only to the individual expressions of human experience, feeling and sensation. Philosophy takes over the role of providing for the needs of spirit.[15] Heidegger laments the demise of art and its purposive import, though he differs from Hegel in his prognosis of the fate of art. Rather than the Hegelian rejection of art, Heidegger holds that, to restore philosophy, art must be restored.

Heidegger embellishes upon what it will take for art to be great; art must be received by a historical people and actualised through its preservation by the people deciding to take it up. Heidegger disagrees with Hegel that great art is gone forever and can no longer be the fulfilment of an absolute need. This has not yet been decided. He reiterates this message in *Origin*, saying that it remains to be seen if art can be an essential and necessary way in which truth happens which is decisive for our historical existence. In fact, contra-Hegel, the possibility of a decisive confrontation with the destitution of our age resides with the return of great art. The premise that great art has devolved into a mere metaphysical abstraction is central to Heidegger's reinvigoration of the concept of art. For art to be restored to its greatness aesthetics must be overcome. Of course, this is an insight that finds its completion in Nietzsche as the culmination of the aestheticisation of art. The point of Nietzsche represents a double end and necessitates a double overcoming, of metaphysics and aesthetics as they run a parallel course in Western history.

In 'Six Basic Developments in the History of Aesthetics' (GA6.1/ NI, section 13), Heidegger shows that how an era is committed to aesthetics is decisive for the history of that era. In other words, art reflects the ethos of an age;[16] furthermore, as aesthetics, art reflects the ethos of metaphysical subjectivity. Heidegger names the first development in his history of aesthetics the 'pre-aesthetic', which corresponds to the great art of the Greeks. In this stage, art was what one might call unselfconscious. Heidegger explains the lack of meditation or reflection on art as being a result of 'such an originally mature and luminous knowledge, such a passion for knowledge, that in their luminous state of knowing they had no need of "aesthetics"' (GA6.1, 78/NI, 80). Heidegger will investigate what such a luminous state of knowledge could entail and how one might regain insight into philosophy and art in such a manner.

The next development is the beginning of aesthetics. Heidegger connects the systematic organisation of philosophy (Plato and Aristotle) with the beginnings of reflective consideration of art, making the powerful claim that 'aesthetics begins with the Greeks only at the moment when their great art and also the great philosophy that flourished along with it comes to an end' (GA6.1, 78/NI, 80). Great art is opposed to aesthetics in much the same way that pre-Socratic thought is opposed to philosophy. For Heidegger, in both situations, something originary has been lost, namely the luminosity of Being. One begins to discern the philosophical subtext of Heidegger's thinking on art: restore the sense of great art and restore great philosophy.

At this point in the development of aesthetics, concepts that mark off the boundaries for all future inquiry into art are determined, much like Heidegger's insistence that the determination of Being as presence which occurred at the beginning of philosophy directs all future inquiry into the question of Being and beings. Briefly, these concepts include the pair *hyle/morphē*, which develops into the matter/form distinction and its relation to *technē*. The *hyle/morphē* pair is determined according to *eidos* or *idea*, setting up an inward and outward distinction, that is, the outward physical appearance is determined by the inward idea or form. How the work of art is experienced as a self-showing, *phainesthai*, is now subsumed under these definitions. The designation of *ekphanestaton* as 'what properly shows itself and is most radiant of all' (GA6.1, 78/NI, 80) relies on the *eidos*, and the work of art is now set up to be judged by the standard of beauty determined by *eidos*. In his new conception of art, Heidegger disturbs these concepts by going back to what lies before these determinations, in part by creating a new conceptual language. Thus, Heidegger's inauguration of the conceptual dualism of earth and world in *Origin* is an enactment of the overcoming of aesthetics through the *logos*. Earth and world uproot traditional understandings of *hyle/morphē*.

The second concept that comes to guide all inquiry into art as aesthetics is *technē*, which, though commonly understood as designating art as well as handicraft, craftsmen and technites (artist-producers), more originally designated a kind of knowledge, that 'which supports and conducts every human irruption into the midst of beings' (GA6.1, 79/NI, 81), a distinction that Heidegger will return to when he attempts to reclaim *technē* as a means of addressing modern technology. Heidegger claims that the ambiguity of the word in its subsequent usages has led to the further obfuscation of the basic position from which the Greeks define art, prompting him to recommend an examination of *technē* in relation to its counter-concept, *physis*, as two types of bringing forth. Heidegger asserts that with the emergence of the *hyle/morphē* distinction, *technē*, which once implied the knowing guidance in bringing forth, is applied specifically to the *eidos* and the beautiful, thus securing the place of aesthetic interpretation in art. Heidegger is sceptical of the way these conceptual frameworks are transferred and applied in the realm of fine art and artworks and says that this 'is reason enough to be dominated by a deep and abiding doubt concerning the trenchancy of these concepts when it comes to discussions about art and works of art' (GA6.1, 80–1/NI, 82–3).[17]

The third development is marked by the beginning of the modern age. In philosophical terms, this is age of reason and certainty, which leads man to believe that his judgement can be the measure of all things and can procure knowledge in every form. The parallel outcome in art theory is that 'taste' becomes the court of judicature. 'Meditation on the beautiful in art now slips markedly, even exclusively, into the relationship of man's state of feeling, aesthesis' (GA6.1, 82/NI, 83). Art becomes the field of the sensuous and feeling. Nothing could be further from the notion of great art that Heidegger begins with. Great art must fill an absolute need and this is exactly what is lost when aesthetics dominates the field of art. Drawing upon

Hegel's understanding of the purpose and meaning of great art and anticipating the next stage of development, Heidegger says that 'art forfeits its essence, loses its immediate relation to the basic task of representing the absolute, i.e. of establishing the absolute definitively as such in the realm of historical man' (GA6.1, 83/NI, 84). Aesthetics represents the erasure of the possibility of thinking great art.

Heidegger marks the fourth stage in the development of aesthetics as the moment when aesthetics reaches its greatest height, which is simultaneously the moment when great art comes to a definitive end: 'In all these relations: art is and remains for us, with regard to its highest determination, something past.'[18] That moment is Hegel's *Lectures on Aesthetics* (1828–29), where aesthetics becomes completely self-conscious, a matter of pure aesthetic enjoyment and subjective expression (*art for art's sake*).[19] Heidegger does point out that this does not mean future individual works of art could not originate and be esteemed, but that art has lost its power to be absolute. Defined as it is, great art must be that which answers an absolute need and reveals beings as a whole, the situation and essence of a historical people as a whole.

In the fifth stage of aesthetics, Heidegger observes that the nineteenth century catches a 'glimpse of the decline of art from its essence' (GA6.1, 84/NI, 85) and, subsequently, there is a backlash in the arena of aesthetics, in which an effort is made to regain the 'collective artwork' (*Gesamtkunstwerk*). Heidegger associates this development primarily with Richard Wagner, who anticipated a melding of the arts into 'the art' that will be a celebration of national community. Heidegger, not opposed to viewing the artwork as a force that gathers together a community or people, is less impressed with the fact that Wagner forges this collective artwork through 'sheer indeterminacy, total dissolution into sheer feeling, a hovering that gradually sinks into nothingness' (GA6.1, 86/NI, 87). Heidegger charges that this is nihilism in its most pessimistic form. Being is expressed as dissolution, without form or law, clarity or definiteness. What is valuable about art changes as well; rather than revealing the truth of Being or displaying poetic originality, the arts are meant to elicit a 'lived experience' (*das Erlebnis*) of sheer feeling and sensual arousal *tout simple*. If the question is whether and how art is still known and willed as the definitive formation and preservation of beings as a whole, the question fails in the collective artwork of the nineteenth century. The collective artwork that emphasises only the measureless, fluid dissolution into feeling, such as Wagnerian music, gives up the possibility of knowledge. Art is examined according to its ability to produce aesthetic states, and these states of feelings are themselves submitted to experiment and observation, i.e. psychology. The aesthetic state becomes one of the characteristics of man, along with the political and the scientific. In Heidegger's assessment, the nineteenth-century culture of the aesthetic man foregrounds what Nietzsche 'is the first to recognize and proclaim with fully clarity: nihilism' (GA6.1, 90 /NI, 90). As opposed to Hegel, who declares art to have fallen victim to nihilism and to have come to an end, Nietzsche deems that religion, morality and philosophy cease to provide the ability to fashion and preserve the absolute. Art, by contrast, is Nietzsche's counter-movement to nihilism, because only art is true to life.

Thus, in the sixth development, aesthetics reaches its ultimate expression through Nietzsche, for whom art becomes a 'physiology of art'. Art is to be the counter-movement to nihilism by establishing new supreme values firmly rooted in the physical realm. It is to prepare new ground for law and measure, and yet can only be properly grasped by way of physiology. Aesthetics becomes the investigation into bodily states and processes and their activating causes by methods of natural science, i.e. applied physiology. States of feelings are to be traced back to excitations of the nervous system, to the vicissitudes of life.

For Nietzsche, the basic aesthetic state is *Rausch* (rapture): a feeling of plenitude and force which brings together the physiological feeling of excess and the power of will.[20] The rapture that is felt in the enjoyment of art points us toward the basic mode of the human being and, more generally, of life, the will to power as the will to preservation and increase. Basically, the Nietzschean desires to surpass art in artworks in favour of art as life. This is how physiology and philosophy come together for Nietzsche – the basic affect of rapture as the essence of art is 'the essence of the metaphysical activity of life' (GA6.1, 103/NI, 102). Thus, we have come full circle, back to the relation of art to philosophy, and, in Nietzsche's case, the aesthetic to the metaphysical.

Preliminarily, we can situate Heidegger's conception of art between Hegel and Nietzsche. Like Nietzsche, Heidegger sees art as a possible solution to the crisis of modernity, its groundlessness, but like Hegel, he sees great art as a thing of the past. Heidegger disagrees with Nietzsche on the essence of art as the aesthetic; and he disagrees with Hegel that art has necessarily come to an end and can no longer be a historical emergence of beings as a whole. For Heidegger the notion of great art must be re-examined. We must return to the essence of art that was meant when it was great and art must once again be seen as that which fulfils an absolute need.

The corresponding insights that Heidegger gleans from these developments read as a shortlist for his own conception of art. Heidegger's reflections on Nietzsche and his conception of the place of art are guidelines for his own conception of the place of art. To recapitulate those insights: (1) art must return to the pre-aesthetic; (2) we must move beyond or investigate the origins of the metaphysical categories that have defined art since the beginning of philosophy, such as *technē/physis* and the determination of art and the beautiful through *eidos*; (3) rather than being a matter of subjective taste, art must fulfil an absolute need; (4) art must be a determinate rather than a dissolutive exploration of sheer feeling; (5) in order to surpass aesthetics, we must reconsider the question of being. In Part II, we will see how these themes are fleshed out in *Origin* and in relation to Heidegger's understanding of the role of the poet/poetic.

## Temporalising the Moment, Eternal Recurrence

What has not yet been determined is how Nietzsche's other fundamental thought, that of the eternal recurrence (*ewige Wiederkehr*), completes his philosophical project and represents the overcoming of nihilism. Heidegger devotes the second volume of *Nietzsche* to this fundamental thought, a thought most fully expressed by Nietzsche in *Thus Spoke Zarathustra*. Heidegger notes that this literary-philosophical work constitutes the centre of Nietzsche's philosophy. *Zarathustra* is the conjunction of art and philosophy, a poeticising/thinking that reveals Nietzsche's greatest thought of eternal recurrence. In *Zarathustra* Nietzsche dramatises his philosophical project, leading the reader through the various developments in philosophical history. This book is fundamental in that it leads past the nihilistic position, envisioning what must be thought afterwards: the eternal return. *Zarathustra* connects Nietzsche's theoretical ideas to different forms of humanity, opening the door to the notion of the transformation of man, or, as the case may be, a people.

The thought of the eternal recurrence is the accomplishment of the revaluation of all values. Heidegger insists upon the centrality of this thought in Nietzsche's project, corroborating his belief through detailed analysis of Nietzsche's unpublished plans for what posthumously becomes *The Will to Power*. Heidegger offers two options for thinking the thought of the eternal recurrence. To think the eternal recurrence of the same nihilistically: 'let us think this thought in its most frightful form: existence as it is without meaning and goal, yet inevitably recurring; existence with no finale to sweep it into nothingness: eternal recurrence', drawing from Nietzsche's statement: 'that is the utterly extreme form of nihilism: the nothing ("meaninglessness") eternally'.[21] This form of the eternal return is merely a circle. But this is not Nietzsche's final word on the eternal return, and Heidegger is a more subtle reader than to allow Nietzsche's fundamental thought to disappear into nihilistic oblivion. The eternal recurrence of the same must be grasped, he says, 'in its character of decision, the character of the moment' (GA6.1, 392/NII, 175). The eternal return is to be thought in conjunction with nihilism, not nihilistically, but creatively, as what is to be overcome (*Überwindenden*). Referring to Nietzsche's own description, 'The doctrine of eternal return as fulfillment of it (i.e. nihilism), *as crisis* [*our emphasis*]', Heidegger elaborates on the unique position that the eternal return represents: 'The doctrine of eternal return is the "critical point", the watershed of an epoch become weightless and searching for a new center of gravity' (GA6.1, 377/NII, 159). Heidegger's understanding of crisis is specific. If this teaching is the 'crisis', then it must face in two opposite directions. Thus, on the one side, there is nihilism: 'the propriative event by which the weight in all things melts away – the fact that a center of gravity is missing' (GA6.1, 377/NII, 159), and on the other? This remains to be thought.

As Heidegger interprets it, the image of the gateway inscribed as 'Moment', given to us in the section entitled 'On the Vision and the Riddle' of *Thus Spoke Zarathustra*, corresponds to these criteria; Heidegger uses it to explain the bi-directionality of the eternal return. It is an image of a gateway with two long avenues, one going forward and one back. Zarathustra has been walking with a dwarf; each is representative of a certain path in thought. Zarathustra is the climber of heights; the dwarf is the one who drags down. At this gateway is the sign, '*Augenblick*', or 'Moment', described by Heidegger as the 'image of time running forward and backward into eternity' (GA6.1, 260/NII, 41). The Moment is the point of departure for both the not yet now of the future and the no longer now of the past. This is the image of the most abysmal thought, the thought of the eternal return. Both paths are infinite. Zarathustra asks the dwarf a series of riddling questions. 'Do you believe that these ways contradict one another eternally?' The dwarf answers, 'Everything straight deceives . . . All truth is curved, time itself is a circle.' But this is too easy. The thought of the eternal return, Heidegger says, is not thought adequately as 'everything turning in a circle'. This must be true as this answer comes from the lowly dwarf, the one who drags down. Zarathustra directs another question to the dwarf, this one pertaining to the gateway itself. What of the Moment? This as well must have always been there. Asking the question from the standpoint of the Moment, the gateway, brings new conditions into the riddle, 'requiring that one adopt a stance of his own within the Moment itself, that is, in time and its temporality' (GA6.1, 263/NII, 44). The difference is minimal, but it makes all the difference.

The interpretation of the eternal return that comes out of the second questioning reflects a certain kind of understanding. Rather than thinking only the two paths to infinity, one must think the moment where these two paths collide. This is to place oneself in the movement, as the Moment, 'performing actions directed toward the future and at the same time accepting and affirming the past' (GA6.1, 277/NII, 56), rather than looking at the circle of the eternal return as a spectator. Heidegger explains, 'whoever stands in the Moment lets what runs counter to itself come to collision, though not to a standstill, by cultivating and sustaining the strife between what is assigned him as *a task* and what has been given him as his *endowment*' (GA6.1, 277/NII, 57, my emphasis).[22] The difference of thinking the Moment lies in how one approaches this most burdensome of thoughts. To stand in the Moment is to be responsible for how and what recurs:

> That which is to come is precisely a matter for decision, since the ring is not closed in some remote infinity but possesses its unbroken closure in the Moment, as the center of the striving; what recurs – if it is to recur – is decided by the Moment and by the force with which the Moment can cope with whatever in it is repelled by such striving . . . eternity is in the Moment, that the Moment is not the fleeting 'now', not an instant of time whizzing by the spectator, but the collision of future and past. (GA6.1, 277–8/NII, 57)

There is hope in this perspective. The Moment embraces everything at once, but not in a way that is indeterminate. Nietzsche speaks of affirmation, the need to affirm all that is and was. Part of the heaviest burden is affirmation, which rests on the decision of how one meets that which returns.[23] Affirming the thought of the eternal return is to be a part of it, to say yes to the infinite movement of temporality, but it is also to affirm one's place within it and understand that it is not a matter of indifference.[24]

The structure of crisis as the condition of the eternal return is manifested as nihilism and the moment of decision. This structure brings two Heideggerian themes together: need and temporality. These conditions remain, for Heidegger, central features of the work of art as an origin, as bearing the possibility of founding a world and a people. Moreover, decision is both the determinate activity of the preservers of the work of art and the factor that will finally create a people for Heidegger. Given these similarities (i.e. temporality, crisis, and the task to be taken up by a future humanity), one may wonder if his interpretation is an endorsement or a critique, if it were not for the few fundamental things that Nietzsche does not think through essentially enough.

Indeed, for Heidegger, to couch the issue in terms of refutation or critique is already misguided: 'the officious will to refute never even approaches a thinker's path' (NIII/IV, 229). The point of Heidegger's analysis of Nietzsche is to build upon his reflection, to think that which remains unthought in Nietzsche's thinking. Heidegger will use the language of *das Aufgegeben* and *das Mitgegeben* to describe how a people takes up its essential nature. The repetition of these exact terms in respect to Nietzsche's *Augenblick* cannot be unintentional. As we will see in Chapter 3, Heidegger determines the content of crisis somewhat differently, illumining his proximity and distance from Nietzsche's position. For Heidegger, Nietzsche is a 'precursor, a transition, a pointing before and behind ... and therefore everywhere ambiguous' (GA8, 21/51).

Heidegger separates himself from Nietzsche through his model of temporality. Nietzsche's Moment is conceived as related to three phases of time in terms of eternity. The Moment is always determined as the constant Now. Though Nietzsche adds the notion of time and movement to his idea of being, temporality as recurrence privileges the Now. What is constant, then, is the present, a true recurrence of the same (temporal moment). Heidegger's thinking must, as Nietzsche's thought does not, overcome the temporality of being thought as presence. Nietzsche's thought tells us what is, now we must listen to what remains unspoken in it. Nietzsche's interpretation of time and crisis produces a particular understanding of the possible progression of man toward the Overman and the preceding 'types' of man. Heidegger's critique and innovations on these Nietzschean themes allows us to interrogate what type of transformations of man or humanity he himself is proposing.

## Transforming Epochs of Thought and Types of Man

> Each division (of development of Platonism) [is] brought into connection with the type of man who comports himself to that world. At the end of Platonism stands a decision concerning the transformation of man ... a decision as to whether at the end of Platonism man as he has been hitherto is to come to an end. (GA6.1, 211/NI, 208)

To transform our essential relation to being is to transform humanity. This connection between essential movements in thought and formations of humanity is made metaphorically in *Thus Spoke Zarathustra*. The final movement of metaphysics is thematised as the image of the bridge between the Last Man and the Overman. On the one side is the Last Man (of the past); on the other is the Overman (of the future). Zarathustra must cross that bridge, symbolising the overcoming of revenge against the sensuous world, becoming and, therefore, time.

Heidegger's 1951/2 lecture course, 'Who is Nietzsche's Zarathustra?', has been called a sympathetic return to Nietzsche.[25] In this lecture Heidegger reiterates the continued importance of Nietzsche for his thinking of overcoming and transformation. There, the Overman represents the transformation of humanity: 'that human being who goes beyond prior humanity solely in order to conduct such humanity for the first time to its essence, an essence that is still unattained, and to place humanity firmly within that essence' (NII, 215). The thought of the eternal return, the heaviest burden, has the power to lift mankind out of its current state of existence and transform it into something more, so that man may accede to its essential nature as will to power to the most extreme degree.

The formulation of the Overman quoted in the preceding paragraph should sound extremely familiar to those with Heideggerian ears; Heidegger continually explains that the task left for humanity is to take up its ownmost, to accede to its essence. But Nietzsche's Overman is not the answer for Heidegger. Why? Because Nietzsche's Overman is still determined by a historical moment beholden to humanism and metaphysics of presence. 'Because Nietzsche recognizes the historic moment in which man takes it on himself to assume dominion over the earth as a whole. Nietzsche is the first thinker to pose the decisive question ... is man, in his essence a man heretofore, prepared to assume dominion over the earth?' (NII, 215). Nietzsche recognised the crucial necessity of a change in the realm of essential thinking, and that this change would correspond to a new form of humanity. Humanity, according to Nietzsche, stands at the peak of decision. As Heidegger explains, Nietzsche makes the assessment that the 'human' is metaphysically determined, and therefore, given Nietzsche's critique, the definition of human as the rational animal is put into question; in other words, the human being's essential nature is not yet determined (GA8, 24/58). Yet, Heidegger recognises the stamping of being on becoming which occurs as the highest gesture of the eternal return, as the supreme will to power: 'That everything recurs is the closest approximation of a world of Becoming to one of Being.' Though 'the space of freedom from revenge is where Nietzsche sees the superman's essential nature' (GA8, 33/88), Heidegger is led to posit that Zarathustra's teaching does not bring redemption from revenge. Revenge is understood as an inherent 'ill will *against* sheer transiency' (NII, 228), and, in that becoming is made to be through will to power, the Overman practises a 'highly spiritualized revenge' rather than the crude revenge against time that Nietzsche diagnoses in Platonism.

Heidegger does not dispute the accuracy of Nietzsche's recognition of this particular phase of world history; the answer, however, is not to embrace this metaphysically laden path but to overcome it. The Overman is associated with the metaphysical assumption of man's domination over the earth. The essence of humanity, for Heidegger, is misunderstood within this metaphysical purview.

> Thus something in Nietzsche's thinking comes to the fore which this thinking itself was no longer able to think. Such remaining behind what it has thought designates the creativity of a thinking. And where a thinking brings metaphysics to completion it points in an exceptional way to things unthought. (NI, 229–30)

Once again, we have an instance of Heidegger following Nietzsche only so far, because it is Heidegger himself who is left the task to think what remains unthought in Nietzsche's thought, as what is opened up by Nietzsche's thought. To think what remains unthought in Nietzsche's thought is the path to overcoming; what remains unthought is Being. Heidegger is charged to think beyond metaphysics, beyond humanism. The Overman is the name for the human essence that corresponds to Being, but what remains to be thought is how these two cohere together 'if Being is no fabrication of human beings and humanity no mere special case among beings' (NII, 231).

In order to engage in this questioning man must hold his nature open for once to the essential relation toward Being. Thinking's proper activity is to 'rip away the fog that conceals beings as such, it must be concerned not to cover over the rift . . . through the rift, torn consciousness is open to admit the Absolute' (WHD, 34/89–90). The metaphysics of subjectivity covers over the rift and impedes our true engagement with Being. Heidegger's task is to initiate another beginning in philosophy that does not cover over the essential relation between the human and Being.

Heidegger's own formulation of the essential nature of man is developed out of a reflection on Nietzsche here, as a response and alternative interpretation of a possible future people. There are three elements to this bridge: that from which one departs, the transition itself, and that toward which one is heading. 'If the preview of the "whither" is missing, the one in transition remains rudderless . . . yet the place to which the one in transition is called first shows itself in the full light of day only when he has gone over to it' (NII, 217). Heidegger, as well, wants a transformed humanity, but not by metaphysical means. Getting on the bridge, thinking Nietzsche's fundamental thoughts, prepares the way toward the future. Nietzsche's thought is the bridge, but the bridge is not sufficient. What comes next is a leap – such a radical departure from what has come before that it initiates a whole new way of thinking.

## Notes

1. Friedrich Nietzsche, *The Will to Power*, trans. Walter Kaufmann and R.J. Hollingdale (New York: Vintage; Reprint edition, 1968), no. 853.
2. The desire for founding a people is problematic especially in light of National Socialism, so much so that addressing the idea of a people, das *Volk*, became philosophical anathema. Philippe Mengue makes this point quite explicitly in 'People and Fabulation', in Nicholas Thoburn and Ian Buchanan, eds, *Deleuze and the Political* (Edinburgh: Edinburgh University Press, 2008), p. 219. Yet, there is a whole tradition of political ontology devoted to conceptualising new modes of being-with. We situate Heidegger's understanding of a people against the Nazi propagation of *völkisch* mythology of blood and soil and Deleuze's criteria of minor and missingness for a people-to-come as a political imperative for resistance.

3. 'The Will to Power as Art' was delivered at the University of Freiburg, winter 1936–37. 'The Eternal Recurrence of the Same' was delivered at the University of Freiburg, summer 1937. Though this series of lectures occurs after the initial version of *Origin*, it is clear that Nietzsche is at the heart of these reflections.

4. For Heidegger, this 'crisis' in thought and of the Western spirit is directly related to the state of politics and world disarray. Heidegger explicitly reiterates and defends his diagnosis of crisis in the short 'Letter to the Rector of Freiburg University, November 4, 1945', where he indicates that he was not alone in such a belief: 'Three addresses by a man of no lesser rank than Paul Valéry ("The Crisis of Spirit," "The Politics of Spirit," "Our Sovereign Good," "The Balance of Intelligence") constitute sufficient proof of the seriousness, concern, and profundity with which the destiny of the West became an object of reflection outside of Germany during these years.' See Richard Wolin, ed., *The Heidegger Controversy: A Critical Reader* (Cambridge, MA: MIT Press, 1993), p. 62.

5. Complicating matters is the fact that Heidegger's interpretation of Nietzsche undergoes a change, from viewing Nietzsche as pointing the way to a new beginning for the West (early 1930's) to seeing him as the final thinker of metaphysics, claiming finally that Nietzsche's metaphysics justifies the technological domination of the earth (post-1938). See Jacques Taminiaux, 'On Heidegger's Interpretation of the Will to Power as Art', *New Nietzsche Studies* 3:1/2 (1999), pp. 1–22.

6. Farrell Krell, 'Analysis', NI, p. 237.

7. Ironically, Jürgen Habermas, in *The Philosophical Discourse of Modernity*, trans. Frederick Lawrence (Cambridge, MA: MIT Press, 1990), will levy the same criticism against Heidegger. According to Habermas, Heidegger also remains a captive of the metaphysical edifice which his philosophy professes to overthrow. Habermas claims that he remains bound to 'the constraints of the paradigm of the philosophy of the subject'.

8. Babette E. Babich, 'Heidegger's Relation to Nietzsche's Thinking: On Connivance, Nihilism, and Value', *New Nietzsche Studies* 3:1/2 (1999), p. 51.

9. Ibid., p. 42.

10. See Martin Heidegger, *Nietzsche Volume 4: Nihilism*, ed. David Farrell Krell (San Francisco: HarperSanFrancisco, 1991).

11. Franz-Hubert Robling investigates the issue of subjectivity in Nietzsche in 'The Force of Plasticity: Some Reflections on the Concern of Rhetorical Subjectivity in the Works of Friedrich Nietzsche', *Nietzsche Studien* 25 (1996), p. 87ff. Nietzsche, well known for his criticism of the traditional notion of the subject, its autonomy and rationality, does not give up the notion of subjectivity altogether. According to Robling,

Nietzsche subscribes to 'rhetorical subjectivity'. Rhetorical subjectivity is focused on continual self-enhancement and self-creation, aiming toward the development of the *Ubermensch*. It is an entirely different form of subjectivity that does not adhere to the metaphysical trappings to which Nietzsche is opposed.

12. Friedrich Nietzsche, *On the Use and Disadvantage of History for Life*, in *Kritsche Studienausgabe* (Berlin: de Gruyter, 1980), p. 251.

13. See the Epilogue to Heidegger's 'The Origin of the Work of Art', in *Off the Beaten Track*, ed. and trans. Julian Young and Kenneth Haynes (Cambridge: Cambridge University Press, 2002).

14. Hegel claims that 'the form of art has ceased to be the supreme need of spirit'. The dissolution of art means that it can no longer be seen as having a monolithic purpose because it is fragmented and a matter of personal, aesthetic experience. Art can no longer fulfil man's highest spiritual needs. See *Hegel's Aesthetics: Lectures on Fine Art*, Vol. 1, trans. T.M. Knox (Oxford: Oxford University Press, 1998), and 'Religion of Art' in *Hegel's Phenomenology of Spirit,* trans. A.V. Miller (Oxford: Oxford University Press, 1976).

15. Heidegger distinguishes Hegel's metaphysics of subjectivity from Nietzsche's in terms of the subject. For Hegel, 'absolute subjectivity' stems from the essence of reason existing in and for itself, whereas, for Nietzsche, man's nature as *animalitas* is taken as guide. For this critique, see NIV, 147, and for more on Heidegger's criticism of Hegel on the issue of art, see David Couzens Hoy, 'The Owl and the Poet: Heidegger's Criticism of Hegel', *Boundary 2* 4:2 (1976), pp. 393–410.

16. In 'The Age of the World Picture', in *Off the Beaten Track*, ed. and trans. Julian Young and Kenneth Haynes (Cambridge: Cambridge University Press, 2002), Heidegger defines five equally essential phenomena that determine the modern period. These are science, machine technology, art's moving into the purview of aesthetics, human activity conceived as culture, and the loss of the gods.

17. In 'The Origin of the Work of Art', Heidegger distinguishes between *technē* and *poiēsis* as two ways of man's bringing forth in order to separate kinds of production that happen in the artwork from that of the technical mastery and control that *technē* comes to imply, 'the kind of knowledge that guides and grounds confrontation with the mastery over beings' (GA6.1, 79/81). In keeping with the hypothesis that Heidegger develops his own conception of art out of the reflections he makes concerning the path of aesthetics, it makes sense that he would introduce some type of distinction to further distance himself from the traditional metaphysical, aesthetic uptake of these terms. Furthermore, in *Origin* Heidegger is seriously attempting to think through Greek art beyond these concepts and returning to a thoughtful discussion of *technē* in relation to *physis*. *Technē*, before it is wrested out of its

relation to *physis*, is associated with letting what is already coming to presence arrive. Heidegger attempts to do justice to the essential connection between *technē* and *physis*, and the work of art is where this relationship is born out. Heidegger's conceptual schema of earth and world bears the mark of the movement *physis*.

18. Citation to Hegel's *Works*, Vol. X, part 1, p. 16 is from GA6.1, 83/NI, 84.

19. Hegel's assessment of art follows a historical trajectory. He identifies the secularisation of art in modernity, the disconnection from its close ties to religion, with its inability to speak to the divine and the absolute. Our intent is merely to situate Hegel in the progression of Heidegger's understanding of the progression of aesthetics.

20. *Rausch*, as the basic aesthetic state, is the unification of two different states: the Apollonian and the Dionysian configured in Friedrich Nietzsche's *Birth of Tragedy*. The former has a tendency to order and measure while the latter is passionate and excessive, and these two states comprise the two elemental forces of the will to power, preservation and enhancement. See Heidegger's 'Rapture as Aesthetic State', beginning at GA6.1, 91/NI, 92.

21. Nietzsche, *The Will to Power*, pp. 35–6.

22. The italicisation indicates the similarity of phrasing that is found in 'Origin'. The concepts of assignment (*Aufgegebene*) and endowment (*Mitgegebene*) will become important for understanding Heidegger's notion of a people and it is significant that this language shows up in such a similar fashion in the context of his interpretation of Nietzsche's eternal return.

23. 'My formula for greatness in a human being is amor fati; that one wants nothing to be different, not forward, not backward, not in all eternity. Not merely bear what is necessary, still less conceal it . . . but love it.' Friedrich Nietzsche, 'Ecce Homo: How One Becomes What One is', in *On the Genealogy of Morals and Ecce Homo* (New York: Vintage Books, 1967 [1888]), II.10.

24. Drawing upon Nietzsche's imperative of *amor fati* and its relation to decision, Gordon Bearn develops an interesting account of a fully affirmative ethics which highlights the necessity to approach life with the intention of the affirmation and intensification of life. See his *Life Drawing: A Deleuzian Ethics of Existence* (New York: Fordham University Press, 2013), pp. 277–95.

25. Farrell Krell, 'Analysis', NII, p. 254.

# 2

# Deleuze's Nietzsche

Given that Heidegger is the great thinker of the end of philosophy as metaphysics, a comparison with Deleuze may not seem to be an immediately forthcoming project. Deleuze supposedly never had the patience for such claims,[1] and is known for characterising his own project in terms of metaphysics, which would seem to render their projects antithetical. Statements such as: 'I feel like a pure metaphysician . . . Bergson says that modern science hasn't found its metaphysics, the metaphysics it would need. It is this metaphysics that interests me',[2] could be interpreted as a rejection of Heidegger's main premise. For some, this rejection has represented the slamming of the door on any productive comparisons. Obviously, we are opposed to such a reading.

Deleuze's qualification, 'it is *this* metaphysics that interests me', necessitates a closer look into what metaphysics actually means for Deleuze. In 1959–60, he gave several lecture courses on Bergson, courses which, notably, were paired with a consideration of Nietzsche. As Ansell Pearson observes:

> Bergson, Deleuze notes in the lecture of 28 March 1960, participates in the Nietzschean moment of philosophy . . . [however] where Nietzsche tells the history or story of how the 'true world' finally became a fable, which is also a story of the devaluation of the highest values and the advent of nihilism, Bergson seeks to reorient metaphysics, to bring science and philosophy into a new rapport.[3]

Deleuze is thinking these two in tension with each other – the resolution of which indicates that overcoming metaphysics (Nietzsche's prerogative) is not the end of metaphysics, but a new kind of metaphysics (Bergson's prerogative), one that would have to be a matter of immanence rather than transcendence. This is exactly what Deleuze gives us in *Difference and Repetition* by unearthing the conditions of real experience.[4]

When one then considers that the reversal of Platonism is an organising aim for Deleuze, indeed the task for contemporary philosophy

(DR, 82/59) – evident from his 1966 lecture entitled 'Reversing Platonism' and remaining a continuous theme through *Difference and Repetition* (1968) and *Logic of Sense* (1969) – the comparison between Deleuze and Heidegger becomes more palpable. Deleuze insists, 'to reverse Platonism is first and foremost to depose essences and to substitute *events* in their place' (LS, 69/53), thus this metaphysics represents the need to pass from a transcendental philosophy to a genetic one, from a consideration of Being to that of Event, providing an even more provocative point of similarity between Heidegger's later concept of *Ereignis* and Deleuze's own elaboration of Event.[5] Miguel de Beistegui's *Truth and Genesis* explores this connection quite thoroughly, arguing for a revival of ontology, or metaphysics, on the basis of a new conception of the transcendental understood as immanent condition of the real. Beistegui sees both Heidegger and Deleuze as complicit in elaborating philosophies of immanence.[6]

Beistegui describes Heidegger's move to *Ereignis* as a move away from metaphysics, primarily understood as *ousiology*, the language of essence and substance. The event for Heidegger is the unfolding that is proper to a thing, but is itself a matter of truth, an epiphanic and poematic rendering of a particular side of being. Beistegui's claim is that the Event, in Deleuze, indicates a far different side of being, being in its genesis, and is thus related to the mathematical side of being, that which is 'in-itself' rather than 'for-us'. What they share is a vision of philosophy's path toward immanence, the need to explore the excess of philosophy as an event of ungrounding.

Ultimately Beistegui concludes that rather than being fundamentally incompatible, the differences between Heidegger and Deleuze's projects are indicative of the fact that they are approaching Being from two sides: truth and genesis. While Beistegui's work is groundbreaking, and a fundamental signpost for our own thinking in these matters, the splitting of the two thinkers along the lines of an epiphantic-poematic elaboration of Being 'for-us' and a mathematical-genetic side of Being 'in itself' makes it difficult to address what we think are several key overlaps between Heidegger and Deleuze. In particular, Deleuze's own encounter with art and the related issue of a people do not appear. As we have claimed in the Introduction, a people-to-come is tied to art for both thinkers, necessitating a re-opening of the relation between Heidegger and Deleuze in terms of art as integral to our understanding of the reframing of ontology in terms of Event. We will endeavour to re-open the question of art and the future of humanity through what we are calling the 'point of Nietzsche'. If, as Deleuze claims, the (Nietzsche-inspired) reversal of Platonism is a matter of moving from essence to event, then the question of the event becomes a question *for us*, a question of who we are and how the event can transform that understanding.[7] By no means are we arguing for the equation of the two philosophers or of their positions concerning the notion of a people-to-come. In arguing for the difference between their interpretations of Nietzsche, matriculated into their conceptions of art, we are simultaneously opening the discussion of a different notion of a people-to-come in Deleuze.

What is both paramount and potentially perplexing is that Nietzsche is equally as significant for the progression of Deleuze's philosophy as for Heidegger's, yet, though both are inspired by Nietzsche's critical and innovative philosophy, their interpretations are significantly different. Delineating the two is crucial for disentangling what is a somewhat uneasy alliance. Deleuze's short 1966 essay, 'Reversing Platonism',[8] is our starting point, having the dual benefit that one can assemble a direct confrontation with Heidegger and emphasise the importance of art for Deleuze's project. It then remains to flesh out Deleuze's full-fledged confrontation with Nietzsche in *Nietzsche and Philosophy* (1962). There we find the predecessors of Deleuze's key ideas of difference (between forces), power (understood as the genetic element that determines these differential relations of forces),[9] and repetition (of the eternal return) as the affirmation of differences, all of which make up the ontology of the Virtual and the Actual which serves as the explanatory framework for Deleuze's philosophic enterprise.

In what follows, we present Deleuze's interpretation of Nietzsche as a rejoinder to Heidegger's claims concerning Nietzsche on these key points: (1) Reversal: not every reversal need be a mere inversion; (2) Subjectivism: according to Deleuze, the will to power operates at the level of pre-individual forces; (3) Theory of forces: Deleuze extends the analysis of forces in a productive way that also distinguishes will to power as something entirely different than force, thus emphasising the will to power as the creative, differential element that produces qualities of being. Difference is primary and the world becomes through its repetition; (4) Eternal return: Deleuze interprets Nietzsche as offering a distinctive interpretation of temporality, not subject to the metaphysics of presence.

How is Deleuze affected by this Nietzsche? He formulates a theory of a differentiated plane of consistency comprised of pure forces or intensities, the basis of his own ontology; he conceives of the positive power of difference and its affirmative repetition as the motor of existence; he formats his own solution to the double bind of oscillating between the radical poles of order and chaos, being and becoming, preservation and enhancement, or necessity and chance, along the lines of Nietzsche's embrace of multiplicity and contradiction.

## Nietzsche, Sage of the Simulacrum

In 'Reversing Platonism', Deleuze dismisses Heidegger's formulation of Nietzsche's reversal of Platonism, 'the abolition of the world of essences and of the world of appearances', saying that 'such a project would not be peculiar to Nietzsche . . . it is doubtful that Nietzsche meant the same thing' (RP, 165). Instead, to reverse Platonism means to bring the motivation of Platonism into the light of day. The great innovation in Nietzsche, according to Deleuze, is the positing of a new kind of being, the simulacrum. In *Difference and Repetition*, Deleuze reiterates that 'overturning Platonism, then, means denying the primacy of original over copy, of model over image; glorifying the reign of simulacra and reflections' (DR, 92/66), eventually connecting this reversal to the pre-eminence of the event in *Logic of Sense*.[10]

In 'Reversing Platonism', Deleuze locates the foundation for the theory of Ideas in Plato's method of division, which he characterises as dialectic of rivalry between pretenders to knowledge and truth. Plato sets up a system in which there are two kinds of images (*eidolon*): copies or icons (*eikones*) and simulacra (*phantasmata*), for which the Platonic Idea serves as a concrete criterion for selection. Deleuze emphasises that the process of selection between rivals is always accompanied by myth, i.e. a 'myth' that founds and justifies the Idea (see DR, 60–9). Myth provides a story of foundation; 'it permits the construction of a model according to which the different pretenders can be judged' (RP, 166), setting up a hierarchy between suitors based upon levels of participation and leading to an infinite degradation that culminates in the simulacrum. Plato separates the eikastic art from the phantastic art, where the eikastic is image-making in conformity with a paradigm, while the phantastic 'appears but does not resemble'[11] because it does not conform to the original in exact proportions. Plato broaches this distinction with regard to craftspeople who seek to make their imitations beautiful rather than true, placing painting and all mimetics in this category. 'Copies or icons (*eikones*) are well-grounded claimants to the transcendent

Idea, authenticated by their internal resemblance to the Idea, whereas "simulacra" (*phantasmata*) are like false claimants, built on a dissimilarity and implying an essential perversion or deviation from the Idea.'[12] There can be good or bad copies, as they approximate the ideal, but the *phantasmata* are of an entirely different order, in which the aim is not to imitate correctly but to seem as if to imitate. Thus, the simulacrum is farthest from the ideal, a completely false pretender as opposed to the true pretenders who approach or participate in the ideal. The sophist practises the art of phantastics,[13] as do craftspeople or artists, and for this reason, Plato is intent upon separating the sophist from the philosopher as the pursuer of truth.

Yet, according to Deleuze, through tracking the false pretender, the sophist, Plato discovers that 'the simulacrum is not just a false copy, but that it places in question the very notion of copy and model' (RP, 167). Deleuze is referring to the fact that by the end of the *Sophist*, the figure of Socrates, the lover of truth and wisdom, is almost indistinguishable from the sophist, the man of rhetorical persuasion and false pretender to truth. The discussion of falsity leads Plato to question the nature of things which are not. Does false opinion opine because 'things which are not' *are not* or because 'things which are not' *are*?[14] The sophist and her art have become quite slippery, causing Plato's dialogue to falter and leading to his admittance of the difficulty which the sophist poses. The simulacrum is supposedly a copy of a copy that has become so altered that it no longer resembles 'well' or 'correctly', yet the simulacrum seems to be geared toward something besides 'that which is' and may then be a good copy of 'that which is not'. But this cannot be for Plato, as it would disrupt the very notion of the true. Deleuze takes this to mean that the simulacrum is less a thing severally removed from the true (that which is) than a phenomenon of a different nature altogether, espousing the power of the false.

According to Deleuze, Platonism does not pursue this conclusion, instead upholding the priority of identity and resemblance and dismissing the simulacrum as worse than a bad copy: 'subordinating difference to the powers of the Same and of the Similar, in declaring difference unthinkable in itself, and in sending difference and the simulacrum back to the bottomless ocean'.[15] The goal of overturning Platonism, Nietzsche's goal, would then entail the affirmation of the simulacrum in itself. Further, one would need to affirm that the simulacrum has a being unto its own and to provide it with its own concept.

Deleuze understands Nietzsche's criticism of Platonism as not merely inverting the sensuous and the supersensuous or abolishing them both in his process of critique, but as calling attention to a different kind of being altogether, a being predicated on internal difference rather than resemblance and internal identity. The sensuous as such is not the one, true being anymore than the supersensuous. This would be a mere reversal. Deleuze's point is that the simulacrum is beyond the dyad sensuous/supersensuous. These are categories that are informed by the metaphysics of resemblance. The simulacrum is a sign of a moving and dissimulative being not based on resemblance, and, as such, it signals that neither the sensuous nor the supersensuous is adequate to the task of expressing reality.

The simulacrum allows a reading of the world based on fundamental disparity or difference rather than similitude and identity. Because Deleuze interprets Nietzsche as dismissing truth in favour of the simulacrum, in other words, upholding falsity and error, he would disagree with Heidegger that Nietzsche remains tied to truth as correctness and, therefore, remains tied to Platonic metaphysics. There is a 'difference in nature' between the copy and the simulacrum. The simulacrum is an 'image without resemblance' (RP, 168), whereas the copy is always caught in the web of representation and resemblance. The simulacrum is predicated upon divergences and changes of kind. It is a matter of production, and, as implied by Plato's own reference to phantastics as the craftsmen's art, creativity.

Though reliant upon Nietzsche's vanquishing of Platonism and upholding of the simulacrum, Deleuze's appropriation of the simulacrum is itself an innovation that twists free. There are several epistemological and ontological consequences of Deleuze's account of the difference between the system of images as copies and simulacra. Simulacra must be motivated and created out of difference rather than sameness. They imply an internal dissimilitude that, in turn, implies a creative and productive dynamism.

> Deleuze consequently defines the simulacrum in terms of an internal dissimilitude or 'disparateness', which in turn implies a new conception of Ideas, no longer as self-identical qualities (the *auto kath'hauto*), but rather as constituting *a pure concept of difference*. An inverted Platonism would necessarily be based on a purely immanent and differential conception of Ideas.[16]

Ideas, according to Deleuze, are immanent, not fixed or eternal; they are the effects produced by the interplay of intensities and multiple forces – through difference. This is not merely conceptual difference but real difference, which lies at the heart of being and that, in fact, produces beings. Difference is not a 'difference from' but fundamental difference that produces ideas,[17] such that the genetic conditions of ideas are not re-presented or copied in them. Between the condition and its construction, there is no resemblance.

The real crux of Deleuze's problematic reveals itself here. Deleuze wants to describe the possibility of interaction between the immanent multiplicities that constitute objects, rather than working at the level of the actualised, 'whole' object. He offers an ontology that explains the process of becoming of entities, rather than an ontology that takes objects or entities as they are, already having been actualised, and describes them as such, according to an external and ideal model that they supposedly replicate. Thus he views the simulacrum as an excellent vehicle for initiating thought about these differences.

The triumph of the simulacrum speaks directly to Deleuze's philosophic concern to explain the multiplicity and productive heterogeneity internal to any system. 'The simulacrum abolishes both [original and copy]. For, of the two divergent series which it interiorizes, none can be assigned as the original, none as the copy. There is no privileged point of view, just as there is no object common to all points of view' (RP, 174). Likewise, there is no origin or foundation, another touchstone for critical engagement with Heidegger. Rather than beings having a greater or lesser amount of being determined by how well they fit the ideal model which produces a strict, hierarchical categorisation of beings, the simulacrum creates a levelling effect that opens up a whole field of possibilities for recognising the communication and transversality between beings.

Deleuze's elaboration of the simulacrum as internally differentiated is a model for his own ontology of difference, as well as an explanation for disparity between the appearance of beings and their virtual, genetic conditions. Thus it can better explain the series of convergences and divergences between beings, the relations in which these beings engage, and potential becomings of beings than the copy/image model can. Following Deleuze's line of thought, art is valued more than truth, as Nietzsche says, because art is the order of the simulacrum, and the simulacrum, the power of the false, is indicative of the genetic conditions of being, that is, becoming.

Moreover, Deleuze links the simulacrum directly to art, which is enormously enticing in terms of our investigation. Though brief, the implications of the following statement are profound: 'the perfect state of the simulacrum is only approached by certain machines or certain works of art'.[18] Given the privileging supplied in this statement, if Deleuze is heralding the triumph of the false as the way to interpret the world, then artworks, of a certain kind, must play centre-stage in the explanation and expression of Being/Becoming. Once the link between ontology and art is solidified, it is necessary that philosophy move through art, which provides us with a clue, to which we will return, for understanding the Laruelle-inspired phrase on the last page of *What is Philosophy?* (1991): 'philosophy needs a nonphilosophy that comprehends it; it needs a nonphilosophical comprehension just as art needs nonart and science needs nonscience' (QP, 206/219).[19]

How the artwork is an exemplar of the simulacrum will be addressed in Chapter 4, where we examine Deleuze's conception of art in light of concepts such as multiplicity, assemblage, becoming, the being of the sensible, and the abstract machine.[20] Our main desire here was to make the argument that Deleuze's encounter with Nietzsche influences his subsequent thinking on art as expressive of the genetic conditions of immanence. For Nietzsche, the activity of life is a dissimulating, seducing power of falsehood, and art raises this power of falsehood to its highest affirmation. 'Our highest thoughts take falsehood into account; moreover, they never stop turning falsehood into a higher power, an affirmative and artistic power that is brought into effect, verified and becomes-true in the work of art' (NP, 119/105). Appearances are no longer the negation of the real in this world but a selection, correction and affirmation of a kind of being. Simulacra are signals of a larger, subterranean and, perhaps, chaotic process. We must not mistake the simulacrum for a copy, and we must apply these standards to the world, seeing simulacra signalling the depth and internal complexity of Being everywhere, rather than merely perceiving a world of representations. This becomes all the more clear in Deleuze's analysis of the eternal return and will to power both in *Nietzsche and Philosophy* and in his other writings on Nietzsche: 'The will to power has its highest level in an intense or intensive form, which is neither coveting nor taking, but giving, creating ... the mask is the most beautiful gift, showing the will to power as a plastic force, as the highest power of art' (ID, 167/119).

## Unveiling Nothing but Force

Nietzsche's thought exerts a profound influence on Deleuze throughout his philosophical development. The issue of overcoming Platonism guides Deleuze toward an alternative canon in Western thought: 'only the philosophies of pure immanence escape Platonism – from the Stoics to Spinoza or Nietzsche' (ECC, 137). Given this priority of immanence, Deleuze will say that the central concern of philosophy is the univocity of being, an ontological levelling where being must be said in the same way for all beings, yet account for the pure positivity of difference. Deleuze's own articulation of immanence, as 'unformed intense matter, the matrix of intensity ... [in which] matter equals energy' (MP, 189/153), is inspired by Nietzschean force.

Deleuze characterises Nietzsche's ontology as a monism of force in statements such as these: 'There is no quantity of reality, all reality is already a quantity of force' and 'All sensibility is only a becoming of forces. There is a cycle of forces in the course of which force becomes' (NP, 45/39–40; 70/63). These two statements summarise Nietzsche's account of immanent being. Reality is comprised of forces, a plurality of forces that does not arise from something like Hegelian negation but as a plenitude that always already is. The sensible is the product of these forces, in other words, the constantly moving arrangements of these forces with respect to one another in their incessant becoming.

That Deleuze interprets Nietzsche's philosophy in terms of force is not unique. Heidegger, as we have seen, understands Nietzsche's will to power as a matter of force. What is unique to Deleuze is the specification of forces and will to power into particular types and qualities: reactive, active, negative and affirmative. What is more, Deleuze, rather than conceiving of will to power as force, conceives of it as something altogether different from forces; the will to power is the differential element that decides, interprets and differentiates forces. Will to power determines the relation of force with force and produces their quality, allowing for the identification of forces and the evaluation of difference between them. Accordingly, the difference between forces is co-present with force, though completely indeterminate and, in this sense, absent as a constant or uniform thing. Thus, we are brought to Deleuze's philosopher's stone, difference in itself. According to Deleuze, what commands Nietzsche's pluralistic monism is difference. Forces of intensity are forces of difference itself (DR, 286/222).

With the interpretation of force presented here, one can draw several parallels to Deleuze's own understanding of being. Deleuze espouses a kind of ontological univocity; Being is said in the same way for all beings, yet Being is the same only in that it differs. Univocity is heterogeneity:

> In effect, the essential in univocity is not that Being is said in a single and same sense, but that it is said, in a single and same sense, of all its individuating differences or intrinsic modalities. Being is the same for all these modalities, but these modalities are not the same. It is 'equal' for all, but they themselves are not equal. It is said of all in a single sense, but they themselves do not have the same sense. (DR, 53/36)

Being is, univocally, difference; it is a continually differentiating process. Therefore, for Deleuze, there *is* only becoming. This bears a great resemblance to the Nietzschean claim that being is becoming. The similarity in these formulations is due to Deleuze's endorsement of Nietzsche's ontology of forces, which serves as the genetic explanation for seemingly stable beings, the becoming beneath being. Deleuze's theorisation of Nietzsche's conception of force anticipates his later conceptualisation of the realm of the Virtual as consisting of pre-individual intensive singularities. Deleuze claims that 'what he [Nietzsche] calls the eternal return is taking us into a dimension as yet unexplored: neither extensive quantity nor local movement, nor physical quality, but a domain of pure intensities' (ID, 170/122). One could say that the Virtual is a more sophisticated account of the world of intensities and their interactions than Nietzsche, according to Deleuze, envisions. Deleuze undertakes to explore this dimension of sub-representative forces, prior to individuation.

In *Nietzsche and Philosophy*, Deleuze begins by claiming that Nietzsche's most general project is the introduction of the concepts of sense and value into philosophy. Sense is juxtaposed to essence. A philosophy that interrogates sense looks for the genetic conditions of phenomena and events rather than looking to explanations from essential categories or models – just the problem that was taken up in 'Reversing Platonism'. A philosophy that poses itself in terms of value is inherently critical according to Deleuze. It necessarily asks the question of the value of values, leading one to the conclusion that value is a matter of interpreting. Therefore Deleuze defines a typology of Nietzschean forces in order to better make sense of 'things.'

> We will never find the sense of something (of a human, a biological or even a physical phenomenon) if we do not know the force which appropriates

the thing, which exploits it, which takes possession of it or is expressed in
it. A phenomenon is not an appearance or even an apparition but a sign,
a symptom which finds its meaning in an existing force. (NP, 3/3)

Forces are quantitative, though every force is itself differential
thereby having its own qualitative relation of quantities. In other
words, because forces are always in relation, they are marked by the
difference in their quantity, which is quality. Deleuze names the qualities of forces 'active' and 'reactive'; these express the relation of force
with force. Active forces are those that are capable of transforming
themselves, 'plastic forces', while reactive forces must be interpreted
in light of their relation to the active. Each event or relation must be
evaluated for its qualities; there is no preset determination of quality.
There is also a tendency for forces to become reactive, in the sense
that intensive force 'tends to . . . cancel itself out in extensity and
underneath quality' (DR, 288/223), because of the very nature of the
active force to transform itself. Reactive forces, on the other hand,
'lose nothing of their force, of their quantity of force, they exercise it
by securing mechanical means and final ends, by fulfilling the conditions of life and the functions and tasks of conservation, adaptation
and utility' (NP, 46/40). Incidentally, Deleuze has just redefined
the two forces of Heidegger's interpretation of the will to power, the
self-enhancing and the preservative, in terms of the active and the
reactive, a point to which we will return when discussing the double
selection of the eternal return and its outcome in the next section.

While active forces are only concerned with acting, with taking
themselves to their own limits, expanding and transforming themselves, reactive forces are by nature dependent upon remaining as
they are, preserving themselves and their force. Reactive forces, then,
in an attempt to do this, separate active forces from what they can do,
thereby making even active forces reactive. In other words, Deleuze is
describing a double tendency toward the reactive. Regardless of the
fact that it may seem that Deleuze, channelling Nietzsche, is advocating the 'noble' qualities of active force, Deleuze is quick to emphasise
that all forces must be affirmed, an idea to which Nietzsche's commitment will be evidenced in the description of the eternal return as
the greatest burden, the return of even the mean and small. To do
otherwise would be to deny existence and to place our hopes and
desires naively in front of reality.

When speaking of force, Deleuze is careful to differentiate force
from will to power, yet not in such a way as to terminate their

relationship. Will to power is inherently connected to force, and may be considered an outgrowth or development from an ontological theory of force.[21] As Deleuze says, 'force is what can, will to power is what wills' (NP, 57/50). Thus, the will to power has its qualities: the affirmative and the negative. 'Affirmation is not action but the power of *becoming active* . . . negation is not reaction but the *power of becoming* reactive' (NP, 61/54), and though there is a deep affinity between the active and the affirmative and the reactive and the negative, they are not the same. The will to power can either affirm or deny the active and the reactive; as such, it is necessary for them to achieve their ends. By determining, it bestows sense and value. Affirmative will to power is the extreme valuation of life, while negative will to power is the extreme depreciation of life. The negative will to power is the will to nothingness, evinced by the becoming-reactive of force. This is the type of becoming that characterises nihilism. Thus, it is through the combination of the two, force and will to power, that it becomes appropriate to speak of the becoming of force.

Deleuze recognises that 'the becoming-reactive, the becoming nihilistic, of force seem to be essential components of the relation of force with force' (NP, 73/64). Therefore, the seeds of nihilism go far deeper than our human endeavours and choices, an interpretation which counters the claims of those who argue that Nietzsche's philosophy is hyper-subjective. Superficially, the will to power has been viewed as an anthropomorphic principle that reinstates man's right to dominate and value the world as he likes. Nietzsche himself quite explicitly rejects egoism as an interpretation of the will, and, according to Deleuze's interpretation, the will to power has no motive or object, nor is it the will to increase power, as Heidegger suggests. '*The will to power is essentially creative and giving*: it does not aspire, it does not seek, it does not desire, and above all it does not desire power. It gives: power is something inexpressible in the will' (NP, 97/85). The will to power is internal to force, not internal to humans. The will wants only to affirm its difference, a difference between forces. Therefore, we can only speak of will to power in the context of a relation of pre-personal forces, not as a separate principle.

Given that there is a double tendency toward becoming-reactive, Deleuze concludes that the problems of producing action, creation and affirmation are critical for philosophy. This is the same species of problem as that of entropy in physics and, transversally, that of the foreclosure of political possibility. In terms of the thermodynamic principle of entropy, the problematic rests with the interpretation of entropy as either the tendency toward disorder resulting in a terminal state of equilibrium, death, or as the initial condition for new, creative organisation. Deleuze's confrontation with Freud rests on this distinction: 'It would be wrong to confuse the two faces of death, as though the death instinct were reduced to a tendency toward increasing entropy or a return to inanimate matter. Every death is double and represents the cancellation of large differences and swarming of little differences in intensity' (DR, 333/259). As Deleuze considers Nietzsche's leading idea of repetition in the eternal return to be grounded on the dissolution of self, this distinction becomes all the more relevant. Death, as the dissolution of the subject, and, as we shall see, becoming-reactive taken to its limit, indicate conditions for the proliferation and dissemination of these 'swarming little differences', where only the excessive and the unequal return. To allay the risk of reducing Deleuze's philosophy to mere mechanical operations of cause and effect that the transposition of the language of entropy from physics may induce, one must emphasise that Deleuze's understanding of creative organisation out of disorder is not solely determined as a closed circuit but by dissemination according to the contingency of situation. In other words, it is selective but not subjectively so, which becomes extremely useful in understanding Deleuze's interpretation of the eternal return and affirmation and in connecting this to the political, as presenting positive possibilities for a politics of affirmation not entirely steered by the intentional subjective act of will but also not fatefully bound to a nihilistic march toward fascist monotony. One question that arises is: 'does this create a problem for the idea of politics – or the need for a revision of the assumption of voluntarism at the heart of the political discussion?'

Importantly, forces serve as the explanation for all things, as a truly immanent ontology would demand. All phenomena, from the most simple to the complex, are signs or symptoms of the difference in force. As a consequence of this immanent ontology, human beings are determined by the same system and qualifications of forces as every other phenomenon. 'The history of a thing is the succession of forces which take possession of it' (NP, 4/3), and human consciousness is no different. A thing has sense and value according to *which* forces take possession of it and *what* the ordering of these relations is, i.e. via will to power. As such, a subjective interpretation of the will to power misinterprets the effect for the cause. This too can be explained within the purview of active and reactive forces.

Ironically, with the triumph or domination of the reactive over the active that has come to characterise humanity, the order of explanation has been reversed. Reactive forces, already controlled by the spirit of the negative, limit active forces: 'seen from the side of reactive forces the differential and genealogical element appears upside down, difference has become negation, affirmation has become contradiction' (NP, 63/56). Therefore the origin, which is nothing other than difference, is inverted; instead of recognising the forces that comprise and create phenomena, the phenomena become the origin of difference, and difference is understood only in relation to identity and sameness.[22]

And yet Deleuze tells us, with reference to Nietzsche's *Genealogy of Morals*, that even though active force is separated from what it can do by a fiction (of moral superiority supported by the *ressentiment* of the weak), the fact that force has become reactive is no less real. The will to power is manifested as a capacity for being affected, an affectivity or sensibility. Therefore, a particular type of will to power will manifest a particular sensibility. Becoming reactive is the will to deny, and the sensibility that characterises humanity is nihilism. Nietzsche diagnoses humanity as a sickness, a skin disease. Deleuze claims that figures of *ressentiment*, bad conscience and the ascetic ideal are all examples of reactive triumph in the human world, and, in fact, are not psychological traits but constitutive of man. Nietzsche's aim is the freeing of thought from nihilism. Reactive forces have become the foundation of modern humanity, thus, to overcome nihilism must mean to overcome humanity: 'a man who would not accuse and depreciate existence – would he still be a man ... would he not already be something other than a man, almost the Overman?' (NP, 40/35).

The problem is that as the tendencies of force have been described there seems to be only becoming-reactive. This, though, cannot be so. If it were, there would be the first sort of entropy, the cancellation of difference and an end to becoming altogether: 'If the universe were capable of permanence and fixity, and if there were in its entire course a single moment of being in the strict sense it could no longer have anything to do with becoming.'[23] For Nietzsche, this is clearly both a matter of practicality, because nihilism is passively self-destructive and annihilative, and an ontological matter, in that reality is itself pure becoming. Nietzsche/Deleuze must explain how reactive forces can become active. To this end, Deleuze asks if there even is another becoming? Can there be another becoming? In response, he unfolds a principle of pure becoming based on ultimate affirmation as the foundation of the eternal return.

But if, as in fact it is, affirmation is the only directive that Nietzsche gives, the question might be posed, 'why should we affirm rather than negate and deny?' This is doubly difficult because of the ontological levelling we have just described. Forces operate on a pre-personal level, thus affirmation and activity cannot operate solely through intentionality. Deleuze's resolution can be expressed by reference to Nietzsche's demand for a new sensibility, an affirmative sensibility. Such a new sensibility begins with the thought of the eternal return, as that which engenders a general attunement or way of approaching experience: 'Only the eternal return can complete nihilism because it makes negation a negation of reactive forces themselves' (NP, 79/70). Thus, the path to becoming active must pass through the affirmation of the reactive. True to Nietzschean logic, everything must be affirmed, even the reactive. Denial then becomes an affirmation.

## Doubling Moment of Affirmation, Eternal Return

According to Deleuze the eternal return has two aspects: (1) as a physical doctrine of the possibility of the passage of time, the eternal return affirms the being of becoming; and (2) as a selective ontology that causes the active alone to return, it affirms being as becoming as the self-affirming of becoming active. In the second aspect, it is further delineated as a complicated doctrine of double affirmation and double selection.

Deleuze, like Heidegger, presents two moments in Nietzsche's discussion of the eternal return – the first, failed or misunderstood attempt, and the second, richer account for those who have ears to hear it. Deleuze interprets Nietzsche's first exposition of the eternal return in terms of the reactive. The reactive man, encompassed by the spirit of revenge, is incapable of acting and makes objects or others responsible for his powerlessness. For this man, that everything returns, even the mean and the small, is unbearable, because the reactive man cannot overcome himself in order to move beyond this doleful vision. The reactive man thinks in terms of the same, in terms of being rather than becoming, and so his vision is the heinous vision of the same returning over and over again. The thought of the eternal return in terms of the reactive puts contradiction and negativity into the eternal return. The first understanding, the false eternal return, is the purely mechanistic view of the return of everything that is as it is: a bare, lifeless repetition. In *Thus Spoke Zarathustra*, the first introduction of the thought of the eternal return is followed by the vision of the Shepherd choking on a black snake. To affirm the eternal return, we must bite off the head and envision 'another becoming, another sensibility: the overman' (NP, 74/65).

According to the richer account, the eternal return is, in fact, the return of that which differs, the becoming of heterogeneous forces. It eliminates the repetition of the same. As we have seen, thinking in terms of the same is born out of reactive forces. The will to remain the same is self-preservative, the reactive that wilfully denies life as becoming:

> According to Nietzsche the eternal return is in no sense a thought of the identical but rather a thought of synthesis, a thought of the absolutely different which calls for a new principle outside science. This principle is that of the reproduction of diversity as such, of the repetition of difference ... We fail to understand the eternal return if we do not oppose it to identity in a particular way. The eternal return is not the permanence of the same, the equilibrium state or the resting place of the identical. It is not the 'same' or the 'one' which comes back in the eternal return but return is itself the one which ought to belong to diversity and to that which differs. (NP, 52–3/46)

Deleuze explains that Nietzsche's account of the eternal return presupposes a critique of a terminal or final state of becoming. The first aspect of the eternal return, that it is a doctrine of pure becoming, rests on the logical conclusion that by virtue of the infinity of past time, if becoming had a final state it would have attained it. Therefore, becoming always is and always has been. There is no present moment where becoming has ceased to become. In other words, there is no pure being. Thus there is no permanence of the same. Everything is in movement and constantly changing. What eternally returns is becoming. Deleuze says that 'all we need to do to think this thought is to stop believing in being as distinct from and opposed to becoming or to believe in the being of becoming itself' (NP, 54/48).

It is interesting that just at this moment in his exposition, Deleuze cites the Nietzschean passage that Heidegger emphasises in his own critique: 'That everything recurs is the closest approximation of a world of becoming to a world of being – high point of the meditation.'[24] Instead of interpreting this passage as a sign of the re-inscription of the metaphysics of presence, Deleuze formulates the problem otherwise as a question of how the past can be constituted and how the present can pass. He questions the logic of the present moment and its passing into a new moment. What separates Deleuze from Heidegger is a difference in their understandings of the temporality of the moment, and what this Now actually means. Deleuze argues that the eternal return is the answer to the problem of passage. The problem is formulated by Deleuze as this:

> The passing moment could never pass if it were not already past and yet to come – at the same time as being present. If the present did not pass of its own accord, if it had to wait for a new present in order to become past, the past in general would never be constituted in time, and this particular present would not pass. (NP, 54/48)

Deleuze's response to this dilemma is to say that the moment must be simultaneously present and past, present and yet to come, seemingly very similar to Heidegger's own position. When discussing the simultaneity of these temporal phases in the Moment, Deleuze also has in mind the same image of two paths that lead to the gateway entitled Moment to which Heidegger refers, but how Deleuze incorporates this moment in Nietzsche into his own interpretation is definitive. Rather than the past and future being assimilated into the present, Deleuze suggests that what one calls the present or the Now is a synthesis of the past and future, it is already passing. Rather than focusing on the present, as itself a being, Deleuze focuses on the passing of the moment, on its necessary and unavoidable relationship to becoming. 'We misinterpret the expression "eternal return" if we understand it as "return of the same." It is not being that returns, but rather the returning itself that constitutes being insofar as it is affirmed of becoming and of that which passes' (NP, 54/48). Further, this second exposition of the eternal return in terms of the Moment is not about our specific relation to it, or our position in relation to the past and future; it is about the synthesis of time itself, an ontological rather than subjective issue. One could also claim that the Moment understood in this way, as including the past, inherently contains that which eludes the present. 'Becoming entails this double structure, this being pulled in both directions at once, and this "at once" is not an identifiable, present moment, but is a "self-contradictory" moment which will forever "elude the present"'.[25] It is a moment of irresolvable self-contradiction, just as the will to power is that which inheres in the relation of forces but remains unidentifiable. Notably, this interpretation of Nietzsche draws him closer to Heidegger's own philosophy, in which truth and being are always oscillating between the concealed and the unconcealed, thus breaking with the priority of presence.

Determining the eternal return in its first aspect puts us in a position to examine its second aspect. According to Deleuze, in its second aspect, the eternal return is an ethical and selective thought that selects for affirmation and becoming active. That the eternal return acts as a selective doctrine is crucial for Deleuze. Without this feature there would be no way to combat or select against reactive forces. The criterion for selection is nothing other than the thought of the eternal return. In other words, it is not you or I who selects but the eternal return itself that selects. The first selection begins with the directive of the eternal return: *whatever you will, will it in such a way that you also will its eternal return*. Initiating this thought, living by it, makes willing and acting something whole. As Deleuze says, 'it makes willing a creation' (NP, 78/69). The first selection is accomplished by the thought of the eternal return eliminating from willing everything that falls outside of the thought. Certain reactive states would not return, because they are unable to perpetuate themselves or become, i.e. little compensations, little pleasures. Certain states would also be fundamentally changed in having been willed in this way, i.e. laziness, stupidity, baseness, cowardice. Yet, there are those reactive forces that go to the limit of what they can do, those that find 'a powerful motor in the nihilistic will [and] resist the first selection' (NP, 78/69). A second selection completes the affirmation of the eternal return in a very different way than the first.

In the second selection, 'it is no longer a question of eliminating ... but of the eternal return making something come into being which cannot do so without changing nature' (NP, 80/71). Negation, the will to deny, is transmuted into affirmation by means of will to power as will to nothingness relating itself to the eternal return. In most cases, the will to nothingness appears in alliance with reactive forces and against active forces, leading it to deny the active forces and turn against itself. Though, in so doing, the will to power, as the becoming reactive of forces, thwarts itself and cannot complete its full becoming, because nihilism as essentially reactive life has the principle of self-preservation or conservation at its core. The will to nothingness as the depreciation and negation of life conserves itself in the grip of the reactive.

When the will to nothingness is related to eternal return, it breaks its alliance with reactive forces, and makes negation a negation of reactive forces themselves. The will to nothingness by the eternal return destroys rather than conserves nihilistic, reactive force. This is self-destruction not as a turning against oneself but as the leading of reactive forces to nothingness. Deleuze describes self-destruction as the completion of nihilism, whereas turning against oneself in the sense of depreciating life and oneself is merely passive nihilism, a nihilism that cannot act. What amounts to an *active* negation is the only way that reactive forces become active. By submitting the reactive in oneself to the test of the eternal return, the self wills its own decline. The negative is transmuted into an active destruction of itself, therefore affirming the eternal return unconditionally. This should be linked to the liberation of difference which is indicative of the doubleness of death developed in relation to Freud: 'cancellation of large differences and swarming of little differences in intensity' (DR, 333/259). It is the transmutation of the reactive and negative into the active and affirmative. Thus, the eternal return produces becoming-active. The eternal return is therefore not only selective thought but also selective being (NP, 80/71). The plastic, self-surpassing force of becoming-active signifies nothing but the return of difference.

## Transforming Sensibility Beyond/Over Man

Nietzsche's two main concepts (eternal return and will to power) point both toward a notion of the transformation of the human engendered from the thought of repetition of difference and beyond the human in terms of a pre-individual realm of being, the swarming differences of intensity, upon which individuals and events are predicated. Nietzsche's positive task is to determine not what humanity is but who overcomes humanity. Overcoming is opposed to preserving. The active destruction initiated by the second selection of the eternal return is the annihilation of the self, the breaking of metaphysical subjectivity, and the triumph of the powers of multiplicity and becoming. Deleuze dramatises this moment in the final section of *Nietzsche and Philosophy*, 'The Overman: Against the Dialectic'. In order to reach the Overman, there must be a double affirmation, as we have seen in the double selection of the eternal return. Deleuze envisions a constellation of three figures: Zarathustra, Ariadne and Dionysus (the Overman). The first affirmation is the relation of Zarathustra to Ariadne, the affirmation of becoming in the first selection of the eternal return. Ariadne, the bride of man, affirms becoming conditionally in relation to the human, willing only that which one would will eternally. But on the other side, in the second selection, Ariadne is the bride of Dionysus, and she, by affirming Dionysus, affirms becoming unconditionally, signalling the triumph of the power of Dionysian multiplicity over the human and over the self. From this perspective, one submits the reactive and preservative in oneself to destruction.

What appeals to Deleuze in Nietzsche's philosophy is 'becoming imperceptible', thinking at the level of multiplicity and forces, which he sees it as advocating, and Deleuze's use of Ariadne as the fulcrum in this scenario is not arbitrary. Becoming-woman represents the dissolution of molar identity necessary for the reinvigoration of philosophy/thought and is a necessary step to becoming-imperceptible. Ariadne represents the threshold to the breaking of metaphysical subjectivity (NP, 213–17, 186–9). However, one must also use her position as a gauge of the impossible possibility of this moment. Ariadne is a figure of extreme self-contradiction. She must live as both the Ariadne-Zarathustra coupling and the Ariadne-Dionysus coupling, affirming both simultaneously. In doing so, she eludes self-presence as she is always between, in passage. It is this double structure of insistent contradiction, connected to what Deleuze will theorise as disjunctive synthesis, which defines the Overman and provides the possibility of creative repetitions, or counter-actualisations of the present.

To live as the Overman is to live impossibly, the both/and rather than the either/or. The position of Ariadne is perhaps the closest that we may come to riding the line between sheer Dionysian ecstasis/ dissolution and the minimal attachment to self that remains necessary to think and to live at all. Nietzsche's philosophy welcomes contradiction, is replete with paradox. In *Thus Spoke Zarathustra* (1883–85), where Nietzsche posits the Overman as the new goal for humanity, the characteristics of this new humanity are quite illuminative: humanity will not be an end but a bridge, thus always in process or becoming; humanity will not have one goal but constantly seek out multiple paths and ways of being; humanity must produce its own goals, must produce itself, constantly engaging the forces of life; humanity must overcome itself, venturing beyond-man.

If the overman is to remain the most powerful being, he must change his leading goals, because that is the only way for him to do justice to the process of changing reality. His goal is undeterminable, not because he has left behind him all contents as inessential. Rather, there cannot be only *one* goal for him, because in the flow of time the most varied contents can and must be considered the dominant goals . . . the overman is to achieve in one person the intensification of the contradictions of all strivings to their extreme.[26]

In Deleuze's view, this is one of Nietzsche's most positive traits. The Overman must incessantly engage in going beyond even herself. Deleuze says that to 'become' it is necessary to have a fascination with multiplicity (MP, 293/239–40). Human beings have this fascination, however latently, because we are immanent to the systematic whole of being. We are multiplicities, and, though tied to an understanding of ourselves based upon identity, unity and subjectivity, the potential for thinking otherwise lies within us. Couple the thought of the eternal return with the new order of the simulacrum and one has a recipe for thinking beyond the human or beneath it to the internal rumblings of the incessantly becoming forces of life that at once comprise and destroy us.

Placing the emphasis on maintaining contradiction rather than the will to power as either self-preservation or self-enhancement allows Nietzsche to slip out of the double bind of either/or that has plagued philosophy and defined metaphysical thinking. Philosophy's problem, according to Deleuze, is to exist in this contradiction, to 'acquire consistency without losing the infinite into which thought plunges' (QP, 45/42). The Janus-faced position that Nietzsche's Overman inhabits is Deleuze's inheritance, one side facing the human and one side facing the infinite. The double structure described here reappears as the model of the Event, issuing from the construction of a plane (or intensive plateau) of immanence. Composed of the surface-effect of language and an underside of affective being, intensity, the event is inescapably doubled. It is simultaneously the creation of sense, generation of thought and thus liberation from corporeality, and also the liberation of alternative forces and desires of the plane of immanence itself, an affect-event, a doubling that is itself flattened into one plane or surface. Deleuze calls this the 'strolling couple, affect-event'.

Deleuze's philosophy leans toward the thought of the infinite, to maintain just enough consistency to become imperceptible. This is one reason why the Overman is untimely, always to come, characterised as it is by a perpetual openness forged out of a wrenching bi-directionality – surprisingly reminiscent of the Heideggerian rift, which is also constituted out of difference. Thus, the issue is not one of dictating a new form of humanity, but of maintaining the conditions of openness. We will return to this outline, this figure as it were, in terms of the concept of a people-to-come which Deleuze and Heidegger share, in order to draw these two thinkers even closer in this strange coupling.

Concomitantly, overcoming is to think beyond the human, toward a more elemental reality that opens upon the becoming of force, speeds and slownesses, dynamism and movement. In other words, the transformation of thought itself requires a sensitivity, or maybe a sensibility, for pure immanence. As Nietzsche says, 'the will to power not a being, not a becoming, but a *pathos* – the most elemental fact from which a becoming and effecting first emerge'.[27] Thus, a return to affect will be central to our claims concerning the formulation of a people-to-come.

> One must still have chaos in oneself to be able to give birth to a dancing star. I say unto you: you still have chaos in yourselves. – Zarathustra

## Notes

1. Badiou, *Deleuze: The Clamor of Being*, p. 5.
2. Gilles Deleuze, '*Je me sens pur métaphysicien*', from a letter reproduced in Arnaud Villani, *La Guêpe et l'orchidée* (Paris: Belin, 1999), p. 130.
3. Keith Ansell Pearson, 'Beyond the Human Condition: An Introduction to Deleuze's Lecture Course', *SubStance* #114, 36:3 (2007), p. 57.
4. These lectures contain 'in embryonic and germinal form some of the essential modes of thought that characterise his contribution in the development of philosophy in post-war France' (ibid.).
5. Beistegui identifies this similarity in 'Eventful Being: On *Ereignis*', chapter 3 of *Truth and Genesis: Philosophy as Differential Ontology* (Bloomington: Indiana University Press, 2004), p. 113.
6. See ibid., p. 337.
7. See Leonard Lawlor, 'The Four Fundamental Aspects of the Reversal of Platonism', in Babette Babich and Dimitri Giney, eds, *The Multidimensionality of Hermeneutic Phenomenology: Essays in Memory of Joseph Kockelmans* (Springer Press, forthcoming). The question that drives Lawlor's investigation is 'what is the event' given Deleuze's characterisation of the reversal of Platonism as the move from essence to event. Lawlor claims that we know 'we have experienced an event when the two questions of its primary origin and its ultimate destination are and remain necessarily unanswerable', when what has happened and what is going to happen become undecidable. What is truly provocative about this claim is Lawlor's further insistence that, absent of this situation, we have not really broken free of Platonism. In

other words, this brings into focus the political dimension of the event; this is what we must aspire to and become. This is a crucial indication of a people-to-come, which strengthens our claims in Chapter 4 concerning features of works of art, such as indeterminancy, chance and diagram, as illuminative of the singularity of the event.

8. Originally published as '*Renverser le platonisme*' in *Revue de Métaphysique et de Morale* 71:4 (1966), pp. 426–38. Deleuze revised the piece and published it in *Logique du sense* (Paris: Minuet, 1969) as '*Platon et la simulacra*'. The version used here is Heath Massey's excellent translation, published as 'Appendix 2' to Len Lawlor's *Thinking Through French Philosophy: The Being of the Question* (Bloomington: Indiana University Press, 2003), pp. 163–78, in which he indicates the revisions or omissions in the 1969 version.

9. Deleuze refers to power as a genetic element determining differential relations in several ways: aleatory point, dark precursor, event, or desire, thought out of an Oedipalised and subjective context.

10. 'To reverse Platonism is first and foremost to depose essences and to substitute events in their place' (LS, 69/53).

11. Plato, *Sophist*, trans. Seth Benardete (Chicago: University of Chicago Press, 1986), 235d–236d.

12. Dan Smith, 'The Concept of the Simulacrum: Deleuze and the Overturning of Platonism', *Continental Philosophy Review* 38:1–2 (2005), pp. 89–123.

13. Plato, *Sophist*, 239d.

14. Ibid., 240e.

15. Lawlor, *Thinking Through French Philosophy*, p. 103, also in LS, p. 253.

16. Smith, 'The Concept of the Simulacrum', p. 89.

17. For the reversal of the causal order between the empirical and ideas, see Gilles Deleuze's *Le Bergsonisme* (Paris: Presses Universitaires de France, 1966).

18. RP, p. 172. The works of art to which Deleuze refers are those that create something entirely new and that validate appearance for its own sake, not for the sake of representing. Machines are assemblages which necessarily link to other assemblages, thus they possess a constant variability or morphological tendency.

19. In *The Non-Philosophy of Gilles Deleuze* (London: Continuum, 2002), Greg Lambert locates the necessity of nonphilosophy for philosophy's continuance in the loss of the pretention to truth and the rule of reason (identifying both Nietzschean nihilism and the shattering of truth through the events of the world wars); the philosopher must either 'invent new [rules], or abandon the game altogether' (p. 74). Philosophy's survival relies on a creative engagement with its outside, with art for instance.

20. By the time Deleuze and Guattari write *A Thousand Plateaus* (1980), the notion of the simulacrum has been transmuted into the language of becomings, thus eliminating the residual reference to representation completely.

21. Keith Ansell Pearson has claimed that the eighteenth-century astronomer and physicist Ruggero Giuseppe Boscovich exerted an influence on Nietzsche's thinking concerning force, specifically as it relates to time: 'Nietzsche's encounter with Boscovich was an important one and may have proved decisive for the later articulations of the doctrines of will to power and eternal return ... [indicating that] as early as 1873 Nietzsche had a well-developed theory of forces'. Keith Ansell Pearson, 'Brave New World of Forces: Thoughts on Nietzsche's 1873 "Time Atom Theory" Fragment & on the Influence of Boscovich on Nietzsche', *Pli* 9 (2000), p. 7. Pearson says that this early fragment reveals Nietzsche's attempts to dispel certain prejudices concerning the reality of time and force, including the understanding of time as a series of discrete (spatialised) points and the understanding of forces as persistent. Force must be seen as a function of time, thus as a matter of becoming. Boscovich conceives of matter as simple, non-extended and indivisible points surrounded by fields of force, the repulsive magnitude of which increases or decreases according to distance. Ansell Pearson also emphasises the importance of compentration, when the distance between two points of matter becomes nothing such that the two occupy the same indivisible point of space – these two elements lead Nietzsche to credit Boscovich with refuting the premise of solid corporeal atoms. Reality is movement and relational force. See also G. Whitlock, 'Examining Nietzsche's "Time Atom Theory" Fragment from 1873', *Nietzsche-Studien* 26 (1997), pp. 350–60. Whitlock has argued that Nietzsche's discovery of finite force is decisive for the eternal return or infinite time. Deleuze is careful to distance Nietzsche from a purely literal mechanical or scientific understanding of force: 'it is true that Nietzsche was interested in the energetics of his time, but this was not the scientific nostalgia of the philosopher' (DR, 243).

22. See 'Origin and the Inverted Image' in NP, pp. 55–8.

23. Nietzsche, *Will to Power*, no. 1066.

24. Ibid., no. 617.

25. Jeffrey Bell, 'Philosophizing the Double-Bind: Deleuze reads Nietzsche', *Philosophy Today* (Winter 1995), p. 9.

26. Wolfgang Müller-Lauter, *Nietzsche: His Philosophy of Contradictions and the Contradictions of His Philosophy*, trans. David Parent (Chicago: University of Indiana Press, 1999), p. 80.

27. Friedrich Nietzsche, *Sämtliche Werke. Kritische Studienausgabe in 13 Bände*, ed. G. Colli and M. Montinari (Berlin: De Gruyter, 1980), p. 259; and *Will to Power*, no. 635.

# PART II

# (Un)Thinking, What must be Thought

# Introduction to Part II

The comparative reading of Heidegger and Deleuze has prepared the path for a discussion of the transformative potential of art as a prelude to the question of the political. Each thinker places the philosophic tradition into question, seeking a transformation, whether as another beginning or a new image of thought, through an engagement with philosophy's limits, which is to say the limits of thought. Thus both are interested in difference: between being and beings, between thought and being, and, as we have argued before, both recognise a fundamental requirement of conceiving these differences outside of the framework of dualism, immanently.[1] Heidegger and Deleuze are invested in articulating modes of thinking that do not transcend the matter to be thought, but instead unfold out of it. In fact the fold is a major trope for both thinkers, and one that indicates the difference between their respective positions.[2] In other words, the issue of thinking for both is the original event of thought's occurrence.

In a 1978 series of lectures on Kant,[3] Deleuze makes a brief, yet illuminative, reference to Heidegger in relation to the organising idea of the unthought, specifically citing his oft-quoted phrase that 'we have not yet begun to think'.[4] Deleuze identifies the problem of time and its relation to thought as a continued legacy passed down through Kant. 'From Kant onward, philosophy will give itself the task of thinking what is not thinkable, instead of giving itself the task of thinking what is exterior (*extérieur*) to thought . . . the direct line from Kant to Heidegger is truly the problem of time and its relation to thought.'[5] The relation between the form of receptivity (time) and the form of activity (thought), a relation which Deleuze, following Kant, describes as heterogeneous and irreducible, essentially implicates the ungroundedness of thought, and it is clear that Deleuze views Heidegger as working within this problematic.[6] Since both recognise the *Ab-grund*, the foundationless or ungrounded, their difference can be thought in terms of how to conceive founding or commencement. How does one begin (to think) again and how does one conceive the relation between thinking and being?

Though Deleuze credits Heidegger with the thought of difference (DR, 89–91/64–6), he also thinks Heidegger is ultimately re-immersed in the thought of sameness, which subordinates difference to the identity of representation, as indicated by his comments concerning Heidegger's misinterpretation of Nietzsche's eternal return as founded repetition rather than creative.[7] This, in fact, leads to Deleuze's major criticism of Heidegger, that of the homology between being and thinking, ultimately implying the primacy of the Same (DR, 188n1/321n11). Rather than remaining with the ideas of incommensurability and irreducible difference, Heidegger seeks a belonging (*Zugehörigkeit*) between the truth of beyng[8] (as the condition of appearance) and thought (this is clear in his thought of *Ereignis*). For Deleuze, this implies that being is ultimately a founded repetition of the Same, whereas Deleuze will argue that, based on the ontological primacy of difference, being is always a creative, singular event.

A correlate to the concern of the problematic grounding of thought is the in/accessibility of the unthinkable 'ground'. For Heidegger, the limit[9] of thought is that which is concealed or withdrawn from thought, the un-thought, and, for Deleuze, the limit is the non-thought within thought signifying the possibility of becoming and the enigmatic genesis of thought. In the next two chapters, we seek to show how the un-thought becomes revealed in and through art. Heidegger views the poietic as expanding or opening the ways in which we think, while Deleuze, taking the Kantian insight to its extreme, considers thought itself to be unremittingly aesthetic.

For Heidegger, disclosing what has not been thought, which during the mid to late 1930s Heidegger begins to articulate as the truth of beyng, requires a radically new way of thinking, one that twists free from its metaphysical heritage. Heidegger names this new form of thinking 'inceptive thinking', which is characterised as responsiveness occurring through the belonging (*Zugehörigkeit*) of *Dasein* to the sway (*Wesung*) of beyng. One of the main sources for understanding inceptive thinking, and what places Heidegger's thinking underway concerning this transformation in thinking, is the happening of truth in the work of art which Heidegger elaborates in his decisive essay, 'The Origin of the Work of Art'. Heidegger's growing insistence of the importance of art for philosophy in the decade of the 1930s, is notably also the period known as the *Kehre*. The nature of the *Kehre* is often misunderstood, in part because there is a double sense of turning at play here. Heidegger's *Kehre* is often used as a descriptor for the historical shift in his thinking, but it is also a term employed by Heidegger to name the turning of being. Following Heidegger, we will refer to the first, historical turning as a shift, while reserving 'turning' or 'the turn' for the ontological phenomenon.[10] Heidegger's 1930s shift in thinking is inaugurated by a deepened engagement with the nature of truth as *aletheia*, leading to Heidegger's epochal formulation of the happening of the truth of beyng (*Wahrheit des Seyns*), the *Kehre* as *Ereignis*, an event of the belonging attunement to being. This period is marked by a turn from the questioning about being in terms of an existential analysis of *Dasein* toward the thinking of being itself, but it is not a change in standpoint from the fundamental issue of *Being and Time*, which is the forgetting of being, or more strongly put, the oblivion of Being.[11] Nonetheless, the nature of the *Kehre* is difficult to encapsulate, a point which is exacerbated by the intertwining of Heidegger's deeply controversial political involvement with National Socialism and the occurrence of these insights. An extremely intellectually active period for Heidegger, he gave his inaugural lecture at Freiburg University, 'What is Metaphysics?' (1930), his 'Rectoral Address' (1933), the Freiburg lecture course *Introduction to Metaphysics* (1935), as well as writing the *Contributions to Philosophy (On the Event)* (1936–38), a private monograph only recently published (1989).

Indicating the increasingly indispensible role he assigns to artworks and the poet in the revelation of the truth of beyng and the instituting of world, Heidegger published 'The Origin of the Work of Art' (1935),[12] gave the lecture, 'Hölderlins Hymnen *Germanien und Der Rhein*', (1934–35), and wrote 'Hölderlin and the Essence of Poetry' (1936).[13] These must be situated in terms of the progression of his thinking from the 'fundamental ontology' of *Being and Time* to the 'beyng historical thinking' (*seynsgeschichtlich Denken*) that characterises *Contributions*.[14] Of particular importance for understanding the development of art in Heidegger's thinking are 'On the Essence of Truth' (1930), and, of course, his Nietzsche lectures, the first volume of which was composed between 1936 and 1939.

Summarily, Heidegger's investigation into the relation of art and the truth of beyng evolves in the 1930s, first in terms of the creative empowered spirit, corresponding to his fervent optimism in the forging of a new humanity and political regime, to an awareness of the need for a more direct engagement with artworks as themselves opening up a site or space for the event of truth that might inaugurate another beginning, lifting modernity from out of the 'abandonment of beyng' (*Seinsverlassenheit*), and finally into despair that there may be no art for such a desperate age. Doing justice to this trajectory is no small task,[15] and we seek to orient our endeavour around the proposition of another beginning, following the path laid out through Heidegger's diagnosis of the history of being ending with Nietzsche and his deeply critical engagement with what he considers the consummation of Western metaphysics in the will to power, which is indicated by the oblivion of being and machination (*Machenschaft*).[16]

Heidegger understands the oblivion of being as an inevitable conclusion of the history of Western thinking preparing the way for another beginning, but his disillusionment with modernity, exacerbated by his political failures, has an effect on the evolution of his thought concerning art and philosophy. Some suggest that the turn toward art represents a retreat, away from the overt politicisation of his project during his rectorship and the enthusiastic embrace of violence and strength verging so disturbingly near to the language and voluntaristic tone of National Socialism. Taking the language of self-assertion found in the 'Rectoral Address' as a prime example, it has become increasingly evident that Heidegger, during this period, located the possibility of renewing humanity, of a new historical founding of being, in an active engagement with National Socialist politics, albeit philosophically informed. Yet, only two years after the 'Rectoral Address', art and the creative ones are seen as those who can bring being to stand, and, though he is still utilising the language of voluntarism, this could be seen as shift away from the political sphere.

For instance, although his 1935 lecture, *Introduction to Metaphysics*, engages the language of violence and action, there is a subtle modification as images of violence are transferred away from the political toward the aesthetic sphere. There, in the context of reading Sophocles' *Antigone* in order to retrieve the sense of the Greek way of interpreting human essence, Heidegger contends that the Greeks understood human beings to be fundamentally *deinon*, which he translates as *Unheimlich* (to be 'not at home' or uncanny) but also associates with violence (GA40, 158–9/159–60). In fact, humans are the most *deinon* (*to deinotaton*) in that they are doubly so because our uncanniness includes a particular vulnerability to the strangeness of the overpowering power of being and the human tendency to violently go beyond itself and that which is familiar. We transcend our own limits through our necessary predisposition to impact the surrounding world through our making, or *technē*. Thus, the human is the uncanniest of the uncanny because it is both violent in the sense of thrown into the overwhelming power of being and the most violence-doing in the midst of the overwhelming. Humans are essentially creators, who lay paths 'into the beings that envelop humanity in their sway' (GA40, 166/168), yet our task is not to get bogged down in our own path-making. Thus, Heidegger conveys the clear sense that the task for humanity is to face risks and actively and dangerously to bring about change in order to found itself, which will be either a matter of victory or defeat. In the following passage, we see this subtle shift, where the task is undoubtedly given over to the creative ones:

> Thus the knower is thrown this way and that between fittingness and un-fittingness, between the wretched and the noble. Every violent taming of the violent is either victory or defeat. Both throw one out of the homely, each in a different way, and they first unfold, each in a different way, the dangerousness of Being ... The one who is violence-doing (*Gewalt-tätige*), the creative one (*Shaffende*), who sets out into the un-said (*Un-gesagte*), who breaks into the un-thought (*Un-gedachte*), who compels what has never happened and makes appear what is unseen, this violence-doing one stands at all times in daring (*toma*). Insofar as he dares the surmounting of Being, he must risk the assault of un-beings, the *mē kalon*, disintegration, un-constancy, un-structure, and unfittingness. The higher the peak of historical Dasein rises, the more gaping is the abyss for the sudden plunge into the unhistorical, which then only flails around in a confusion that has no way out and at the same time has no site. (GA40, 170/172)

The tone of the text evokes subjective wilfulness, yet there are indications that Heidegger is attempting to think beyond this, an endeavour at which he will be more successful with the onset of his fuller engagement with Hölderlin and art. As we have explained, Heidegger develops the idea that humans are the uncanniest in their relation to violence, which is a matter of both going beyond limits and of being exposed to the overwhelmingness of beings as a whole; thus our uncanniness is characterised by the struggle between *technē*, our violence-doing or, more literally, making, and *dikē*, the overwhelming-power of being. Notably, Heidegger will maintain this relation, transposing it to the work of art as that which opens a space, as in a fissure or gap (*Riss*).[17] *Dikē*, which Heidegger translates as *Fug*, is a fittingness not determined by *Dasein* but that which belongs to being, the direction that the overwhelming gives to its sway; what is fitting is not the known and it is not of our making, and what is unfitting is to be lulled into a forgetfulness of this, to be content with the already understood. To launch oneself into the uncanny, which is the overwhelming power of being, is, paradoxically, to accede to one's essence more fully than if one were to remain comfortably attached to that which is known. Thus that which is most *deinon*, most strange, which is to reach beyond the limits of our understanding and familiarity into that which is foreign, is essentially related the task of the humanity, of becoming who we are.

After presenting multiple oppositions (the wretched and noble, victory and defeat) which set up at least two possibilities of the *deinon*, Heidegger launches into his discussion of the creative ones, conceived as those who dare, risk and stand – all positive terms at this point. In other words, *deinon* is the essence of the human, yet Heidegger implies multiple ways of being *deinon*. Is it the demeanour of the creative ones that we must understand as the method of *deinon* to be desired? What is it that the creative ones bring? How do they approach the sway of being differently or more intensely? Within these questions is the latent seed of Heidegger's later thought concerning both who we are and the attitude or attunement that we must cultivate in order to become that which we are. It seems that the creative one is able to hold herself out into the maelstrom, to undergo this exposure in a way that maintains openness to it, and that this is the essential point which gets carried over, though transformed significantly as we shall see, into his thinking of the work of art. Thus the danger of the doubleness of *deinon* is an indication that we destroy ourselves, in the original sense of our essence as *deinon*, in our own attempt to do violence to the violent or strange. In other words, there is a double possibility to our essence as *deinon*: Are we to do violence, to assert, to claim, to lay paths in being, and thus to surpass our limits in this way, or are we to undo ourselves, our security in our surroundings and knowledge, thereby putting ourselves in question yet more within the strangeness of being?

Now following the association of the creative with standing firm in the daring, Heidegger links this risk, this way of being, to the most radical departure from the fitting, at least as one possibility. In this passage the creative one must thrust herself into the sway, and it seems that the creative ones are more able, or willing, to do so. Thus they risk the most, to be swept away by the unremitting flow of that which abjures determination, on the precipice between the fitting and the unfitting. Because one is on the limits, beyond one's understanding, the danger is greater that one will plunge into the unhistorical. But what is the unhistorical? It is the stagnation of time that implies the application of a standard of a being to *dikē*, which would be a fundamental contradiction since *dikē* is always in movement, displaced and displacing. One could interpret this as Heidegger excusing his own extreme political blindness, or, as recognising the limits of a thinking which attempts to make being submit, even in terms of art or the 'creative ones', and as an admonishment to approach the unsaid and the unthought in ways which do not attempt to destroy its strangeness. We are inclined to the more generous of interpretations, given that maintaining this non-appropriative relation to that which is strange, in other words letting it be, is exactly what Heidegger begins to develop in terms of 'earth' in *Origin*. There, it is the work of art itself, rather than the creative one, in which this strife takes place. This is significant in that the work of art can be a means by which its preservers, a people, come to stand in the truth of beyng and begin to cultivate an attunement to this strangeness, to let it be and thus be transposed into their essential nature – to be *deinon*. *Origin* reflects a shift away from the language of resoluteness and violence of this period – thus, we can see Heidegger's disillusionment productively channelled into a renewed attempt to eradicate the subjective residues in his thinking.

In his proceeding works, Heidegger gives up the language of compelling, daring and projecting for the gentler language of receiving and listening, yet the idea of placing oneself in the unknown, to remain vigilantly exposed to that which is foreign and unknown, the unthought, remains central to his thinking. In other words, several of these themes remain at the forefront of Heidegger's thought, while others will recede, indicative of the struggle he undergoes in relation to a misplaced bravado concerning the power of philosophy to intercede in the actual political events occurring around him. In the following chapter, we will explore the development of what remains to be thought, which is not some 'thing' or 'a being', but the very truth of beyng understood through being-historical thinking prepared by thinking through the origin of the work of art. One could say that this marks an entrance into Heidegger's understanding of the task of philosophy as a kind of (un)thinking, which requires the insertion of that which is outside of thought in order to be attuned to the truth of being and begin to think anew.

## Notes

1. For Deleuze's recognition of Heidegger's important role in thinking difference in itself see Leonard Lawlor and Janae Sholtz, 'Heidegger and Deleuze', in *The Bloomsbury Companion to Heidegger* (New York: Bloomsbury, 2013), pp. 417–24.

2. Deleuze sees the Heideggerian fold as a sameness, or neat alignment, between being and beings, as well as thought and being, whereas, for him, the fold is symmetrical, more of a zigzag. Therefore, the founding event of thought is conceived very differently. Rather than a relation of belonging resonance between Dasein and being, Deleuze conceives this relation in terms of the violence of an encounter that is both unrepeatable and eschews resemblance between the matter and thought.

3. The context for this lecture is Kant's modern conception of time, which Deleuze claims indicates 'a radical reversal in the position of the problem of time in relation to philosophy'. Whereas classical understandings subordinate time to movement, leading to circular models of time as eternity, Kant thinks time as a straight line, the present as caesura with no correspondence between before and after – time out of joint. These models speak to different understandings of limit; the first model leading to a view of the human as eluding the limit through transgression and then the re-establishment of equilibrium through atonement. This cyclical time 'carries out the act of limitation'; it binds. Time, as a line, indicates a passage to the limit. Reaching the limit is both the ungrounding of thought and the discovery of the limit as founding kernel, a passage from chaos to order. See *Les Cours de Gilles Deleuze*: Kant 14/03/1978; Kant 21/03/1978; Kant 28/03/1978; available at <http://www.webdeleuze.com/php/sommaire.html> (accessed 11 July 2014).

4. Deleuze refers to Heidegger's question, 'what calls for thinking?' several times. See DR 188/144, but also 25–3/195–6, 259/200, 353/275. See also F, 124/116.

5. *Les Cours de Gilles Deleuze*: Kant 28/03/1978, p. 8.

6. Illustrating Deleuze's awareness of the problem of ground, in his most direct engagement with Heidegger (DR, 89–91/64–6), he cites Heidegger's 'On the Essence of Ground' and 'What is Metaphysics?', both in *Pathmarks*, ed. William McNeil (Cambridge: Cambridge University Press, 1998), pp. 97–135; pp. 82–96.

7. See Chapter 2. For Deleuze's criticism of Heidegger's reading, see DR 91/66; NP, 211n1/220n31; DR, 85/60. See also Lawlor and Sholtz, 'Heidegger and Deleuze', pp. 420–1 for the significance of different conceptions of repetition.

8. Marking the shift in Heidegger's thought beginning in 1930s, Heidegger switches from *sein* to the archaic spelling, *seyn*, to indicate its

anteriority to the metaphysical concept of being. We will use *beyng* to remain faithful to Heidegger's intent. See John Sallis' explanation in 'Grounders of the Abyss', in Charles E. Scott et al., eds, *Companion to Heidegger's Contributions to Philosophy* (Bloomington: Indiana University Press, 2001), pp. 184 and 196, n12.

9. 'The *peras* is Greek philosophy is not *limit* in the sense of the outer boundary, the point where something ends. The limit is always what limits, defines.' Heidegger, 'On the Essence and Concept of *Physis*', in *Pathmarks*, p. 206.

10. In a 1962 letter, Heidegger writes, '*Das Denken der Kehre* ist *eine Wendung in meinem Denken ...*' (The thinking of the turning *is* a turn [shift] in my thinking ...). See the preface to William Richardson's *Heidegger: Through Phenomenology to Thought* (New York: Fordham University Press, 2003), pp. xxii/xxiii.

11. James Risser, ed., *Heidegger Toward the Turn: Essays on the Work of the 1930s* (New York: SUNY Press, 1999), p. 3. He does begin to develop this problematic in terms of the 'withdrawal' of being.

12. There are three versions: the Frankfurt or first version (1935), recently translated into English as 'Of the Origin of the Work of Art (first elaboration)', trans. Markus Zisselsberger, in *Epochē* 12:2 (2008); the second version, an unauthorised French translation of the lecture given in 1935 in Freiburg: *De l'origine de l'oeuvre d'art. Première version (1935)*, ed. E. Martineau (Paris: Authentica, 1987); and the third version written in 1936 and first published as *Holzweg* in 1950. This version has gone through several publications and revisions, with Heidegger adding the '*Nachwort*' after 1936 but before the 1950 publication and adding the '*Zusatz*' before 1956. These changes as well as the editing of several passages appear in what is commonly called the Reclam-edition: *Der Ursprung des Kunstwerkes* (Stuttgart: Reclam-Bibliothek, 1960). The most recent editions of *Holzweg* (GA 5) include these additions as well as working notes that Heidegger added in 1950 and is translated in *Off the Beaten Track*. These versions were crafted between 1935 and 1937, just previous to his lectures on Nietzsche and just following his exit from the National Socialist Party.

13. Heidegger continues his profound engagement with Hölderlin in 'Hölderlins Hymne "Andenken"' (Winter Semester 1941–42) and 'Hölderlins Hymne "Der Ister"' (Summer Semester 1942). Also, in six essays written between 1936 and 1968, published in *Elucidations of Hölderlin's Poetry*.

14. For an excellent introduction to the *Beiträge* and comparison to *Being and Time*, see Daniela Vallega-Neu, *Heidegger's Contributions to Philosophy: An Introduction* (Bloomington: Indiana University Press, 2003).

15. Hermeneutically, this period represents an impossibly dense

interpretative knot which cannot be solved by a merely linear reading of the texts. The overlapping and interwoven nature of Heidegger's thinking of this period means that where one begins is less important than the more challenging task of thinking the interconnected nature of what is presented. We enter Heidegger's thinking from the historicity of being opened up by his consideration of Nietzsche and from the place of the artwork and its relation to truth.

16. Machination is identified with modern technology's ability to secure beings in their perfect disposability in service of the sheer expansion of power (NIII, 175).
17. See GA40, n65.

# 3

# Heidegger on Art and Ontology

To repeat and retrieve (*wieder-holen*) the inception of our historical-spiritual Dasein, in order to transform it into the other inception . . . the inception is repeated when . . . the inception is begun again more originally, and with all the strangeness, darkness, insecurity that a genuine inception brings.[1] (GA40, 42/41)

Through his historical excavation of being (*thinking-beyng-historically*), Heidegger determines that metaphysics is in its final stage, an age of nihilism ushered in by Nietzsche as the final entanglement in metaphysics. Human beings have become disconnected from the origins of thought and the richness of being. Overcoming metaphysics necessitates the need for another beginning, nothing short of a radical leap. What might constitute such a leap into another beginning is really the issue. The leap is a founding and the broadest leap is that of thinking (GA65, section 120). In *Contributions*, Heidegger devotes an entire fugue (chapter) to this issue, beginning with some general characteristics of the leap in section 115. The leap requires abandoning the familiar, which is to say, an acknowledgement of the utmost abandonment of being, the attunement of deep awe, and releasement into belongingness brought about through the awareness of one's condition of complete thrownness, which would amount to a return to our essence as *deinon*.

But we must take a step away from the specific constitution of the leap in order to see Heidegger's trajectory more clearly. As Heidegger begins to think the possibility of another beginning, there are three significant, intertwining factors: (1) the necessity of returning to the Greek origins of thought, in order to retrieve something of the original sense of the historical essence of *Dasein*;[2] (2) his devotion to Hölderlin, the German poet who both experienced the oblivion of being (the flight of the gods) and founded the possibility of another beginning both in terms of the German/Greek relation and in light of the hinting toward the gods, which initiates the possibility for new decisions about the god/human relation;[3] (3)

his commitment to art as providing the path through to this other beginning.

To appreciate the significance of Heidegger's insistence on establishing a new relationship to the essence of art requires a certain digression. That is, an analysis of Heidegger's engagement with technology and attention to his particular historical locatedness. As prepared through our reading of Nietzsche, we have illumined Heidegger as one of the great diagnosticians of the state of modernity, the essence of which is tied to what he calls technological thinking. The crisis of our age is the utter and complete oblivion of being within this technological thinking. Yet, the way out of this particular mode of thought is also foreseen within the essence of technology. This double recognition establishes the precedent for a reflection on art, as art is the alternative to which we turn in order to overturn the priority of technological thinking. With this backdrop, we may then explore how thinking through the essence of the work of art prepares the grounding attunement (*Grundstimmung*) which may awaken our sensitivity to *Ereignis*.[4]

The proposed digression into the essence of technology is consistent with our prior claim of Heidegger's shift in emphases; another beginning will involve a return to the origins of Western thought in order to understand its historical trajectory, a repetition (*wiederholen*) that unearths what remains unthought or has been forgotten from the beginning. In other words, only through understanding the course of Western thought since the Greeks in its historical unfolding are we able to overcome metaphysics and begin again.

According to Heidegger, the issue of origin is itself already bifurcated and, thus, ambiguous. The beginning of metaphysics (Plato) is not the first beginning. The more primordial beginning is found in the thought of the pre-Socratics. Heidegger claims, 'it belongs to the *first* commencement, to throw so much brightness around itself that it needs no limping explanations' (NIII, 113). The residue of this space that the Greeks first measured out resides within the *logos* of the pre-Socratics. There are fundamental words that reveal the guiding insights and commitments of the Greeks, which have either been forgotten in their richness or dramatically altered and transformed from their original meanings. Thus, Heidegger will situate his later project in terms of language and its primordiality, shifting away from his prior phenomenological interrogation of *Dasein*.

It is remarkable that, while Heidegger privileges the origins of thought, there is no simple going backwards. The move to rediscover these origins is predicated on Heidegger's retracing of the error into which Western metaphysics has plunged, but also being mindful of our present situation. This does require a look back to the foundations of thought, a strategy Heidegger employs with respect to truth as *aletheia*, art as *poiesis*, language as *logos*, and the emerging into presence of *physis*, but it also requires a different way of thinking and a different attunement to the world. The origins of thought must be creatively and reflectively incorporated into our present awareness, an awareness that we must still produce.

Heidegger refers to the necessary change in awareness as preparation for the leap or *transition* (*Ubergang*) from the first beginning to the other beginning (GA65, S117, 228/180). Our thinking must be attuned in order to prepare for the leap. If wonder is the grounding attunement of the first (Greek) beginning, Heidegger claims that the grounding attunement of the other beginning will be characterised by several names: startled dismay (*Erschrecken*), reservedness (*Verhaltenheit*), awe (*Scheu*), intimation and deep foreboding,[5] all of which speak to the crisis or distress that characterises our epoch. To enter into this new era, we must be able to experience our distress rather than cover it over, preparing the way to the thinking of *Gelassenheit*.[6]

The second section of the chapter concerns how art accomplishes such a necessary transformation in awareness and explores both the ontological (the truth of beyng) and ontical (the founding of a people) dimensions opened through such a transformation, returning to these two elements in Chapter 5, 'Heidegger and the Political', in order to elucidate the structure for Heidegger's conception of a people-to-come.

## From Ruins, Another Beginning – A Digression

> No transformation (*Wandel*) comes without an anticipatory escort (*vorausweisendes Geleit*). But how does an escort draw near unless Appropriation (*Ereignis*) opens which, calling, needing, envisions human beings, that is, sees and in this seeing brings mortals to the path of thinking, poeticizing, building. (GA7, 98/110)

Heidegger proposes two conditions for transformation: *Geleite* and *Ereignis*. As Heidegger often speaks of the poet and the thinker as those who are the most susceptible to Being and who will, in effect, lead the way to 'another beginning', we can assume that the 'anticipatory escorts' will be either one or both of these. Yet, *Ereignis* ushers in the escort by opening a space whereby a new path can be revealed. In other words, something must happen in order that human beings have 'ears to hear' and 'eyes to see' the poets and thinkers who offer a new path. That Heidegger expresses doubts concerning the possibility of a true historical founding through art in our age echoes the observations of untimely thinkers such as Nietzsche and Hölderlin. The destitution of our age is linked to the fact that a 'people', those who would be able to hear the poetic word of the poet, echoing Paul Klee, are missing. Whence, Heidegger's overwhelming concern with thinking the conditions for the transformation of humanity governed by the insistent questions 'Who are we?' and 'How can we become a people?'[7]

The issue of 'who we are' is a central theme of *Introduction to Metaphysics*, to which we would like to return for a moment. There we learned that the fundamental situation for human beings is one of striving against an overwhelming power which renders us strange and vulnerable, compelling us to try to shape and limit this vastness. Heidegger characterised this as a struggle between *dikē* and *technē*. Of course, Heidegger is enacting a return to the Greeks in these passages, but to what ends? It is because the Greeks understood something that we moderns have forgotten. The overwhelming power of being, the fittingness meted out by being (*dikē*), was present and acknowledged by the Greeks and met by the fundamental attunement of awe and wonder. Now, it seems that our essential tendency to route paths in being has obscured our original experience of it; our activity, as *technē*, has taken over. Given that *technē* is an existential feature of human beings, this oblivion is seen as merely the march of progress, humanity's vanquishing of the uncertain and unknown. Thus Heidegger sets the task for humanity as a kind of retrieval, the taking up of its essential historical destiny through remembrance of this essential relation to being.

To return and take up that which is 'ownmost', first requires the recognition of the oblivion of being. Because of the special doubleness of the uncanny essence of human beings, this oblivion passes by us and remains unthought. Therefore, Heidegger argues, the recognition of the oblivion of being only besieges us in the time of greatest need or danger, in crisis. It is in this moment that we are brought in to our 'ownmost', which is a realisation of our relationship to Being in which we both belong to Being and are needed by Being. This enowning event (*Ereignis*) can only happen out of the most extreme danger.

According to Heidegger, we face just such a danger: the technisation of thought itself. The paradox is that this critical stage of thought, wrought as it is from the nihilistic will, jeopardises the core of human endeavours yet is an essential outgrowth of those endeavours. The age of technology 'realizes, actualizes, the modern metaphysics for which to will is to posit being as an object and the object as rational, hence calculable'.[8] As such, the technisation of thought and deed is the essential possibility of Western metaphysics. Technological thinking is the ultimate and most persevering danger because metaphysics in this final form is characterised by the oblivion of the strangeness of being. Every being is seen as knowable, calculable and controllable – constantly present. The question of the being of beings is effaced and forgotten within it. The essence of humanity itself is at stake:

> The fixating of truth within the *Gestell* and of thought as calculative thought would exile man from his essence. There would be no more relation to the opening, for the possible would be identical to the real. A human being fully adapted to the technological world would no longer be human, for being would no longer be for him worthy of questioning.[9]

Technology as the metaphysically determined expression of *technē* objectifies everything, including human beings. This objectification eliminates the question, which is to say the possible and, thus, the future. Not only would the grounding attunement which opened the first space for philosophy, wonder, be lost, but human beings would no longer provide openings or clearings in which being could come to presence. However, our relationship to technology is an ambiguous one. The acute withdrawal of being also offers the possibility of an opening in which questions can be thought anew and, as we shall see, in which the truth of beyng can once more be glimpsed. In effect, Heidegger views crisis as something that *could* open up a space for genuine thinking, as the unyielding force of technology indicates the point where the whole of philosophy is gathered in completion as a task for thinking.

There are several places that Heidegger explicitly outlines the practical indices of the age of technology, many of which are found in or are connected to his political writings. Heidegger saw Europe's problems as the effect of the technisation of thinking and living. Planetary homogenisation of modes of living and thinking, constant mobilisation of cultural and artistic activity, uprooting and neutralisation of space and time, insensibility to suffering, loss of a sense of proximity and distance, rapid circulation of information, politics subservient to bureaucracy, stockpiling and total mobilisation, comprise the face of the age of technology.[10]

In *Introduction to Metaphysics*, he describes the darkening of the earth, the transformation of men into a mass, the hatred and suspicion of everything free and creative, as part of the spiritual decline of the earth as a *present* concern. The situation that he envisions constitutes much of his explanation for the urgency of his, albeit unfortunate, political involvements of the early 1930s. This crisis, which Heidegger took to be a culminating point in the history of metaphysics, loomed ominously close to home, both philosophically and geographically.[11] He most definitely interpreted the political situation of the day in terms of his own philosophical-historical diagnosis.

In his Rectoral Address, 'The Self Assertion of the German University', Heidegger is enthusiastically committed to a renewal of the spiritual-historical mission of Germany guided by the principles of National Socialism as the solution to the nihilistic age of technology. He advocates a direct relationship between universities and political leadership, and, though he remains loyal to the primacy of knowledge and philosophy, the boundaries between philosophy and a hazardous politics are dangerously blurred. Critics point to the fact that Heidegger stresses the need for spiritual and intellectual leadership which it will be his duty to provide as rector,[12] yet this leadership should be subordinated to the spiritual mission of the German people.[13] Passages concerning Germany's spiritual mission such as this: 'the spiritual world of a people . . . is the power that comes from preserving at the most profound level the forces that are rooted in the earth and blood of a *Volk*' (R, 35) are oft times assumed to be point blank endorsements of National Socialism, some going so far as to contend that, by not 'explaining what he understood by "people" or "earth" (let alone "blood"), Heidegger encouraged his audience to interpret his words in terms of the reigning political context'.[14] At this point, these kinds of critiques of Heidegger's political involvement are ubiquitous and not without merit, yet to take such a stance and neither address the evolution of Heidegger's thinking on these matters nor the complex the intersection of his thought on art and ontology of this period would also be remiss.

When consulting his 1954 essay, 'The Question Concerning Technology', one finds that the tenor of his diagnosis of modernity changes little, but the solution that Heidegger offers in the quest to overcome metaphysics, nihilism and the domination of technology represents a deviation from his prior political endeavours. One, we claim, which better encapsulates his permanent and persevering philosophical viewpoint. Here, the saving power comes through understanding the essence of technology itself, which is not directly linked to political engagement of the sort emphasised in 1933, but is related to art. This is significant because, already as early as 1934 immediately following his exit from the rectorship, Heidegger begins to lecture on Hölderlin and produces *Origin*, which is generally acknowledged to be his definitive treatise on art.[15] That he maintains his stance concerning the importance of art in the complementary pieces, 'The Question Concerning Technology' and 'The Turning', is significant, indicating that we must not shelve Heidegger's views of the 1930s in their entirety, as many have done, nor immediately implicate the concepts and language coming out of that period in National Socialist politics. Neither can we separate his views on art from their political content. In light of these findings, one may be more apt to reconsider or at least consider just what Heidegger means when he continues to use the language of *Volk*, earth and historical-spiritual mission in his philosophical writings, specifically in relation to art.

Heidegger's aim in 'The Question Concerning Technology' is to open a free relationship to the essence of technology. He explains that this essence is itself nothing technological, but has actually been covered over through the increasing domination of the instrumental understanding of technology. Though we will not attempt a complete explication of Heidegger's derivation, it is important to note that he traces the evolution of *technē* in terms of the progression of metaphysics and the transformation of our understanding of basic human experiences. Tracing back to Aristotle's four causes, Heidegger finds that these modes or causes, as ways of occasioning something, are gathered under the term bringing forth (*Her-vorbringen*),[16] which is to say *poiesis*. Bringing forth is essentially a matter of revealing that which was not before present. Given that every bringing forth is a revealing, *technē* also shares in this fundamental trait; hence, it is also a mode of *aletheia* (GA7, 13/12). Accordingly, the essence of technology concerns a mode of revealing, rather than just an instrumental concern for producing certain ends. Yet the mode of revealing of modern technology differs from the bringing forth of *poiesis*. Rather, the mode of revealing that Heidegger claims dominates modernity is 'challenging' (*Herausfordern*), 'which puts to nature the unreasonable demand that it supply energy that can be extracted and stored as such' (GA7, 15/14). Technology as challenging-revealing produces a relationship to beings and to the earth such that they are wielded according to what can be extracted from them and in such a way as to increase power or productivity, thereby affecting what can be revealed about them. In the age of technology, the earth would be revealed as a diamond mine to be excavated or land to be fracked, the field that was formerly cultivated and maintained would now be seen as part of the mechanised food industry, or giving birth would be seen as the production of citizens for statistical, economic or military fodder. Essentially beings are unconcealed as 'standing reserve', and nature is revealed as 'to-be-ordered'. Heidegger insists that this ordering-revealing of modern technology is larger than the human will. Human beings are swept up in this mode of revealing, challenged to order and exploit, as part of the destining of being. This framework which sets upon man to order and reveal the real through which we understand the world Heidegger names *Ge-stell*: 'The challenging claim which gathers man thither to order the self-revealing as standing-reserve' (GA7, 20/19). *Ge-stell* is the essence of modern technology, a mode of revealing that sets humans upon a particular trajectory, a destiny. Unfortunately, that destiny forecloses possibilities rather than opening them.

The essence of modern technology as a 'challenging-revealing' contains the promise of a twofold ambiguity. As challenging, technology covers over the truth of beings other than as 'to-be-used'. The more original connection of *technē* to bringing forth, this essence of technology, is inherently covered over by the violence of challenging. Other possibilities, of experiencing the world, of revealing, of destining, are blocked. Yet, as a mode of revealing, modern technology still participates in the essence of truth and attests to the relation between the truth of beyng and human beings; that our highest dignity 'lies in keeping watch over the unconcealment' (GA7, 33/32). By opening ourselves to that first claim, we may, possibly, accede to another beginning and a new relation to the earth.

Yet, this is not so simple. Fundamentally, the challenging-revealing of *Ge-stell* blocks this possibility by its very method of revealing: 'man, thus under way, is continually approaching the brink of the possibility of pursuing and pushing forward nothing but what is revealed in ordering, and of deriving all his standards on this basis' (GA7, 26/26). As well, modern humanity suffers from two delusions that represent the greatest danger as they threaten to cover over the ability to encounter its essence. First, humans, approaching the world as standing-reserve, are themselves also taken as standing reserve. To counter this objectification of self, human beings draw strict distinctions between mere objects and themselves, attempting to exalt their own status and in the process diminishing that of the external world. Second, because of such a self-serving delusion, our perspective concerning the world is severely limited, and human beings only and everywhere encounter themselves and their modes of calculating, interests and measure (GA7, 27/27). Therefore, *Ge-stell* not only endangers human beings' relationships to themselves, it conceals all other modes of revealing. Ordering-revealing becomes the only kind of revealing that is possible. Moreover, *Ge-stell* conceals revealing as such, blocking the holding-sway of truth wherein unconcealment comes to pass. As a mode of revealing, it belongs to the history of being, but as the particular mode of revealing that it is, technology conceals the truth of beyng. Thus, 'the essence of technology, as a destining of revealing, is the danger' (GA7, 29/28).

Yet, the ambiguous essence of technology contains both the greatest danger *and* the saving power. Enframing technology still remains a granting of being, and the saving power must extend from this destining that claims us. That is to say, there is no 'way out' of *Ge-stell* except through it.[17] The question becomes, 'How does danger turn into a saving power?' As if foreshadowing his answer to the question, Heidegger poetically claims that these two possibilities 'draw past each other like the paths of two stars in the course of the heavens' (GA7, 34/33).

Heidegger claims that enframing technology holds within itself the possibility of its overcoming, because in its essence it is a revealing, and it reveals even as it conceals. When Heidegger writes, 'when we look (*blicken*) into the ambiguous essence of technology, we behold (*erblicken*) the constellation, the stellar course of the mystery . . . the constellation in which revealing and concealing, in which the coming to presence of truth, come to pass' (GA7, 34/33), he is invoking this moment of what passes in the *Ge-stell* as a necessary condition for moving to a new stage of thought. The saving power grows because we experience the profundity of oblivion and concealment, that most elusive yet essential element of *aletheia*. Ensconced in darkness, unconcealment is a bestowal which human beings may then bring forth into the open. We draw nearer to the truth of beyng.

The risk is not recognising that which is being granted through this danger. It seems that it may pass too quickly, as a glimpse or flash, descriptions that resonate in the multiple forms of *Blick* throughout this section. To be prepared for this moment, we need another mode of access, to which Heidegger's final words in the essay respond:

> Because the essence of technology is nothing technological, essential reflection upon technology and decisive confrontation with it must happen in a realm that is, on the one hand, akin to the essence of technology and, on the other, fundamentally different from it. Such a realm is art. (GA7, 36/35)

In 'The Turning', Heidegger focuses expressly on the resonances of the concealment of being with the ambiguity of *Ge-stell*. If concealment belongs to the truth of beyng, and *Ge-stell*, as a mode of revealing of being, also contains this essential element of concealment, then the revealing of the concealment of the oblivion of being actually comes about through recognising *Ge-stell* as a particular mode of revealing that entraps the truth of beyng. The coming to presence of this danger, the revealing of the revealing-concealing essence of *Ge-stell*, happens as the 'possibility of a turning in which . . . the truth of the coming to presence of Being will expressly turn in – turn homeward – into whatever it is' (GA11, 118/41). This turning, which is nothing willed or controlled by human ordering, is a moment of bare exposure to concealment. Oblivion reaches its limit as it were and 'compels thinking so that thinking is set out into the original sway of being as withdrawal'.[18] The fact that being withdraws in the mode of revealing that is *Ge-stell* allows the possibility of a new relation between humans and being, an opening out of the recognition of human finitude and the temporality of being, where we may realise that concealment and revelation are equiprimordial dispensations of being. In other words, within the estrangement of being in *Ge-stell* lies the possibility of bringing about a reversal whereby the truth of beyng as concealment is revealed. This turning event (*kehriges Ereignis*) is a 'radically inverted movement of being, grounded in finitude, that stands over and against the metaphysical ideal of being as full presence and intelligibility'.[19]

This event cannot be forced but must be realised, experienced, and this is why the age of technology is to be the longest of the metaphysical epochs. What saving power can prepare for another beginning? Heidegger answers, 'Through thinking, we first learn to dwell in the realm in which there comes to pass the restorative surmounting of the destining of being, the surmounting of Enframing' (GA11, 118/41). Yet, as Heidegger infamously claims, we have not yet begun to think, nor have we established an attunement to being and to ourselves that lets us think outside of the parameters of calculative thinking. That the answer to another beginning lies in our thinking differently, and yet our thinking is determined by its historical interpretations and decisions which themselves have led to a certain blindness concerning what is fundamental and essential, presents somewhat of an impasse: how are we to begin thinking alternatively or outside of this framework? The modern thinker must discover how and through what medium to bring about this other beginning. If the transition begins with inceptive thinking, to think beyng historically, then thinking must 'remain exposed to the experience of this concealment and thus let it occur'.[20] This is precisely the attunement brought about through understanding the happening of truth in the work of art, as countermeasure to the wilful dominance and emphasis on presence as pure and total unconcealment which characterises technological thinking. This is why Heidegger places such emphasis on learning to dwell poetically upon the earth. Pondering the poetical allows us to draw nearer to the essence of technology, and prepares us to *recognise* the moment of the arrival of another destining, *Ereignis*.

For this unpredictable future event, two moments must conjoin: (1) the in-turning of being where through its oblivion, in the mode of revealing called *Ge-stell*, the truth of beyng is revealed out of its very estrangement, and (2) preparedness through attuned thinking. And, at each moment when Heidegger begins to contemplate the possibility of another beginning, he turns to a reflection on art. Plausibly, he is searching for a different mode of thinking, one that remains outside of the metaphysical determination of calculation and rational certitude, but this is only a cursory explanation. As explained in the first chapter, Heidegger recognises that aesthetics has come to a similar place of crisis as metaphysics. It is not enough to appeal to art; aesthetics must be overcome through a deeper engagement with the essence of art, as well as the poetic essence of language. Being gives itself in language, and Heidegger views poetic language (*Dichtung*) as an *Ursprache*, a place where being is spoken originally and anew. In 'What are Poets For?', Heidegger tells us that poets operate most fundamentally in times of distress. It is when the gods have fled, in the oblivion of being, that poets open a new clearing by naming the holy from out of which new gods can arise. The poet is poised to attend to the call of being, laying out the realm from which a people gains its view of itself. Hence, to establish a new relationship with being and transform our relationship to the earth, we must return to the original bond between *aletheia, poiesis* and language. Listening to poetic *logos* and poetic thinking will be proposed as our cultivating activities, as that which is and brings forth our ownmost, arising from within us as an authentic response to being.

## Event, Art as the Saving Power

As we have intimated before, the issue of art is complicated by the fact that it is a place where Heidegger's ontological project and the political converge. This is no where clearer than in 'Hölderlins Hymnen *Germanien* und *Der Rhein*': 'Poetry as instituting effects the ground of the possibility for the settling of humans on earth between it and the gods, that is *for becoming historical and so able to be a people*' (GA36, 216). Consequently, two interrelated questions stand in the background of our discussion of the significance of art. First, if one characterises the essence of the work of art as an event or happening of truth, does it give us insight into the nature of *Ereignis*, and if so, to what degree? This question arises from our intuition that what is essential about art starts Heidegger on his path of thinking about *Ereignis*. Second, for whom can the experience of art be an event, as one that opens a space for *Ereignis*? This question cuts to the heart of our inquiry because of its political trajectory. As a preliminary answer to the first question, we submit that the essential feature of the work of art which Heidegger develops in *Origin* is that it brings the concealedness of being into the Open, bringing those who experience the work of art nearer to the heart of *aletheia*. A more complete response entails an investigation into Heidegger's understanding of the essence of art, its disclosive purpose, and connection to the philosophic project of overcoming metaphysics and the issuance of a new, post-technological epoch of thinking. Our thinking in terms of the second question is that the answer lies in investigating the work of art as a place (*Ort*) that gathers, and overlaying this image, as Heidegger does, onto the spatial inferences of a *polis*, in terms of homeland (*Heimat*) and dwelling – the subject of Chapter 5.[21]

The first step to bringing art to its status of saving power, which is to say to initiate *Dasein* into a true, more authentic, relationship to being out of which history can begin anew, is to reclaim the essence of art. 'Everything depends upon our taking the right leap forward' and this right leap consists in the 'extraction of a sufficient preliminary concept of the work of art' (*Of*, 332). *Origin* represents Heidegger's most vivid analysis of the happening of truth as *aletheia*. In *Origin* this happening is figured as the dichotomous relationship between world and earth, revealing the essence of truth as a movement of unconcealment and concealment. Heidegger also characterises the work of art as opening up a world *for a people*, transposing a people into their ownmost, their endowment. The work works doubly as an original disclosure of truth (*Offenbarkeit*) and as the founding a people (*Offenlichkeit*).[22] Finally, poetry, as the privileged art form, links two major Heideggerian themes: the primordiality of language and the creative disclosure of truth in the artwork. Hence, *Origin* brings several themes together: truth, art, the founding of a people, and the role of language, providing the design for the commencement of another beginning.

*Origin* is often cited as Heidegger's attempt to move beyond the existential analysis of individual *Dasein* and the residual humanism found in *Being and Time*. The introduction of earth as the counterpart to world and the understanding of the artwork as producing a collective understanding for a particular people are two indices of this. The work of art tells us something about the truth of beyng that the analysis of world alone does not, namely about that which eludes us and remains beyond the purview of, and concealed from, our human endeavours. The addition of earth reflects this element of being that is absolutely other or foreign to us, and it is through the work of art that we become open to this foreignness as foreign, that we are able to see the earth as earth. Given what Heidegger has claimed concerning the obliteration of our relation to the earth through the enframing power of technology, and that he claims that a people can only become authentic and achieve its ownmost through a more authentic relation to earth, the artwork, as that which reveals earth as earth, has the potential to open up a world for a people, thus bestowing upon a people its future outlook.

*Origin* also marks a turning away from *Being and Time*'s question of the meaning of being, which is determined on the basis of the clearing opened by *Dasein* to the presencing of the truth of beyng through the space opened up by the work or art, a progression that begins in the early 1930s. In 'On the Essence of Truth' (1930), *eksistent Dasein* opens a space due to its comportment of receptive engagement, wherein being can enter and show itself as it is, but that opening is empty without the upsurgent presence of being flowing into it. The open comportment of *Dasein* involves reciprocity with 'the Open' (*das Offene*).[23] Thus, Heidegger begins to develop the relation of belonging. Yet, the Open is more primordial than *Dasein*;

it is not something that *Dasein* lets happen but that which *Dasein* happens in, the *Da*.

De-emphasising *Dasein*, and its meaning-giving activities, allows Heidegger to focus on the fact that being gives itself and that the Open is an event that happens to us. *Dasein* is necessary to hold open the space of the happening of being. Yet the Open must be grounded in freedom, and freedom is a bestowal of being, not a consequence of human willing. Freedom is letting-beings-be, which is 'to engage oneself with the open region and its openness into which every being comes to stand' (GA9, 188/144). *Ek-sistent Dasein* is surrounded by the disclosure of beings and is granted the possibility of truth. The issue for Heidegger is: will human beings accede to their essence, as *Dasein*, and how?[24]

From 'On the Essence of Truth' to *Origin*, Heidegger's formulation of this relationship between *Dasein*, being and freedom changes. In *Origin*, the work, rather than *Dasein*, opens a space for this free belonging.[25] It is the free space in which *Dasein* can occur. As well, the *Da* of the work of art opens the possibility of transforming the *Dasein* of a people. In other words, Heidegger is no longer working under the assumption of the individual *Dasein*. The work of art gives a common world that operates as a space for gathering a people in an authentic relationship to earth and world. Poetry (*Dichtung*) has a privileged position in this process; since language is fundamentally a shared experience, the poetic provides the place for communion, for the gathering of a people.

## The Happening of Truth in the Work: Strife Between Earth and World

Discussing the work of art as an opening onto being brings us to one of the central issues of *Origin*, the relationship between the work of art and truth. Heidegger has determined that the being of the work of art is different than that of either things or equipment; more than materiality and more self-sufficient than the equipmental, the work of art lets us know what things are in themselves, revealing the truth of beings. 'The artwork opens up, in its own way, the being of beings. This opening up, i.e., unconcealing, of the truth of beings, happens in the work. In the artwork, the truth of beings has set itself to the work' (H, 28/19). Two things stand out from this passage: first, truth and the artwork are kinds of things that have an event-like nature, and second, the artwork exists as a being that captures this event or happening in a special way. It holds open the happening of the truth of beyng. Moreover, given that the origin of the work of art must be understood through the primordial affinity between *technē* and *poiesis* as modes of bringing forth, what happens in this opening of the artwork is itself essentially related to the disclosedness of the revealing/concealing essence of truth.

Let us examine how Heidegger comes to understand the unique essence of the work of art – the work as a happening of truth. In his first two examples, Van Gogh's painting of a pair of peasant shoes and a poem by C.F. Meyer, 'The Roman Fountain', Heidegger concludes that the work-being of the work may not be thought as a combination of equipment and thing, but must be thought in itself (H, 28/18). The first example, the peasant shoes, sets him on his path. By taking what seems to be a piece of equipment, a pair of shoes, and intending to discuss its nature as equipmentality in the work, Heidegger finds that Van Gogh's painting, itself a depiction of equipment, is first, rather obviously, not itself equipmental, and, further, that it gives us something far beyond mere representation:

> From the dark opening of the well-worn inside of the shoes the toil of the worker's tread stares forth. In the crudely solid heaviness of the shoes accumulates the tenacity of the slow trudge through the far-stretching and ever-uniform furrows of the field swept by raw wind. On the leather lies the dampness and richness of the soil. Under the soles slides the loneliness of the field-path as evening falls. The shoes vibrate with the silent call of the earth. (H, 23/14)

Heidegger's description is a repudiation of the representational function of art, which is necessary if he is going to reclaim art for the purposes of emancipating our thinking from the technological manner of representing beings as objects for our consumption.[26] The world of the peasant woman, her daily toil, and the elements against which she toils appear, showing that the work concerns the general essence of things as a whole, not the reproduction of a particular being (H, 26/16). If anything, this example indicates that a work of art is meta-representational, revealing a richness of being that does not merely show up as immediately present at hand. The painting overflows the image of the shoes themselves. Gadamer, drawing upon Heidegger, writes that the distinctiveness of the artwork is that it enriches and increases the being of whatever is presented;[27] in essence, the work goes beyond the being of what is presented, letting appear a region of beings, a set of relations both human and nonhuman, out of which any being comes to have its particular look. As a revealing of these relations it is a happening of truth and, most importantly, as the next example will illustrate, the opening instituted by the work is a gathering which reveals relations for the first time.

Heidegger clarifies the work-being of the work once again with a final example, one entirely removed from the genre of representational art – the Greek temple. Though itself a well-worn example, the passage bears repeating, as it is definitive for Heidegger's understanding of how truth sets itself into the work, the originating power of the work, as well as for understanding the ontological and political power of the work of art:

> It is the temple work that first structures and simultaneously gathers around itself the unity of those paths and relations in which birth and death, disaster and blessing, victory and disgrace, endurance and decline acquire for the human being the shape of its destiny. The all-governing expanse of these open relations is the world of this historical people. From and within this expanse the people first returns to itself for the completion of its vocation.
>
> Standing there, the building rests on the rocky ground. This resting of the work draws out of the rock the darkness of its unstructured yet unforced support. Standing there, the building holds its place against the storm raging above it and so first makes the storm visible in its violence. The gleam and luster of the stone . . . in fact first brings forth the light of day, the breadth of the sky, the darkness of the night. The temple's firm towering makes visible the invisible space of the air. The steadfastness of the work stands out against the surge of the tide and, in its own repose, brings out the raging of the surf. Tree, grass, eagle and bull, snake and cricket first enter their distinctive shapes and thus come to appearance . . . the Greeks called this coming forth and rising up in itself and in all things *Φύσις*. At the same time *Φύσις* lights up that on which and in which man bases his dwelling. We call this the earth. (H, 31–2/20–1)

This passage brings together many of the key themes of Heidegger's philosophy, and admittedly we can here only gesture at its richness. Heidegger presents two essential traits of the happening of truth in the work of art: the setting-up of world (*Er-richten*) and the setting-forth (*Herstellung*) of the earth. The work is a happening out of which world and earth come to presence. In *Being and Time* the world is the referential whole of how things are for us, a shared totality of significance. A world is made up of references whereby things are understood as having a for-structure: the hammer is 'for' hammering, the roof is 'for' shelter, and each of these is determined by its utility for us. *Dasein,* by gaining a more authentic awareness of world, understands its ownmost possibilities. Here, Heidegger's reference to world is more poetic, even verging on the prophetic, and the possibility of world seems closely tied to a transformed relation to being: 'world is that always-nonobjectual to which we are subject as long as the paths of birth and death, blessing and curse, keep us transported (enraptured) into being' (H, 33–4/23). By world, Heidegger understands the essential relations, paths and decisions that give meaning to our existence and provide the context from which we judge and measure the importance and significance of things and come to understand the structural positions within the social order.[28] The temple, with its enclosed god-figure, indicates to a people what is holy. It is also a location where rites, blessings and sacrifices are performed. These activities foster the growth of values and beliefs, giving a people its view of itself.

Whereas, vis-à-vis *Being and Time,* the world becomes visible in the breakdown of equipment, the work of art gives access to world in a different way. Breakdown provides a momentary glimpse that becomes covered over once one resumes everyday activities. The work allows the open of the world to remain open; because the work is itself in repose, it reveals the world in a way that the breakdown of equipment cannot. It stands within itself, unlike equipment which is always directed toward some other end, and this repose is that of self-sufficiency related to its ability to maintain itself and keep open its opening. Now, if the essential function of the artwork were rep-resentational, works of art would merely be reflections of already set values and practices rather than genuine modes of *Ein-richten.* Yet, given Heidegger's explanation of the work as a place where beings first acquire their look, we can see that the work of art holds open the open of world as a space for new worlds or the revision of meanings, and so can initiate a caesura or break in history. 'The establishment of truth in the work is the bringing forth of a being of a kind which never was before and never will be again' (H, 50/37). This is the worlding of world. In ascribing to the work the ability to found a world, Heidegger bestows a profound power on the work of art. The work can change the outlook of those who embrace it.

The second essential trait of the work is the setting-forth (*Herstellung*) of the earth. The concept of the earth provides a coun-terpart to that of world, and it takes on several significances within the course of these lectures. As the temple example illustrates, the earth is both related to the rising up of *physis*, nature, and a literal place within which human beings dwell. However, Heidegger implies that it is not merely to be understood as the astronomical planet or the sum of physical beings. Earth is as much a structural concept as world. Earth, Heidegger enigmatically tells us, is 'that in which the arising of everything that arises is brought back' (H, 31/21). He describes it as sheltering, which means in part that, unlike world, it does not give itself in terms of meanings and significances related to our human endeavours. On the contrary, it is mute and meaningless, and, if it has significance at all, it does not come from human projections. Anticipating our discussion of poets, the earth has been closely tied to the equally enigmatic concept of the holy.[29]

In relation to the work itself, the setting-forth of earth is presented as the setting-forth of the work-material out of which the work is made. A work is literally brought forth out of some material, whether stone, wood, metal, colour or language. As mute colour, stone, wood, etc., the earth 'shatters every attempt to penetrate it'; it is 'essentially undisclosable' and 'self-secluding' (H, 35–6/25). We become aware of our inability to ever completely capture the nature of the material.[30] The earth is apprehended as earth only when understood as that which withdraws from disclosure. It is therefore essentially at odds with unconcealment, though, paradoxically, its concealing nature becomes unconcealed in the work. Heidegger insists that, similar to the needful belonging of being and language, the earth needs the setting-up of world in order to be itself or at least to reveal itself. As he says, the 'temple-work, in setting up a world, does not let the material disappear' but instead 'the rock comes to bear and rest and so first becomes rock, the metal comes to glitter and shimmer, the colors to shine' (H, 35/24). In other words, the sensuous qualities appear for themselves. The work moves the earth into the open, so that the earth can be disclosed as earth rather than slipping away in an infinite, sensible stream of rising and passing away. Great art is able to maintain the 'dignity and splendor' (its holy unintelligibility) of the earth, to bring it into the light without using it up.

The setting-forth of the earth happens in conjunction with the setting-up of world as a unity. Heidegger evokes this unity by referring to the temple's particular groundedness, its protrusion from the ground yet ostensible difference from the natural horizon brings into relief these surroundings, the mute elements that form a constant barrage against it. In fact, because of the intrusion of the temple, nature becomes apparent to us: 'the temple's firm towering makes visible the invisible space of the air'. The earth is vividly displayed as crashing against world, in a tense and oppositional relationship described as an enactment of strife: 'the storm visible in its violence', and 'the surge of the tide . . . the raging of the surf' (H, 31/21). The holy repose of the temple exists in stark contrast to the unremitting forces of wind and wave.

These two traits are equiprimordial and irreducible. As such, the essence of the work is conceived as essential opposition, the generative force of bringing forth. The essential oppositional traits comprise a unity which speaks to the activity of the work, its inner movement. In this relation of strife, each carries the other beyond itself, bringing forward that which is 'extra-ordinary (*Un-geheure*)' and 'overflowing' (*Überfluss*) (H, 62/47). Self-assertion (*Selbstbehauptung*) now belongs to the work of art itself. Strife is an irreducible element of the work that remains an open opposition, an ontological dispensation in which both earth and world are heightened, or amplified. The clearing (*Lichtung*) resulting from the strife lets this oppositional relation itself appear, bringing earth and world more fully into their essences. With the addition of earth to world, and in conceiving the work of art as this space of active tension, Heidegger provides a richer, more complicated account of the truth of beyng. This relation is reminiscent of the *dikē/technē* opposition Heidegger develops in relation to the *Antigone*. The self-sustaining stream of boundary setting of the earth was formerly a trait attributed to *dikē* and the ability to create paths and bestow significance, the essence of the human as *technē*.

What is decisively important is to understand the temple as an intensive site in which things come to pass and appear – a becoming. The vital function of the temple is a gathering, a unifying that brings together the human and nature in a co-determining relation: 'the temple first gives to things their look, and to men their outlook' (H, 32/21). Rather than considering works of art as inert objects, it would be well to understand this oppositional unity of world and earth as a *happening*, an event. As a happening, the free of the Open as understood through *Origin* is thus characterised by activity – the activity of the strife between earth and world *and* the activity of preserving, to which we will return.

Heidegger describes the process by which this happening is preserved as a translation of the strife between earth and world into a *Riss*. The *Riss* is the site of intimacy of world, which demands openness and decisiveness, and earth, which 'strives to preserve its closedness ... [carrying] the contestants into the source of their unity, their common ground' (H, 51/38). Most often translated as rift, as in fissure or cleft, *Riss* can also be understood as design, which designates the sense that earth and world remain in perpetual tension, and, through their mutuality, establish a border space – an in-between. The tension between these two opposing forces remains intensive, creating an outline (*Auf-riss*) which marks the fundamental features of this rising up of the Open, which, 'set back into the earth and fixed in place' (H, 51/38), becomes figure (*Gestalt*). In the emergence of the figure, the truth of the opening of beings, the sway of beyng, is illuminated. After explaining the relationship between earth and world, Heidegger then considers that what remains to be thought is the essence of truth itself: 'until now the assertion that truth is set to work ... remains merely provisional' (H, 39/27).

## THE CONCEALED ESSENCE OF TRUTH

Truth is one of the basic concepts of Heidegger's philosophy.[31] His first basic intervention with the concept comes in Section 44 of *Being and Time*, where he critiques the traditional (correspondence) understanding of truth. The upshot of this work is that those concepts of truth based on correctness and judgement are understood as secondary structures dependent on the ancient Greek understanding of *aletheia*. Focusing on the alpha-privative contained in *a-letheia*, Heidegger understands truth as disclosure, or unconcealment. In 'On the Essence of Truth' (1930), he revises and deepens his investigation of *aletheia,* focusing on concealment as the non-essence, or pre-essential essence, of truth (GA9, 194/148). The Greeks understood *aletheia* as unconcealing, but did not ask about that from out of which truth presences – 'concealing as a fundamental occurrence has sunk into forgottenness' (GA9, 195/149).

Heidegger discovers the concealment at the heart of unconcealment through his contemplation of freedom as letting-beings-be, which is to say the disclosure of beings. He explains that historical *Dasein* can, in letting beings be, also not let them be as they are. In fact, our mode of comportment to this or that being and our tendency to comport to that which is most familiar closes us off to the openedness of beings as a whole. To this end, the openedness of beings as a whole prevails more essentially in the unfamiliar. Therefore, the freedom that brings *Dasein* into accord with beings is doubly bound to concealment, both as that which is covered over through our comportment and in terms of the unfamiliar. 'The concealment of beings as a whole, untruth proper, is older than every openedness of this or that being. It is also older than letting-be itself which in disclosing already holds concealed and comports itself toward concealing' (GA9, 194–5/148). Heidegger finds that un-truth, as the pre-essential essence of truth, points to a still unthought domain of the truth of being.

Given that Heidegger claims decisions of history arise from the way that the original essence of truth unfolds, a more original unfolding of the essence of truth, such as the disclosure of the unthought of *aletheia*, would present the possibility for a leap into another beginning. To think more profoundly about truth, toward its pre-essential essence, concealment, is to verge upon a new site of history. The possibility for human beings to enter into their historical essence (to become a people) is given in the thinking of *aletheia* as both disclosure *and* concealedness, presence and radical, even double, absence.

It seems to us that 'On the Essence of Truth' lies in the background of *Origin*, evincing a call to which *Origin* is the response. That call is to discover a means to open a space for the freedom of letting-be in order that the truth of beyng, its duality as unconcealment and concealment, can come to presence. Though in the 1930 essay, Heidegger bequeaths philosophical thinking the special propensity for 'resolute openness that does not disrupt the concealing but entreats its unbroken essence into the open region of understanding' (GA9, 199/152), by the mid-30s he has come to understand the necessity for a thinking oriented by the poetic. Concealment, first thought through in 'On the Essence of Truth', is thematically fulfilled in *Origin*, figured in and through the concept of earth.

> In the midst of beings as a whole an open place comes to presence. There is a clearing . . . Only this clearing grants us human beings access to those beings that we ourselves are not and admittance to the being that we ourselves are . . . But even to be *concealed* is something that being can only do within the scope of the illuminated. (H, 42/30)

In order to initiate this new mode of thinking that takes its beginning from another comportment to beings as a whole, 'there must be a being in which the openness takes its stand and achieves constancy' (H, 50/36), a place where the normal fleetingness of concealment can be preserved along with the unconcealment which is more generally visible in *aletheia*. The work of art provides the occasion, the open space, to think this radical absence and so lets us glimpse the infinite possibility of concealment out of which unconcealment arises. Works of art possess the inherent possibility of bringing about the unfamiliar, which is where the openedness of beings as a whole prevails over our essential gravitation toward the readily available, or present-at-hand. The essence of the work of art consists in its propensity for the extraordinary – the possibility of rising above the usual. Hence, the work, as the clearing where beings become unconcealed for the first time, is an original happening of truth, which is to say, *poiesis*: 'All art, as the letting happen of the advent of the truth of beings, is, in essence, poetry' (H, 59/44). It is in this respect that Heidegger considers not just the origin of the work of art, but the work of art as an origin.

## Origin of the Work and the Work as an Origin

Through contemplating the origin of the work of art, its poetic essence, Heidegger reveals the work as an origin, a founding of an original happening of truth. As a founding event, the work of art is simultaneously bestowal, grounding, and beginning. What distinguishes *poiesis* from other forms of disclosure is that it is bringing forth not in accordance with a particular idea or model in mind, as in the kind of epistemic knowledge that guides the production of artifacts or tools. *Poiesis* is a revealing characterised by its projective power. Projection implies extension outwards and going beyond what is there, thus the work is a bestowal in that it overflows or is in excess of what is present and available. The conflict between world and earth is like an upsurge that opens a space for the emergence of being.[32] It is excessive to the present in that the opening that is created, the *Riss*, which is then fixed in the figure of the work, is not a representation of this or that being, but a genuine opening from which being bestows itself in and through the work. Poetry is a clearing projection which allows beings to shine and sound for the first time (H, 60/45). This indicates the singularity of the work as well – as that which was never before and will be never again.

Poeticising projection is also a founding in the sense of grounding history because of its relation to coming preservers. Heidegger moves from how being is bestowed and thus transformed in the work because the 'an open place is thrown open, a place in which everything is other than it was' to how *we* are transformed in the work: 'we transport ourselves out of the habitual and into what is opened up in the work' (H, 59/44) – in other words, we become attuned to the granting of being that happens in and through the work. The projection of truth is an opening up of a certain historical humanity that provides the possibility of a ground for that humanity.

Finally, art, as *poiesis*, is founding as a beginning, where beginning is characterised by the suddenness of a leap – a leaping ahead.[33] In order to come to this particular interpretation of beginning, Heidegger connects the leap to the notion of origin as a spontaneous or sudden uprising, intending the play between *Entspringen* (arising), *Sprung* (leap) and *Ursprung* (origin). Art, because its essence is poetry, is itself an origin, not an origin in the sense of before but in the sense of beginning. Heidegger distinguishes the beginning as origin from the idea of the primitive. The primitive lacks the bestowing grounding leap, which is to say, has no history. In an earlier version of *Origin*, he says that the primitive is incapable of liberating itself, which would imply that this beginning is also a type of liberation or freedom. This makes some sense in light of the fact that what we need to escape is the inexorable juggernaut of our past, which is a weighty sediment that becomes covered over and seemingly impenetrable over time.

The work of art in these three senses provides the possibility of the sudden break with the continuity of the past. Art is a leap ahead of, or beyond, that which is recognised and usual, and though it is founding in all three senses, it is most properly a beginning because a beginning always includes what is leapt-over. It includes the veiled within it, and this is exactly what the work reveals to us, the veiled within the present, the unsaid-concealed past providing for the future.

Now we can understand how art can be the origin of a new *Grundstimmung* for another beginning. The work of art provides the grounding attunement that lets one begin to let-beings-be in two ways: (1) the work of art opens our eyes to the essential relation of unconcealment and concealment. The work of art represents a kind of being that is neither merely a thing nor equipment to be used, and through contemplating the work, a fuller vision of being occurs. The work allows earth to be earth, which enframing technological thinking has made impossible otherwise. (2) The origin of the work is poetry, a clearing projection which establishes an open space, a rift, in which the happening of truth occurs. It is an event that unfolds the truth of beyng and, with it, the essential belonging of thinking and saying to that unfolding (prefiguring Heidegger's thinking of *Ereignis*). The possibility of a break with the past inheres in the work, because the break must be prefaced by the establishment of a new *Grundstimmung* and the work provides this new attunement.

The particularity of the work of art lies in the presentation of earth. There may be other ways truth is established,[34] but the revealing of earth as earth remains the privilege of the work of art. In his 1950 lecture 'Erde und Himmel', Heidegger writes: 'art, as the pointing that allows the appearance of what is invisible, is the highest kind of showing' (GA4, 162/186). As we began the chapter, what remains to be thought is the withdrawal of beyng. That which withdraws into non-presence is figured by the earth. The original self-withdrawal of being is sheltered in the appearance of the strife between world and earth.

Because in all its aspects, earth is the *Ab-grund* of our thinking, it is the central concept around which the overcoming of technology and the saving power of art must gather. 'In all this appearance it clings to itself and remains unexplained and concealed.'[35] In other words, part of what it is to be earthy is to resist the penetrative grasp of calculation and analysability, to remain essentially undisclosed, and thus preparing the way for thinking the withdrawal of being.

> What unifies the different senses of the concept of Earth, what links them to the body, to *Stimmung*, to the 'dwelling', or to the habitation as well as to the 'thingliness' of the work of art, is the unique thought of a non-foundational foundation. And consequently, what technology most persistently forgets . . . is precisely this ever implicit, non-occuring, non-formalizable, non-exteriorizable, non-available dimension, this place and medium of all proximity which is prior to all manifestation, the Earthly ground upon which the world lies without being founded in it.[36]

In Chapter 5, we will return to the concept of earth, elaborating on its various senses in order to provide a critical context that activates the political implications involved in *Origin* and that extends to Heidegger's work as a whole.

## Poets, Language, Thinking: the Logos of Poeticising-Thought

Our account of *Origin* has omitted one crucial element, language. The decision to postpone this discussion rests on a twofold reasoning. First, reserving language for the finale serves as a punctuation indicating the singular importance of language for Heidegger. Second, the discussion of language leads to a more focused discussion of the privilege of poetry, the role of the poet, and to Hölderlin's ontological/ontic role as the poet who names the oblivion of being, providing the possibility of another beginning and a German people-to-come.

106

Toward the end of *Origin*, Heidegger pronounces that all art is in essence poetry, initiating a reflection on the intimate link between art and language. Though all the arts are essential modes of bringing forth, poesy occupies a privileged position among the arts because of its connection to the most primordial form of *poiesis*, the projection of being through language. All other art forms happen 'in the open of saying and naming' (H, 61/46).

In order to understand this connection, we need the 'right concept of language' (H, 60/45), which is to say an understanding of the distinction between propositional language (*Aussage*), which typifies our everyday language (*Gerede*), and saying (*Sage*), which indicates original (*ursprünglich*) or inceptive (*anfänglich*) language. Language, in its most primordial sense, 'brings beings, as beings, for the first time, into the open' (H, 60/46), thus it is a prior condition for using language propositionally. The theme of the fallenness of our everyday language resonates throughout Heidegger's philosophy and his critique is well known. By and large, we use language as a tool for transferring information and re-presenting ideas. Thus our statements are referential, directed toward some intention or about some particular beings, which in fact cover over the inceptive essence of language. Recalling Heidegger's own formulation of the nearness yet unavailability of the endowment, human beings live in language, but do not hear its essence: 'everyday language is a forgotten and therefore used up poem' (PLT, 208). Poetic saying, on the other hand, retains the poietic, projective origin of language. Rather than taking control or forcing according to the dictate of a prior ordering, or set of concepts, poetry lets words ring out in their uniqueness. It clears a place, a region in which the sway of beyng is disclosed, and, because it is not easily assimilated, holds open the truth of beyng.

The leap that Heidegger sees as necessary for the transformation of thinking is directly connected to language, because both poeticising and thinking move within the common element of language: 'All reflective thinking is poetic, and all poetry in turn is a kind of thinking' (OWL, 136). It is with this in mind that we return to a portion of the quote with which we began the chapter:

> *To recapture, to repeat (wieder-holen), the beginning of our historical-spiritual existence, in order to transform it into a new beginning.*

The leap is a leap back into language, a founding repetition which returns to the primordial place of the unity of thought and poetic *logos*. In the 'Anaximander Fragment', referring to the beginning of thinking prior to the beginning of philosophy, Heidegger claims the intimate belonging together of *poiesis* and thought: 'Thinking is primordial poetry, prior to all poesy' (EGT, 19). In *this* beginning, *poiesis* and thinking are not separated. The clarity of presentation, or disclosure, for the Greeks originally happened in *poiesis* prior to the dominance of *technē*. In other words, thinking is essentially poetic, but original thinking is what has been covered over in philosophy's pursuit of *technē*. If there is to be another beginning, it will be another level of thinking taking place at the primordial level which thinks the belonging of poetry and thinking.[37]

The belonging together of poeticising and thinking happens through language, but language itself is doubly concealed, both in terms what has been forgotten and in terms of its own withdrawing essence. The first difficulty in reflecting on language is its nearness, its ubiquity. It is language itself that speaks, according to Heidegger, but our discussion of it, taking it as an object for thought, bars us from actually entering into the speaking of language. Secondly, language is the earth of our disclosure, as well as the medium of history and endowment; it carries within it its own dimension of withdrawal, where its resources are hidden, i.e. the sound of spoken language, its rhythm and accents, carry a material weight which escapes signification, eludes transmission and withdraws from the clarity of sense.[38]

We must seek the speaking of language in what is spoken, and what is spoken most purely is the poem. Poetic language can be transformative because it can return to language the feature of primordial disclosure, giving words back their novelty and beautiful unfamiliarity. As Heidegger explains, 'poetic images are imaginings in a distinctive sense . . . imaginings that are visible inclusions of the alien in the sight of the familiar' (PLT, 226). How can we understand what these visible inclusions of the alien are? First, the poetic, as a mode of revealing *logos* not intended for easy consumption or propositional directedness, opens up the ambiguity of language. By allowing the difference which inheres in the word to become visible, poetic language reflects the multiplicity of meanings that inhabit the word, the unsaid within the said. Poetry also lets the invisible appear, the spacing in between beings, the relation between beings that amplifies and transforms beings as a being together. In the later period of his writing, Heidegger conceives this gathering in terms of the fourfold (*Geviert*), complicating his own schema by introducing a more multiple framework. In the essay, 'Language', Heidegger uses a poem by Trakl to reveal the gathering power of the poem, the calling into presence of these elements through the poetic image (PLT, 187–210):

*A Winter's Evening*

When snow falls against the window,
Long sounds the evening bell . . .
For so many has the table
Been prepared, the house set in order.

From their wandering, many
Come on dark paths to this gateway.
The tree of grace is flowering in gold
Out of the cool sap of the earth.

In stillness, wanderer, step in:
Grief has worn the threshold into stone.
But see: in pure light, glowing
There on the table: bread and wine.

What we hear, according to Heidegger, is the calling into word, the gathering, of the fourfold of earth, sky, divinity and mortals. The poem releases the mundane, the table, bread, wine, the tolling of the evening bell, lustrous in their simplicity, their one-ness, with snow-filled sky and the earthiness of the hearth. Together these elements, indicative of the fourfold schema, resonate, invoking an appearance of the whole that exceeds their separated beings: 'Its luminous joining decides the brightening of the world into its own' (PLT, 205). In addition, the poem reveals the 'difference between', which is the space opened up by their inhering together: 'the pure, limpid brightness of world and the simple gleaming of things go through their between, the dif-ference' (PLT, 205). Therefore, really what we are able to see through the purity of the poem is difference itself, the invisible between that lets the elements of the fourfold shine. So, it is by virtue of the poietic, projective utterance that being is meted out and the unspoken comes to presence.

The poetic word and thinking are both thought by Heidegger as essential gatherings, sharing a creative task of bringing being to word through the original disclosure of language. 'Multiplicity (*Mehrdeutigkeit*) of meanings is the element (*Element*) in which all thought must move in order to be strict thought' (WHD, 75/71). Thinking, as with the poetic, recalls the difference at the heart of this gathering and is a matter of decision about what is gathered together, of ascertaining the unity of the gathered. Through poetical thinking, a thinking that retains its connection to *poiesis* as the free disclosure of beings in the open, language itself opens up as itself. Rather than being a tool for description and analysis, the creative essence of language becomes once more apparent, and language becomes once more the site of revealing of being and the original jointures of being become illuminated.

Human beings are then the caretakers of being, and language is that which shelters and preserves being. If our language is to provide a shelter for being, the space opened up through language must allow the truth of beyng to resound freely, which implies the silence of listening and the need for reticent hearing. Poetic saying/thinking is 'a listening response to beyng's withdrawal'[39] which can be precipitated by attunement through the poetic, the patient opening of language through the poem – allowing a historical opening of the truth of beyng. When we listen attentively, attuned-ly, we can experience the amplification of beyng. Heidegger's main resource for exemplifying this is the poems, albeit of a very select number of poets of whom Hölderlin ranks supreme.

Heidegger maintains that the poet has a unique receptivity, and thus acts as a mediator of the primordial and unspoken.[40] The poet responds to the withdrawal of being, and, in the absence of the gods, the space of the holy is opened up which provides the possibility for a new founding. Heidegger claims that the role of the poet is to dwell in the absence of the fleeing gods, the abyss of being, and prepare the way for coming gods, by naming the holy. In the absence of the gods, parallel to the withdrawal of beyng, the poet must open a space for the return of the gods, that is, it is the poet's job to question and thereby keep open the vicinity of thought for that which remains unspoken and unthought.

The poet is therefore essential in the founding of a people. In his 1934/35 lecture *Hölderlins Hymnen 'Germanien' und 'Der Rhein'*, Heidegger makes this connection explicit, explaining that it is the poet who originally discovers the essential disposition (*Grundstimmung*) of a nation (*Volk*), and that Hölderlin is the poet who will establish the *Grundstimmung* out of which the German people can understand itself and its place on this earth. In both cases, whether regarding the work or the poet, the *Stimmung* is the letting-be of beings that occurs only in the free space of the Open. While Heidegger explicitly invokes Hölderlin as the poet/thinker who makes the connection between the Germans and the Greeks, which we shall explore in more detail in Chapter 5 in order to develop an understanding of the link between art and the political, Hölderlin's import and status as the poet of poets is also predicated on the fact that he is a poet who poeticises about what it means to be a poet and about the poet's relation to the thinker. Heidegger thinks that the historical determination of philosophy as a whole is linked to the necessity of making Hölderlin's words be heard (GA65, 422/334; see also 401/318).

Thus, one vital thing Heidegger hopes to learn from Hölderlin is how to think (and dwell) poetically.[41] This is something one can only learn from the poetry itself, and Heidegger devotes himself to elucidating Hölderlin's poetry in numerous lectures and reflections, which for lack of space we cannot embark upon here. Heidegger's overarching point is that contemplating the essence of *poiesis* changes our relationship to thinking, allowing thinking to open and gather around a place opened by the inaugural words, such as Trakl's 'Winter's Evening', of the poet, as anticipatory escort. So, at the end of metaphysics, we have to think; and to truly think, one must think what has not been thought. Thinking is not about possessing knowledge, but about the movement of thinking itself, a passage through the unthought and creative upsurging of beyng through the word.

The *Ursprache* that the poet makes available gives a people its ground. But the ground must be thoughtfully prepared. Invoking the 'unmediated word', Heidegger says that the poet's words resonate but do not give themselves. The holy remains something unmediated and mysterious, a direct bequeathal of vicinity of being, but being itself remains shrouded and must be determined through the work of the thinker, who interprets or makes available the work of the poet (GA39, 286). The thinker and the poet thus establish a community of needful belonging: 'For now there must be thinkers so that the poet's word may be perceptible' (GA4, 30/48).

But the determination of history requires more: a people able to hear this thinking of being. What is important is insisting upon certain way of taking up language and history, both resolutely and questioningly. Otherwise, the sense of how one can enter into (hear) the event of one's destiny remains opaque. The poet and thinker are thus joined by the preservers, who listen and must be ready for the message. The role of the preservers is crucial for the completion of the work's work, which 'only becomes actual in preserving' (H, 62/47). The preservation of the work entails making a decision to take up the significance of the work. Through the shared experience, a common understanding forms around the work. To preserve the work and to become a people are intertwined in that becoming a people is a matter of making a decision to listen to the words of the poet or attend to the place that has been opened through the work of art.

Out of the relationship between art, the poet and the thinker, Heidegger posits the necessity of human essence as poetic dwelling, thus human beings become preservers of being – through attunement, language and decision. By placing ourselves into the space opened up by the poet, we can open ourselves to the concealing nature of truth, as *physis*, which was primordially experienced in the first beginning of thinking. To dwell poetically is to attune oneself to in-finite relations, which Heidegger thematises using the fourfold, and to listen to the gathering destiny of these relations. The poet grounds existence which is not yet but arises out of this gathering of paths and relations. 'Everything with which man is endowed must be fetched forth from out of the closed ground and explicitly set upon this ground' (H, 63/47). The medium through which the sojourn takes place is language, which is one of the poles, the primary pole, around which a *polis* gathers. When being is gathered in a certain historical moment, Heidegger claims, the possibility for decision arises.

At the time he wrote *Origin*, Heidegger held the opinion that it remained to be seen whether the art of Hölderlin would found a world, whether the Germans would unite by deciding for Hölderlin's path. This was a path which returned the Germans to the remembrance of the Greek past; a path enjoined by Heidegger's nostalgia, and even mourning, for the greatness of Greek art.[42] Given that the overcoming of aesthetics required a return to the greatness of Greek art, it has been claimed that Heidegger is either unconcerned or sceptical about the artistic innovations of his own age. His statements concerning modern and abstract art only strengthen this view.[43] Yet, Heidegger does begin to think the possibility of plural paths, 'a few other great beginnings',[44] and we can speculate that one such path centres around Paul Klee (1879–1940), an artist ultimately attuned to the changes, turmoil and confusion of his time – a painter/poet looking to the future rather than the past.

## Klee Plateau: The (Deferred) Possibility of (Art's) Other Beginning

In Klee something has happened that none of us yet grasps.[45]

Heidegger began to discuss Klee's work in the 1950s, but it was his encounter with Ernst Beyeler's private collection of Klee paintings in

1956 which had the most profound effect,[46] enough for him to consider the incompleteness of his own thinking on art in light of Klee's work. Heinrich Petzet, Heidegger's art historian student with whom he had ongoing conversations about Klee, confirms that Heidegger intended a rejoinder to *Origin* vis-à-vis Klee.[47] When Heidegger looked at Klee's paintings, what was it that made him, if only momentarily, consider rethinking his understanding of art?

Since Heidegger never did offer his definitive word or publish on Klee,[48] their encounter remains deferred, such that any thinking on their relationship must remain an imaginative projection. Yet the profundity of Klee's impact on Heidegger is irresistible for a project such as ours. What is it that Klee's work brings forth for Heidegger? Heidegger's notes provide some insight: 'Something never seen before is visible in these paintings.' There are very few commentators who have taken up the task of interpreting these lines. Dennis Schmidt's *Between Word and Image* is one such sustained engagement.[49] Schmidt reads Heidegger's encounter with Klee as transformative and suggests that it signalled the possibility of thinking beyond the confines of Western art, beyond the distortions of modern technicity that dominated the majority of modern art, and contributed to Heidegger's rethinking of art according to *Ereignis*, rather than remaining with the language of the strife between earth and world.[50] As Heidegger was searching to find *logos* adequate to the event, he was drawn to Klee's work. For Schmidt, Klee opens up the space between the image and the word, thus engaging the struggle of thought's emergence, and his play of image and word sheds light on the poverty of language at the heart of philosophy: 'this hesitation, a sort of stutter of language, a hesitation of reticence, should characterise the beginnings of any philosophical reflections upon the image'.[51] Another possible interpretation is offered by John Sallis, who recently orchestrated a conference and exhibition on Klee's work and its philosophical implications.[52] Sallis explains that Klee was able to bring forth what we do not ordinarily see but is somehow present in our perception through the simplicity of line, as well as a multiplicity of techniques. Klee's 1939 painting *Ein Tor* (*A Gate*) was influential for Heidegger for this very reason. Sallis interprets the painting as depicting the centrality of death as a gate through which we all must pass, thus making visible the confrontation with the Nothing which discloses the *Abgrund*. Yet, we wonder about the selection of this painting in particular. It certainly synchronises well with Heidegger, and it is true that Klee's concerns about death became ever more explicit as his own debilitating illness encroached,[53] but Klee is also the painter of whimsical creatures,

THE INVENTION OF A PEOPLE

mixtures of the machinic and the natural, cosmic landscapes, and pure schemas of colour.

The possibility that Klee holds the key to a new view of the relation between being and thought is one that we wish to explore further, though in slightly different terms. Though Heidegger may have been sceptical of Klee's ability to theoretically grasp the significance of his own work,[54] we shall give him more credit. According to Klee that 'something' which has not yet been grasped to which Heidegger refers was the emergence of the visible itself. Klee's oft-quoted (by Deleuze specifically) phrase, 'art does not reproduce the visible; rather, it makes visible'[55] provides a window onto his art-making, one that echoes the disclosive, rather than reproductive, power of art. Klee understood painting as the illumina-tive disclosure of the dynamics of life, making creation/genesis visible through the kinetic movement between point-line-plane-dimensionality: 'Everything (the world) is of a dynamic nature.'[56] Along these lines, what is made visible is not some part of our perceptual world which we have ignored or with which we are inauthentically engaged, but the pre-perceptual or the genesis of the sensible/visible itself. Klee's self-awareness also extended to his historical untimeliness, for he knew that there was no community of preservers prepared for his art, which means that he was painting, lamentably, much as Hölderlin was writing, for a future people.

Heidegger considers the disappearance of the object in Klee's paint-ing, its abstractness: 'when one does away with the image-character – what is "seen." What one "sees" is "production" (Hervorbringen)'. Schmidt interprets this to mean that Heidegger understands Klee as making visible the genesis of things and that this rendering of emer-gence, Ereignis, is what makes Klee's work beautiful for Heidegger.[57] So, Heidegger recognises that Klee's works made visible the inconspicu-ous tension of emerging and withdrawing; however, the key feature of Klee's painting for Heidegger is the illumination of this movement in terms of the phenomenological, the genetic conditions of appearance. Deleuze also credits Klee with making visible the forces of genesis, finding his paintings to be indicative of the primacy of immanence and becoming. Deleuze does not consider the impact of forces rendered through the artwork in terms of beauty, but rather as shock or distur-bance. Our intuition is that the difference lies in the way that Heidegger may be mapping Klee's work back on to his own understanding of Ereignis as an openness that gives itself over to Dasein, while, for Deleuze, Klee's work reveals the entirely impersonal real conditions of the event. Deleuze credits Klee with a powerful insight, a vision of the

114

cusp of creation or, one might say, an intimate awareness of the event in which chaos becomes order – this grey point, as Klee christens it,[58] haunts many of his paintings as a deep, spherical abyss.

Heidegger also thought that Klee's work sacrificed the image itself in the process. Our following hypothesis concerning this claim causes us to return to *Origin*. For Heidegger, the strife between earth and world, tropes of concealment and unconcealment in their intimate sway, has a *dénouement*, the *Riss*, as the opening from which a figure comes to stand. So, though art is not about representing objects, it is about the emergence of a figure. From this perspective, Klee's work is either deficient or it is disruptive. Klee's ultimate intention is not the accomplished figure. He is interested in capturing the emergence of form,[59] or the transition from chaos to order through visible media. Thus, his work is cosmogenetic,[60] rather than cosmological, a difference which we think separates Klee's project from the criticism which Heidegger levies (of being too cosmological) and to which we shall return when addressing Klee's significance for Deleuze in the next chapter.

Klee's *Magic Garden* (reproduced on the cover of this book), exemplifies the cosmogenetic tendencies of his work. It discloses the dynamic emergence from chaotic immanence, resembling a 'primordial substance worn and textured by its own history. A cosmic eruption seems to have spewed forth forms . . . Although excused from the laws of gravity, each of these forms occupies a designated place in a new universe.'[61] Certainly, one can identify human artefacts, goblets, architecture, but these are not privileged, centred beings; the force of genesis itself is the overarching construct, as it is as much the case that things recede into the maelstrom of the chaotic sensible. Equally conspicuous is the immanence from whence they arise, evinced by a striking luminosity that seems to seep up from some inner depth, and the intimate, necessary connection between the two. Further, if we were to keep within the earth/world paradigm, we could say that there is a reversal of priority here. Earth becomes the dominant figure, in such a way that addresses its nature as abyssal, the shifting beneath our feet. In this respect, we ask, 'Does Klee's work reach deeper into the abyss by virtue of its cosmogenetic tendencies, and this in a way that implies an even more radical disclosure than Heidegger is able to grant?' Klee, fascinated with the forces of creation (or, granting poetic license with the title of the Klee on our cover, the magic of creation), makes these visible through the deconstruction or deformation of formal elements, i.e. experimentation and inventiveness with the line, re-compositions, and, foremost, presentation of a fantastical imaginary.

Julian Young charges that Heidegger's recognition of the importance of Klee's work precipitates his conclusion of *Origin*'s incompleteness because it frustrates one of the criteria, in that it does not meet the communal condition, which is to say the gathering together of a culture to witness the presencing of world.[62] It may be the case that what arises in Klee is not 'world' in the sense of the greatness of Greek art. Yet, rather than excluding Klee's work from the categorisation of 'great art', as a happening of the truth of beyng, we contend that Klee's work precipitates a new way of understanding our human relation to being, and thus may be an extension of Heidegger's claims.

We submit that Klee's work does speak to the emergence of a new world, the world of a dispersed, missing people − or, as we shall see with Deleuze, the criteria of missingness as included and constitutive of a conception of community. Of course, this does present a challenge to the view of the presencing of world from *Origin*, and even the idea of the future gathering of a people, but if we couple this with the absence that seems implicit in *Ereignis*, which has never arrived and for which we are still preparing, we see that *Ereignis* is figured as 'to come', envisioned through waiting, which discloses its own absence.

In any case, Klee's grey point is what we shall call a point of indeterminacy between Heidegger and Deleuze, a point where Heidegger could have taken another path and where Deleuze begins a more radical account of genesis which extends beyond the genesis of the human and of thinking, inscribing thought into the fabric of genesis itself. If we were to place Deleuze within Heidegger's *Gestalt*, we would say that, for Deleuze, the *Riss* is everywhere. In the next chapter, we will address art from Deleuze's perspective. For him, Klee's work invokes the radical inhuman forces of becoming, forces that envelop, define and exceed us. A key difference between Heidegger and Deleuze rests on this point, which is to say that, for Deleuze, the *Ereignis* disclosed in Klee's paintings is not an enowning of human beings. Perhaps Heidegger was not willing to think *Ereignis* as exceeding the human so radically, where world recedes and earth or the cosmic thrusts itself forward so intensely.[63] We think that this is just what Deleuze is prepared to do. We will engage the work of art from what Deleuze calls the being of the sensible, which, similar to Heidegger, is disclosed and even preserved through the work of art. In this respect, Klee's grey point is a point of intersection which then bursts into divergent lines (paths) for these two thinkers. The hypothesis that we have been developing could be put in this Heideggerian framework: Modern art, neither merely dictated by the forces of technology, nor attempting a repetition of the

Greek model of greatness to which Heidegger is beholden in *Origin*, reveals new dimensions of earth (as *physis*, as cosmogenetic) in its pure aspect of becoming.

Klee's paintings dismantle myths and disfigure images both as social commentary and as a means to open up the figure to other possible worlds.[64] As such, Klee's works overflow the possibilities of disclosure, liberating magical, fanciful, impossible worlds – a new vision of the cosmos. Our contention is that Klee's art overflows *aletheia*, embracing the pure power of invention, or the powers of the false. He is an untimely portent, an inventor of new earths and new worlds, which explains Deleuze's fascination with Klee's last words in *On Modern Art*: 'We still lack the ultimate power, for: the people are not with us (*uns trägt kein Volk*). But we seek a people.'[65] For Deleuze, to seek a people is to be an inventor, a *fabulator*. Referring back to Deleuze and Heidegger's divergence concerning Nietzsche, we might say that a people-to-come is erected on the powers of the false rather than on a founding disclosure of *aletheia*.

With Deleuze the abyssal nature of thought is the correlate of an ontology of pure difference and radical becoming. In *Cinema I*, Deleuze suggests a de-centred perception of the world that splits the subject from its position of objective onlooker and causes the viewer and the work of art to embark upon a vacillating union that eludes these very designations of subjective and objective. Contesting Heidegger's privileging of *logos*, Deleuze seeks to articulate a kind of discourse that goes beyond language itself, one comprised of heterogeneous elements that exceed the word. The assemblages that comprise discourse are not necessarily linguistic, nor do they privilege linguistic art forms. Moreover, rather than widening the scope of meaning, Deleuze focuses on the a-signifying capacity of the artwork, what Anne Sauvagnargues calls a semiotics of the affect.[66] In fact, artworks are primarily explorations of the realm of sensibility that prefigures signification. In other words, Deleuze's thinking about art is erected on a different edifice than that of Heidegger. In Deleuze's philosophy, art is linked to the rhythmic becomings that precede and exceed the human. Utilising the innovations which he finds in Nietzsche's diagnosis of a new kind of being, that of the simulacrum, Deleuze presents a metaphysical picture that emphasises the creative and the contingent, positive markers of the powers of the false. For Deleuze, to embrace the powers of the false is to be an inventor, a fabulator, but not of myth. Myth is too foundational. Rather, of the *le petit recit*, the minor and impossible, the cosmic elementality of an imaginary garden or the fluctuations of crystallising water. In the following chapter,

117

these elements are articulated in terms of geophilosophy, in which the grounded earth gives way to the cosmic becomings of which it is comprised.

## Notes

1. The primally earlier (*die anfängliche Frühe*), which comes forth only later, is central to Heidegger's understanding of destining, as an arrival or granting appropriation – *das Ereignis*. See GA4, 23/22 and OWL, 127.
2. See Dennis Schmidt, *On Germans and Other Greeks: Tragedy and Ethical Life* (Bloomington: Indiana University Press, 2001).
3. Daniela Vallega-Neu makes this point, along with offering an insightful distinction between the poet (the founder of historical beyng) and the thinker (the one who brings to light what is sheltered in these poetic words). See her 'Poetic Saying', in Scott, ed., *Companion to Heidegger's Contributions to Philosophy*, pp. 75–6, 106.
4. Heidegger makes use of both the root word *eigen*, as 'one's own', and *augen*, as 'eye', which is connected to the *Augenblick*, notably referred to in his Nietzsche lectures. The prefix *er-* has the sense of bringing forth; therefore, *Ereignis* is the bringing forth of the proper or what is ownmost corresponding to the particular temporality of the Moment with its twofold structure previously described as both encapsulating the past and as glimpsing the future in one and the same instant: destiny coming to us from the past.
5. Heidegger refrains from naming the grounding attunement, opting instead for this multiplicity of descriptors. This is often confusing because Heidegger himself may use one term or another, and different translations of his work will privilege one over another. Heidegger actually addresses this in *Contributions*: 'the grounding attunement of another beginning can hardly ever be known by merely one name' (GA 65, 14–15/16). Struggling to find a word for this attunement speaks to its nature as ungraspable and to the state of oblivion that makes such an attunement so elusive for us. I believe that it is Heidegger's hope that by layering these words, he may evoke a sense or feeling of this attunement without directly naming and thus foreclosing it.
6. Though Heidegger does not propose *Gelassenheit* as a formal concept until the late 1950s, this concept is fundamentally in play as early as the 1930s, as its origins lay progressively in the thinking of clearing elicited through thinking the relation of earth and world and the fundamental attunement of reservedness found in the *Beiträge*. In *Heidegger and the Will: On the Way to Gelassenheit* (Evanston: Northwestern University Press, 2007), Brett Davis traces the progression of Heidegger's concepts

from *Being and Time* to *Gelassenheit*, illustrating the progressive pulling away from the language of willing. Davis understands Heidegger's transition from resoluteness (*Entschlossenheit*), as an example of his entanglement in a philosophy of the will, to reservedness (in the *Beitrage*), as a 'restraining' of the will, an active passivity. Of course, we would add to this the development of the notion of earth and the comportment toward it that is developed in *Origin.*

7. We emphasise the link between three concepts – transformation of humanity, the 'we', and 'people' – in order to express the continuity in Heidegger's thought on these matters. Even when Heidegger speaks of world-historical being and the transformation of humanity, *Ereignis* is always singular and situated, justifying to some extent the designation of a particular 'we' or even 'peoples'. For Heidegger on the necessity of the transformation of humanity, see *Beitrage*: GA65, 475/334, and *Grundfragen der Philosophie*: GA 45/214.

8. Michel Haar, *The Song of the Earth: Heidegger and the Grounds of the History of Being*, trans. Reginald Lilly (Bloomington: Indiana University Press, 1993), p. 82.

9. Ibid., p. 87.

10. 'In 1930 Ernst Jünger's "Total Mobilization" appeared   I discussed these writings at this time   and attempted to show how in them an essential comprehension of Nietzsche's metaphysics is expressed. Total mobilization, aside from expressing 'total war' where all resources are employed, represents the readiness for mobilization, and hence, the stockpiling of all resources and the cultivation of a mentality that views all things as resource.' Martin Heidegger, 'The Rectorship 1933–1934: Facts and Thoughts (1945)', in Gunther Neske and Emil Kettering, eds, *Martin Heidegger and National Socialism* (New York: Paragon House, 1990), pp. 15–32.

11. According to Heidegger, Germany is centrally positioned both philo-sophically and geographically to reinvigorate philosophy and bring about an essential change in humanity. Infamously, Heidegger describes this world stage in terms of Germany caught in the pincers between Bolshevism and Americanism, both metaphysically and literally sur-rounded on all sides. See GA40, 40–1/40–1.

12. With its 'knowledge service' (*Wissensdienst*), the university was to provide a counterpart to the labour service (*Arbeitdienst*) and military service (*Wehrdienst*) of the German state. Bambach points to the paral-lel between this tri-partite division and that of Plato's in the *Republic*, arguing that this is yet another sign of the militant and hierarchi-cal society that Heidegger is endorsing. He claims that by invoking Plato's goal of the formation of the perfect *polis*, Heidegger directs his listeners to draw connections to the aims and desires of the present German state. Charles Bambach, 'Plato's *Staat* and Heidegger's *Volk*',

in *Heidegger's Roots: Nietzsche, National Socialism, and the Greeks* (Ithaca, NY: Cornell University Press, 2005), pp. 99–107. This claim can be countered by pointing out that Heidegger specifically denies the interpretation of the *polis* in the modern sense of state and power in *Parmenides*.

13. Heidegger emphasises the spiritual mission and a spiritual essence, in a purported effort to counter both militarism and the notion of racial essence (see *Der Spiegel* interview: 'Only a God Can Save Us Now', in Wolin, ed., *The Heidegger Controversy*, pp. 91–116).

14. Catherine Zuckert, 'Martin Heidegger: His Philosophy and His Politics,' *Political Theory* 18:1 (1990), p. 55.

15. In the chapter's final section, we address the (deferred) possibility of Heidegger's revision of this view on the basis of his encounter with Paul Klee's artwork.

16. Summarily, Heidegger's derivation begins with an analysis of causality in which he takes Aristotle's four causes to be the definitive account that shapes inquiries concerning *technē*. His suspicion is that there has been a loss of the original sense of causality, not the least of which is the primary emphasis on efficient cause which comes to set the standard for all causality. Moving from the Latin *causa* to the Greek *aitia*, he connects causality with 'being responsible' for bringing something into appearance – moving toward a more original sense of causality and foreshadowing his own return to the language of the fourfold in his later works. He then asks about what unites these different causes, and brings these ways of 'causing' together through reference to Diotima in Plato's *Symposium* (205b): 'Every occasion for whatever passes over and goes forward into presencing from that which is not presencing is *poiesis*, is bringing-forth' (GA7, 12/10).

17. 'Technology will not be struck down; and it most certainly will not be destroyed' (GA11, 116/38).

18. Vallega-Neu, *Heidegger's Contributions*, p. 69. This formulation is quite similar to the method of double affirmation which transforms reactive forces into actives forces by taking the reactive to its own limit.

19. Thomas Sheehan, '*Kehre* and *Ereignis*: A Prolegomenon to *Introduction to Metaphysics*', in Gregory Fried and Richard Polt, eds, *A Companion to Martin Heidegger's Introduction to Metaphysics* (New Haven: Yale University Press, 2001), p. 3.

20. Vallega-Neu, *Heidegger's Contributions*, p. 71.

21. Heidegger names three steps on the path of his thinking: Meaning (*Sinn*), Truth (*Wahrheit*), and Place (*Ort*) (VS, 344/347).

22. These are closely intertwined, as evidenced by Heidegger's trade on the semantic proximity of two senses of openness, *Offenbarkeit* (revealedness) and *Offenlichkeit* (public-ness), to describe the transformative happening that the work of art engenders. Public-ness is the

transformation of the public: 'The only relation it has to the "public audience" – where such a thing exists – is that it destroys the latter and the greatness of the work of art is measured by this power of destruction' (*Of*, 332).

23. In this lecture, Heidegger develops the concept of the Open as a name for being, complicated by the fact that *Dasein*'s comportment is also a standing-open (*Offenständigkeit*). Though clearing and Open are sometimes used interchangeably – 'Clearing (*Lichtung*) means "to open" ... The clearing is the presupposition for getting light and dark. It is the free, the open' (GA89, 13/16); or in 'The End of Philosophy and the Task of Thinking': 'The clearing is the open region for everything that becomes present and absent' (BW, 442) – the Open, characterised as a region opposed to but calling forth *Dasein*'s own openness, is the more foundational concept.: Therefore, we refer to *das Offene* as what is opened in particular openings, or clearings. In *Origin*, Heidegger speaks of the opening of the open as the clearing (*Lichtung*), again, reflecting that the Open is the more primordial. See John Krummel, 'Spatiality in the Later Heidegger: Turning – Clearing – Letting', *Existentia: An International Journal of Philosophy* XVI (2006), pp. 405–24.

24. Haar claims that transforming the essence of human beings is Heidegger's unwavering task. Michael Haar, *Heidegger and the Essence of Man*, trans. William McNeill (Albany: State University of New York Press, 1993).

25. This move away from the *Da* of *Dasein* as the Open to the *Da* of the work as the clearing of Truth (the Open) is even evidenced in the revisions of *Origin*. In the third version, those passages in the original version, the unofficial French version, where *Dasein* is linked to the Open, are altered to speak directly of the Open in terms of its relation to the work. (*Of*, 29, 31; H, 32–3/22–3).

26. See Martin Heidegger, 'The Age of the World Picture', in *The Question Concerning Technology and Other Essays*, trans. William Lovitt (New York: Harper & Row Publishing, 1977), pp. 129–34.

27. Hans-Georg Gadamer, *Truth and Method* (New York: Continuum International Publishing Group, 1989), pp. 130–1.

28. Julian Young outlines these 'simple and essential decisions' in terms of one's proper place in the overall social structure; the example of the temple represents an *Au-einandersetzung* which establishes these different positions and modes of obligation. See Young, *Heidegger's Philosophy of Art* (Cambridge: Cambridge University Press, 2001), pp. 26–8.

29. Young identifies the fundamental character of earth as the 'principle of holiness', which signifies an 'epistemological depth', and all that is denied, refused, or occluded from thought. He also connects it with the ungraspable, the mysterious or secret, and the Other (ibid., pp. 38–41).

THE INVENTION OF A PEOPLE

30. Ibid., p. 48.
31. For more on truth as Heidegger's central concept, see Walter Biemel, *Martin Heidegger* (Rembek bei Hamburg: Rowohll Verlag, 1998).
32. One of the implications of Heidegger's account of truth as *aletheia* is that truth is always a disclosure, not a reprising of what is already known: 'Truth will never be gathered from what is present and ordinary' (H, 62/47).
33. In the French (*Ofr*, 43), it is *saut fondatif*, original leap, which signifies the both the originality and the foundational aspect of the leap.
34. In *Introduction to Metaphysics*, Heidegger speaks of the world-making *polemos* sustained equally by creators, poets, thinkers, statesmen. By *Origin*, statesmen are no longer mentioned.
35. Vincent Vycinas, *Earth and Gods: An Introduction to the Philosophy of Martin Heidegger* (The Hague: Martin Nijhoff, 1961), p. 163.
36. Haar, *Song of the Earth*, p. 64.
37. See Robert Bernasconi, 'Poet of Poets. Poet of the Germans', in *Heidegger in Question: The Art of Existing* (Humanities Press International, Inc., 1993), p. 146.
38. For more on the materiality of speech and the incommunicability that grounds communicability, see Jacques Derrida's *Speech and Phenomena*, trans. David B. Allison (Evanston: Northwestern University Press, 1973) as well as Leonard Lawlor's *Derrida and Husserl: The Basic Problem of Phenomenology* (Bloomington: Indiana Press, 2002).
39. Vallega-Neu, 'Poeitic Saying', *Heidegger's Contributions*, p. 72.
40. 'The poet is the one on whom the hint of the gods befalls first and passes this on through their poetry' (GA39, 32) (quoted from ibid., p. 106).
41. See Heidegger, 'Hölderlin and the Essence of Poetry', GA4, 33–48/51–65.
42. In the 'Afterword' to *Origin*, Heidegger calls the foregoing considerations a reflection on the enigma of art, presents the worst case scenario of art's death if we cannot get out of the aesthetic or subjective, and, appealing to Hegel's absolute rationalism, questions if art is any longer an essential and necessary way that truth happens (H, 66/50-1).
43. Heidegger viewed abstract art as reinforcing the technological rather than revealing world. See H.W. Petzet, *Encounters and Dialogues with Martin Heidegger*, trans. Parvis Emad and Kenneth Maly (Chicago: University of Chicago, 1993), p. 66.
44. While some claim that this phrase, appearing only in 'Hölderlin's Earth and Heaven' (GA4, 201/177), refers to the Asiatic and is evidence of Heidegger's openness to intercultural dialogue, others insist on the anomalous nature of the statement and claim his ongoing allegiance to a European context for his thought. See Lin Ma, *Heidegger on*

*East-West Dialogue: Anticipating the Event* (New York: Routledge, 2008), pp. 92–9.

45. A statement made by Heidegger upon viewing Klee's work. Petzet, *Encounters and Dialogues*, pp. 142, 150.

46. According to his art historian student, Heinrich Petzet, who conversed with Heidegger regularly in the 1950s concerning Klee, this viewing was decisive (see ibid., pp. 146–7).

47. Ibid., p. 149.

48. Heidegger did write a seminar prospectus *Bild und Image* (1960), coupling Klee's 1924 Jena manifesto, 'On Modern Art', with Heraclitus (Petzet, *Encounters and Dialogues*, p. 59). He made fragmentary notes during his visit to a 1956 private exhibition of Klee's works, which are known as the '*Notizen zu Klee*', a large portion of which is published in Günter Seubold, *Kunst als Ereignis* (Bonn: Bouvier Verlag, 1996), as well as in Seubold's 'Heidegger's *nachgelassene Klee-Notizen*', *Heidegger Studies* 9 (1993), pp. 5–12. All direct quotes from Heidegger's notebooks are retrieved from Dennis Schmidt's translations in *Between Word and Image* (Bloomington: Indiana University Press, 2013).

49. See also Young, *Heidegger's Philosophy of Art*, pp. 158–62; Iain Thomson, *Heidegger, Art and Postmodernism* (New York: Cambridge University Press, 2011); Stephen Watson, 'Heidegger, Paul Klee, and the Origin of the Work of Art', *The Review of Metaphysics* 60:2 (2006), pp. 327–57; Otto Pöggeler, 'Heidegger und Klee – Überlegungen zur Kunst', *Studia Phaenomenologica* 3 (2003), pp. 197–208; Pöggeler, *Bild und Technik: Heidegger, Klee und die Moderne Kunst* (Munich: Wilhem Fink Verlag, 2002).

50. See Schmidt, *Between Word and Image*, pp. 79 and 92–9. Reinforcing this reading, in a margin note from 1960 (GA5, 42), Heidegger suggests that truth as primal conflict between earth and world should be replaced by *Ereignis*. Reference found in Young, *Heidegger's Philosophy of Art*, p. 64.

51. Schmidt, *Between Word and Image*, p. 14.

52. *Paul Klee: Philosophical Vision; From Nature to Art* (2012); organised by the McMullen Museum in collaboration with the Zentrum Paul Klee, curated by John Sallis in consultation with Claude Cernuschi and Jeffery Howe and held at Boston College.

53. Sallis interview available at <http://at.bc.edu/curatorscut> (accessed 11 July 2014). In *Death and Fire* (1940), the central figure is a skull outlined in thick black lines, its features formed by the German word for death, *Tod*. Death, seemingly out of sync with a reading of Klee as primarily concerned with productivity and genesis, is the 'darker side of the movement that operates in Klee's work' (Schmidt, *Between Word and Image*, p. 95). Klee dramatised death toward the end of his life,

and when his debilitating disease forced him to alter his style to simpler forms.

54. Heidegger found Klee's artistic self-description too neo-Kantian, overly concerned with form, and too cosmological (Watson, 'Heidegger, Paul Klee, and the Origin', p. 327; also Petzet, *Encounters and Dialogues*, p. 148). Our understanding is that Klee's formalism is but an entrance to the pre-formal. His work is about generativity, and any reference to form gives way to the dynamic tension of forces. Thus he is interested in the pre-ontological (in the sense of its coming-to-be). The purely formal is produces the invisible, pictorially.

55. Paul Klee, *Schöpferische Konfession* (*Creative Credo*), ed. Kasimir Edschmid (Berlin: E. Reiss, 1920), Section I.

56. Paul Klee, *Notebooks Volume I: The Thinking Eye*, trans. Ralph Manheim (London: Lund Humphries, 1961), p. 5.

57. Schmidt, *Between Word and Image*, pp. 92–3.

58. Jena lecture, 1924: 'The Grey Point has the double function of being both chaos and at the same time rhythm insofar as it dynamically jumps over itself.' Paul Klee, *Paul Klee* (New York: Parkstone International, 2012), p. 150.

59. 'The principles and paths towards form.' Klee, *Notebooks*, p. 17.

60. 'The point of coming to be and passing away.' Klee, *Notebooks*, p. 3.

61. From <http://www.guggenheim.org/new-york/collections/collection-online/artwork/2160> (accessed 11 July 2014).

62. Young, *Heidegger's Philosophy of Art*, p. 65.

63. There are readings of Heidegger's *Ereignis* as radically contextual and singular, which, by invoking the fourfold, as emphasise that every appearance concerns a multiplicity of factors that coalesce into a situational whole. The fourfold moves the concept of *Ereignis* away from the prioritisation of the human, as the human becomes merely one of the dimensions of disclosure. This view brings Heidegger much closer to Deleuze's account of the singularity. See the work of Jussi Backman, *Complicated Presence: Heidegger and the Postmetaphysical Unity of Being*, forthcoming from SUNY Press.

64. See Watson, 'Heidegger, Paul Klee, and the Origin', p. 350.

65. Paul Klee, *On Modern Art* (London: Faber & Faber, 1948), p. 55.

66. Anne Sauvagnargues, *Deleuze and Art*, trans. Samantha Bankston (London: Bloomsbury Press, 2013).

*4*

# Deleuze on Art and Ontology

## Axelos Plateau: From Earth to the Cosmic

*I feel myself tremble, the old earth, on me who am more and more yours!*
*The earth melts*[1]

We interpret Deleuze's claim that Heidegger got the wrong people and the wrong earth as pertaining to the deepest elements of their philosophies, specifically to the radical transformation they effect in the nature of ontology. From his initial considerations of ontological difference, Heidegger develops a discourse of the truth of beyng characterised by the duality of unconcealing openness, manifesting as world, and an irreducible concealedness, an impenetrability figured through earth. We claim Deleuze's affinity for the cosmic as a rejoinder to these ontological figures. The cosmic invokes an ontology of pre-individual forces and becomings, an ontology of the (micro)cosmic as an elementality that prefigures the appearing of world and earth.[2]

Readers of Heidegger may too hastily dismiss Deleuze on this point, given that, for Heidegger, cosmos indicates merely an aggregate of planetary beings which he opposes to the significance of world. For this reason, we insist upon the distinction between cosmos and the cosmic. The cosmic is also opposed to classical notions of cosmos as a beautiful unity composed according to a superior principle of order, as in Plato's *Timaeus*, or as an indicator of universal humanity, as in Kantian cosmopolitanism. Rather, it is the impersonal, inhuman level of force and flows, a constant flux of matter-energy. The cosmic indicates the priority of the abyss, a perpetual ungrounding. The cosmic mobilises the intensive micro-features that rupture the earth, sanctioning imaginative projections beyond the earth which open onto the universe: 'child of this earth; yet also child of the Universe; issue of a star among stars'.[3] The cosmic signals those processes that create order out of chaos to create *cosmoi* – a bridge or *milieu*.

In his late philosophy, Heidegger does introduce a new concept, the planetary, which could be seen as an intermediary in moving us from

125

earth to the cosmic. Extending beyond 'world' as culturally and linguistically immanent, Heidegger appeals to the planetary, seemingly as a positive future path for thinking:

> [we are] obliged not to give up the effort to practice planetary thinking along a stretch of the road, be it ever so short. Here too no prophetic talents and demeanor are needed to realize that there are in store for planetary building encounters for which participants are by no means equal today. This is equally true of the European and of the East Asiatic languages and, above all, for the area of a possible conversation between them. Neither of the two is able by itself to open up this area and to establish it.[4]

At once this affirms Heidegger's reading of the history of metaphysics and reflects the openness to other cultures and modes of thinking characteristic of his later works. Planetary thinking signals the need for thinking the encounter between worlds, rather than remaining within an enclosure of one's own world and, thus, would require that Western thinking think the ground and the limit of its own thought, and that other cultures (of thinking) must do the same. Heidegger recognises the need to build and dwell in a technological age that draws the boundaries of the earth closer all the while succumbing to models of the gigantic and machinic. This later turn in his thought has been read as attempt to extend his ontological project in response to criticisms of its having a narrowly European/Germanic focus. Yet, planetary thinking remains problematic if this conversation parallels the pattern of sojourn into the foreign in order to return to one's own, the foreign or other as 'useful',[5] and it does seem that dwelling is ineluctably bound to the earth, a localisable and solid foundation that must be built but is nevertheless a goal, a homecoming and establishment of the hearth. Deleuze, on the other hand, imagines a thinking that takes flight from the earth and a concomitant rhizomatics that frustrates both the rooted and the rootless, nomadic wanderings. In tracing a path between the two, the bridge that we imagine comes in the persona of Kostos Axelos.

> The stars set our motives and the meteors – it is not a matter of enumerating them – mix their light, combine, come close to and recede from one another and from the rest of the mortals of which they are part even as they elude them.[6]

Axelos was instrumental in Heidegger's dissemination into French thought and actively engaged in the French intellectual scene.[7] The journal *Arguments*, which he edited between 1958 and 1962, engaged the Heideggerian legacy of world and technology, through the recurrent theme of *mondialisation*.[8] In 1964 Axelos wrote *Vers la pensée planétaire: Le devenir-pensée du monde et le devenir-monde de la pensée*, followed by *Le Jeu du monde* (1969), and *Arguments d'une recherche* (1969), all published by *Les Éditions de Minuit*. To say the least, themes of world, technology, and how to think both *with* and *beyond* Heidegger were 'in the air'. In 1970, Deleuze wrote an enthusiastic review of all three aforementioned books entitled '*Faille et feux locaux, Kostas Axelos*'[9] in which he claims 'Axelos is to Heidegger what a kind of zen is to the Buddha' (ID, 225/161). Deleuze admired Axelos' thought, enough to enthusiastically proclaim him as the conveyor of a new thinking, a new pluralism which identifies the epiphenomenal, fragmentary nature of being as constant becoming (ID, 105–8/74–6).

In *Vers la pensée planétaire* and *Le Jeu du monde*, Axelos works through the encounter of global technology and modern human beings. In many respects, he faithfully follows Heidegger's thought, identifying the planetary era with a levelling, flattening calculation that has forsaken the needful relation of the human and world, and agreeing with Heidegger's diagnoses of the metaphysical roots of the technological (*le technique*). Yet, rather than thinking beyond the technological, Deleuze understands Axelos to be philosophising within it: this flattening 'has the most bizarre effect: it revitalizes the elementary forces in the raw play of their dimensions; it liberates the unthought nothing in a counter-power which is multidimensional play' (ID, 225/160). The planetary concerns the necessary interplay of relations between the human and world, what Axelos calls *le jeu* (the game),[10] but it also concerns the interplay between world (*le monde*) and the cosmos (*le monde cosmique*).[11] Deleuze views this as a significant difference between the planetary, in Axelos' writing, and world, in Heidegger's. Axelos understanding of the planetary diverges significantly from the Heideggerian world in its emphasis on the discordance of the unity between being and the human, necessitating a new relation with the Outside. This point is notably emphasised by Deleuze, who identifies the triple particularity of disarray, disequilibrium and indifference as significant features of the planetary that set it apart from world and the existential of being-in-the-world (ID, 219/157–8).

Axelos considers himself to be moving in directions that remain opaque or only suggestive in Heidegger's thinking; this is especially the case with regard to the *Ab-grund*, which becomes a primary figure in Axelos' ontological picture. He mentions that Heidegger 'sometimes admits a little timidly that the essence of Being is the game itself' and refers to Heidegger's hesitance about the lack of determination of the Game, which demands thinking being as abyss.[12] In theorising the abyss, it is ultimately indetermination (that 'the "because" is drowned in the game') and the role of chance or radical contingency (as an encounter that is not restricted or reinterpreted as fortuitous) that Axelos asks us to consider.[13] Deleuze understands Axelos' extension of the *Ab-grund* as an implicit critique of Heidegger, in that thinking without origin or destination means without point of departure or point of arrival, even between Being (*l'être*) and being (*l'étant*) (i.e. ontological difference) (ID, 222/159). In other words, Deleuze sees in Axelos' philosophy an affirmation of difference as the highest thought. This is the same critique Deleuze and Guattari levy against Heidegger in *What is Philosophy?*[14]

*Le Jeu* is ontological, an 'errant rhythm' surpassing world and thought,[15] and a characteristic of the infinite plurality of thinking in its interplay with being. Planetary thinking is non-unifying, a perpetual play of heterogeneous and multiple realms: art, politics, religion, science and technology, *les grandes puissances*,[16] within which we are incessantly oscillating and playing on several levels.[17] Axelos' emphasis on the fragmentary, non-totalisable and irreducibly relational nature of the planetary indicates a system of open dynamics, conducive to unforeseeable yet incessant becoming: 'The course of thinking is never exhaustive and never complete; there are lines of flight which escape from all parts into the indefinite and unlimited.'[18] It is in this respect that we can understand Deleuze's claim that Axelos' planetary is the culmination of pataphysics (ID, 107/75),[19] as that which seeks the epiphenomenal, the exceptional, that exceeds all metaphysical systems. He insists on a perpetual openness and questioning equal to 'the becoming of a fragmentary and fragmented wholeness of the multidimensional and open world'.[20] Though Axelos echoes Heidegger by proposing *poéticité* as a countervailing mode of thought necessary to think *technique*, he breaks with Heidegger to the degree that he does not think world and Being separately.[21] In other words, Axelos explicitly theorises the radical transformations of modernity, from within *technique*, an ever-progressing oscillation between thinking and epiphenomena. Deleuze reads the planetary as an impersonal and contingent becoming of the world, which includes the human realm of significance but always in light of multiple levels of relation that exceed and affect us – impersonal modes of connection that govern the movement and play of the universe itself.

Deleuze recognised Axelos' revisions of the planetary as important innovations on Heidegger's ontology, which mirror his own understanding of the open dynamism of being as becoming – especially errancy and game.[22] Therefore, Axelos represents a conceptual bridge which leads us away from the Heideggerian figuration of world and earth and necessitates a new figure, one that even surpasses that of the planetary – which, we believe, remains mired for Deleuze in the residue of Heidegger's thinking – toward the cosmic. Axelos' conceptualisation of the planetary allows us to understand the necessity with which Deleuze approaches the need to think the cosmic as opposed to merely the earth, both as indicative of an even more radical fluidity and contingency and as a way of prioritising the abyssal nature of thought and becoming beyond where Heidegger was willing to go. This transition signals a new approach to ontology, an ontology of becoming, for which Deleuze finds fruitful inspiration in the attention to creation and process in artists such as Klee. Deleuze explicitly links the cosmic to art; artists, especially the modern artists, have an affinity with the cosmic and must become cosmic artisans and inventors of worlds. We will return to this point in the final chapter. The following sections of this chapter explore Deleuze's radicalisation of ontology, which we are linking to the figure of the cosmic, in order to understand his positioning of art.

## Situating Art in Deleuze's Philosophy

The aesthetic is central to Deleuze's thinking. As Dorothea Olkowski claims, 'to leave out of their accounts altogether Deleuze's constant and insistent articulation of the work of visual artists, composers, poets, prose-writers as if they serve only to provide examples of concepts developed by philosophers and scientists . . . is to miss the point of much of what Deleuze is about.'[23] This centrality of art is readily apparent from taking an inventory of Deleuze's writings. From his focus in the 1960s on the importance of literature to his shift in the 1980s to the plastic arts, music and cinema, Deleuze uses art to fuel the development of thinking on ontological, political and epistemological issues. In other words, he dramatises the shadow that art and philosophy share throughout his writing, and the development of his ontological picture is bound to his engagement with various art forms. Though we do not seek here to outline the complete chronological and thematic development of Deleuze's thinking on art, we will provide markers as to how his perpetually developing theory of art contributes to the various stages of his thinking. Sauvagnargues' *Deleuze and Art* gives an account of this progression, extracting elements that indicate the status of art in order to interrogate their empirical function within Deleuze's philosophy, and we draw from this insightful analysis with respect to the intersection of philosophical concepts and this progression. Briefly, Sauvagnargues identifies three general phases in Deleuze's engagement with art: (1) his early writings, from *Coldness and Cruelty* (1967) and *Proust and Signs* (1972) to *Kafka: Toward a Minor Literature* (1975), which privilege literature as a disjunctive encounter, allowing for a novel practice of interpretation through symptomology and leading to the recognition of anomalous and a-grammatical aspects of language itself; (2) the eventual abandonment of the interpretive position altogether, toward a philosophy of the machinic functioning of art, which, along with his introduction to Guattari and the political events of the late 1960s, initiates a shift toward the political implications of art as experimentation;[24] (3) a semiotics of creativity that approaches art as the composition of material forces and intensive variations, delivering art and literature from all signifying hermeneutics and exposing thought to its own radical incapacity through the shock of sensibility, initiated in *A Thousand Plateaus* (1980) and explicitly thematised in *Francis Bacon: The Logic of Sensation* (1981), *Cinema I: The Movement-Image* (1983) and *Cinema II: The Time-Image* (1985).

The common thread running through Deleuze's theories of art is the underlying emphasis on the capture and manipulation of forces, which returns us to Nietzsche. In the 1983 preface to the English edition of *Nietzsche and Philosophy*, Deleuze emphasises Nietzsche's great importance for artists, but, given what we have said concerning the centrality of art for Deleuze, this statement folds over into his philosophy as a whole. In Chapter 1 we claimed that Nietzsche's philosophy, particularly his positing of the triumph of the simulacrum and his ontology of forces, is the inspiration for several key Deleuzian ideas. Nietzsche's overturning of Platonism entails the affirmation of the simulacrum and the provision of its own concept. Recall that, on Deleuze's account, the simulacrum places the structure of model and copy into question, eviscerating the priority of the metaphysics of representation. The simulacrum indicates a new kind of being, one determined by an internally differentiated heterogeneity. Rather than approximating an ideal model, the simulacrum reveals beings in proximity that undergo processes of transformation, perpetually changing in kind rather than moving farther and farther from the truth. The simulacrum contributes to Deleuze's elaboration of a different ontological model, as well as an image of thought reconfiguring the notion of the Idea as problematic, heterogeneous and agonistic. Deleuze wants to describe the possibility of interaction between the internal, heterogeneous elements that actually constitute objects. Beginning with the notion of multiplicity, Deleuze systematises the innovations of the simulacrum. His ontology is geared to explain the processes of becoming of particular entities. Deleuze's theory of a differential plane of consistency comprised of pure forces and intensities puts the innovations of the simulacrum to work.

Also recall that Deleuze establishes a special relation between the simulacrum and the work of art: 'the perfect state of the simulacrum is only approached by certain machines or certain works of art' (RP, 172). This too is carried through in Deleuze's subsequent thinking, as art becomes the window onto the ontological picture where multiplicities and becomings occur. In what follows, we address a constellation of concepts that comprise Deleuze's ontology, beginning with multiplicity as the 'being' of the simulacrum, assemblage as successive to the simulacrum, the rhizome as the privileged image of the horizontal topology of multiplicities, assemblages developed in the context of the geophilosophy of *A Thousand Plateaus*, and ending with the abstract machine as carrying through the transgressive, transversal power portended by the simulacrum.

## From Multiplicity, Unfolding Events

Deleuze first introduces the term multiplicity in *Bergsonism* (1966), drawing a distinction between the 'multiple' and a 'multiplicity', or 'multiplicities'. The Multiple belongs to a numerical system and presupposes similarity, while Deleuze is attempting to describe a system defined by heterogeneity, or differences in kind, which cannot be defined in terms of numbers. In other words, numerical counting that yields the Multiple assumes an overall likeness of kind of things counted. The distinction between ontological orders typified by essence (resemblance) versus difference is at play here. Essences are explained by resemblance to other entities via certain invariable traits. The ways in which they differ are of less importance. Their being in its singularity does not show up, so to speak, nor does the process which gave rise to them. A multiplicity, on the contrary, is a thing that can be determined by its internal variation. For Deleuze, 'everything is a multiplicity ... even the many is a multiplicity; even the one is a multiplicity' (DR, 236/182). Deleuze is influenced as well by Bernhard Riemann, who distinguishes between two kinds of multiplicities, discrete and continuous. When the former kind of multiplicity is divided, its parts are merely smaller measurable units. For instance, when a line is divided equally there are merely two parts of the same line, or if one were to divide an hour into smaller units, then one would get smaller units of time, minutes. With continuous multiplicities, one cannot divide the multiplicity without a change in kind: 'one can divide movement into the gallop, trot, and walk, but in such a way that what is divided changes in nature at each moment of the division' (MP, 603/483). Multiplicity of this kind reflects a form of progressive differentiation. Riemann's innovation was to conceptualise a 'realm of abstract spaces with a variable number of dimensions, spaces which could be studied without the need to embed them into a higher-dimensional space'.[25] These two traits put forward by Riemann, variable dimensions and the absence of a supplementary dimension that imposes an external unity, are integral features of Deleuze's multiplicity. Deleuze says that Bergson gives Riemann's account of multiplicity renewed range and distribution by associating continuous multiplicity with duration, from which Deleuze derives his notion of the univocity of being. Rather than difference as a twofold duality between Being and beings, Being is univocal differentiating difference.

In *Difference and Repetition* (1968), Deleuze applies multiplicity to the Idea: 'an Idea is a "complex theme," an internal multiplicity – in other worlds, a system of multiple, non-localizable connections between differential elements which are incarnated in real relations and actual terms' (DR, 237/183). Rather than transcendent and immutable, the Idea is immanent and transmutable, which necessitates that Deleuze must explain how genesis and transformation happen within a system of immanence. The Deleuzian distinction of the virtual and the actual, at least in part, accomplishes this task. The virtual and the actual are not two different levels of being. The virtual is the intensive structure that inheres within the actual and gives rise to the extensive actual, and it is altogether real. The multiplicity of the Idea resides virtually within it as it is actualised. The simulacrum presupposes such a heterogeneous, virtual multiplicity that acts as the explanation for its being.

Deleuze provides even greater nuance to the understanding of multiplicity by introducing the process of different/ciation, the determination of the virtual content of the Idea, illuminating the double nature of a bi-directional event: 'an ideal half, which reaches into the virtual and is constituted both by differential relations and by concomitant singularities; and an actual half, constituted both by the qualities that incarnate those relations and by the parts that incarnate those singularities' (ID, 140/100), 'giving us a world perhaps understood as a fourfold' (ID, 144/103).

Deleuze's ontological plane is a manifold of intensive multiplicities that continuously folds, unfolds and refolds, a single field of interaction in which the intensive tends toward the limits of virtuality and actuality. As opposed to Heidegger, being is not a relation or gathering of things that differ, even if these differents are formal structures; rather, it is the pure structure of relation, or *difference in itself* (dx/dy). Intensity, expressed as a difference in degrees of force, is the problematic field of being (plane of immanence), which resolves itself into extensive actualisations. The individuation of these intensity differentials explains how Deleuze's system can be both univocal and immanent, as well as differenciated and genetic.

After the publication of *Difference and Repetition*, Deleuze abandons the concept of the simulacrum in favour of the concept of the assemblage (*l'agencement*).[26] Historically, *l'agencement* has primarily an artistic sense, that of a beautiful arrangement of figures or rhythms, which is particularly interesting given our contention that ontology and art should be thought together in Deleuze. But Deleuze also extends the sense of assemblage to include elements of the machinic.[27] Consequently, he moves even farther away from the ideas of the resemblance in that things no longer *simulate* but rather *actualise* immanent Ideas, through the selection of various singularities from among the virtual multiplicity corresponding to the particularities of the situation and its demands. Assemblages are open-ended and contingent because there is no logical necessity to the contact between the series that are swept up.

The concept of assemblage works to disrupt certain anthropocentric paradigms of relation. Deleuze contrasts two types of relation, filiation and alliance, used to describe the interaction and generative propensities between beings in order to emphasise the specificity and priority he gives to assemblage. Alliance refers to the union between kinship groups, marriage, while filiation refers to descent, or the reproduction within a particular union. Traditional couplings operate by filiation and assemblages operate by alliance. Deleuze argues that the primary focus in explaining the genealogy of a particular being has been filiation, where beings are always referred to as within a certain line of descent and understood in terms of degrees of sameness. This genealogical ordering occludes the moment of alliance, the entrance of the other into the group. In other words, the exogamous relation is ignored in favour of relations of filial resemblance. Deleuze associates this with a prejudice for the mechanical repetition of representation over a creative repetition that carries with it novelty and difference.

Because the hierarchy of beings does not exist on an ontological level (see MP, 296/242), alliance is a much better way of conceiving the relations and productions that ensue between beings. Deleuze therefore focuses on those types of things that do not follow the filiation model: contagion, proliferation, propagation, contamination. These are unnatural nuptials, at least from the perspective of filiation, which create a zone of proximity between heterogeneous kinds. In Deleuze's well-known example of the exchange between wasp and orchid, there are two heterogeneous series that form an alliance. The orchid mimics the body of the female wasp, luring the wasp to copulate with it and, thus, pollinate. Referring back to the simulacrum, the orchid's imitation of the wasp is neither good nor bad, but rather of an entirely different order which results in a transformation of both series – the figure of the orchid responding to the wasp's body and the promulgation of the wasp-species.

By unhinging generation from filiation, Deleuze can speak of assemblages that cross species and transcend the division of the organic and inorganic. Encounters such as these form the basis for understanding the important Deleuzian concept of becoming/s. The encounter between heterogeneous series transforms both entities, without assimilating them, through the mutual capture of forces and intensities that characterise both. In terms of human becomings, the notion of assemblage allows for the entrance of the inhuman into relations hitherto unavailable to systems of filiation.[28] It allows questions concerning who 'we' are as human beings to be reconceived: 'What might occur between animals and humans, what processes, desires, identities, might circulate in the interspace where animal and human come together?'[29]

The hierarchical architectonic of beings that places humans on top is also challenged; 'man is no longer the eminent term in the series' (MP, 288/235), but is a body made up of affects that may enter into composition with other affects of other bodies. Every assemblage is itself a multiplicity, containing a coagulation of forces and intensities that are imperceptible. Bodies, whether human, plant or animal, are made of multiplicities and defined by affects, so there is an immanent plane on which they can meet, exchange and interact; this molecular world of intensive forces, which is presupposed with the assemblage, is reminiscent of a Nietzschean ontology of force. Deleuze 'assigns art the task of providing access to this corporeality below the level of organization'.[30] Since art is the paradigmatic place where these forces are captured, liberated and unleashed, art is a window onto the vital flux of immanent life.

In *A Thousand Plateaus*, Deleuze gathers the features of multiplicity and assemblage through the rhizome, creating an image, likened to the growth of weeds, of a non-centralised and heterogeneous manner of interactions and relations which are always defined by the outside, by deterritorialising forces which flow through this immanent, horizontal system/plane. 'The principal characteristics of a rhizome: unlike trees or their roots, the rhizome connects any point to any other point, and its traits are not necessarily linked to traits of the same nature; it brings into play very different regimes of signs, and even nonsign states.'[31] The rhizome becomes the privileged image of a horizontal topology of multiplicities and assemblages. Rhizomatics acknowledges heterogeneous relations and systems, opening thought to polyvalence and aberrations. The emphasis on the heterogeneity of connecting series preserves the idea of multiplicity within a unity. In terms of connections, the rhizome operates transversally rather than being bound linearly or vertically, which means that there are more possibilities for connecting between assemblages and strata of organisation. Without vertical hierarchy, the rhizome indicates networks without preferential order; thus rhizomatic organisation resists structures of domination. Of particular significance given our meta-discussion of the nature of beginnings, transformation and origins, the rhizomatic structure suggests that there may be several beginnings and that there is no privileged point of origin – it is always in the middle, an intermezzo. Because rhizome suggests that multiplicities are provisional and fluctuating rather than presupposing constituted organisations, it is a concept that refers to relational forces rather than forms. Therefore, 'the rhizome serves as a methodological precondition for the definition of art as a capture of forces and the logic of semiotic sensation'.[32]

## FROM THE MACHINIC IN LITERATURE TO THE ABSTRACT MACHINE

The final piece to our ontological picture is the abstract machine, as that which provides the minimal amount of consistency and maximal amount of flexibility in an assemblage. Every plane of consistency, comprised of relative exterior and interior milieus of strata, involves an abstract machine that guides the possibilities of the unfolding of multiplicities on that plane. Before going deeper into this discussion, and though we have already introduced the *machinic* as a descriptor of assemblages, it is worthwhile to spend a moment developing its context, as it returns us to the integral relation between Deleuze's philosophy and art, in this case, literature.

Our engagement with Deleuze on art is situated toward what we take to be the middle and end of his aesthetic/philosophic purview, as he develops the political implications of art (*à la* Kafka) and what can be called the semiotics of creativity (*à la* Bacon). As we have noted, Deleuze's interest in art, and choice of particular art forms, changes over the course of his thinking. As early as *Coldness and Cruelty* (1967), Deleuze understands literature in terms of a symptomology of the intensities and forces present within the social order. Initially, symptomology is a method of making sensible that nexus of force and power underlying substances and effects, reflecting a genealogical mode of interpretation understood as a clinical practice of reading or mapping affects. Thereby symptomology exposes and diagnoses particular ways of being or states of forces, leading to the call for experimentation and the proliferation of new subjectivities. Sauvagnargues locates the deepening of the status of the sign in Deleuze's collaborative efforts with Guattari in *Kafka*, where Deleuze becomes less interested in the intellectual status of signs (interpretation) and more concerned about the ethology and material effectiveness of the sign, as well as its impersonal and collective uses. The engagement with literature as machine leads to the critique of interpretation based on the internal coherence of the text/sign, and eventually to a theory of art that is independent of it altogether, art as the capture of forces and the creation of new blocs of sensation.

The concept of machine appears in *Anti-Oedipus, Kafka,* and *A Thousand Plateaus*, significantly all co-authored by Félix Guattari. Guattari had developed this concept as early as 1965, emphasising its 'vital, mechanistic, and concrete features against structure'.[33] In *Anti-Oedipus*, this resistance to structure plays itself out in relation to desire, which, rather than being derived through the Oedipal structure, is limited by it. Desire is not expressive, nor is it signifying; it is productive, and should be conceived in terms of the machine, whereby desire is produced through the interplay of the material flows of the body and their interruption. The machine is that which first cuts or interrupts the continual flow, which in turn conditions the continuity of desire. Each machine is connected to another machine for which it becomes something to be produced, coded and interrupted. Privileging the machine over structure suggests that modes of external connection are the genetic conditions of necessarily relational systems and points to a constant variation at the bottom of signifying systems as well as the possibility of traversing or connecting several different systems.

In *Kafka*, Deleuze and Guattari propose the text as machine, through which they theorise a revolutionary and political use for literature. Therein, the machinic indicates a principle of external functioning that is opposed to the internal signification of the text. What distinguishes Deleuze's interaction with literature in *Kafka* is its decidedly collective and transgressive foci, wherein a twofold force of literature prevails: (1) that it is created through an exploration of the margins of social production and language, and (2) that it has the ability to capture or connect, inventively, with social and political forces that operate within the major codifications of language, but which are not necessarily apparent or sanctioned by the major discourse/language/norms. Deleuze and Guattari categorise this potentiality of the text under the term 'minor literature', to which we will return in the final chapter.

The assumption of a politically relevant role for literature rests on Deleuze's critical stance toward the immanence of power and language, whereby the social body is constituted and maintained by the space of possible linguistic utterances underwritten and sustained by the assumption of language as universal and normative. Deleuze and Guattari understand literature as having a special relation to decoding the dominant symbolic structures of language. The machine replaces models of structural linguistics and master signifiers which impose a certain order related to systems of power and dominance,[34] which will later be re-deployed in relation to material composition to replace accounts reliant upon hylomorphism and internal order. The text literally becomes a means of connecting various sign systems, whether linguistic, social or political, exposing the power relations that instantiate the façade of the singularisation of meaning. Through its multiple outlets and points of connection, literature has the potential to be a disruptive force that cuts through the dominant (majoritarian) language, devising new and deviant uses (experimentation), and opening political spaces.

Thus, to recap, the theory of writing and reading developed in *Kafka* signifies a new function for literature, which also reflects a transformed view of the potential of art and its relation to philosophy. With the advent of this new use for literature, Deleuze presents a programme for making his own philosophy operational and experimental: 'when one writes, the only question is which other machine the literary machine can be plugged into, must be plugged into in order to work' (MP, 10/4). Philosophy, as well as literature, become modes of transformation that capture various forces and engage with heterogeneous genres in order to produce new affects, forces and concepts. Deleuze's intent is to produce a philosophy capable of detaching from the dominant forms of power, and he finds his solution in the realm of aesthetics, particularly the literary machine which generates new codes and is graced with the force of invention.

Deleuze celebrates those artists who tap into this potential and advocates the kind of impersonal experimentation that becomes available through considering the machinic function of literature. And while Deleuze never abandons his position concerning the emancipatory potential of literature, moving toward this machinic image and its a-subjective, even non-linguistic elements paves the way for considering other modes of art for these self-same emancipatory, machinic elements.[35] Following the progression of his engagement with art, Sauvagnargues claims, Deleuze realises that 'semiotics requires a philosophy of art that is not reducible to the order of signification and discourse',[36] which, in effect, leads to the turn to painting and cinema.

This transition turns upon *A Thousand Plateaus*, where Deleuze and Guattari apply themselves to a critique of semiotics, taking specific issue with Chomsky's presupposition of an underlying universal grammar, which results in one of the most powerful yet elusive concepts, the *abstract* machine. Inaugurating *A Thousand Plateaus*, Deleuze and Guattari write:

> Our criticism of these linguistic models is not that they are too abstract but, on the contrary, that they are not abstract enough, they do not read the abstract machine that connects language to the semantic and pragmatic contents of statements, to collective assemblages of enunciation, to a whole micropolitics of the social field. (MP, 14/7)

The detachment of language from its master signifiers, its minoritisation by substitution of the variable for the invariant, which begins in *Kafka*, is deepened through this appeal to the abstract machine, which, functionally, assembles discursive and non-discursive signs and, philosophically, indicates a method of conceptualising future becomings. Consequently, we propose the *abstract* machine as another layer to this analysis, important in that it invokes the virtual

potentialities of any assemblage. In other words, an assemblage operates according to functions that can be called machinic, but is also
guided by a particular abstract machine. By comprehending art as
abstract machine, we can understand Deleuze's insistence of the role
of art in creating new peoples and new earths.

Following Hjelmslev's innovations in interpretation of semiotic
practice, Deleuze and Guattari explain that our systems of meaning
and language are constructed by means of a double-articulation of
content and expression, both of which have their own form and
substance (see MP, 58–60/43–5). Both content and expression are
related to matter, which is the baseline for all thought and activity.
Content refers to formed matters, either as a chosen *substance* or
as an ordered substance, which is *form*. Expression, which refers to
functional structures, is also double, either in terms of the form of
organisation or the substance of the compounds which are formed.
Thus, in actuality, double articulation is itself doubled, and Deleuze
and Guattari emphasise that this renders the pure distinction
between these two arbitrary.[37] What this means is that both regimes
are thoroughly inundated, comprised of both content and expression, thus they are immanent to all assemblages. Though the concept
of the abstract machine is developed in the context of the extension
of Hjelmslev's critique of linguistics, Deleuze and Guattari see him
as a Spinozist geologist and a dark prince (precursor), extending
his linguistic theory to the processes of stratification as such.[38] By
this theoretical complexification, Deleuze and Guattari expose the
derivative nature of the traditional duality of substance and form,
countering this duality with that of matter and function. Substance
and form already imply the presence of ordering as 'stratification'.
In other words, substances already suggest the organisation of matters,
and forms are certain assemblages of substances that operate by
repetitious codings (MP, 70/53), which implies that these are not
primordial categories. Moreover, assemblages are always double-
sided, both containing forms of expression or regimes of signs (semiotic systems) and forms of content or regimes of bodies (physical
systems), what we might consider as replacing the old distinction
between thought and being.

As Guattari contends elsewhere, that each content and expression
has a form suggests that there must be a 'formal machine transversal
to every modality of Expression and Content'.[39] The commonality
that brings content and expression together is the abstract machine.
In other words, the abstract machine subtends both (MP, 176/141),

and form, itself, is subtended by function at the level of the abstract machine. Therefore, content and expression do not have universal essences, nor do they pre-exist their articulations, indicating that these systems are immanent and may be relationally involved with each other and that signification and subjectification are both involved in the same system of stratification and destratification that characterise the earth and organisms.

By drawing on linguistic theorists such as Hjelmslev and Markov, Deleuze presents an alternative theory of language as constantly variable, what Olkowski calls '*langue*-vibration',[40] which would, in effect, suggest that all language has the propensities of slippage and transformation, rather than being reducible to an ultimate universal grammar *à la* Chomsky. In the *Abécédaire*,[41] Deleuze explicitly pits literature against linguistics along these very lines:

> According to linguistics, *langue* is in a state of equilibrium, which thus can be an object of science. All the rest, all the variations are set aside as belonging to *parole*. But a writer knows well that a language is a system that is by nature far from equilibrium, a system in a perpetual state of imbalance. (*Abécédaire*, S is for Style)

Of course, the artist/writer is still necessary to break down the hegemonic forms that language has taken within a particular culture. It is the writer's style that distinguishes her writing from everyday speech, allowing the vibratory elements of language to burst forth. Writers have the ability to make language stutter, whether by detour through non-sense and novelty (Lewis Carroll), taking language it its limits (Artaud, Joyce), or by the force of sobriety, a whittling away of symbolic and metaphorical guise (Kafka).[42]

Deleuze and Guattari also think that this mode of explanation has ramifications for the dominance of the discursive in our understanding of expression. Modalities of expression do not necessarily have to be linguistic or discursive, though we tend to think of them as such when content and expression are merely opposed. When one recognises the codings and functions that make up the form of expression, the heterogeneity of expressive materials is revealed. In *Chaosmosis*, Guattari differentiates between expression, which is normally considered to be discursive, and enunciative substances, which are expressive without necessarily being linguistic, to emphasise this heterogeneity: biological codings, machinic (non-semiotically formed matter), linguistic expressions, incorporeal dimensions.[43] Attending to the intersection of these domains reveals possibilities and a complexity that has been neglected in traditional theories focused on the logic of discursivity. The Signifier and Being with a capital B have been the great reducers of ontological polyvocality. 'Being is like an imprisonment which blinds us to the richness and multivalence of Universes of value which, nevertheless, proliferate under our noses. There is an ethical choice in favour of the richness of the possible.'[44]

Deleuze and Guattari offer descriptions of several regimes of signification and their relation to certain social or political outcomes, each containing form of content and form of expression which creates particular systems of signifiance and subjectification. The signifying system is a network of interrelated interpretations and signs, while the post-signifying system is a system of subjectification. The conjunction of these two regimes dominates the contemporary understanding of the individual, its landscape or world, and the socio-political framework. They will thematise this interrelation of signification and body through the figure of faciality. Dismantling the face becomes the key to moving beyond or escaping these rigidified and power-laden systems. This is, of course, why Deleuze is fascinated by Bacon's repetitive distortions of human bodies and faces.

Deleuze and Guattari emphasise the possibilities for destratification, and, in particular, the defacialisation of the subject, through a-signifying regimes that do not operate by representation and identity. Such is the potential of the abstract machine, and, as we shall see, such is the realm of the artwork. The Deleuzian emphasis on a-signification results from the corresponding critique of representative, semiotic systems as dominating our view of reality and limiting the possibilities therein. The 'complexity of the given' arises from the enunciative assemblages of incorporeal universes of value, discursive orderings, existential territories and material, non-discursive forces.[45] This complexity is reflected in the difficulty of conceiving and even describing the abstract machine, which is clear by the reversion to negative descriptors here:

> An abstract machine in itself is not physical or corporeal [cf. Guattari – it is an incorporeal complexity enabling possibility or freedom of movement], any more than it is semiotic; it is *diagrammatic* (it knows nothing of the distinction between the artificial and natural either). It operates by *matter*, not by substance; by *function*, not by form. The abstract machine is pure Matter-Function – a diagram independent of the forms and substances, expressions and contents it will distribute. (MP, 176/141)

That the abstract machine operates according to another register than the semiotic is an important distinction, one that demands our attention for several reasons. First, locating the abstract machine outside of the system of semiotics opens our discussion to the level of a-signifying or non-discursive force. With respect to our project, we are particularly interested in Deleuze's linkage of art at the onto-logical level to a logic of forces, and for this reason, our forthcoming discussion of art concentrates on the moment when Deleuze moves the farthest away from sense and language to develop this logic of sensation, which is a study of the a-signifying, vital forces at work in the artwork – the sign as affective force. Second, this is an important point of divergence between Heidegger and Deleuze, one which we believe allows Deleuze's philosophy to better address the inventive and transformative potential of art forms without reference back to the poetic or needing to interpret other art forms via an analogy with language. Third, what Deleuze and Guattari replace the semiotic with – the diagrammatic – is significant as it offers a bridge between different forms of art, whereas the semiotic remains indebted to language. Specifically, we are able to engage one of the main foci in Deleuze's theory of painting, the non-narrative, non-figurative, non-illustrative Figure, by determining its diagrammatic nature.

Before moving to consider how art can be an abstract machine, we must determine *how the abstract machine guides the possibilities of unfolding*. As we have explained, beyond mere assemblage, the abstract machine is the condition from which assemblages arise. It is a transcendental condition, in the sense of a pre-individual horizon from out of which the empirical is generated, out of the forms and substance that occur in various strata, but not in the definitive sense of pre-constituting the direction of the connections and relations of the strata – there are creative and contingent potentials involved in the mechanisms of abstract machines. They are virtual systems of potential connections understood as an internal multiplicity which can then become incarnate in actual terms.

> When we speak of abstract machines, by 'abstract' we can also under-stand 'extract' in the sense of extracting. They are montages capable of relating all the heterogeneous levels that they traverse [material, cogni-tive, affective and social] . . . the different components are swept up and reshaped by a sort of dynamism.[46]

The plane of consistency is thus occupied and drawn by the abstract machine (MP, 90/70), which constructs repetitious orderings, or what one might call rhythms, by extracting codes from various domains and re-coupling these codes. Deleuze insists that there is no one abstract machine that constitutes the form of the universe. Abstract machines are singular and immanent to a given assemblage; the abstract machine is like a motor that inhabits each machinic plane of consistency out of which that plane unfolds, assembling and disassembling its assemblages.

The suggestion that the abstract machine is involved in a dynamic process is underscored by the theoretical breakdown of the content/expression and substance/form dyads. There are 'intermediate states between content and expression ... the levels, equilibrium and exchanges through which a stratified system passes' (MP, 59/44). The dynamism of the machine is in part related to the fact that there is no necessary outcome prescribed by it and in part by the heterogeneity of levels that it connects. Its singularity and creativity resides in a particular manner of layering and ordering of the stratified and destratified. Occupying that space between chaos and order, there are no necessary connections but neither is there complete randomness: there are rules, rules of 'plan(n)ing' (*la 'planification'*), which guarantee that continuities, emissions and combinations, and conjunctions do not occur in just any fashion (MP, 90–1/70–1). Therefore, abstract machines are endowed with a directive though not determining power, what Deleuze and Guattari call a deterritorialising piloting role (*rôle pilote*), opposing this role to both territorial indexes (*indices*) or reterritorialised icons (*icônes*) (MP, 177n38/142n41). In other words, the abstract machine is always characterised by its journeying, relaying through and between strata.

The creative or contingent potential of abstract machines is indicated by the abstract line, or line of flight, whose function is equally definitive, if not primary (MP, 176n36/141n38), of the assemblage. It accounts for the genetic potential and complexity inherent in rhizomatic planes of immanence and the possibility of heterogeneous becomings of assemblages and multiplicities:

> Multiplicities are defined by the abstract line, the line of flight or deterritorialization according to which they change in nature and connect with other multiplicities ... The line of flight marks: the reality of a finite number of dimensions that the multiplicity effectively fills; the impossibility of a supplementary dimension, unless the multiplicity is transformed by the line of flight.

The capabilities of cutting across stratifications (MP, 66/50) and mapping out heterogeneous elements indicate the diagrammatic nature of the abstract machine, and its lines of flight render it transversal, meaning that the abstract machine can exceed its original parameters – the assemblage can escape itself, as the abstract machine is not bound to one level or expression of the universe. Thus, the abstract machine's diagrammatic nature means that it is incorporeal yet real, in other words, virtual. As diagrammatic, the abstract machine offers suggestions that extend beyond the actualisations of the strata. Thus, the abstract machine operates according to the logic of the virtualities that comprise the plane of immanence. Though it is the condition of substances and forms (actualisations) that populate the plane, its reach far exceeds these particular accretions, opening different degrees of movement that reside, though virtually, on the plane of consistency.

What this means is that the abstract machine is a deterritorialising agent, because it is a diagram for moving beyond the already mapped out plane and because it provides the connective force for moving between strata and stratified substances. Its function is actually to break down matters locked in substances, mapping out routes of escape and alternative virtualities. In fact, an inherent possibility of machinic heterogeneity is breakdown or catastrophe. In this way it constitutes the birth of new order, corresponding to new functions and codings. Therefore, abstract machines are, potentially, constructions of 'a real yet to come, a new reality' (MP, 177/142).

As matter-function the abstract machine can make new connections between and within substance-form. It liberates the parts of the machine (of the world) in order to remake the world. It takes assemblages and restructures them, liberates singularities, reconnects to different assemblages, deterritorialising the concrete world, and constructing an abstract machine is to construct a real experience, because the abstract machine determines the *real* conditions of experience. Deleuze holds that there is an initial diagrammatic function within philosophy, the elaboration of a pre-philosophical plane of immanence, prior to concepts, and Ian Buchanan treats the abstract machine as an earlier code-word for the concept, thus the carving out of planes of immanence as the creation of a context for competing concepts (voices) would be philosophy's singular task. Such an elaboration determines the concepts that follow, determines our thinking and what is actualisable. Buchanan describes this as an agonistic theatre of philosophy.[47] Yet, our claim is that the abstract machine and its lines of flight manifest in their most potent form through works of art. On the outset, these seem to be competing claims, and it is true that Deleuze very clearly separates the production of concepts and the production of affects and percepts as the respective purviews of philosophy and art. We believe that the contradiction dissolves when referring concepts and affects back to their mutual genetic conditions, laid bare in Deleuze's geophilosophy. Starting with the unformed or decoded earth, all beings and systems of meanings are accretions, constructions, which have the potentiality to be deconstructed or decoded. These assemblages become fixed and concretised, their essentiality unopposed, and this is a problem. Yet double (double) articulation reveals the level of continuous variation inherent in ostensibly fixed forms, allowing Deleuze to posit an unfixing of these forms, which is accomplished by and through the abstract machine and its lines of flight. Philosophy intersects with the creative impetus of the artwork in this regard. This is the final message of *What is Philosophy?*: Art and philosophy 'share the same shadow',[48] the chaotic swirl of the forces of being that must be harnessed through the selection on planes of immanence. Deleuze's numerous references to the provocation of thought from the outside, the dark precursor, the violence done to thinking, are clear indications that concept creation begins elsewhere, in the sensuous other of philosophy, and that this other is always present as the ineluctable double of our thinking.

## Capture, Art as Abstract Machine

Immediately following *A Thousand Plateaus*, Deleuze published *Francis Bacon: The Logic of Sensation* (1981), one of his most, if not the most, significant texts on aesthetics. There, he develops philosophic concepts which correspond to the sensible aggregates of painting as well as other art forms. Though specifically focused on an analysis of the paintings of Francis Bacon, the logic of sensation developed therein provides the basis for understanding the community of the arts in terms of rhythm and as centred on the common problem of capturing forces (laying bare the underlying cadences of sense and perception). In what follows, we address the theory of sensation that Deleuze develops with respect to art, then consider how the elements of art(s) express the being of the sensible.

We began this chapter by returning to Deleuze's claim that the work of art is the perfect form of the simulacrum, which we posit now in terms of how the work of art is the perfect form of the abstract machine. Abstract machines include all the possible modalities and lines of flight available to a given system or assemblage. As such, they are deterritorialising diagrams that suggest other ways of being for that assemblage, degrees of freedom from actual, present states. In itself, this offers a method of analysis that multiplies the registers by which we can understand any given system of relations. Yet, as we have emphasised, there are rules. Take a simple object such as a bicycle. There are a myriad number of states or positions available to the bicycle and these are all part of its overall diagrammatic nature. We could sketch these different states and then layer them on top of one another to obtain what might serve as an image of its abstract machine. The bicycle is determined by its form and material, i.e. aluminium or titanium, the number of gears, the size of tyres, and also its condition, being well-oiled, tyres inflated, etc. These determine degrees of freedom for the bicycle and, at any moment, it may enter into an encounter that would actualise one of these states – a child could pick it up, a car could run it over, the road could be rocky or slick, a bully could be chasing a child causing them to peddle faster, it could be left out in the rain. All of these could unleash the potentialities of the bicycle. What could not happen, without serious modification to the bike, or the power of E.T., is that it levitates and flies off into the sunset. The bicycle is limited in this way.

But what of art? It is relatively uncontroversial to suggest that the form an artwork takes is not limited by any particular function, or conception of what it must be or do. The view that art is not bound to a pre-given conceptual framework was already proposed by Kant, for whom aesthetic pleasure is derived from the free play of the imagination initiated by the fact that works of art are not the kind of objects that we place under a concept or category. This determination relies on the fact that the aesthetic attitude is characterised by disinterestedness, which means that we are not judging aesthetic objects by measures of practicality or in correlation to experience.

For Deleuze, the stakes are somewhat different. The abstract machine of art can bypass the level of stratification and ordering that normally envelopes our encounters (experience), moving directly to the level of material or intensive potentials. In so far as encounters between disparate or heterogeneous series are generally understood under the auspices of capture, where forces and codes are exchanged in a mutual becoming, the encounter with the work of art is a space which captures and connects material forces in ways that do not exist in our already stratified and coded interactions. In light of our conceptual framework, this means that works of art are inventions of new abstract machines which act as relays for creative connections of flows and matters, rather than mappings or plans of existing states of affairs. Artworks are blocs of sensation, which reveal (as signs of) the imperceptible forces at work within the plane of immanence. They are machinic operators that connect heterogeneous and multiple modes of force yielding novel and multifarious sensible encounters which, by passing through us, give a shock to thought and initiate material becomings. This view differs dramatically from Kant's in that the encounter is not purely one of aesthetic appreciation. Art literally creates new modes of being, connecting material, cognitive, affective and social forces, producing new sensations and laying bare the genetic conditions of sensation in the process.

Rather than referring us to a kind of pleasurable cognitive dissonance, the fact that artworks are free from conceptual limitations allows us to think more deeply about the difference between perception and sensation. Drawing from the phenomenological tradition, citing the work of Maldiney and Merleau-Ponty,[49] Deleuze distinguishes sensation and perception as co-extensive aesthetic dimensions, the latter referring to a secondary rational organisation of the former, primary non-rational dimension of sensation. Perception assumes the discernment of distinct objects from a manifold of sensory information (object-unifying process), while sensation is a direct experience that does not pass through these organising capacities. Deleuze links Bacon and Cézanne, in particular, as aiming to develop the priority and imperative of attaining the level of sense experience (*le sentir*) directly, or as Bacon says, to record the fact. Further, Deleuze locates Bacon's work within what he takes to be the indicative problematic of the modernity, that is the imperative to escape the domain of representation (domain of perception), or, in painterly terms, to go beyond the level of figuration, in order to attain the sensation directly. The problem is how to access this dimension given that perceptual organisation is fundamentally automatic to us, thus the world is always already represented. The goal, then, is the reversal of the occlusion of sensation by perception.

Sensation is indicative of a further, 'more profound and almost unlivable Power' – rhythm as the synthesis of chaotic intensities. Daniel Smith outlines Deleuze's reading of Kant's theory of perception[50] in his excellent introduction to *Logic of Sensation*, stating Deleuze's conclusion thus: 'the foundation of perceptual synthesis is aesthetic comprehension, but the ground on which this foundation rests is the evaluation of rhythm',[51] which ultimately leads imagination to experience its limits (the sublime) and the catastrophic collapse of coordinates in general. The realisation of the linkage between sensation and rhythm happens in relation to the role that Kant lays out for aesthetic comprehension in perception itself, which leads to the recognition that constant variation or rhythm is the condition for all perception. The recognition of variation or chaos at the heart of perception meets with different ends for Kant and Deleuze. Whereas Kant is able to find sure footing with the introduction of guiding Ideas guaranteed through the faculty of reason, Deleuze focuses upon the constituted nature of ideas, thematising the fragile relation between chaos and order subtending them. Beyond a theory of perception, then, Deleuze indicates the imperative for a logic of sensation, where such a logic refers back to force:

> Force is closely related to sensation: for a sensation to exist, a force must be exerted on a body, on a point of the wave. But if force is the condition of sensation, it is nonetheless not the force that is sensed, since the sensation gives something completely different from the forces that condition it. (FB, 57/48)

Forces are intensities which are un-sensible yet, perhaps paradoxically, can only be sensed through the sign. The sign is the first point of sensation that is perceptible to the conscious mind. Therefore, a sign is something that can only be felt or sensed and also constitutes the limit of the faculty of sensibility. The empirical or sensible is the product of the becoming of these forces, in other words, the constantly moving arrangements of these forces with respect to one another in their incessant becoming. Deleuze, following Nietzsche, says that 'all sensibility is only a becoming of forces. There is a cycle of forces in the course of which force "becomes"' (NP, 72/63). Thus, the sign is already a composite of elements (intensities) that are more or less virtual in the sense of being indiscernible, or imperceptible. The sign points back toward an infinite number of singularities, 'in short, points to a pure aesthetic lying at the limit of sensibility: an immanent Idea or differential field beyond the norms of common sense and recognition'.[52] A sign is, then, an effect of the relations of forces and intensities which constitute the ideal genetic elements of perception.

Works of art make different levels of force communicate via the linking of multiple material and sensational levels through a variety of techniques. Deleuze refers to artworks as blocs of sensations, indicating the ineluctable status of relational multiplicity that acts as a monument in which otherwise passing and imperceptible genetic components come to stand. Therefore, we must understand the artwork as a *sign* of that which is insensible: intensive force constituting the transcendental realm of the sensible. For Deleuze, affect, sign, sensation and image, interchangeably refer to works of art which themselves infer the being of sensation. Works of art are involved in a double process of becoming, both creating sensible beings and revealing the being of the sensible.

Finally, these functions of the work of art are related to the task for thinking. Deleuze presents a theory of the faculties in which each faculty is taken to its limit or threshold, provoking or forcing a movement or passage to another faculty. The passage from one faculty to another, which constitutes thought, has its origin in sensibility. It is in this respect that Deleuze can say that everything, all thinking, begins with sensibility (DR, 188/144). Works of art, then, are signs which expressly let the process of actualisation of immanent Ideas come to stand in them, revealing the virtual multiplicity beyond and underneath the sensible: 'poets, artists, make a slit in the umbrella, they tear open the firmament itself, to let in a bit of free and windy chaos and to frame in a sudden light a vision that appears through the rent' (QP, 191/203). In thinking the conditions of thinking, the non-thinking within thinking, the being of the sensible itself is what must be thought, and art makes visible this being.

Art is uniquely suited to the task of provoking or inciting thought in that it specifically dismantles and reassembles sensible components of reality or connects to conditions of the real and the plane of immanence in its infinite, genetic movement. Artworks attest to the genetic conditions (the being) of sensation, which makes art a point of access to the impossible task of thinking that which cannot be thought, that is the intensive (ontology of forces) which exists below the level of perception. Thus, the artwork gives sensible form and expression to what is not itself sensible. In the world of the painter, this is to paint forces, rather than objects of representation. To paint (capture) intensive forces is to create an affect that makes us sense these unsensible forces. The same logic applies in other forms of art: the musician must render the non-sonorous sonorous and the poet or writer must inspire imperceptible feelings and unremembered memories,[53] each creating new, specific compositions. Artworks, by making this level of reality visible, have the potential to prepare a new way of thinking and, as well, allow an affective engagement with becoming. The artistic affect, as a pure perception or *sentiendum*, denotes a new compound that creates a passage of intensity on the body, a becoming of the body. The affect confounds perception and understanding, awakening thought because of its novelty – it is a shock to thought. This violence is a provocation, where thought has to form new conceptual schemas to account for such a shock. Therefore, new affects are like the dark precursors to thought. In other words, art not only reveals, in the sense of making visible the conditions of thought, but, in the creation of new and particular sensations, it expands what can be thought.

## Art as Abstract Machine: Diagrammatism and the Diagram

Our claim is that works of art work in a way parallel to the abstract machine; they are generative and diagrammatic. Moreover, if the abstract machine is linked to earth and geophilosophy, marking the priority of immanence, thus also is art, a fact that will become apparent in discussing the artwork as a kind of framing or territory first instanced in the natural world by animals. To support these correlations, we consider how art, like an abstract machine, constitutes the real conditions for new experiences and new constructions of the real, which concomitantly requires that we consider how art is both an agent of deterritorialisation and the instantiation of order. Our starting point in answering these questions lies in Deleuze's characterisation of painting and the nature of the canvas, leading to why Deleuze identifies the need to prioritise Bacon's Figure and the specific elements involved in producing it, and finally to the function of the diagram, once again exemplified through Bacon's style.

In chapter 11 of *Logic of Sensation*, 'Painting before Painting', Deleuze begins by elaborating the existential conditions of the painter. Similar to Heidegger's understanding of *Dasein* as always already thrown into a world, the painter does not create *ex nihilo*; the painter engages in a world filled with perceptual and figurative givens, those things in his head, around him or in his studio. Deleuze relays this viewpoint through his disputation of the emptiness of the seemingly blank surface of the canvas. As Deleuze contends, the canvas with which any painter begins is already populated with images, ideas, directives, in short, the significance of a prefigured world, which Deleuze labels clichés of representation. The painter's task is to break free of these; otherwise, there is no creation of which to speak. Deleuze often refers to Cézanne with regard to the difficulty of liberating sensation from the cliché. To paint one truly new sensation, this was Cézanne's lifelong struggle – not to reproduce an image of an apple, but to convey a unique, unrepeatable sensation of apple-ness. The painter is always involved in a process of selection, limitation and elimination of some or all of the clichés with which she finds herself confronted, and this process is a struggle, requiring the painter to devise means to combat the relentless onslaught of clichés and take pains not to fall back into the world of re-presentation or imitation (FB, 83–4/71–2). Given this existential starting point, Deleuze can say that the principal feature of painting is always deformation, which is reminiscent of the fundamental deterritorialising function of the abstract machine. This is a feature that can easily be extended to all art forms, because each will deal with its own forms of cliché. Therefore, we can say that artworks are by nature deterritorialising machines. For Deleuze, this is especially true of music. Though musical compositions are made up of refrains, which have a repetitive structure, the being of music resides in the deterritorialisation of the refrain (MP, 368/300). Otherwise, all that exists is the monotony of repetitive marks/sounds/beats.

Deleuze is interested in methods of bypassing the figurative, narrative, and illustrative aspects of painting, which only occlude its potentials, in order to reveal the being of the sensible as well as the forces of which sensation are comprised through the various captures and deformations that the painter pushes clichés beyond (FB, 57/48). This is why Deleuze is particularly interested in modernist painting. Modernism is marked by its self-conscious response to social and political upheaval and to the overall disruption of metaphysical and philosophical paradigms – in a word, to crisis. Modern painting breaks away from the demands of representation to deal with the conditions of perception, to try to paint the deformation of objects, the movement and forces of nature and sensation itself. The crisis of modernity is literally transposed into the figures of modern painting through what Deleuze calls the passage through catastrophe, which we address in relation to the concept of the diagram. Preliminarily, the diagram is that which allows something to emerge, whether through the canvas, the frame, the sculpture or even the musical refrain. Philosophically, the diagram is the 'in between', marking the event of becoming.

Deleuze identifies three great paths that fall within the modern function of painting to embrace chaotic intensity in order to depict the genesis of pictorial order and go beyond figuration: abstraction, abstract expressionism and the Figural, which is Bacon's path. Each of these has its merits with regard to revealing the chaotic and eliminating the representative, narrative aspects of the work, and each has a particular relation to the diagram as a technical component of painting. But it is Bacon to whom Deleuze pays special homage, primarily because he sees Bacon's construction of the Figure as most fully able to express the being of the sensible – the 'almost unlivable Power (*puissance*)' (FB, 39/47) of an intensive, vibratory being. Abstraction reduces chaos to a minimum by making it the transmission of a spiritual expression, thus form is transmuted into symbolic code. Abstract expressionism, as in Pollock's works, celebrates catastrophe from which there is no return, a complete abandonment of form (FB, 96–8/84–6). Neither of these expresses the rhythmic interchange which captures the necessary collapse of form *and* the germ of its creation as fully as Bacon.

For Deleuze, the fundamental role of painting in releasing the visual from its representative function implies that all painting is involved in hysteria (FB, chapter 7), the scrambling of material and bodily organisation through the liberation of colour and line from its representative function leading to a collapse of visual coordinates, a point in which the 'eye becomes virtually the polyvalent indeterminate organ: sees the bodywithoutorgans (the Figure) as a pure presence' (FB, 54/45). Yet, painting cannot remain hysterical, it converts hysteria in order to establish new coordinates. In other words, painting must pass through the catastrophic loss of coordinates in order to renew the visual field; this is accomplished through the diagram which is technically both the initiation of hysteria and the tool for its conversion: 'The diagram is indeed a chaos, a catastrophe, but it is also a germ of order or rhythm. It is a violent chaos in relation to the figurative givens, but it is a germ of rhythm in relation to the new ordering of the painting' (FB, 95–6/83). The diagram technically precedes painting, as the first attempt of the painter to deal with the clichés within the canvas.

Deleuze introduces the diagram through the work and self-described practice of Francis Bacon.[54] Bacon explains his artwork as an attempt to capture the random forces of nature that work upon bodies. In order to elude clichéd figuration, Bacon would begin by throwing paint on the canvas haphazardly. The fact that 'these marks, these traits, are irrational, involuntary, accidental, free, random' (FB, 94/82) is very significant, suggesting that the Figure is marked by chance and contingency. Rather than beginning with set forms, the practice of creating an open space of random marks suggests possible forms and multiple paths for his paintings, and raises the accidental to the most prominent form of causation. For Bacon, the diagram is a form of preparation, as both the idea that inspires the work at its inception, and those initial, physical marks that constitute the beginning of the work. These can be a sketch, outline, or movement, any act that initiates and gestures at a future figure. These preparatory marks inspire the work, but they do not represent the last word of the work. Thrown paint, slash-marks, detailed pencilings, charcoal smudges, all these remain to be moved, elaborated, calmed, traced and erased. These diagrammatic 'asignifying marks and nonrepresentative zones (FB, 95/82) intervene between the chaotic intensive field and the form which arises, suggesting rather than determining a Figure.

The diagram is a paradoxical origin because it cannot be represented, yet sets up certain givens within which the painting must arise. As an event that paintings pass through with the dual function of disrupting figuration and initiating the emergence of the entirely new, it is an unfounded beginning from the middle. It is the point of contact between the formed and unformed, the actual and virtual. In other words, the diagram is a gateway between the chaos and order, which preserves the machinic prerogatives of chance and contingency over those of natural progression or essential ordering. In this way, it exemplifies the directive yet not determinative force of an abstract machine. The canvas opens itself up to an emergence of form out of these splatters and plasterings. 'It is like the emergence of another world' (FB, 94/82). These marks cut across, and into, the infinity of gross forms. These are the initial acts of painting that attest to the pre-figural, abyssal ground out of which the Figure arises. The ground created through the diagram threatens to engulf the canvas. Yet, at the same time, the diagram offers what Deleuze calls the possibility of 'fact', which is the possibility of a new, uninhibited sensation or *affect*. By eliminating clichéd representations, Bacon begins to paint the 'fact' (*being*) of sensation.

The diagram is thus the motor of the painting, in the same way that the abstract machine is defined as a transformative agent. In the final chapter of *Logic of Sensation*, 'The Eye and Hand', Deleuze explains that the diagram involves the modulation and passage between forms, occupying the transversal element of the abstract machine. The aleatory brush strokes of Bacon's paintings

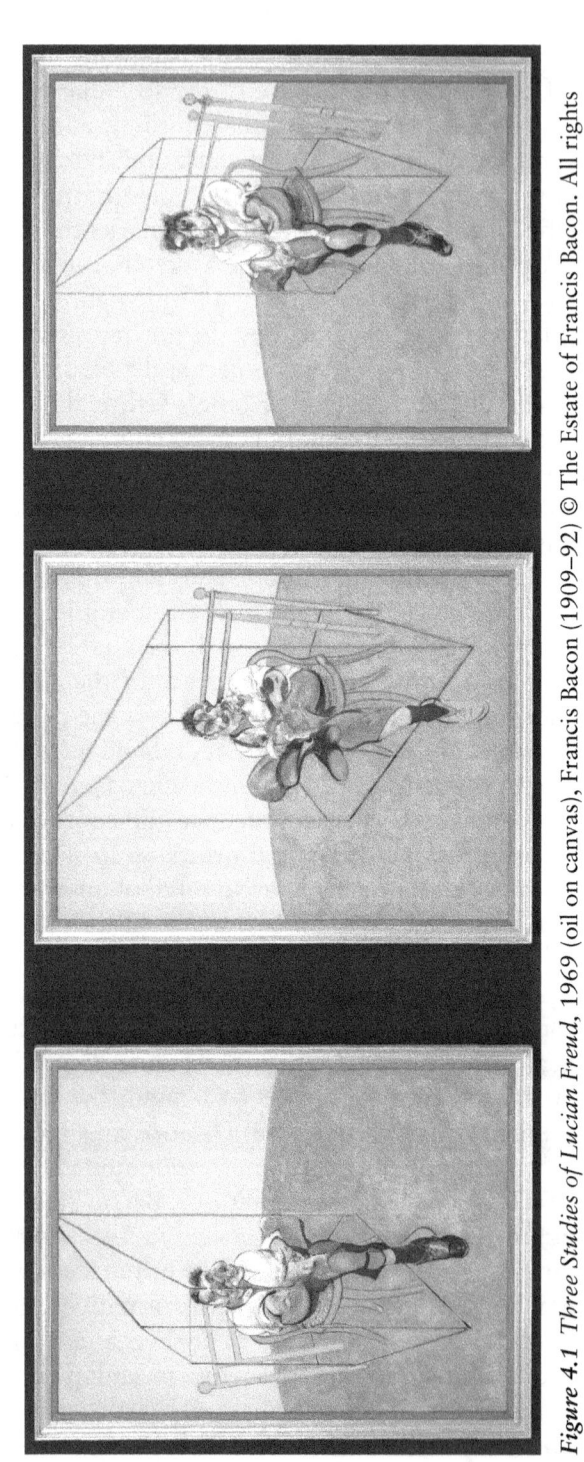

*Figure 4.1* *Three Studies of Lucian Freud*, 1969 (oil on canvas), Francis Bacon (1909–92) © The Estate of Francis Bacon. All rights reserved. DACS, London / ARS, NY 2014. Photo © Christie's Images / The Bridgeman Art Library.

The triptych is the culminating example of multiple levels of rhythm which become visible in Bacon's work. Triptychs are indicative of the passage of force and movement – they establish an intense *rapport* which, as Deleuze emphasises, is not based on narrative depiction. In *Francis Bacon: Logique de la sensation*, Deleuze refers to no less than twenty of Bacon's triptychs, many of which are reproduced in their original vibrancy and occupy pride of place in the centre of the book. We have chosen one of the first triptychs to which he refers in order to offer some fidelity to Deleuze's intent.

offer several opportunities for the figure to break free, degrees of possibility, one or many of which may be selected. There are lines of flight suggested by the marks and zones of indetermination in Bacon's painting. Traditionally, lines of flight lead the eye beyond the visible depictions in the painting itself. They allow the eye to fly off the canvas, engendering the experience of passage or the force of movement. The desire to capture the force of movement is one reason why Bacon's favourite métier is the triptych, paintings comprised of three separated panels, in which he finds similarities to the cinematic image.

## ENGAGING BACON'S WORK: *THREE STUDIES OF LUCIAN FREUD* (1969)

We have given a predominantly theoretical explanation of the logic of sensation, yet, if we are to show fidelity to Deleuze's thought, we must engage with affect on different terms; the *sentiendum* must be felt rather than thought. Deleuze achieves this in *Logic of Sensation* (in the original two volume text) by coupling his writing with Bacon's paintings, inviting an interactive experience of these visual components in resonance with his conceptual analysis. Thus, the beauty of *Logic of Sensation* is that it is more than a *logos*; it is also an exposure to the violence of force through visual sensation. Bacon's works are vivid encounters in which gravity pulls on human bodies, pressure contorts their features, open-mouthed figures attest to the force of the scream, the figure contracts or dilates to express dissipation (FB, 37/29). One can actually see these forces in the paintings and they are absolutely necessary for encountering Deleuze's text. Though we cannot replicate this experience in its entirety, we can follow Deleuze by linking our explanation to one of Bacon's works, and we have chosen the triptych *Three Studies of Lucian Freud*, for its multiple techniques.

Bacon's paintings include several aspects which reflect the self-conscious avoidance of figuration and the clichés of representation in order to produce a direct apprehension of the sensation. In particular, the multiple techniques of isolation, resonance and separation taken separately or together lead us to experience the Figure in its pure capacity as a rhythmic being. At the most basic level, Bacon's paintings are comprised of three components: (1) surrounding fields of colour, usually monochromatic backgrounds, (2) the Figure, and (3) the contour which encloses the Figure. These components work to isolate the Figure, which is the simplest technique to ward off the cliché, by its divorce from any symbolic order or narrative. These elements are readily apparent within the triptych of Lucian Freud. The monochromatic orange and brown zones, colours uncommonly sedate for Bacon's vibrant palate, saturate the background, forming a shallow depth which envelops and curls around the figure of Freud. These fields of colour press into the figures, contracting them, while the figures themselves press outward against the foreground in strangely contorted and unmanageable positions. Freud's body is encaged within a square of thin brush strokes, the contour which acts as a thin, permeable boundary between the Figure and field, a motor (FB, 44/36) that gets things moving. In this case, the contour marks the space of passage resulting from the competing forces of the field upon the Figure, and the Figures strain against the field, animating the quite literal attempt of the Figure to escape itself by depicting one foot stepping beyond its enclosure. Deleuze claims that 'it is the confrontation of Figure and field, their solitary wrestling in shallow depth that rips the painting away from all narratives as well as from all symbolization' (FB, xxxii). There is nothing else besides the elements immersed in a shallow depth struggling against each other. Through the force of isolation the only thing that exists is the immobilised Figure and what it is undergoing, or what passes over, through and around it. This immobilisation reveals a kind of movement in-place, which points toward the 'actions of invisible forces upon the body (hence the bodily deformations which are due to this more profound cause)' (FB, 45/36). Hence what seems to be an 'extraordinary agitation of the head in not derived from movement but rather from the forces of pressure, dilation, contraction, flattening, and elongation that are exerted on the immobile head' (FB, 59/50). The mottled and deformed face, which seem to swerve in multiple directions at once, convey the violence of sensation for which Bacon is perhaps best known, and, though often associated with his series of heads or self-portraits, this affect is also present in his more complex triptychs. For Deleuze, Bacon's work is the most marvellous response to the question of how to render invisible forces visible, which, as Deleuze emphasises, Klee also identifies as the task of painting (FB, 57/48). In Bacon's work, this particular visibility (of the invisible) is obtained through the repose (isolation) of the Figure, allowing the visible spectacle to become a sign of the forces exerted upon it.

The second type of forces, those of deformation, are also obtained through form at rest (*la forme au repos*), such as a Figure merely sitting in a chair. Bacon contorts this natural posture through the Figure's awkward, painfully crossed legs and folded, contracted body. One gets the sense that the tension wrought from the contracted body may at any moment cause it to expand and lose itself entirely, and Bacon's Figures are often deformed to the point of losing themselves or flirting with the saturation of colour they are enveloped by, flesh falling away from bone, features melting down the face, Figures sinking into and between crumpled clothing (forces of dissipation) – until what remains is the inexorable materiality and fact of the body, the body without organs and its participation in the almost unlivable Power of rhythm at the cusp of chaos. At the level of the an-organised body, there is only intensive reality, a dynamic force field of speeds and intensities, a Bergsonian duration of indivisible continuity of movement. Rhythm is both the vibration/oscillation of intensities on the plane of immanence and an ordering of these intensities which make these forces appear.

Ultimately, the contorted, spasmodic episodes of the Figure make visible the systolic-diastolic relation between the field and Figure, the fact that there is an immanent and breathable proximity between the two which is perpetually open to exchange, the rhythmic ground of all sensation. 'This ground, this rhythmic unity of the senses, can be discovered only by going beyond the organism' (FB, 47/39). At the same time, if the Figure disappeared, it would be impossible for these profound forces to become visible, because the Figure also strives against them (a clue to Deleuze's aversion to abstraction). We can draw a parallel to the generative strife in Heidegger's *Origin*. In order for the invisible, the power of rhythm, to become visible, the Figure must remain in tension, bound up in a struggle between competing forces. If, as Deleuze says, 'the struggle with the shadow [invisible forces] is the only struggle' (FB, 62/52), it is because in this confrontation the Figure releases a defiant force of its own, 'an act of vital faith'. This is the power of the scream (FB, 60/51), not as an indication of horror but as an unleashing of force which defies, to scream *at* rather than *before*, in an affirmation of life ('life screams at death') which ushers in the forces of the future and makes visible the resistance to the present that Deleuze adamantly claims we lack. Again, a parallel to Heidegger arises. With reference to Bacon's screaming Pope, Deleuze says that because Bacon painted the scream and not the thing that causes the horror, the horror is multiplied (FB, 43/34). He screams before the invisible, at nothing, neutralising the horror as it is not about anything, which resembles Heidegger's anxiety, as that which is felt in the face of or before the nothing.[55] The void or abyss that cannot be filled is the mute and formless region which cannot be expressed in language – this is the outside.[56]

Moving from the vibration that ensues within the single Figure, Deleuze defines a second order of complexity in Bacon's paintings, the resonance of two sensations: coupling. Bacon understands the coupled figures to present a matter of fact, rather than be involved in a narrative event. The couple accentuates or makes visible the relational nature of sensation and, even though resonance exists even in simple sensation, the couple dramatises the 'combat of energies' that results in the emergence of something beyond either. His wrestling nudes exemplify the sheer proximity of two intertwined Figures, presenting the reality of confrontation and struggle as a matter of fact. Finally, the third order of complexity, and Bacon's most preferred method of painting, consists in the triptych. Bacon's triptychs are often studies of the same Figure with slight variations on each of the three panels, which Deleuze understands to confer a great mobility to the painting, indicating their circular rather than linear nature. These are not stories; they are vibratory encounters that happen by virtue of their separation. The triptych, according to Deleuze, is replete with rhythm, which is to say that its fundamental aspect is the distribution of three rhythms: *active* characterised by increasing variation; *passive* with a decreasing variation; and *attendant* (*témoin*), whether in the traditional mode of an actual personage, or as the horizontal element which draws the eye across the panels (FB, 74/63). In the case of our triptych, the horizontal created through the juxtaposed colour saturations focuses the eye directly to the contraction of the body, what must then be addressed in terms of the variations between Figures on the panels to determine the active or passive rhythms which abound. At a second level, the attendant function may circulate through the painting, operating on or animating one or more of the Figures which causes the visible attendant to give way to either passive or active rhythmic attendants.[57] Finally, there are opposable rhythms between the figures themselves. One figure will be slumped (descending), while a figure on another panel will be leaping (ascending). There can be oppositions between the diastolic and systolic as well. In the case of the Freud triptych, the opposition is between the naked and the clothed, a contrast between the exposed shoulder and contracted head on the left to the covered one with relaxed head on the right (FB, 76/65). Deleuze spends a good part of two chapters (9 and 10) parsing the complexities of these rhythms. What is decisive for us is

158

that the triptych, as a multiplicity of rhythmic passages, represents a move beyond variation or rhythm dependent on the Figure, to rhythm itself becoming the Figure (FB, 70/60). The triptych makes visible the passage of sensation, moving us beyond the Figure and even beyond the limits of a canvas. Whereas the line of flight, technically the vanishing point, generally indicates the end of visibility and an imagined beyond of the canvas, the triptychs circulate between each other via these lines, activating various rhythms and becomings. If we are to find a model for understanding the abstract machine, in its selective and connective yet non-determinative role, we may begin by looking to Deleuze's analysis of the triptych.

Of course, Deleuze mentions other artists whose work confronts chaos in order to bring to visibility the germ of creation and a new order. Rhythm is a métier of the artist, who works to creatively assemble and disassemble forces in order to produce a unique bloc of sensation, an affect. So it is style that separates the artist, style which amplifies the creative assemblage of forces into the birth of a unique affect: Van Gogh's pulsating sunflower, Cézanne's unadulterated apple, Messiaen's deterritorialised birdsong, or Bacon's screaming liberation. When speaking of the passage to the chaos-germ of order, Deleuze cites Klee's work as among those which treat this generative moment explicitly. For Deleuze, Klee's main painterly agenda is to make visible the force of creation: 'Klee's "chaos," the vanishing "gray point," and the chance that this gray point will "leap over itself" and unlock dimensions of sensation' (FB, 96/83–4). The operative word in this quote is 'chance'. The gray point, present in some form in most of Klee's paintings (like the deep abysmal point which draws us into *Magic Garden*), is like a black hole that sustains a promise for the entire canvas and is equally the place of proliferation and the horror of being swallowed up. It is a 'mobile equilibrium, a center of balance, suspended over a veritable chaos of sensations',[58] which provides a foundation from which 'it is able to reach out into dimensions far removed from conscious endeavor'.[59] Reappearing in *What is Philosophy?* as the final example of the non-thought which resides within the heart of thought, it summons an indeterminate blindness, a dark precursor unleashing unknowable forces that may unhinge us from the tyranny of the present.

Deleuze also cites Kandinsky's use of the transversal line as a positive example of the possibilities for liberation, through the freeing of the line: 'In Kandinsky, there were nomadic lines without contour next to abstract geometric lines' (FB, 98/86). For Kandinsky, the artwork embodies living forces, each point and its matriculation into line encapsulates living being: 'the fundamental source of every line remains the same – force'. Kandinsky's synaesthetic attempts to render visible the musical underscore his attention to the rhythmic underpinnings of the sensible. Kandinsky explains that he aspires to generate reverberations, new beings and resonances, through the repetitions of line and point.[60] He views the internal necessity of his work as stemming from the reality of forces that populate the world, which then intervene on the canvas through the visibilities of colour and form, crashing into each other in relations of tension. What is lacking, and what clearly draws Deleuze to Bacon, is attention to indeterminacy and chance. We should therefore think of these as privileged, and absolutely necessary, elements of art as abstract machine or art as related to a people-to-come.

## From Frame to Framing: De/Territorialising the Refrain/Cosmos

We have seen how the diagram functions like an abstract machine within painting by introducing chance and indeterminacy into the visual field to deterritorialise clichés. Just as moving through the aspects of the Figure pointed beyond its rhythms to the Figure of rhythm itself, we aim to move beyond the diagram within the frame to the framing function of artworks leading to the relationship between art and nature, an aesthetic ontology where artworks, as the becoming-expressive of territorial refrains, become dynamic, diagrammatic exchanges between milieu and territory. To move beyond the frame (of painting), the diagram must be considered essentially in its framing/deframing mobilisation which becomes the basic figure of the merging of art and life. In our discussion of geophilosophy, we presented the forces of territorialisation and deterritorialisation as essential to the construction of surfaces which bear the events and singularities that diversify the world, and posited the aesthetic as deeply connected to the movements and forces of the earth. The connection between art and life is made explicit in *A Thousand Plateaus*, chapter 11: The Refrain.

Deleuze and Guattari identify three basic components of the refrain: point of order, circle of control, and line of flight.[61] At the most basic level, the earth, as elements, forces and singularities in relation to one another, is composed of milieus. These milieus are established through the repetition of certain activities, patterns, or sonorous components which become ordered based on the relations and responses of living beings. For example, the interaction between leaf and water or the spider/fly relation will comprise vibratory blocs establishing a milieu. The repetitious orderings derived from terrestrial (and cosmic) forces form the rhythmic regularity which signifies a point of order of the refrain.

At a second level,[62] these milieus become territories when the components cease to be merely functional and become instead expressive. Deleuze and Guattari explain this staking out of territory as the establishment of the infra-assemblage of the refrain, the circle of control. For example, the bird sings to announce its presence and ward off other males, or arranges leaves in patterns to mark its territory, as is the case with the brown stagemaker (MP, 387/315); the components of the milieu are now used to organise and demarcate space. This is the basis of the refrain, a repetition of elements establishing a boundary – the refrain is a frame and the origin of the circle is always found within the between spaces of milieus. Deleuze asks, rather rhetorically, 'can this becoming be called Art?' (MP, 388/316). The framing of these sensible elements, as the animal carves out an abode, is *art brut*. Deleuze takes this to mean that art, rather than originating from human action and expression as *technē*, begins with the animal. 'Music is not the privilege of human beings: the universe, the cosmos, is made of refrains; the question in music is that of a power of deterritorialisation permeating nature, animals, the elements, and deserts as much as human beings' (MP, 380/309). We are at once reminded of Heidegger's now infamous claim that animals are world-poor.[63] Given that the work of art is a matter of strife between world and earth, Deleuze is here directly at odds with Heidegger. Either animals have some form of world, Jacob Uexküll's claim,[64] or art is not what Heidegger thinks it to be. The poverty of the animal, its deprivation, is understood by Heidegger in contrast to the being of the human as *soon logon ekhon*, its dwelling in *logos*. Though more should be said concerning this, it must suffice for now to mention that Deleuze is able to include animals because he has unhinged art from *logos*.

Following Deleuze and Guattari's tripartite distinction, the refrain of territory is merely the material for the becoming of art; we must still consider the line of flight, or the opening of the territory to the outside. '*Art brut*' becomes truly musical only *beyond* the frame, through its deterritorialisation or detachment from this original possessive intent. Just as 'music is a creative, active operation, which consists in deterritorializing the refrain' (TP, 369/300),[65] beyond a repetitious, vibratory intensity, the unequal (difference) must enter in. The territorial refrain must enter into counterpoint with elements external to it (MP, 390/317): an enemy approaches, rain falls, the 'bird sings an impromptu aria at the break of day, and thus opens its territory to other milieu'.[66] These events create melodic landscapes and the bird's song no longer remains a marking of territory but becomes a series of motifs and counterpoints, a style. The initial organisation of milieu is that point of order, the demarcation of a territorial boundary as the circle, and the opening of the bird's song to the outside, as marker of the break of day, the line of flight.

The debate among ornithologists as to whether we can consider these songs as instinctual or a kind of free play is interesting because it raises the question of where the shift from the territorial to the deterritorialisation that constitutes music happens. Messiaen, well known for his symphonies modelled on birdsongs, claims that birds are not only virtuosos but are artists in their territorial songs, and Bogue refers to Messiaen to suggest an answer, a bridge between what we may call *music brut* and human music. He explains that the changes and manipulations necessary for humans to even interact with the songs (i.e. slowing down, adapting of tone) reflect a transformation, a becoming-bird of music, rather than an imitation.[67] It is less a clear distinction than a zone of indetermination, which constitutes the very nature of the becoming of music. Deleuze says that music moves us beyond the bodily refrain/frame (FB, 55/47), through the liberation of the purest intensities according to music's airy flights. This release from materiality is closely connected to cosmic becoming. This liberation of the elemental constitutes a means of reconnecting with the elements and intensities from which our myriad refrains have been constituted. The freeing of the refrain/frame completes the musical gesture. Art exceeds its nascent moment and draws its specificity from its ability to draw us into deterritorialisations, deframings. The material forces, which are now framed and combined, are cut away from their environments, released as blocs of sensation which enjoy an existence independent of their original signification. The superfluity and independence from any expressivity other than itself is essential to art.

Rather than the Enframed (*Ge-stell*), there is *Framing*, an exemplar of the double, rhythmic function of the frame. The movements of the refrain punctuate the permeability of 'framing', the capture of the force of rhythm running parallel to our discussion of the diagram in painting and indicative of the deterritorialising function of the abstract machine. Framing preserves what would otherwise be transitive and fleeting. Just as the creation of a territory provides a place for certain habits to form and behaviours to arise, the artwork, as the capture of forces, preserves the fleetingness of the being of the sensible. Yet the specificity of art is that it is always also a matter of deframing (*décadrage*), or allowing the a-systematic – chaos – to reassert itself (QP, 179/188), which Deleuze elucidates in *What is Philosophy?*

There, Deleuze sets the planes of art, science and philosophy on separate but equal footings – each operates by establishing a particular domain of order, and, at first, it seems that the purpose of each is purely the battle (*lutter*) against chaos: 'we require just a little order to protect us from chaos' (QP, 198/201). Each plane casts a protective yet tentative net over chaos, or, as Deleuze's says, an *ombrelle*, which, significantly, is not an umbrella such as one would take in the rain, as commonly translated. It is, rather, a parasol which is used to protect from the searing rays of the sun. The sun, while it is impossible to look at directly, is illumination. In terms of life, it is necessity itself. Likewise, chaos, though unthinkable, is what we need. The larger battle, which equally besieges thought, is against opinion. Given the particular nature of opinion to calcify, to become immobile, lifeless *Urdoxa*, a concerted effort of resistance to every present instantiation is called for and the need to invent forces of the future. Citing Lawrence's violently poetic text, Deleuze affirms that artists 'tear open the firmament itself, to let in a bit of free and windy chaos' (QP, 191/203). Art is not chaos, but it does tarry with it a bit longer, 'to frame in a sudden light' (QP, 191/203) the unthinkable and impossible in a vision or pure Sensation. Each art, through the capture of forces and the establishment of new flows, is essentially a framing of chaos but equally a deframing. This is the breath of fresh sunlit air that lays bare our opinion-making, preparing the path for the affirmation of the powers of the false, which is to say the possibility of affirming its own inventiveness. Though art, philosophy and science all erect planes over chaos, it is art that also allows the force of the formless appear. Art draws our attention to the fact that the frame opens out and is built from the outside. Therefore, the frame does not enclose or limit, but exposes. A work is the utmost vulnerability of form to its unleashing; it must perform, as it were, acrobatic feats.

The framing of the conditions of the sensible and the provoking of new affects demands the acknowledgement of the beyond the frame, even within the frame. In this context, Bacon's paintings are important in that the Figure, field and contour never remain completely intact. 'The contour as a "place" is in fact the place of exchange . . . like a membrane through which there is a double exchange of flows' (FB, 21/13). Yet, in moving beyond the frame of painting, Deleuze shows that rhythm, the vibratory power of diastole and systole, characterises the world as a whole. Sensation is vibration that has been demarcated. It is the cut in the flow of vibration that produces the sensation.

Emphasising this a-signifying, rhythmic element levels the prioritisation of one art over others, which allows us to bypass the priority of language emphasised by Heidegger. Every art has its own means of expression and medium, therefore there is no one way that forces are presented or these effects of deformation, contraction, dissipation and movement – in short, rhythms – are brought about. Clearing the way for new coordinates to arise in the canvas, musical counterpoint that goes beyond the original parameters of the refrain, or the breaking of genre in film by altering the style and sequence of images, are all methods for passing through catastrophe toward new order and establishing new rhythms. Through their individual methods of passage, they each reveal the chaotic, intensive being which underlies the world that we know as an organised world of form and solidity. In this revealing, the plane of art/composition is unparalleled. Artists construct abstract machines that offer new programmes of reality, producing new sensations and new bodily configurations.[68] The work of art, like the abstract machine, initiates transformation (of a system), destabilises a given network of relations (opinions), and introduces the possibility of new and different futures – and the artwork is exemplary in its ability to do this. Artworks are permanently renegotiating their conditions, and, in that the imaginative space of the artwork constitutes a freedom that is unavailable in everyday practice, they embody the spirit of experimentation. In other words, artworks can be truly and wholly creative, creating new affects, which, like Deleuze's enigmatic emerald water sprites, are operators of transformation which illumine the possibility of a different world.

This question of world returns us to the relation of Deleuze and Heidegger. For both, artworks are instantiations, the bringing to presence of that which is concealed or invisible. But *what* comes to stand separates these two thinkers at the level of ontological vision. For Deleuze, the work of art does not bring forth a new order of signification, a Heideggerian world, but instead calls forth new rhythmic beings, affects operating at the level of what cannot be thought, only felt, to change what can be thought. Art is critical and creative in making the being of the sensible, the composition of forces, visible. It is creative because rhythm establishes measure which introduces a new order into the world, and critical because the foundation of perceptual experience is revealed to be a constantly fluctuating variation. And, while artworks are these inventions of new rhythms, they are also points of connection between us and the universe.

This view is corroborated in *What is Philosophy?*, where Deleuze introduces the relationship between works of art, as beings of sensation, to other physical bodies as a 'house-territory system' (QP, 174/183). This is a combinatory vision that marries the territorial activities of the animal and the nuanced frames of the artist, while illuminating the dynamic interaction between what we consider to be familiar or homely and the rest of existence. The 'house' is presented in juxtaposition to Merleau-Ponty's concept of flesh, in an implicit critique of the phenomenological intertwining of the lived body (*corps vécu*) and world. The house replaces the flesh as the intermediary between the inner and outer worlds, as a means for Deleuze to underscore that works of art are compounds (framings) of nonhuman forces which exist beyond the perceptions and affectivity of the human body.[69] Deleuze reasserts the nonhuman dimension of the aesthetic: 'If nature is like art, this is always because it combines these two living elements in every way: House and Universe, *Heimlich* and *Unheimlich*, territory and deterritorialization, finite melodic compounds and the great infinite plane of composition' (QP, 176/186). Art is a way that humans and animals alike experience the world, carve out spaces for ourselves by and through which we orient ourselves and our bodies, framing forces in order to create sensible landscapes.

The house also serves as a figure for the 'structuring, modulating, and shifting configuration of forces within the artwork'.[70] Deleuze writes of the jointures between and within the frame, the interlocking of which becomes a metaphor for the composite nature of the bloc of sensations and the equivalent of musical point and counterpoint of the heterogeneous forces at work in the composite (QP, 177/187). As well, its windows suggest the intimate belonging together of art and its outside. Not only does the house communicate with the landscape, that milieu which immediately surrounds the house, but it opens onto the universe, the cosmos: 'the house does not shelter us from cosmic forces; at most it filters and selects them' (QP, 173/182). The openness of the house to the universe is crucial in that it reflects the resonance which works of art enter into and the reverberations, or counterpoints, that can exist to infinity: 'an infinite symphonic plane of composition' (QP, 176/185). This exposure and release to the outside constitutes the deframing (*décadrage*) moment which proliferates more affects and becomings.[71]

Initially, the parallel between the Heidegger and Deleuze, in that both understand the work of art as an open confrontation between the *Heimlich* and *Unheimlich* which makes visible the invisible (or concealed), seems itself uncanny. Heidegger calls for the setting-into-work of the *Unheimlich* in order that the truth of beyng comes to stand, thus setting up a vision for *Dasein*, for a people, out of and in relation to the overwhelming power of being.[72] *Dasein* is forced beyond itself in order to create the work, which then brings *Dasein* into essential belonging with being. For Deleuze, art is also described as a coming to stand (QP, 155/164), a Monument in fact. Yet, for Deleuze, it is the work which forces the human beyond itself, creating zones of indetermination which become the launching points for inhuman becomings. In other words, their accounts enjoin an inverse relation. Can we then distinguish the two in terms of which way we step across the threshold, *into* or *out of* the house?

Additionally, Deleuze transcribes that which Heidegger appoints to be the work of *Dasein*, to be *deinon* (or *unheimlich*), to all of nature. Deleuze is not disagreeing with Heidegger about the nature of human beings, just radically expanding this phenomenon beyond the human. Basically, the most primitive to the most complex bodily structures participate in rhythm, which is the infinite movement between the *Heimlich* and the *Unheimlich*. Remember that this is Deleuze's critique: Heidegger fixes the movement of territorialisation and deterritorialisation between Being and being. Of course, for Heidegger, human beings are further distinguished by the kind of home-making of which they are capable: they dwell, and *Dasein* dwells in language. Yet, it is precisely this that Deleuze eschews when it comes to the decisive characterisation of art as the capture of forces. The House, for Deleuze, is a composition of forces via materiality, an a-significatory, rhythmic being. Rather than returning *Dasein* to its internal relation to language, the work of art, as the passage from the finite to the infinite, illuminates the outside to our *logos*. Correspondently, a people does not look inside itself to pull out something hidden that is more meaningful, greater and purposeful, but is created in responding to the outside, a perpetual becoming other – not a historical becoming, but a cosmic becoming which arrives from the future, as the outside, rather than the past. Rather than a dwelling, Deleuze's house is an *atelier* from which to launch toward the Universe, a passage from the finite to the infinite.

## Affect, Becoming and Indirect Discourse

> It should be said of all art that, in relation to percepts or visions they give us, artists are the presenters of affects, the inventors and creators of affects. They not only create them in their work, they give them to us and make us become with them. (QP, 166/175)

Becomings are set in motion by the invention of affects. Artists construct new affects and percepts by arranging the vibratory materials of paint and colour, stone, sound, and the extent to which the artwork uniquely produces affect happens according to the artist's style. A Deleuzian people-to-come must be a people with a new sensitivity for the power of the affect and its rhythmic force, which, in relation to the House-Universe description, Deleuze intimates as a 'cosmic sensibility' (QP, 171/182). In our reference to affect, we have assumed its existence as a thing or entity rather than as a quality or experience, that is, a *being affected*. The idea of the artwork as an affect requires explanation. Deleuze derives his understanding of affect from Spinoza, noting that in the *Ethics* one finds two words dealing with affection, *affectio* and *affectus*. Rather than translating them both as 'affection' as many have done, Deleuze seeks to relay the difference. He deems that *affectus* refers to the affect while *affectio* refers to affection. Affection is a state of a body, an effect that occurs with the mixture of two bodies, while the affect denotes the variation or passage from one degree of power (*conatus*) to another. Also utilising Spinoza's understanding of bodies as composed of movement and rest and defined by the power of being affected, Deleuze claims that affect denotes the 'continuous variation of someone's force of existing'.[73] While affection (*affectio*) indicates the nature of the affected body more than the affecting body, the affect allows one to think both the passage of intensity that is incurred on the body and the independence of the affecting body. It is both an effect that a given object or practice has on its beholder and also a self-sufficient element in the world which is not dependent upon a subject.

Just as there are two moments in the diagram, affect is also charged with duplicity. The artistic affect is sometimes referred as that which stands on its own as a pure being of sensation, *the affecting*, and sometimes as a passage of intensity across a body. Artworks produce affects, but does this mean that they are themselves affects or that they affect bodies? The answer is both. The artwork stands on its own as an affect, but it also enters into a relation with the bodies that it encounters, namely our own. The important factor to remember about Deleuze's specific use of 'affect' is that it arises through works of art and passes through subjects who encounter them. As a passage, affect names the risings and fallings of bodies. As a matter of relations between bodies, affect extends beyond the human and the beyond the human extends to us. In other words, the power of being affected is not uniquely human – an instance of the expansion of the potentially transformative power of art beyond Heidegger's philosophy: 'Life alone creates such zones where living beings whirl around, and only art can reach and penetrate them in its enterprise of co-creation . . . art itself lives on these zones of indetermination' (QP, 164/173). As such, art is a catalyst for becoming, transforming our understanding of what it means to be human, or rather our understanding of the place of the human in this universe.[74] Thus, humans become with the affects of the world, connecting with other bodies via affect.

It is, in fact, the independence of the affect that generates the dynamics of radical becoming, because, wholly detached from subjective moorings, the affect (and percept) engage the human subject in the inhuman, in an otherness beyond human *others*. Deleuze maintains that this standing up on its own is the only law of creation, and, obviously, for forces to become something other than passing sensations, they must maintain a consistency. Art as monument is a compound of percepts and affects which 'owe their preservation only to themselves' (QP, 158/168). Why? Deleuze's idiosyncratic use of percept as opposed to perception and affect as opposed to affection (which we have already broached) is the issue, and must also be situated with respect to Deleuze's view of phenomenology. Though Deleuze grants that phenomenology goes farther in resisting clichés and *Urdoxa* than a those kinds of perception reliant on the transcendent and the subject who knows, he claims that 'it too goes in search of original opinions which bind us to the world as to our homeland (earth)' (QP, 141/149). By invoking the primordial lived, phenomenology seeks to renew perception and affections, yet,

Deleuze argues, by making immanence immanent to a transcendental subject, the cycle of opinion and cliché formation remains intact. He maintains that the only way to convey the pure being of sensation is to 'fight against the machine that produces [clichés]' (QP, 142/150). This is why Deleuze contends that the aim of art must be to wrest the percept away from the perceptions of objects or the perceiving subject and the affect away from its connection to affection as the transition from one state to another. Percepts and affects are such that they are extricated from their subjective associations, released from resemblance, signification, or memory, so that they 'are autonomous and sufficient beings that no longer owe anything to those who experience or have experienced them' (QP, 158/168). They enjoy what Bogue calls a 'free-floating existence', which means that they are liberated for undetermined becomings and adventures.

The purity of the sensation is the source of its power: 'the monument does not commemorate or celebrate something that happened but confides to the ear of the future the persistent sensations that embody the event' (QP, 167/176). Part of an artwork's being able to stand on its own entails that it does not represent sensations but generates sensations all of its own. Each work of art is itself a singularity. The self-sufficiency of the artwork and the independence of the affect are key in that something new is being produced and released into the world: 'Sensations, percepts, and affects are *beings* whose validity lies in themselves and exceeds any lived', (QP, 154–5/164) existing in the absence of the human.

There are several clear departures from Heidegger resulting from this discussion. For Deleuze, the work of art is a wandering affect, in which uprootedness is an affirmation, whereas for Heidegger the artwork must remain embedded in its world, even as it opens new vistas of that world, if it is to remain an opening onto the truth of being. This distinction will be important for illuminating the differences between their visions of a people-to-come. As well, what gets preserved and even who does the preserving is of great interest in relation to Heidegger, who saves pride of place for the 'preservers' who will determine if a work of art engenders a people. Where, for Heidegger, the artwork must be decided for, i.e. preserved, *by* a people, for Deleuze, the work of art is the material preservation of pure sensations disentangled from their past, their human saga or instantiation, which acts as a creative fabulation, an event that speaks to the liberation of sensation from its human bonds and through which the human can become other than itself. Therefore, the encounter with the work of art should not be thought in terms of preserving but instead as becoming, a radical phenomenological *epoché* where even the subject is removed and all that is left is phenomena, as if in a world without others. What kind of mad becomings can this engender? We have some idea because Deleuze enacts this thought experiment – or, rather, he submits thought to this experiment (see the next section). The affect and percept are the human's nonhuman becomings. We are speaking of obtaining to immanence, not lived perception but life or existence within a zone where animal and human, material and sensation, pass into each other, a zone of indetermination, which is the opposite of a return to origins. 'It is always a question of freeing life where it is imprisoned' (QP, 162/171), shattering lived perceptions. As Deleuze poetically writes: 'the task of all art is to extract new harmonies that raise them to the height of the earth's song and the cry of humanity' (QP, 167/176), which is a counterpart to his suggestion that we must become equal to the event. Affects launch new rhythms, which energise our thinking and multiply the possibilities in our worlds, and the affect may potentially sweep us outside of pre-coded strata, deterritorialising us and preparing us for new becomings. As in Heidegger's case, art wrests us out of our habitual ways of thinking, yet the dismantling of our subjective coordinates must go much deeper than Heidegger, or phenomenology, allows.

## BECOMING OF THOUGHT: EMERGENT SENSITIVITY TO THE AFFECT-EVENT

We have presented the diagram, and the affect that emerges, as a point of passage to a 'yet to come'. It is an event that one does not go through untouched or unchanged – an *affect-event*. On this journey of becoming, we may not recognise ourselves on the way back (QP, 181/191), positioning us for the question: what might a people be who pass through diagrams and experience the instituting power of the abstract machine? In beginning to answer this question, we must remember that Deleuze insists that art only prepares or forewarns of a people-to-come, rather than providing its model. The future of philosophy calls us to think through new affects, to think the pure being of sensation, in order that a new thinking and a new people emerge. Thinking would then follow the path of the diagrammatic, embracing mobility and indeterminacy as the perpetual motor of becoming other than itself, which leads us to posit the cultivation of sensitivity to the affect-event as a kind of preparation. Such a sensibility would amplify our attunement to connectivity and singularisation on the plane of immanence, which means that we must construct a new *logos*, a logic that accounts for the affect-event.

In 'Michel Tournier and the World without Others' (LS, 350–72/301–21), Deleuze experiments with just such a perverse logic. The shift in thought adequate to this perverse logic is catalysed by the melting away of all signifying coordinates, most of all those that comprise our communal understanding, our humanity. Tournier's novel, *Vendredi ou les Limbes du Pacifique* (*Friday*), a reworking of the classic Defoe novel of a man marooned and struggling with his solitude, provides Deleuze with the platform for his thought experiment: what would the world be without others. What we witness with Robinson's journey is a flattening of ontology, where Robinson becomes one with animals, plants and stones,[75] participating in the same elemental flux. Robinson's metamorphosis leads us to consider an immanent reality that does not refer back to a subject, or, at most, refers to a completely altered subjectivity.

The significance of Deleuze's choice of Tournier's over Defoe's version lies in how Robinson deals with his solitude. Rather than reproducing society, artifacts and work, *à la* Defoe, Tournier's Robinson submits to the brute depths and elemental nature of the island, engendering a quasi-mystical relationship with her, Esperanza; his adventure signals a decomposition of the world, a *sortie sans retour*. Robinson abandons culture, communes with the elements, even tarries in animality, before returning to the respite of language – he writes laws, a penal code. Yet, this is not the final stage for Robinson, and, if it were, the novel would not do what Deleuze needs it to do. The recalcitrance of Friday, a native whom Robinson attempts to domesticate and enslave, toward the newly established rule of law, initiates a role reversal. Then, under the tutelage of Friday, Robinson begins another adventure, that of joyful living. Friday is not encountered as other, but as 'something wholly other than the Other', as one who 'dissolves objects, bodies, and the earth' (LS, 368/317). Robinson's solipsism leads to the discovery that 'the presence of others', which signifies a world of concerns that can easily become one's own and that through which one's perception is formed, 'is a distraction'.[76] So earth, as 'a great body retaining and organizing the elements', is only earth to the extent that it is guided by the structural Other, i.e. the assumption of Others which guarantees the whole transcendental field, reminiscent of a Heideggerian world of referentiality (see LS, 355–9/305–9). Robinson's recognition generates the double, the suspicion that there is another world, not coordinated by others as a structural given: 'another Speranza might be hidden beneath his cultivated island' (LS, 367/316), another Speranza that signals a new, less human, more elemental Robinson. Here, Deleuze opposes this 'logic of the structural Other'[77] to a perverse logic that leads to a strange elemental world, a world purely populated by affects and events.

Through an intensification brought on by isolation, elements are carried outside of themselves and doubled,[78] detaching and effecting strange mixtures of aerial earth, water and fire, or terrestrial fire, water and air. The double arises at the moment of dissolution of the Other-structure: 'it is at the surface that doubles and ethereal Images first rise up ... doubles without resemblance and elements without constraint' (LS, 366/315). The ethereal double is neither earth/depth nor its inverse as height but something in between, an energetic, flowing surface that is rather an escape from the solidity and formedness of earth.

It is the intervention of Friday which reveals the sense and aim of Robinson's metamorphosis. Friday 'indicates another, supposedly true world, an irreducible double which alone is genuine and in this other world, a double of the Other who no longer is and cannot be. Not an Other, but something wholly other than Other' (LS, 368/317). Friday literally explodes the last vestiges of Robinson's ordered world, revealing a way of life guided by an 'underlying wholeness, an implicit principle'[79] characterised by 'pure elements and [dissolved] objects, bodies and earth' (LS, 368/317). The priority for Deleuze is not in the discovery of the Double as Image or idea, but in the pure elements that it reveals: 'the discovery of the free Elements, which are more radical than Images or Doubles since these latter are formed by them' (LS, 367/316).

Friday's complete refusal to abide by orders and significations ushers in a new way of addressing the elements, where they are opened up to a seething, living becoming, epitomised by the 'inhuman music [created from the skull of Andoar] ... at once the deep voice of earth, the harmony of the spheres, and the hoarse lament of the dead goat ... wherein the naked elements combined – earth, tree, and wind'.[80] This is an entirely different realm, a world of molecular combination, and what Deleuze explicitly calls 'cosmic surface energy' (LS, 351/302). Necessarily, we would have to refer to this as something other than earth – *the cosmic*.

Under Friday's influence, Robinson realises that 'a body which is accepted and rejoiced in . . . is not only a better instrument for dealing with the external world but also a sturdy and loyal companion'.[81] Of course, this focus suggests that it is not a matter of being thought but of being felt, a matter of affect. For an affect to be felt, it must connect to another body, and it is the variation of intensity that is felt. This power to force existence to its limit is *conatus*. *Conatus* can only extend to its limit when decoupled from reactive forces, from sedentary forces in order to be free for errant, deviant or extraordinary encounters, effected here through its uncoupling from the other-structure. Partly, this is about adopting an attitude, a way of being in the world. Deleuze says, 'Stop thinking of yourself as an ego (*moi*) in order to live as a flow (*flux*), a set of flows in relation with other flows, outside of oneself and within oneself' (ECC, 51/68), but equally important is what one encounters. Deleuze broadly advocates experimentation, placing oneself in new situations and thereby accessing one's unknown potentials. In 'Of the Refrain' (see MP, 427–8/345–6), it is clear that that task of modernity, of the cosmic artisan, is to free the molecular. It is also clear that this move explodes the elemental in the name of pure force and movement, opening the elements to their seething, inner becoming. Therefore, the perverse logic of the affect operates according to a sensitivity to immanence and an amplification of multimodal perception.

Deleuze's investigation of art in *Logic of Sensation* and the distinctive role that he gives the artist in *Logic of Sense* intersect at this point: 'The artist is not only the patient and doctor of civilization, but also its pervert' (LS, 278/238). As patient, the artist's sensibility is such that he or she is susceptible to this other dimension of fluid, cosmic becoming. As doctor, the artist diagnoses and thus reveals this dimension through 'harnessing forces' in her works, turning her 'attention to the microscopic, to crystals, molecules, atoms, and particles . . . nothing but immanent movement' (MP, 416/337), revealing the intensive being of the sensible. Finally, as the perverse is typified by momentary alliances of bodies, doubles and elements, the artist fulfils the role of the pervert, creating new blocs of sensation, affects which take on independent life and momentum, through which we are affected. In this respect, perverse logic, which here has nothing to do with sexual deviance or clinical perversion, is not a stable identification, but rather a sensitivity to the movement of affects on the plane of immanence. It is the adventure itself, becoming, an explosion of errant thinking predicated on the liberation and recombination of elements, described by Deleuze as 'an extraordinary art of surfaces' (LS, 158/133).

New thought, which is the only thing worthy of being called thought, only occurs with the adventure of the affect, the liberation of elements to re-form, connect, flow – this intensive level of existence is what must be liberated for thinking to happen. One hears a foreboding (and perhaps exhilarating) echo of this in de Beistegui's claim that 'when exposed to the brute and intensive forces of anorganic Life, the activity of thought becomes dangerous'.[82] The faculties, pushed to their limits, transform themselves, become other than themselves; thus, what we are after is a new sense, or kind, of sensibility and a new concept, or kind, of perverse thought. In other words, the affect-event is simultaneously the genesis of sense, thus providing a necessary anchor for the subject, and a creative process that exceeds and overflows the subject. The transcendental field/metaphysical plane that is opened up is a creative plane where the intensive gets taken back up, selectively and creatively, generating new affects, sending subject and world into a process of becoming, transformation and overcoming. The moment of liberation/dissipation is equally a dis-organisation, an involution which frees affects and speeds and plunges the ego into chaotic intensity. It is nothing less than the possibility of thought itself. Therefore, true creativity, the becoming of thought, requires a sensitivity, or maybe a *sensibility*, for pure immanence. Immanence creates a levelling effect that opens up a whole field of possibilities for recognising the communication and transversality between beings. This new register liberates the elements for the adventure of the affect, which in turn is the adventure of thought.

## METHODS OF BECOMING: DISRUPTION, DE-CENTRING AND INDIRECT DISCOURSE

The sensibility for immanence is encountered in what may be called the inhuman trajectory of art (and politics). The elimination of the humanist privilege is indicated by the interconnection of art and life in *A Thousand Plateaus* as the becoming expressive of territory (framing in nature), and is reiterated in *What is Philosophy?*, using a commensurate architectural language. It is not the human that is essentially *Unheimlich*, but the human being experiences the *Unheimlich* as its core via immanent participation in the becoming of the world. Becoming happens by engaging with the truly unknown (*l'inconnu*) as something wholly other than Other.

Throughout his work, Deleuze is drawn to artists of a particular ilk, those who live, breathe, and create on the boundaries of chaotic intensity, situating themselves within the maelstrom of psychic dissonance and cultural upheaval in congress with the unknown. Their maladies are re-inscribed by Deleuze as signals of their untimely timeliness. Of course, one of the most dramatic examples is Artaud, for whom the boundaries between reality and fantasy were unequivocally blurred. It is well documented that Deleuze attributes to certain figures, chiefly artists, special insight, an ability to move beyond the theatre of representation and engage in the movement of pure immanence.[83] It is a dangerous precipice, an almost unlivable place to inhabit which verges upon the unthinkable, and, of course, this is what is fascinating about these journeys to what remains otherwise unknown. The collapse of visual coordinates and the destruction of clichés (Bacon's diagrams) is one path toward becoming other, as is enacting a radical de-centring of the subject from its world of signifying coordinates (Tournier). The refrain which flows through Deleuze's writing is the affirmation of a liberating dis-organisation.

One final method, which summons Deleuze's own style and engages us once again in the complexities of his handling of language, is free indirect discourse (*discours indirect libre*). Utilised by early nineteenth-century novelists such as Jane Austen, and made explicit in modernist literature by authors such as Flaubert, Zola, Woolf and James, Deleuze's appropriation of this literary device is unique and even subversive. The notion in literary narrative refers to the portrayal of first-person speech in an indirect third-person manner, commonly evidenced by a narrator presenting a character's internal thoughts or the merging of perspectives of several characters. Woolf's *To the Lighthouse* is considered a paradigm of this modernist style. Here the narrator gives way to the inner reflections of one of the characters, which themselves are confounded by the impersonal 'one', lending to the merging of perspectives:

> But this morning everything seemed so extraordinarily queer that a question like Nancy's – What does one send to the Lighthouse? – opened doors in one's mind that went banging and swinging to and fro and made one keep asking, in a stupefied gape, What does one send? What does one do? Why is one sitting here after all?[84]

The method allows access to the subtle inner worlds of characters, layering complexity into plots by offering the perspective of what remains unsaid but thought. Deleuze, however, understands and employs free indirect discourse as a philosophical and political act that allows philosophy to challenge the dominance of hegemonic (major) language regimes and to engage the unintelligible depth of the living. Woolf's writing is indicative of the rhizomatic and collective nature of the minor.[85]

Deleuze's appropriation of the device is dependent on his characterisation of language in terms of the order-word. According to Deleuze, language is not about individual expression, but about the transmission of commands, related to the fact that all language is primarily indirect: 'Language is not content to go from a first party to a second party, from one who has seen to one who has not, but necessarily goes from a second party to a third party, neither of whom has seen' (MP, 97/76–7). Indirect discourse is the condition of communicability (MP, 97/76), which, channelling Heidegger, also means that we participate in language, rather than being the originators of language. Referring to both the extrinsic and intrinsic relations between action and speech discovered by J.L. Austin, Deleuze claims that language is a system of control predicated on the transmission of implicit propositions which demand obedience and imply certain incorporeal transformations and attributes, which limit and control subjects. The free indirect is a means by which to disrupt this system of language, by 'slipping another expressing subject into a statement which already has an expressing statement' (TRM, 371). For Deleuze, it is not enough to show the social nature of enunciation – enunciation itself as a collective assemblage needs to be revealed. The value of the free indirect, in this regard, is that it blurs the boundaries of speech and speaker, making us aware of the multiplicity of voices which inhere in enunciations and incorporeal transformations that occur through the order-words of language (MP, 101/80). In Deleuze, one finds several variations, all loosely bound to this intent, which is why one finds such diverse opinions on the free indirect in Deleuze scholarship.

In particular, Hughes understands free indirect discourse to be Deleuze's unfailing mode of expression throughout his entire *oeuvre*, a style of approaching everything through detour, i.e. indirectly.[86] He points to the way in which Deleuze detours through philosophical figures without clearly demarcating these interpolations, such that one is left to wonder, for example, exactly what is Deleuzian and what is Bergsonian in *Bergsonism*. Hughes argues that, however essential Deleuze's critical engagements and polemics with these philosophers, one must always keep in mind that they are indices of a larger structure,[87] the progression of a philosophic point of view and a desire to think and write philosophy differently. Hughes also insists that this detour-esque style happens with the development of philosophical concepts as well – when speaking of ideas, Deleuze detours through mathematics, and so on.

What is most interesting is Hughes' insight into why Deleuze employs this style of the indirect, particularly provocative in that this insight is developed from the context of Heidegger's observations concerning the immense and powerful influence of history which lead him to a new application of the phenomenological reduction. Heidegger's critique of Husserl concerns an oversight concerning the radical and continuing impact of the past within the present: 'What has been handed down it hands over to obviousness; it bars access to those original "well-springs" out of which the traditional categories and concepts were in part genuinely drawn' (GA2, 29/19). As Hughes explains, Heidegger extends the Husserlian reduction to include the bracketing of history, so that both the natural attitude and philosophical concepts must undergo the reduction. Connecting Deleuze to this trajectory, he says that Deleuze recognises the need to further extend the phenomenological reduction beyond the conceptual history of language to natural language itself, because the subject/predicate structure of language imposes its own series of arresting connections onto becoming. Language orders how we speak of bodies and imposes limits on what bodies can become, which is just the situation that Deleuze and Guattari address through the idea of the order-word in *A Thousand Plateaus*. Thus, Hughes identifies as Deleuze's central ambition the desire to find means for adequately expressing the movements of becoming and thought, 'to speak of the unintelligible depth of living' rather than the arrest of bodies.[88] Hughes equates this reduction with the need to invent an entirely new philosophic discourse, to speak differently. Direct discourse is discounted from the start, because, 'as soon as you directly represent thought in language, you have lost it. Deleuze therefore gives to philosophy an enormous aesthetic dimension'[89] wherein thought must move through other dimensions, to speak indirectly of itself.

Hughes' interpretation of free indirect discourse as a method of detours is helpful in that it reveals an underlying consistency of searching for new philosophic expression adequate to immanence while providing context for the myriad variations in the kinds of detouring that one finds throughout Deleuze's work. In our view, the free indirect undergoes several metamorphoses in Deleuze's work:

opening creative spaces for the unthought to arrive in philosophic discourse; de-centring the authorial function, therewith introducing indeterminacy into any authorship; unearthing the senseless murmurings and incomprehensible utterances within language; and finally disrupting the purely linguistic nature of discourse.

Similarly, Zourabichvili equates free indirect discourse with the act of fabulation (*acte de fabulation*),[90] understanding it as a mode of discourse which typifies Deleuze's style of engagement with other philosophers and philosophic positions. Deleuze enters into the philosophy of another and establishes a kind of comingled presence, 'a manner of placing his voice in the speech of the other which ends by confounding itself with its inverse ... *l'écriture à deux*',[91] a double becoming which opens a space for what the other [philosopher] left unthought to arise through the intermingling of voices. *L'écriture à deux* is most literal in Deleuze's collaborations with Guattari, where the author as subject is rendered moot: 'To reach, not the point where one no longer says I, but the point where it is no longer of any importance whether one says I. We are no longer ourselves ... we have been aided, inspired, multiplied' (MP, 9/3). In other words, free indirect discourse multiplies enunciation, which points to a multiplicity of voices and an ineliminable variation of sense.

These characteristics are generally referred to minor literature, as an indication of its propensity to evoke the collective, or language as an impersonal milieu, which may disrupt the order-words that direct and limit information according to hegemonic regimes of power. Earlier, we claimed that the detachment of language from its master signifiers, its minoritisation by substitution of the variable for the invariant, begins in *Kafka*. Kafka's liberation of language and establishment of the minor constitutes an exemplary instance of the free indirect.[92] His tales of bureaucratic machines make visible the order-words which command us, and his wrenched and stilted use of the major language opens a language within a language, a language torn from sense. Gregor's deterioration in Kafka's *Metamorphosis* from human thoughts and expressions to incomprehensible, guttural noise is also an excellent image for the sliding scale of free indirect discourse and its power to reveal an inner seething of language, its murmuring, senseless materiality and the unformed material of expression.

Additionally, Massumi understands free indirect discourse in terms of the primacy of expression, liberated from the communicative or informational models of language. Therefore, what the figural is to the representational figure, expression is to communication. Expression cannot be attributed to a particular speaker; it is 'abroad in the world', to be taken up in various modes and degrees of capture.[93] The freeing of expression from its moorings in both subject and context makes it something of a wandering affect. In our view, it is with regard to the affect that free indirect discourse takes on its most unique and liberating hue by multiplying the ways in which discourse can be indirect. We may begin to think of a discourse which happens not through language but through the affect, thus free indirect discourse moves through literature's twisting of language, cinema's images and visual silences,[94] and music's sonorous release. This sense of the indirect truly evinces the uniqueness of Deleuze's position. Deleuze's philosophy takes a detour through art, in order that *logos* may take a detour through the affect. In this sense, free indirect discourse is the freeing of discourse *from* language. Deleuze steadily moves us toward such an understanding, through his appeal to the concept of the abstract machine, which, functionally, assembles discursive and non-discursive signs. These non-discursive signs refer to Guattari's distinction between expression, normally considered to be discursive, and enunciative substances, which, he says, are expressive without necessarily being linguistic. This distinction is made visible by the conceptualisation of the abstract machine as that which connects radically heterogeneous series, of both content and expression. The heterogeneity of expressive materials includes biological codings, machinic non-semiotically formed matter, linguistic expressions and affective dimensions. The intersection of these domains reveals possibilities neglected in traditional theories focused on the logic of discursivity. Free indirect discourse includes the heterogeneity of enunciative acts which are beyond discursivity, a *logos* of the affect simultaneous to the *logos* of sense and language. Deleuze's philosophic detour through art is therefore a more radical departure than Heidegger's in that he does not remain with or return to even poetic language. Rather than the unconcealment of truth, art reveals the being of the sensible and the priority of the affect in producing and transforming thought. The difference between Heidegger's and Deleuze's appeals to language are indicative of their political stances. The French sociologist Pierre Bourdieu, one of Deleuze's contemporaries, argues that Heidegger's phenomenological reduction of ordinary language, through which the more originary or authentic sense of *logos* is unearthed, inserts a particular form of political conservatism within the formal structures

of philosophic discourse.[95] Heidegger's procedure of establishing
an association through alliteration and resemblance of form and
sound to establish quasi-material relations between signifieds (for
example, *Denken* = *Danken*), and his philological and polyphonic
reading of these morphological connections, simultaneously evokes
and revokes the ordinary in favour of the deeper, more authentic
sense.[96] Bourdieu links this to the creation of a reservoir of forms of
apperception of a social world, 'of commonplaces which enshrine the
principles of vision of the social world common to a whole group'.[97]
Deleuze's emphasis on the free indirect, and in particular, Kafka's
bastardised use of German, suggests the opposite stance, an anarchic
indictment of originality and authenticity.

## Notes

1. Arthur Rimbaud, 'What does it matter to us, my heart', *Collected Poems*, trans. Oliver Bernard (New York: Penguin, 1962).
2. See John Sellars, 'The Point of View of the Cosmos: Deleuze, Romanticism, Stoicism', *Pli* 8 (1999), pp. 1–24.
3. Paul Klee, *Pedagogical Sketchbook*, trans. Sibyl Moholy-Nagy (London: Faber & Faber, 1968), p. 9.
4. Martin Heidegger, *The Question of Being*, trans. William Kluback and Jean T. Wilde (Connecticut: College and University Press, 1958), p. 107.
5. See, for instance, Evan Thompson, 'Planetary Thinking/Planetary Building: An Essay on Martin Heidegger and Nishitani Keiji', *Philosophy East and West* 36:3 (1986), pp. 235–52.
6. Kostos Axelos, *Vers la pensée planétaire* (Paris: Les Éditions de Minuit, 1964), p. 15 (my translation).
7. Axelos edited the journal *Arguments* between 1958 and 1962 and a book series of the same name with *Éditions de Minuit*, which published Deleuze's *Spinoza et le probleme de l'expression* and his presentation of Sacher-Masoch's *Venus in Furs*, as well as Jean Beaufret's four-volume *Dialogue avec Heidegger*. He acted as an interpreter for Heidegger at Cerisy-la-Salle in 1955 and translated Heidegger's 'What is Philosophy?' ('*Qu'est-ce que la philosophie?*' trans. Kostas Axelos and Jean Beaufret, in Martin Heidegger, *Questions I et II* [Paris: Gallimard, 1968], pp. 317–46). For a more detailed account of Axelos' influence on the French intellectual scene, see Stuart Elden, 'Kostas Axelos and the World of the Arguments Circle,' in J. Bourg, ed., *After the Deluge: New Perspectives on Postwar French Intellectual and Cultural History of Postwar France* (Lanham: Lexington Books, 2004), pp. 125–48; also Axelos, 'Planetary Interlude', trans. Sally Hess, *Yale*

*French Studies* 41, Game, Play, Literature (1968), pp. 6–18, one of the few English translations of excerpts from *Vers la pensée planétaire.*

8. 'To the *mondialisation* of problems we must respond with the *mondialisation* of thought and action'; the West 'must propose or offer (*proposer*) to the East and South to make a unity of the human world.' Pierre Fougeyrollas, '*Thèses sur la mondialisation*', *Arguments* 15 (1959), pp. 38–9. The 1960 manifesto of *Arguments* announces: 'second half of the twentieth century: a planetary age of technology; iron age of a new industrial civilization; new age of the human'. 'Manifeste no. 2 (1960)', in *Arguments* (Paris: Les Éditions de Minuit, 1960), p. xxx.

9. Originally published as '*Faille et Feux locaux: Kostas Axelos*', *Critique* 26:275 (1970), reprinted in *L'île déserte et autre texte*, pp. 217–25; Eng. title: 'The Fissure of Anaxagoras and the Local Fires of Heraclitus', ID, 56–61.

10. See Axelos, *Vers la pensée planétaire*, p. 21.

11. Kostas Axelos, *Le Jeu du monde* (Paris: Les Éditions de Minuit, 1969), p. 254. Deleuze cites Axelos directly (ID, 219/157). The distinction between *le monde* and *le monde cosmique*, which is obscured in the English translation where cosmos and world are commonly used interchangeably, is significant in light of our insistence on separating cosmos from cosmic. The translation of *le monde cosmique* as cosmos negates this difference. *Cosmique* has the sense of astral, celestial, universal, while *le cosmos* signifies world, nature or universe.

12. References from Axelos, *Vers la pensée planétaire*, pp. 22, notes 1 and 2; Martin Heidegger, *Identitat und Differenz* (Pfullingen: Neske, 1957), p. 64. Axelos is referring to Heidegger's reference to *Vorspiel* (playing-forth) (GA11, 46); Martin Heidegger, *Le Principe de raison* (Paris: Gallimard, 1962), p. 241. Translated as 'The *Geschick* of being: a child that plays ... Why does it play, the great child of the world-play Heraclitus brought into view in the *aiôn*? It plays, because it plays. The "because" withers away in the play. The play is without "why".' Martin Heidegger, *The Principle of Reason*, trans. Reginald Lilly (Bloomington: Indiana University Press, 1991).

13. Axelos, 'Planetary Interlude', pp. 8 and 14.

14. 'Heidegger betrays the movement of deterritorialization because he fixes it once and for all between being and beings' (QP, 91/95).

15. Axelos, *Vers la pensée planétaire*, pp. 30, 34–5.

16. Ibid., p. 16.

17. Axelos, 'Planetary Interlude', pp. 10–11.

18. Axelos, *Vers la pensée planétaire*, p. 14. Technically, lines of flight are elements of the image, referring to the dynamics in paintings and related to the *pointe de fuite*, the vanishing point or place where the visible line leads the eye beyond the frame. Lines of flight (*lignes de fuites*) become an important part of Deleuze's lexicon during his collaboration with

Guattari, signifying the potential in any multiplicity (assemblage) to go beyond itself (escape, leak, flee), and thus cause a change in kind – the creative (or liberatory in terms of the political) event. It is often associated with nomadism (see 'Pensée Nomade', ID, 356/255).

19. Pataphysics, coined by Alfred Jarry in the late 1800s, is the study of what is beyond metaphysics, a system in which there are no rules, only exceptions: variance (*anomalos*), alliance (*syzygia*), and deviance (*clinamen*), often defined as a poetics of an imaginary science. Jarry was known for equalising multiple systems of thought, a stylistic mélange of languages, slang, and the synthesis of poetic and scientific discourse. Pataphysics' flouting of the principle of non-contradiction, and emphasis on experimentation, levity and openness, were influential for Absurdism, Dada, Futurism, Surrealism, Theatre of Cruelty and Situationism. One might call it the original theory of the *inoperable*. See Alfred Jarry, *Adventures in 'Pataphysics: Collected Works I*, trans. Antony Melville (London: Atlas Press, 2001).

20. Kostas Axelos, *Horizons du monde* (Paris: Minuit, 1974), p. 13.

21. SeeKostas Axelos, '*Heidegger et le destin de la philosophie.*' *Réponses énigmatiques* (Paris: Minuit, 2005).

22. Though there is evidence that Axelos and Deleuze were close friends through the 1950s (Dosse, *Intersecting Lives*, pp. 99 and 120), they parted philosophical ways with the advent of Deleuze's collaboration with Guattari and the publication of *Anti-Oedipus* (ibid., pp. 208 and 559n12), seemingly over Deleuze's progression toward a more radical ontology of immanence and the inhuman.

23. Dorothea Olkowski, 'Beside Us, In Memory', *Man and World* 29 (1996), pp. 283–92, n5. Olkowski stands as a paradigm of thinking Deleuze's philosophical oeuvre through the aesthetical. In her work, she both insists that Deleuze's philosophy is grounded on aesthetics by emphasising the importance of sensibility and enacts a Deleuzian aesthetic imperative by folding art and artists into her own philosophising. This is patently true for *The Ruin of Representation* (California: University of California Press, 1999) in which Olkowski characterises Deleuze's philosophy as fundamentally creative, while unfolding the idea of the creative act through reference to contemporary art. See also 'Deleuze's Aesthetics of Sensation' in Daniel Smith and Henry Somers-Hall, eds, *The Cambridge Companion to Deleuze* (Cambridge: Cambridge University Press, 2012), pp. 265–85.

24. Sauvagnargues, *Deleuze and Art*, chapter 5.

25. Manuel DeLanda, *Intensive Science and Virtual Philosophy* (London: Continuum Press, 2002), p. 12.

26. See 'Letter-Preface to Jean-Clet Martin' in TRM.

27. Deleuze and Guattari follow Francisco Varela's definition of a machine as 'the set of inter-relations of its components independent of the

components themselves'. Machines are characterised by a set of relations, or flows, and not by their particular materiality.

28. See the example of Little Hans (MP, 314–15/257–8).
29. Jeffrey Jerome Cohen, *Medieval Identity Machines, Medieval Cultures* (Minneapolis: University of Minnesota Press, 2003), p. 42.
30. Sauvagnargues, *Deleuze and Art*, p. 60.
31. See Introduction to MP.
32. Sauvagnargues, *Deleuze and Art*, p. 126.
33. Ibid., p. 91.
34. For more on Deleuze's criticism of linguistics, see Jean-Jacques Lecercle, *Deleuze and Language* (New York: Palgrave Macmillan, 2002).
35. See Sauvagnargues, *Deleuze and Art*, chapter 5.
36. Ibid., p. 10.
37. Ian Buchanan does a good job of teasing out the implications of this in his *Deleuzism: A Metacommentary* (Durham, NC: Duke University Press, 2000), chapter 5, 'Assemblages and Utopia', in particular pp. 121–5; see also MP, 59/44.
38. MP, 57–8/43. See also, Buchanan, *Deleuzism*, p. 121.
39. Félix Guattari, *Chaosmosis: An Ethico-Aesthetic Paradigm*, trans. Julian Pefanis (Bloomington: Indiana University Press, 1995), p. 23.
40. Dorothea Olkowski, *Gilles Deleuze and the Ruin of Representation* (Berkeley: University of California, 1999), p. 229.
41. *Abécédaire* is an eight-hour series of interviews between Deleuze and Claire Parnet, directed by Pierre-André Boutang in 1988–9. Each episode is developed around a concept beginning with one of the letters of the alphabet.
42. For more on Kafka's style of sobriety as invention, see Gregory Flaxman, *Gilles Deleuze and the Fabulation of Philosophy* (Minneapolis: University of Minnesota Press, 2012), pp. 207–36.
43. Guattari, *Chaosmosis,* pp. 24–5.
44. Ibid., p. 29.
45. Ibid., pp. 58–9. Schizoanalysis is the process by which these diverse cartographies that comprise any situation are examined and the complexity of the given, its ontological heterogeneity, is acknowledged.
46. Ibid., p. 35.
47. Buchanan, *Deleuzism*, pp. 57 and 71n63.
48. See final paragraph beginning with italics, QP, 205–6/218.
49. See FB, chapter 6.
50. See '*Quatre Leçons sur Kant*', available at <http://www.webdeleuze.com/sommaire.html> accessed 15 July 2014.
51. Smith, 'Translator's Introduction', FB, xix.
52. Daniel Smith, 'Deleuze's Theory of Sensation: Overcoming the Kantian Dualism', in Paul Patton, ed., *Deleuze: A Critical Reader* (Oxford: Blackwell, 1996), p. 34.

53. Deleuze claims that Proust's art is to extract an experience of the essence of a past situation. As such, it is not the situation represented or repeated in narrative form, but a composite of affects that elicits a sense generated out of the past.
54. See David Sylvester's *Interviews with Francis Bacon* (London: Thames & Hudson, 2002).
55. I thank Len Lawlor for leading me to this point.
56. See Greg Lambert, *The Non-Philosophy of Gilles Deleuze* (New York: Continuum, 2002), p. 117.
57. See Francis Bacon's *Triptyque, deux figures couches sur un lit avec témoins* (1968). Collection Particulière, New York (referred to as No. 5 in FB). The 2002 Seuil edition of *Francis Bacon: logique de la sensation* reproduces a limited number of the paintings, mainly the triptychs, to which Deleuze refers, including this one.
58. Lambert, *The Non-Philosophy of Gilles Deleuze*, pp. 58–60.
59. Klee, *On Modern Art*, p. 29.
60. Wassily Kandinsky, 'Point and Line to Plane', in *Complete Writings on Art* (Boston: Da Capo Press, 1994), pp. 659 and 611.
61. Ronald Bogue, *Deleuze's Way: Essays in Transverse Ethics and Aesthetics* (Aldershot: Ashgate, 2007), p. 27.
62. These are not temporally successive processes, but instead happen in multiple contexts in tandem and moving in multiple directions.
63. See Martin Heidegger's 1929/30 lecture course, *Fundamental Concepts of Metaphysics: World, Finitude, Solitude*, trans. William McNeill and Nicholas Walker (Indiana: Indiana University Press, 2001). For criticisms surrounding this position, see Jacques Derrida, *De l'esprit: Heidegger et la question* (Paris: Galilee, 1987); Giorgio Agamben, *The Open: Man and Animal* (Stanford: Stanford University Press, 2004); Len Lawlor, *This is Not Sufficient: An Essay on Animality and Human Nature in Derrida* (New York: Columbia University Press, 2007); William McNeill, 'Life Beyond the Organism: Animal Being in Heidegger's Freiburg Lectures, 1929–30', in H. Peter Steeves, ed., *Animal Others: On Ethics, Ontology, and Animal Life* (Albany: SUNY Press, 1999), pp. 197–248; Simon Glendinning, 'Heidegger and the Question of Animality', *International Journal of Philosophic Studies* 4:1 (1996), pp. 67–86; 18–30; Stuart Elden, 'Heidegger's Animals', *Continental Philosophy Review* 39:3 (2006), pp. 273–91; Gerard Kuperus, 'Attunement, Deprivation, and Drive: Heidegger and Animality', in C. Painter and C. Lotz, eds, *Phenomenology and the Nonhuman Animal* (Dordrecht: Springer, 2007). Andrew Mitchell writes beautifully about Heidegger's rethinking of animality, specifically his 1958 Trakl essay 'Language in the Poem', in which he develops a *pathos* between human wanderer and the animal. See his 'Heidegger's

Later Thinking on Animality: The End of World Poverty', *Gatherings: The Heidegger Circle Annual*, 1 (2011), pp. 74–85.

64. See Jacob Uexküll, 'A Stroll through the Worlds of Animals and Man', in Claire Schiller, ed., *Instinctive Behaviour: The Development of a Modern Concept* (New York: International University Press, 1957), pp. 5–80 and Jacob Uexküll, 'The New Concept of *Umwelt*: A Link Between Science and the Humanities', *Semiotica* 134 (2001), pp. 111–23.

65. For an interpretation of music according to this Deleuzian framework, see Richard Pinhas, 'Cosmos, Rhythm and Plane (Approach to Sonorous Production)', trans. C. Kerslake, first published in the web journal *Synaesthesie* in 1999; Ronald Bogue's work in this area is seminal, see his *Deleuze on Music, Painting, and the Arts* (New York: Routledge, 2003).

66. Bogue, *Deleuze on Music, Painting, and the Arts*, p. 17.

67. Bogue, *Deleuze's Way*, pp. 29–30.

68. For more on this relationship, see Stephen Zepke, *Art as Abstract: Machine Ontology and Aesthetics in Deleuze and Guattari* (New York: Routledge, 2005).

69. See Bogue, *Deleuze on Music, Painting, and the Arts*, pp. 166–7.

70. Ibid., p. 168.

71. Here, Deleuze references deframing as a concept developed by Pascal Bonitzer to highlight new relationships (new emotions and affects) created by 'disjointed, crushed or fragmented' planes in cinema (QP, 178n28/232n28). See Pascal Bonitzer, *Le champ aveugle: essais sur le cinéma* (Paris: Gallimard-Cahiers du Cinéma, 1982).

72. For a reading of the struggle between man and being in terms of *deinon*, National Socialism, and the saving power of art, see John Caputo, 'Heidegger's Revolution', in *Heidegger Towards the Turn: Essays on the Work of the 1930s* (New York: SUNY Press, 1999), pp. 64–7 in particular.

73. Gilles Deleuze, Lecture Transcripts on Spinoza's Concept of Affect (released by Emilie and Julien Deleuze, p. 4; available at <http://www.webdeleuze.com/php/sommaire.html> (accessed 15 July 2014).

74. As opposed to Kant, for whom the sublime leads us back to the superiority of our rationality, Deleuze takes the aesthetic moment as a moment of un-grounding from which we do not and should not 'recover'.

75. Michel Tournier, *Friday*, trans. Norman Denny (Baltimore: Johns Hopkins University Press, 1997 [1967]), p. 201.

76. Ibid., p. 38.

77. See Jack Reynolds, 'Deleuze's Other-Structure: Beyond The Master-Slave Dialectic, But At What Cost?', *Symposium* 12:1 (2008), pp. 67–88.

78. Intensification is taken from Deleuze's interpretation of Spinoza's ethology, an art of living 'making it possible to harmoniously combine the solicitations of the affect and concept to intensify the coincidence of greater reason and more joy' (Dosse, *Intersecting Lives*, p. 149). Intensification must be prefaced by the removal of certain obstacles and is linked to experimentation.
79. Tournier, *Friday*, p. 182.
80. Ibid., pp. 198–9.
81. Ibid., p. 183.
82. Miguel de Beistegui, *Immanence: Deleuze and Philosophy* (Edinburgh: Edinburgh University Press, 2012), p. 69.
83. QP, chapter 7 is replete with a dizzying number of references to artists whose aesthetic figures enter into strange becomings: Messiaen, Cézanne, André Dhotel, Goya, Daumier and Redon's strivings for the pure sensation; Virginia Woolf's 'saturate every atom'; and the cosmic deterritorialisations of Boulez, Mahler, Berg, Bartók and Cage.
84. Virginia Woolf, *To the Lighthouse* (London: Penguin, 1993 [1927]), p. 214.
85. Deleuze and Guattari make reference to Woolf throughout MP, claiming that she 'made all of her life and work a passage, a becoming' (MP, 308/252). Particularly, they express admiration for her ability to experience herself as a multiplicity through her writing and enter into variable relations of becoming (MP, 293/239), citing her method 'to reduce oneself to an abstract line, a trait, in order to find one's zone of indiscernibility with other traits, and in this way enter the haecceity' (MP, 342/280). Woolf's use of indirect discourse is critical to her ability of intermingling thought processes and inserting herself into them while remaining, as it were, at the 'edge of the crowd' (MP, 42/29). Deleuze and Guattari describe her writing as a passage through immanence occurring by the saturation of each scene with multiplicity, gliding between internal and external perspectives, and slipping between voices: to 'eliminate everything that exceeds the moment, but put in everything that it includes' (MP, 342/280).
86. Joe Hughes, *Deleuze's Difference and Repetition: A Reader's Guide* (London: Bloomsbury Academic, 2009), p. 14.
87. Ibid., p. 17.
88. Ibid., pp. 20–2. See also Claire Colebrook, *Philosophy and Poststructuralist Thought: From Kant to Deleuze* (Edinburgh: Edinburgh University Press, 2005).
89. Hughes, *A Reader's Guide*, p. 23.
90. Zourabichvili, *Deleuze: Une philosophie de l'événement*, p. 51.
91. Ibid., p. 6.
92. See Flaxman, *Gilles Deleuze and the Fabulation of Philosophy*, pp. 217–26.

93. Brian Massumi, ed., *A Shock to Thought* (New York: Routledge, 2002), p. xxi.
94. See Louis-Georges Schwartz. 'Free Indirect Discourse in Deleuze's Cinema', *SubStance* 34:3, Issue 108, *French Cinema Studies* 1920s to the Present (2005), pp. 107–35.
95. Bourdieu's claim should be read within the context of his overarching position concerning the conservative tendency which marks Heidegger's endeavour to combat what he saw as the lowering of standards and levelling-down tendencies presenting themselves through the university and more generally in the increasingly technologically inundated masses by returning to prior values and deeper meaningfulness.
96. See Pierre Bourdieu, *The Political Ontology of Martin Heidegger* (Stanford: Stanford University Press, 1988), pp. 70–87.
97. Ibid., p. 80.

# PART III

# (Un)Earthing a People-to-come

# Introduction to Part III

*Through the concept of Earth a gap is sketched in being that cannot recoup, a fissure, a 'chaos' in the sense of chasm (béance) that opens itself in a quite diurnal manner.*[1]

For both Heidegger and Deleuze, the trope of earth as indicative of another ontological understanding, and its extension through the cosmic, is set up through considering art. At the same time, their discussions of art operate as pivotal loci for their conceptualisations of the people-to-come, a place in which the political becomes. The various *topoi* that each develops indicate a relation to a people-to-come. We are not alone in thinking the political as place. De Beistegui speaks of the perpetual movements of the space of politics as dis-placement and re-placement, 'places (*Orter*) of being understood as points of intensification, in which presence itself has come for a time to crystallize',[2] where words, things and actions come together. These final chapters follow the etchings of these *topoi* – earth, homeland, milieu, territory – presenting an image, however shadowy, of the political future that each envisions. We have three objectives: first, to define and interrogate Heidegger's specific sense of a people-to-come drawn from his analysis of art as a gathering place (*Ort*) for the historical destiny of a people which constructs the earth as homeland (*Heimat*); second, to combine the elements of the cosmic and the minor, which Deleuze associates with a people-to-come, into a coherent, and ultimately flexible, model of a people; and third, to further delineate the sense in which Deleuze's work is a completion and displacement of Heidegger. This final piece hinges on the fact that, though Heidegger and Deleuze both insist on this space of the unthought, their ontological dispensations determine what kind of people emerge: wanderers or nomads, which we understand as conceptual personae indicative of new paths, or images, of thought.

We claim that the earth is the centrepiece of Heidegger's later philosophy and demands another kind of thinking, what one might hazard to call a new image of thought, or perhaps a *bastard reasoning*. The earth embodies multiple senses of the unthought, the not yet thought, the essentially undisclosed, or the unfamiliar (*Unheimlich*). Therefore, earth provokes a multiple reading that does not reduce to the logic of oneness or non-contradiction; it is an increasingly complicated concept and is deployed in several different philosophical contexts, all nascent in *Origin*.

Most generally, the introduction of earth signifies a shift in Heidegger's thinking solely in terms of *Dasein*'s relation to its world toward the relation to both world and what lies beyond world, that element which does not concern or eludes the for-the-sake-of-which. The element of earth adds another dimension to our understanding of beings that are *not Dasein*. The earth, described as an impotence of the will (H, 36/25), is that which is beyond our control, unknown and ungraspable. This is emphasised by the sense of earth as mute work-material. The hardness of the stone in the statue, the shine of the colour in the painting, and the rhythm of the language in the poem are not in themselves signifying. They attest to an elemental-ity that resists the disclosure of world. Heidegger will insist that earth is that which is self-secluding and must be grasped in itself, as self-secluding. We must let the earth be earth, and correspond-ingly, let beings outside of our world be themselves, resisting the all-too-human urge to define, master and shape them according to our worldview. This is to more essentially belong to being and is the basis of the fundamental attunement of *Gelassenheit*. Thus, the thought of letting-be is being developed through the concept of earth. Moreover, the earth is indicative of that which remains necessarily mysterious and unthought, thus our understanding of the nature of truth as *aletheia* is enriched by it.

Haar delimits four general trajectories with regard to earth in Heidegger's work: (1) as the essence of *physis* unthought by the Greeks, specifically, the dimension of withdrawal which holds sway in un-concealing; (2) as corresponding to what is called 'nature', as essential difference and the inexhaustible richness of natural beings forgotten by the world; (3) as representing the 'material' of the work which appears as it is only within the artwork; (4) as the 'terrestrial' (*heimatliche Grund*), the homeland to be won.[3] In Heidegger schol-arship, often one finds one of these senses emphasised at the expense of the others.[4] Yet, if to think the earth is a new way of thinking, to think as a gathering of multiple senses that are not lost when unified under one concept, this concept sustains them all simultaneously. We can understand this kind of thinking as a *polemos*, a struggle between separation and belonging together that reflects the same kind of necessary tension as that between the earth and world within the work.[5] To think is to gather but it is also the de-cision in gathering, which is to set apart (*aus-einandersetzung*) and determine how things belong together. By the same token, gathering into unity must maintain what is gathered as separate, otherwise what is gathered loses its character. This peculiar gathering makes its appearance in several contexts in Heidegger's later thought and returns in relation to the gathering of a people through the clearing place of art, the splitting edge where everything is brought together.[6]

## Notes

1. Haar, *The Song of the Earth*, p. 12.
2. Miguel de Beistegui, *Heidegger and the Political: Dystopias* (New York: Routledge, 1998), p. 7.
3. See Haar, *The Song of the Earth*.
4. Julian Young, in his *Heidegger's Philosophy of Art*, emphasises the mysterious nature of 'earth' and its connection to the holy, or Nature, with little to no reference to its political connotations. John Sallis also approaches earth apolitically in *Echoes After Heidegger* (Bloomington: Indiana University Press, 1990). By contrast, in *Heidegger's Roots: Nietzsche, National Socialism, and the Greeks*, Charles Bambach emphasises, almost exclusively, the political undertones to Heidegger's writings on art and earth, connecting earth to a similar autochthony that drives National Socialism.
5. See Rodolphe Gasché, 'Toward an Ethics of *Auseinandersetzung*', in *The Honor of Thinking: Critique, Theory, Philosophy* (Stanford: Stanford University Press, 2007).
6. Heidegger understands *Ort* as originally indicating the extremity of the knife edge. See Beistegui, *Heidegger and the Political*, p. 7.

# 5

# Heidegger and the Political

Having mentioned earth in terms of concealment, the otherness of beings, the work-material, we turn to earth as homeland, with the express understanding that these other senses do not fall away completely. This final sense of earth opens up the political context of *Origin*. Heidegger's detractors most often assume a coherence between Heidegger's use of earth as *Heimat* and that of the rhetoric of *Blut* and *Boden* championed by nationalist ideologues. In fact, there are many who associate earth with National Socialism and its intellectual predecessors *tout court*, claiming that Heidegger's choice of earth as a fundamental concept betrays his involvement in and inheritance from this tradition.[1]

First, it should be noted that the language of rootedness, tied to a romanticised vision of the rural and pastoral, does not originate with but is eventually co-opted by reactionary ideologues. For instance, Beistegui identifies the emphasis on Germanic rootedness as a response to the decline of culture in Ferdinand Tönnes' 1887 *Gemeinschaft und Gesellschaft*, which decries the battle between rural communities tied together by blood, place and spirit and artificial (rootless) associations based on interests indicative of a decadent urbanism.[2] Heidegger is no doubt persuaded that such a crisis or battle exists, as his reflections on the decadence of thought, machination, and his general distaste for city life indicate. Embracing the Hölderlinian-Nietzschean diagnoses of the crisis and danger befalling Western Europe, Heidegger sees Germany as a central figure in the historical future of the West, and in this respect he was caught up in the politics of the day. He also saw National Socialism as harbouring a possibility for great transformation on a spiritual and intellectual level. Heidegger's employment of the language of German rootedness and *arché* is undeniably a feature of his speeches of 1933–34 and plays out in his philosophic texts of the 1930s and 1940s, yet one must question whether he finds the impetus for returning to the Greeks in the same types of autochthonous thinking as his contemporaries, predicated as they were on the worst forms of biological racism.[3]

It is the case that Heidegger is particularly influenced by Hölderlin's preoccupation with the retrieval of German origins and the return of the Germans to their authentic rootedness, in light of an increasingly rootless modern world. Yet, Hölderlin, long before the uptake of his ideas in the twentieth century, had suggested that his work and thought about the need for the renewal of German essence had fallen on deaf ears. Heidegger often refers to 'those who have the ears to hear', a theme echoed in the sonorous imagery of attunement, and of hearing the call. One could say that, for Heidegger, National Socialism had the unfortunate disposition of a similar deafness. That belonging (*gehören*) is enjoined to hearing (*hören*), which is brought about through silence (*Schweigen*), indicates that the attentiveness of Hölderlin as opposed to the deafness of National Socialism will help ground a *Volk*. Silence 'gives rise to a genuine potentiality-for-hearing (*Hörenkonnen*) and to a being-with-one-another that is transparent' (GA2, 165/154); it provides the essential possibility of communication (and community).

Some take a more sociological view, casting their scrutiny toward the outlook and presuppositions of an entire generation. In this respect, Bourdieu provides a valuable insight into the *Zeitgeist*, and, in particular, the lexicon that would have formed the conceptual background for social positions and attitudes.[4] Heidegger, communicating in the midst of these particular ideologically connected words which generated a 'field of simultaneously possible stances in which his own position will be defined negatively and differentially', was simultaneously bound to this field of language and determined to 'undermine in advance any inadmissible interpretations'.[5] Heidegger knows this, which is why he takes such care: this 'frontier is the one that separates the layman from the professional'.[6] Therefore, one should begin by pulling apart the distinct sense in which Heidegger employs this language, which is what we endeavour to do in the following.

What has given pause to many is the way in which Heidegger glorifies the destiny of Germany. Beistegui argues that this is a direct outgrowth of the move from the possibility of authenticity of individual *Dasein*, as a solipsistic encounter with one's self, to a shared temporality and the possibility of the authenticity of the 'we' in *Being and Time*. There, the language of authenticity and resoluteness involves the association of history (*Geschichte*) with destiny (*Geschick*): 'These fates have already been guided in advance, in our being-with-one-another in the same world and in our resoluteness for definite possibilities' (GA2, 508/352). As this passage suggests, it is not enough to merely be-with-one-another; becoming a people (*Volk*) or community (*Gemeinschaft*) is predicated on resoluteness for definite possibilities. 'What this means is that a people is not simply given, but is constituted through communication and struggle, through efforts and decisions, through a common resoluteness.'[7] Beistegui notes that the ontological determination of authenticity undergoes a slippage here which casts the possibility of authenticity in an ontic light. This formulation avoids the problem of ontological closure, because, if the authenticity of the 'we' remains predicated on the logic of being-toward-death as a common horizon, it would lead to the plurality of existence being absorbed into the immanence of the Same. The authenticity of a people resides in its ability to take up its common history, but not as a simple reiteration or as something 'present-to-hand'. Resoluteness demands a deconstruction of the history of ontology and a reawakening to the forgotten essence of the German people, the temporally ecstatic nature of that essence, and thus the future as constructed from the possibilities inherited as historical destiny. With the relation of history as destiny, the concept of authenticity takes a decidedly political turn, a *German* destiny and a *German* resoluteness. The emphasis on communication and struggle restores the possibility of singularity, but at another cost: complicity with the political voluntarism of the movement and the desire to produce this renewed sense of the national from out of the movement. This is the project that Heidegger envisions in the 'Rectoral Address: The Self-Assertion of the University'. In that speech, he calls for a renewed relation of the will to science to its historical origin or essence, *technē*. The authentic existence of the German people rests on the possibility of taking up a questioning attitude toward *technē* as the originally disclosive attitude of historical *Dasein*. Beistegui calls this Heidegger's techno-politics.[8] Heidegger himself quickly comes to realise its failure, recognising the need to move to a more primordial understanding of *technē*. In other words, resoluteness is defined here through a clipped horizon which fails to think the historical in relation to an even more ontologically primordial expression, which from *Introduction to Metaphysics* (1935) on is associated with art. There are two major events that mark this shift: (1) Heidegger's 1934 year-long seminar uniquely devoted to Hölderlin's *Dichtung*, and (2) the publication of 'The Origin of the Work of Art', in which Heidegger develops earth as the ontological counterpart to world, a paradoxical mode of revealedness indicating a level of being which surpasses our significations and remains opposed to the technical.

Heidegger's engagement with Hölderlin's *Dichtung* concerns the elaboration of a specific sense of *Heimat*, one which 'corresponds to the elaboration of the national question according to its proper ground (not soil, or the blood, but the earth and the divine)',[9] while *Origin* offers the possibility of transformation, becoming a historical people, through art rather than political action. One can read Heidegger's introduction of this discussion on art as a clear denial of the politics of the day and as favouring the attempt to address the overcoming of metaphysics and the transformation of human *Dasein* philosophically or by other means. Our point is that, rather than being analogous to the kind of autochthonous thinking of *Blut* and *Boden*, the concept of earth acts as a rejoinder to the techno-politicised vision of the character of a people. In relation to *Bodenständigkeit*, *Blut* and *Boden*, all of which are clearly rhetorical categories within the Party, Heidegger's discourse of earth is an attempt to offer a new understanding of what it is to be enrooted. Rootedness is understood in relation to art and, in particular, poetic language/dwelling, and the notion of origin or autochthony is circumscribed by Heidegger's own formulation of temporality. In other words, though he may be influenced or inspired by the idea of a return to the subterranean earth, the *chthonic*, we must look at how Heidegger himself conceptualises the earth as a homeland.

## *Hölderlin's* Heimat *and* Origin's Earth

Heidegger interprets Hölderlin as giving voice to the destitution of the age and to Germany's place within this historic moment of the radical abandonment of being and the whittling down of all meaningfulness into ubiquity and everydayness. What has been lost is the ability to hold open the question, to engage in the kind of wonder which characterises the most primordial experience of being. Most importantly, Hölderlin's poetry attests to the belonging of *Dasein* to the earth and the need to establish a new relationship to the earth as the proper ground from which a homeland will rise.

In his 1934 lecture course, 'Hölderlins Hymnen *Germanien* und *Der Rhein*', Heidegger addresses this relationship between earth, a people and homeland, interpreting the significance of the river in Hölderlin's *Der Rhein* as the creative projection of a German

197

homeland, where, in the encounter with the excess of being, the river establishes its own limits:

> Now the river creates the space imprinted by the land and the bounded place of settlement, of commerce, of arable land for the people and the preservation of their immediate *Dasein*. The river is not a body of water that only flows past the place of human beings. Rather, its flowing as landforming *first creates* the possibility of the grounding of the dwelling of human beings. The river is not just by way of comparison, but is as itself a founder and poet. (GA39, 264, emphasis added)

The river is itself a demigod, intermediate between god and man, the equivalent of the poet or founder. The river-demigod-poet is the emblem of poetic dwelling, both flowing away and remaining ensconced in the earth, a theme taken up again in Heidegger's reading of *Der Ister*. The river '*first creates the possibility of the grounding of human dwelling*', which would be the transformation of earth into homeland. Imperatively, from Heidegger's reading, it is not a foregone conclusion that the homeland exists. There is always a sense of the 'not yet' that accompanies this concept; the homeland has not yet been envisioned. This chafes against the National Socialist mythology of an intact, yet infiltrated, homeland that merely needs to excise its impurities. In his well-known poem, 'Homecoming', Hölderlin poeticises the homeland as something that is both near and yet to come, punctuated by a wandering return and silent waiting for holy names which are lacking. Heidegger interprets this to mean that countrymen (Germans) 'must first become at home in the still withheld essence of their homeland' (GA4, 14/33), requiring the brightening earth to bestow the place in which a people can be 'at home'. Here, Heidegger is even more explicit that homecoming is the poet's vocation, that the poet prepares that which is held in reserve, holding open in the poetic word the dark depths for the bestowal of light, a 'pure opening' which *first imparts* the truth of beyng. What is homelike is the nearness to the origin, where origin preserves itself as an ever-renewing and ever-repeating mystery, as other, as earth, and the task of remembering this essential hiddenness is solely that of the poet. Through remembrance that there is a first beginning, the poet brings the event of wonder into the world of the people, and the people become themselves (historical) for the first time. Most importantly, in order to poeticise purely, the poet receives rather than conceives, not from her own ego, but from out of that which essentially prevails. Notably, Heidegger comes out strongly against the notion of poet as genius, as this view is shrouded in a subjectivist metaphysics that occludes rather than opens the truth of being (see GA65, 52/43). Any founding that the poet accomplishes is clearly understood as a bestowal, such that it is the river who is the poet (GA53, 203/165).

Furthermore, Heidegger's understanding of Hölderlin is always linked to the post-metaphysical project he envisions as philosophy's task. When Heidegger refers to Hölderlin's use of 'secret place' in the fifth stanza of *Germanien*, he asks if the poet can find in his homeland the place for establishing the great beginning where the infinite relation of heaven, man, earth and god will correspond. As we have seen, Heidegger's reference to establishing a beginning is related to the task that awaits us in light of our overcoming of metaphysics. In effect, for Heidegger, the idea of beginning and origin must always be directed toward the future. Beginning also has a special affinity to the sense of origin (*arché*) established through the work of art in *Origin*. As our analysis of this concept has shown, origin is a special designation for Heidegger, one that far surpasses the sort of simplistic autochthonous thinking of origin as something merely to be recovered. Importantly, the work originates 'for the first time', and not as an anticipation or description of something already there or as a repetition of the past, though all the elements from which new decisions and paths are made come out of the already-there, self-secluding ground.

If Heidegger is engaging in the politics of enrootedness, it is not that of those longing for a nostalgic return to a once great past; it is nothing already present or already known, to be extricated or purified, and there is no simple return to an original source. Heidegger's philosophic position runs directly counter to the National Socialist rhetoric of German greatness and returning to the soil and blood. Moreover, as both *Germanien* and *Der Rhein* and Heidegger's account of 'Homecoming' make clear, the founding of a people happens through a kind of poetic creation, not through political edict or fervour.

Heidegger's studies of Hölderlin provide an indispensible context for understanding the power of *poiesis* to convey something outside of the traditional metaphysical paradigm and propel us toward our initial intuition that Heidegger is attempting to engage with and operate within an affective realm. Indeed, one of the things we saw in Chapter 3 was that another beginning would require the establishment of a new grounding attunement. Nevertheless, though the poetic treatment of Hölderlin provides a metaphorical and affective context for understanding the becoming of a historical people, *Origin*, as Heidegger's own philosophical opening, helps us fill in the intrinsically enigmatic lacuna of such a poetically spoken account – this is, as it were, to repeat the already established relation that Heidegger sets up between the poet and the thinker: 'for there must first be thinkers so that the poet's word may be perceptible'. Ideally, Heidegger envisions a people-to-come 'of poetry and of thought' (GA4, 30/48).

Though the notion of homeland is only infrequently alluded to in *Origin*, this particular sense of earth is fundamental to its underlying political emphasis. It opens *Origin* up to a wider discussion of the work of art as a *real* and localisable historical beginning and what it means to become a people (*Volk*). Becoming a people is a matter of a community's resoluteness to take up *its* language, *its* (philosophic) history and, ultimately, the question of being from its particular locatedness. These issues are all circumscribed within the space that art opens, as a (potential) origin or *beginning of history*: 'The temple work opens up a world while, at the same time, setting this world back onto the earth which itself first comes forth as homeland (*heimatliche Grund*)' (H, 32/21). Heidegger writes that 'the temple first gives to things their look, and to men their outlook on themselves' (H, 32/21), meaning that it gathers together words, things and actions in a particular place. These quotations offer an insight into the work of the artwork in relation to homeland, which is to erect a standard of measure and give guidance into what is essential. The work of the temple is to lay out the parameters of what is holy for the Greeks, how that people will worship and conduct themselves, and to provide a relational measure. In other words, the work of art brings what is important for a people to the fore.

But this passage reflects a double criterion for becoming a people: beyond the disclosure of being-with-one-another, a world, the work of art also discloses the otherwise secluded earth as the elemental ground out of which a people arises. Bringing earth and world together in the work establishes a relation that inflects both. By providing a place in which world remains engaged with and set within the elementality and repose of earth, the earth becomes present and meaningful for us, and the artwork changes the earth from mere land or soil to a homeland. Homeland is something over and above the geographical place where certain inhabitants live; it is a specific relationship that these inhabitants have to the earth that has been inflected by their world of projects, meanings and history. The artwork, because of its connection with earth, can become the site for a community to resolutely take up its possibilities and make decisions in relation to its destinal horizon.

So, to be attuned to one's homeland is to become enrooted, grounded, in the earth. How is the enrootedness to be accomplished? In order to answer this question, we turn to Heidegger's formulation, *heimatliche Grund*. *Grund* designates the need for groundedness and the importance of understanding one's origins. Heidegger interprets this enrootedness in terms of awareness of the history of being and the philosophical heritage that is one's own. Not only does Heidegger's critique of the history of metaphysics show that the path to this earth has been obscured, leading to humanity's loss of identity and essential connection to being, but earth, by its very nature, is self-concealing and withdraws itself. *Grund* is the basis or ground, but always in reserve and concealed. It is a nourishing soil, but one which has been forgotten. Consequently, just as essential to Heidegger's notion of *Grund* and grounding is *Ab-Grund*, the abyss. In fact for Heidegger, the ground is always an abyss, a foundationless foundation. The play between *Grund* and *Ab-Grund* is endemic to being itself, and as belonging to being, man's nature also resonates to this sway. In *Origin*, the earth is named the abyssal (*Abgrundig*), signifying that a ground must be established; it is not already there. The earth is a ground that first emerges in the work as a ground for art and for history: 'Thus this ground first finds itself grounded as the supporting ground' (H, 62–3/ 47). Art is a beginning of history because it is capable of once more transposing humanity into its endowment, the essential relation to its past and its earth, by the fact of its very disclosure of the concealing nature of earth as *Ab-Grund*. Yet, earth, even as abyssal, is not just *Grund*, it is *heimatliche Grund*. As *heimatliche Grund*, earth is not monolithic and should not just be understood as a universal totality, the same for all humanity, or merely a structural prop for ontological concerns. A people has *its* earth, a homeland, just as in *Origin* Heidegger stresses that a people has its world and that language is always of *a* people. In Chapter 3, we asked the question, for who can the experience of art be an event. It is now clear that the work of art has to be thought in terms of a particular people and a particular history.

Parallel to the sense of *Grund* as *Ab-Grund*, *Heim* exceeds its common determination as natality or the biological and is 'more closely associated with the ungraspable nearness and simplicity of the familiar abode than with the notion of birth'.[10] *Heimat* as home or place of habitation is thought doubly as *Heimisch* (familiar) and *Heimlich* (secret or intimate). Translating these two with 'native' obliterates the initial sense of 'to inhabit'. Rather than something to which we feel a natural attachment, as in native, or natal, the earth is an abode or dwelling which one comes to inhabit, and which must be grounded. In that this discussion of homeland is beholden to Heidegger's understanding of Hölderlin, we must take seriously his pronouncement of how man dwells on the earth, that is, poetically, if man is to dwell according to his essence or ownmost.

As a place of dwelling, earth resonates with the sense of *polis* that Heidegger puts forward in *Parmenides*, the dwelling or gathering place (*Ort*) of a people. The *politeia* is the metaphysical determination of the *topos* of the *polis*. *Polis* is the abode of the essence of historical man that discloses and conceals beings wherein the Being of man in its relations to beings has gathered. The *polis* is the *Da* of a people, and dwelling in the *polis* is a sojourn on earth. It is a pole or centre around which everything is gathered and assigned to man. In *Origin* the work is a gathering place (*Ort*) like the *polis* of ancient Greece, and the *polis* serves the same function as the work of art, the gathering together of all the essential determinations of a people. As a gathering place, the *polis* (and the work of art for that matter) is the centre or unification of the relations of man to beings and has a temporal and local determination. The *polis* or the work as das *Ort* (place) is both literal location and a matter of metaphysical and historical determinations.

Homeland can literally refer to the location where one is born and raised, but can never be reduced to this. The givenness of homeland is never merely understood in terms of place, but also in terms of time. A homeland, for Heidegger, is a matter of history, and history is preserved in language. Therefore, when Heidegger declares that a *Volk* is determined by its relationship to the soil of the earth (*Erdboden*), this is not merely geographical or a matter of the terrain and climate which determines the thrownness of our existence, but includes the accretions which are found in language. It is language that preserves our history and our being. Heidegger emphasises that our being happens in language, we *are* in language, and this is always a particular language that connects us to those others who are in that language as well. We happen, and we become historical in language. The connection between the earth and language is not inadvertent. Language is specific and belongs to a people, therefore, one's philosophic inheritance, and relationship to being, are always particular. The question of one's homeland becomes a question of the appropriate relationship to language, a question that dovetails with both Heidegger's discussion of the importance of Hölderlin (for the Germans) and poetry as the original language (*Ursprache*) of any historical people. Having the proper relation to language is crucially related to the becoming-historical of a people. By taking language up as our dwelling, as the house of being and history, rather than as merely functional, we enter into our possibility of becoming historical.

In this next quotation from *Origin*, Heidegger emphasises the local or regional character of earth and its connection to a people: 'The truly poeticizing projection is the opening up of that in which human existence (*Dasein*), as historical, is already thrown (*geworfen*). This is the earth (and, for a historical people, its earth), the self-closing ground upon which it rests, along with everything which – though hidden from itself – it already is' (H, 62/47). This should be read alongside the following rather elusive passage from *Origin* bringing the crucial themes of the given (or the earth), history and a people together:

> Whenever art happens, whenever, that is, there is a beginning, a thrust enters history and history either begins or resumes [begins anew]. History, here, does not mean a sequence of events in time, no matter how important ... History is the transporting (*entrucken*) of a people into its appointed task (*Aufgegebenes*) as the entry into its endowment (*Mitgegebenes*). (H, 64/49)

*Gegeben*, the root of two words in this passage, has the multiple senses of the given, the pre-existing, endowment, the appointed or given task. Heidegger's definition of a people is said here, as the relation between *das Aufgegebene* and *das Mitgegebene*. The question is what is given and what is 'the given'. In other words, the question of what is given over is contingent on our understanding of what the given itself is. Consulting *Being and Time*, we can relate the given to thrownness, one's pre-existing situation and one's past, as well as the place (earth as *Ort*) into which one is thrown.

In this passage it is clear that the given is both a task and an endowment, meaning that the given is not immediately present. The entry into one's endowment is not itself 'a given', and so uncovering what is given also becomes a task for the future. There is work to be done for earth to become a homeland, now understood as a dwelling;

the work of the work of art grounds the earth in order for it to come to presence as earth and homeland. *Heim* is not a *Boden*, a ground of biological vital rootedness.[11] *Heimat* as a native destiny is chosen and learned. The true fatherland is not the earth where one is born, but the earth that one understands and preserves, 'which means he knows how to preserve the secret mixture of native spontaneity and restitution of the past'.[12] Accordingly, Heidegger's conception of a people necessitates that it be more than the literal location or present factual existence of a people. It also stands to reason that when earth becomes a homeland, or a people are transported into its appointed task, a beginning happens. Thus, the importance of the idea of *becoming* a people for Heidegger's philosophy is demonstrated.

The earth as endowment resonates with the notion of one's proper (*Eigentlichkeit*), a theme that is inherent in the notion of *Ereignis*, and resurfaces explicitly in *Contributions*. An endowment would be what is most properly one's own, one's inheritance or property. As we have seen, the happening of *Dasein*'s belongingness to being, *Ereignis*, is predicated on man's rekindling of his essential nature. Therefore, the question of 'who we are' is an essential one. In *Contributions*, Heidegger sets out the stakes in this question. Mindfulness of being demands mindfulness of who we are. But who is the 'we'? Here, Heidegger acknowledges that the 'we' is ambiguous. He asks, do we mean the human being as such or ourselves as our own people (GA65, 48/40)? What becomes apparent from *Contributions* is that Heidegger is asking at the same time what it means to be human and what it means to be a people. When taken to be a question about *when* and *if* we will be ourselves, the question becomes historical. Indeed, the question is always historical because *Dasein* is always already historical. But the question is universally a question for any peoples: 'we are not the only ones but are a people with other peoples' (GA65, 48/40). We can speak of a general, ontological understanding of human being's essence as related to being, but this structure will always be grounded in a particular earth, producing a particular people. As we shall see, it is necessary to understand Heidegger's philosophic path in light of both the general and the particular, as his philosophic position vacillates between the two, especially when ensconced in political concerns. His ontological and general understanding of the proper is represented in the following quotations: 'The selfhood of the human being – of the historical human being as the selfhood of a people – is a realm of occurrences, a realm in which human beings are appropriated to themselves only if they themselves reach the open time-space wherein appropriation can occur', and 'the most proper "being" of humans is therefore grounded in a belonging to the truth of being' (GA65, 51/42). This is to say that until human beings gain ontological awareness, move beyond the oblivion of being, they have not found their essential natures. At the same time, this general directive offers no solid guidance as to what it means to accede to one's proper until linked to the now clarified sense of earth. In 'Hölderlin and the Essence of Poetry', Heidegger says that 'man is *he* who he *is* precisely in the attestation of his own existence', and that to which he must testify is 'his belonging to the earth' (GA4, 36/54), made possible through a particular history and language. Earth as homeland repeats the dual structure of the general and the particular. It refers to the general designation of a path toward another beginning for all of Western metaphysics and the specific peoples who comprise Western Europe. The ontological interpretation of earth is reinforced in 'On the Essence of Truth', where Heidegger mentions both *being transported* and an *endowment*. There, it is the inevitability of the mystery, the self-concealing essence of being that one is transposed or transported into, and the endowment is that of the correspondence between humans and being that is granted by Freedom. But elsewhere Heidegger also insists that what is proper is 'determined out of what is essential in the sense of the original-unique' (GA65, 66/53). In other words, each people is transported into being in a particular and unique manner and has a particular earth: 'In its origin and destiny this people is unique, corresponding with the uniqueness of be-ing itself, whose truth this people must ground once and for all in a unique site and a unique moment' (GA65, 97/77). Notice what has happened here. The ungrounding, or uprooting, of humanity is, likewise, both general and particular. As the inheritors of the same metaphysical tradition, Western humanity shares in a common rootlessness, but its manifestations are different according to the particular inheritance and world that one shares with others. Being enrooted is no longer thought in terms of *Blut* and *Boden* autochthony, or only in terms of the Germans. Heidegger says that resisting uprootedness (*Entwurzelung*) is preparing for those who will create new sites within being itself. The transformation into enrootedness (*Verwurzelung*) is the province of the future ones, 'who create in being new locations out of which a constancy in the strife of earth and world will eventuate again' (GA65, 62/49–50). Of course, we know to whom Heidegger is referring: the poets and thinkers.[13]

From *Origin* we learn that every historical *Volk* has an endowment and a task. Endowment has to be learned, through being enraptured in the appointed task. When taken alone, these statements are cryptic at best. In order to explain the passages in *Origin* concerning the transposition of a people into its endowment, we bring our attention back, in what we hope will be a creative repetition (*weiderholen*), to Heidegger's analysis of Hölderlin, given that for Heidegger the specific path for the Germans in attaining their proper comes from Hölderlin, *and* it is also from Hölderlin that Heidegger derives the structural account of homeland. In other words, Hölderlin provides the essential model for the path to attaining one's proper generally, and, more specifically, indicates the path of the Germans in fulfilling their specific destiny through the relationship of the Germans and to the Greeks.

## The Wandering Return

Hölderlin's own experience of travelling taught him that journeying abroad gave him a greater understanding of his own essence: 'for him the journeying abroad to the foreign land remained essential for the return home into the law of his own particular song' (GA4, 83/108). Heidegger refers to this as the law of destiny, which he claims is directly expressed by Hölderlin through his poetry (GA4, 87/112). Generally speaking, the task is to think the unthought in one's historical essence. This can only happen by struggling with what is foreign. The way to one's proper is to be transported into the strange (*Unheimlich*), to be disrupted and have what is common challenged, and, indeed, Heidegger does formulate human being's essential nature in this way elsewhere as well (i.e. the human as *deinon* in *Introduction of Metaphysics*). Man is the uncanny one, the one who is not at home and therefore seeks out what is other in order to create and build a dwelling on the earth. Importantly, to dwell is not to become secure or familiar, as one might assume. Through confrontation with the uncanny and the strange, human beings reach their own limits, thus understanding what is proper to themselves: 'The ground is won in which a people founds its historical dwelling in which it becomes unfamiliar in being in order to become serious about the uncanny of Being' (*Of*, 337). This is a huge insight into what it means to be a people for Heidegger. To be a people, and dwell in being, is not to remain within the familiar, nor is it a matter of simply returning to some lost origin. What is proper to man is to be *Unheimlich*, constantly seeking beyond the limits of the familiar.

In *Hölderlin's Hymn 'The Ister'*, Heidegger explains that the foreign is not arbitrary, as some indeterminate or manifold other of one's own; in other words, it is not just otherness in general. This relationship involves the particular foreign other that set one's own on its path. The foreign of one's own is a specific relationship. Through the poet's work, this encounter is made. The hymn involves the singing of coming into one's own. In this particular case and with this particular poet, one's own is whatever belongs to the fatherland of the Germans, and the other of the Germans is the Greek.[14] History, as a transformative leap into another beginning will happen in relation to the Greeks as the 'other' of the German. Another beginning is possible by understanding the Greeks as that which the Germans must come to terms with in order to be transported into their own endowment, although Heidegger explicitly denies the simple return to Greek origins: 'This is the "paradox." Since we fight the cause of the Greeks, but on the opposite front, we become not Greek but German' (GA39, 293). The earth must become a homeland, by going out into the foreign essence of the Greek (for the Germans) and then returning to their earth, transfixed or transposed into their own essence. Essentially, 'Hölderlin's poetry opened up the mood which enabled Germans to experience (*erfahren*) the departure of the old gods. But it could also elicit a mood in which Germans could be carried away (*entrücken*) to new gods and carried back (*einrücken*) to their earthly homeland.'[15]

According to Heidegger, to be transported and carried away is exactly what the Germans need to enter into their endowment. Through the encounter with the Greeks poeticised in Hölderlin's poetry, the Germans are supposed to learn their task, and, thus, be transported into their endowment, their proper. Following Hölderlin, and relying specifically on his letters to Casimir Böhlendorf, Heidegger gathers that only in so far as the Germans are transported into the fire of heaven (as that which is proper to the Greeks and foreign to themselves) can they get clarity of presentation, their own endowment.[16]

The fires of heaven and the clarity of presentation refer to the duality of the Dionysian and the Apollonian depicted by Nietzsche, and more profoundly addressed by Hölderlin. The clarity of presentation, which is Apollonian world-structuring, is the endowment of the Germans, while the foray into the Dionysian, being touched by the self-concealing powers of being, is their task. This is exactly the opposite of the Greeks, who possessed the endowment of the Dionysian and the task of the Apollonian. Heidegger claims that the 'native trait of the Germans, however, does not become authentically their own as long as this ability to grasp is not tested by the need to grasp the ungraspable' (GA4, 88/113). The movement through what the Germans encounter as foreign to themselves, the fire of heaven, is an essential component of the process of coming to dwell in the German homeland. In other words, as we have claimed, it is not just a German people becoming once again enrooted in its soil *or* merely revisiting Greek philosophy. There is a transformation of both that must happen for the Germans to become a people.

Here and elsewhere, Hölderlin's law of destining arises from a relation of the foreign and one's own, a wandering movement of going out and return: 'Coming to be at home is thus a passage through the foreign' (GA53, 60/49). Yet, Heidegger says that instead of purely heralding the joys of return, Hölderlin's poem is bracketed by trepidation brought about by the 'not' in the last stanza. Indeed homecoming is not a matter of *simply* arriving or returning: 'the one returning home has not yet reached his homeland simply by arriving there' (GA4, 13/32). If one must seek what is near, it is not immediately given. The countrymen must first 'become at home in the still withheld essence of their homeland' (GA4, 14/33), which, in turn, requires that they know the homeland's specific nature. Those who have not gone out or sought have no access to what is most proper to them without the help of the one who seeks what is most proper and best in the homeland. They require the seeker to show them the nature of their homeland. When Heidegger writes that 'to compose is to find' (GA4, 15/34), there is no doubt of who the seeker is; it is the poet, to whom the people must learn to listen. The poet, in going out and opening himself to those elements of the holy, is animated by what Heidegger refers to as the poetic spirit, which, in turn, allows the poet to ground the poetic dwelling of man. Then 'the *spirit* itself dwells in the grounding ground' and will 'be "naturally" *at home*' (GA4, 91/115). True dwelling is poetic, and something that the poet must first accomplish in order to point out the poetic essence of dwelling to others: 'the poetic dwelling of the poet precedes the poetic dwelling of man' (GA4, 91/115).

In this respect, Heidegger's analysis of Hölderlin's 'The Wanderer' is illuminative. As the title suggests, the poem is about one who journeys away from home and seeks new experiences through wandering. Heidegger says that 'the returning wanderer has become more experienced in the being of the gods, that is, of the joyful ones' (GA4, 20/39) and brings this experience back. The poet/wanderer must learn about those joyful ones, the angels of earth, light and aether, as those which brighten up the hearth/homeland, so that its original essence can be seen. With a clearer view of what Heidegger names the 'highest' or 'holy', the poet can see the earth *as* homeland. This is to see the homeland's own special nature and what is highest in it, thus indicating that the return is the final goal. Fundamentally, the poet/wanderer's activity of going out into the foreign must always end in return. Returning completes the process of finding one's proper, which, as we know, is a prerequisite for the initiation of another beginning.

The poet and the poetical open a clearing onto being for which a people can decide or not, and it is the intersection with the work of art that makes Heidegger's notion of a people unique, representing a break with past understandings of what it means to be a people. For him, a people, for which he is advocating, has not arrived and is, thus, to come. The distinction between a people and a mere public is thus a difference in attunement, of having the ears to hear (*horen*) in order that they may belong together (*gehoren*). A public goes about its everyday business, always thinking only in terms of its tasks. A people think in terms of both tasks and endowment. A people becomes *historical* in taking up the task of learning its endowment.

## *Reflections on* Geist *and* Volk

Though the inclination may be to have done with Heidegger's language of a *Volk*, we understand the question of a people, the 'we', to be central to his thinking and to the possibility of engaging another beginning. He follows a path opened by Hölderlin, asking not only who we are but whether we will be at all (GA65, 51/41). Heidegger's commitment to the question of a people stems from the fact that he believes that belonging to a people is essential for one's existence and authenticity. In 1934, just after Heidegger resigns the rectorship, the first lecture course that he gives is *Logik*. He renews the question 'Who are we?' claiming that it is not through a combination or accumulation of I's that the *Volk* is defined, but the very essence of the I is determined by the essence of the *Volk* (GA38, S13). He lays out three different conceptions of *Volk*, corresponding to body (*Körper*), soul (*Seele*) and spirit (*Geist*). *Volk als Körper* is race understood as blood relations and rank, denoting a kind of purity of origin and habitation. Thus, *Volkskörper* is a people considered as a brute body, physical and numerical. Membership in a *Volk* by these standards is limited to literal physical boundaries, both of the land and of blood. *Volk als Seele* involves cultural practices: *Volkslieden* (singing), *Volksfesten* (public festivals) and *Gebrauchen* (needs or employment), which leave an allegorical impression of its inhabitants. Rather than random settlements of men in a certain area, a people on this level comes together through its interactions and shared activities as well as by the particular way that the land and resources are used. *Volk als Geist* translates as spirit-mind, and Heidegger follows Hegel in linking *Geist* to history. The *Geist* of a nation is the mediation of its historical past, the shared history of a people. Heidegger admits that *Volk* is itself ambiguous, and though he does reject any idea of *Volk* that is exclusively bodily, he critiques all three conceptions of *Volk* and attempts to think them in some form of unity (GA38, 67–8). None of these categories is adequate, because body and soul are already metaphysically determined, as is spirit (GA65, 53/43). If anything, Heidegger is attempting to offer a new conception of *Volk* that will be linked to a conception of the *spiritual* rather than *spirit*. One can interpret Heidegger's coupling of the spiritual and a people as an attempt to distance himself from other notions of *Volk* being perpetuated, those that would define *Volk* in terms of biology and racial heritage as well as the metaphysics of mind/body.

Heidegger's understanding of the temporality of *Dasein* necessarily affects this aspect of a *Volk*. Emphasising the futural possibility of this *Volk*, Heidegger insists that it is not as if the spiritual *Volk* exists already; it is, rather, by its nature always a matter of decision and therefore always coming or to come. In other words, the particular path of a people's belonging is a coming together that renews itself, thus homeland always has the potential to be something new and the tradition of homeland is never closed. To be historical/spiritual is to resolutely and thoughtfully take up the past in anticipation of the future. To take up the past is to think that of the past that has yet to be thought. A *Volk* has a spiritual world, as the language and history through which its people approach being; in this sense, a people is bound to its earth and its past. It is rooted in traditions and language, but, as our prior analysis has shown, it is also more than this past, more than its traditions and its rootedness. To recognise spirit in terms of presence to itself, or in the fullness of an accessible past, would be to forget the question of being and ontological difference: Being will never coincide with beings. In order to perpetuate the difference between spirit in a metaphysical sense and the spiritual, Heidegger thinks the spiritual in terms of the un-thought wealth of language and history. The emphasis on the earth and a people in *Origin* speaks to this issue: though earth cannot be interpreted wholesale as the physical, it does imply distance from the metaphysical. Language is a vessel of the past that has its own physical, persevering existence. Language and history are spiritual but not otherworldly. Also, as we have seen, earth as the hidden or concealed implies that which lies beyond our common understanding and technological grasp of things. Therefore, it is a particular concealed aspect of language that relates it to origins and history.

As we know, Heidegger's insistence on the spiritual mission of Germany and Germany's privileged place in the transition of Western philosophy into another beginning is problematic and worrisome. There are two separate problems. First, does Heidegger's emphasis on the Germans preclude his philosophy's wider application? Second, is Heidegger's emphasis on the gathering of a people toward their spiritual mission, though it runs clear of biological racism, a form of spiritual or metaphysical racism grounded on the logic of inclusion? This, of course, draws near to the worry of our thinkers of community, Bataille, Nancy, and Blanchot, for whom the thinking of community on the basis of identity or Sameness inevitably leads to exclusionary and deleterious totalitarian political formations.[17] For these thinkers, the propensity toward totalitarianism does not originate in Heidegger's philosophy; rather, it is a metaphysical dispensation, gleaned from the formulation of being in terms of sameness and purity, which then becomes instantiated in communal relations and social existence through foundational violence and maintained through the logic of exclusion. Ironically, Heidegger stands at the end of a metaphysical tradition in which this tendency is latent. The apprehension is that imbuing both thought and being with the characteristics of gathering and belonging is to repeat the tendency for totalitarianism at the heart of philosophy.

In response to the first problematic, Heidegger is explicit about Germany's centrality even after his political involvement is over. In 1943, he writes, 'the planet is in flames. The essence of man is out of joint. Only from the Germans can there come a world-historical reflection – if, that is, they find and preserve their "Germanness"' (see G55, *Heraklit*). Though Heidegger is clear that all of Europe is heir to the historicity of metaphysics, he gives an infamous account of Europe that places Germany at the centre: caught between the pincers of America and Russia. Many point to this passage as evidence of Heidegger's ethnocentrism and complicity with National Socialism.

Even as the whole of Europe inherits the legacy of metaphysics, Germany is the source that these others surround. So, Germany, as the most metaphysical of nations at the heart of this world-historical moment, is poised to take up the mission of overcoming the technisation of humanity. Nonetheless, being at the centre does not exonerate Germany of Europe's ills. Germany's centrality is not an exalted position but one of highest culpability, as most metaphysical and, therefore, most beholden to metaphysics' destined unfolding.

Because of Heidegger's commitment to Hölderlin and the renewal of German essence, the language of the opening of a clearing by the strife between earth and world also takes on a suspiciously political hue. If the earth is what is mysterious and foreign, while the world is the ordering prior to contact with this earth, then the truth would be the outcome of this interaction, the transporting of a people, a German people, into its endowment, as a specifically German truth. This presents a problem for those who would like to derive an overarching, non-political reading of the structures of earth and world. The difficulty is not Heidegger's conjoining of art and a *Volk*, but that he 'employs the idea of *the* people'.[18] If the transposition of a people into their endowment refers to a new German people, then there is a very specific sense in which poetry, in particular the poetry of Hölderlin, applies only to a German people. How much of *Origin* can be applicable outside of this context and how we are to understand Heidegger's reliance on Hölderlin, in order to bring Heidegger's understanding of the artwork into conversation with a more contemporary audience and contemporary philosophers who emphasise the relation between art and philosophy? Can we separate this philosophy from its specificity to Germans. That is to say, is Heidegger saying something essential when he talks about thinking and poeticising?

This dilemma goes to the heart of the issue as to whether Heidegger's formula for the becoming of a people can be structurally applied to other historical peoples and, also, if art has the significance he grants it in relation to the founding of a people. In the posthumously published *Der Spiegel* interview conducted in 1966, Heidegger admits that he does allocate a special task to the Germans in this configuration, though only when considered in dialogue with Hölderlin. Yet he also says that the 'law of encounter (*Auseinandersetzung*) between the foreign and one's own is the fundamental truth of history' (GA53, 61/49), indicating that the ontological structure is trans-historic. Heidegger's later thought definitely reflects the attempt to think along these lines, as opposed to the ontic determinations of *the* people. He speaks less of the spiritual mission of the Germans, referring more often to the world-historical task that lies before us. Homeland is also reconfigured as 'nearness to being'. Though still emphasising the need to return to Greek origins, it is usually in the context of its relation to Western philosophy in general, and, while the movement of remembrance as well as trans-figuration of these Greek origins remains consistent in Heidegger's thinking, it is *Dasein* as a whole that must accede to that which is proper to it, however concealed.

Though Heidegger never gives up the centrality of the Germans in this process, the 'Letter on Humanism' reveals that Heidegger expands his view by situating the Germans in a larger Western destiny which potentially even includes consideration of the Orient:

> But even the West is not thought regionally as the Occident in contrast to the Orient, not merely as Europe, but rather world-historically out of nearness to the source. We have still scarcely begun to think of the myste-rious relations to the East which found expression in Hölderlin's poetry. German is not spoken to the world so that the world might be reformed through the German essence; rather, it is spoken to the Germans so that from a fateful belongingness to the nations (*Völkern*) they might become world-historical along with them. (Wm, 335/218)

In *Contributions*, the complex nature of Heidegger's historical vision is exposed, as he at once names the great end of Western philoso-phy (German idealism and Nietzsche) a philosophy of the German people, which is *prima facie* true, yet immediately says that this says nothing about the essence of philosophy itself, insisting that speaking of the philosophy of a people has nothing to do with natural aptitude or capacity but instead is a matter of genuinely relating philosophy to the proper origins and history.[19] *Contributions* also marks the begin-ning of his thinking of *Ereignis*, where his formulation of *Ereignis* is denuded of consideration of the Germans, as is the case in his subse-quent work, where he further elaborates a properly world-historical event, anticipated as a conjunction of four dimensions of being, the fourfold (*Ge-viert*).

So, Heidegger's work does warrant consideration, however ten-tative and careful, of its wider application and world-historical nature. It is clear that Heidegger does not just address the problem of German identity, however occupied he was with this problem during the 1930s. Even while considering the German relatedness to the Greeks, he simultaneously offers a programme for another way of thinking and being that can be extracted from its particular application to Germany, developing a notion of *Dasein*, the wanderer, who encounters the strange and unfamiliar, in order to return home, to dwell. This does not indicate a resting in place and a notion of nation, people or homeland that is stagnant or even related to specific, pre-ordained boundaries. To think this would be to disregard what Heidegger clearly illustrates in *Origin* and elsewhere, that the origin is something to be made, and that a people must learn its endowment. Humans become at home by confronting and tarrying with the *Unheimlich*. Return to the homeland cannot be a return to something already there, and thus the return is never to an already determined, original place. If one interprets this movement as indicative of what it means to be human, becoming at home is more like a continual process of wandering. *Dasein* dwells poetically, creatively, which means that dwelling is itself a matter of movement and process. Though Heidegger maintains the idea of specific peoples that have a relation to their earth and homeland, what these peoples may be is open to change, there to be negotiated and created. Human beings are *deinon* because they belong to being and its overwhelming power. This is an ontological condition that determines human existence as a whole. Therefore, there could be other relationships that establish their own beginnings. We may be able to apply Heidegger's formula to peoples other than the Germans, based on the fact that Western European philosophy as a whole shares a common history, the Greeks. In this case, the German path is but one path, which itself remains a question open for the future.

The more difficult question is whether we can transpose this model beyond those relations that exist within the Western tradition.[20] If Heidegger's philosophy truly permits the possibility of *other* beginnings, then a reading of Hölderlin that generalises the structure of the founding of a homeland and the national character of thought to other earths and other peoples is warranted. Yet, there is real debate about whether Heidegger opens himself up to other relationships besides that of the Greek and, potentially expanded, the West. His interest in Asian philosophy, as well as his selective interest in modern art, has been cited as evidence of this.[21] Heidegger's self-expressed affinity with Zen Buddhist D.T. Suzuki is sometimes offered as evidence of the possibility of finding inspiration for another beginning outside of the Western inheritance of the technological understanding of being.[22] Given the constraints of our project, we cannot faithfully speak to the wealth of scholarship that has grown up around these issues, though it is clear that there is a growing contingent of philosophers who seek to move Heidegger beyond Occidental boundaries.[23] The general theme within this line of thinking is that overcoming metaphysics may be accomplished by looking toward or by greater approximation to Eastern philosophy. Yet, Heidegger's thinking, in our opinion, does not achieve nor directly yield this encounter. In fact, it has been argued that Heidegger's use of Eastern texts, primarily the *Taoteching*, reflects his philosophical preoccupations with Being, emptiness and nothingness, rather than considering the Taoist contexts of the Chinese counterparts of these words.[24] As well, he most often turns these dialogic encounters back over to a Greco-German context.

Minimally, one can say that there is a danger in appropriating Heidegger beyond the boundary of his provincialism and the essential enrootedness of his thought which is twofold at least. First, one must consider whether the global import of Heidegger's hermeneutical model of renewal and return runs the risk of imposing a Western framework upon other traditions, thus perpetuating the advancement of control and mastery of being that it is meant to avoid. Second, the move from the historical to the trans-historical runs afoul of the specificity of Heidegger's thinking, whether the equivocation lies within his own thinking or not. By Heidegger's standard, the asymmetrical relation as a model of a relation to the foreign cannot be an arbitrary one nor can it be thought in the manner of otherness in general. It is not enough that one pursue the unfamiliar; one must tarry with a particular unfamiliar, the other that helps one become oneself. Heidegger's insistence on the particular starting point of the Greeks for Western philosophy means that thought is bound to this particular historical circuit and results in him thinking that the return to the Greeks is necessary.

Even if we found that this model could be applied to other beginnings, ones outside of the Greeks, the model of return and renewal remains unchanged. Heidegger's project is bound by world history that is in the process of unfolding itself, out of necessity toward a destiny. In other words, this opening toward other relations still remains bound to a hermeneutics of discovery from within this encircled whole. The necessity of the circular movement of return to a particular historical form disguises the relativity of the movement. Regardless of its applicability, the trouble lies in the model itself. That a people is open to change and free to recreate itself from its interaction with its 'other' does not preclude the fact that Heidegger is bound to a concept of origin that Deleuze adamantly rejects. Structurally, it seems that the only reason to go out, to seek the other, is to return home. Deleuze is critical of exactly this bounding of movement, however infinite, because it retains a particularly obstinate and vicious, though subtle, form of teleology. Freed from this, the model of a people takes on an entirely different structural nature, one that operates through the unpredictable and indicates a version of difference that moves beyond 'differing between' toward 'difference in itself'. Which leads us to a more fundamental question: is Heidegger's philosophy inherently exclusionary based on the logic of autochthony, even if autochthony must now be viewed as an ontological structure of perpetual renewal?

In answer to this problematic, we begin by referring to Jacques Derrida's deconstructive analysis of Heidegger's concept of spirit in *Of Spirit*, which is important for several reasons: first, Heidegger's usage of the spiritual in political speeches marred the context almost irrevocably. Whereas many commentators preferred to distance themselves entirely, Derrida attempts to disentangle Heidegger's language from the National Socialist *Zeitgeist* by providing a breakdown of the spiritual, which perpetuates a genuinely philosophical encounter. Second, Derrida's analysis brings us back to the issue of difference in Heidegger's philosophy, now accentuating the concurrence between thought and spirit as the site of unification. The particular contours gathering in this conception highlight what is at stake for a logic of autochthony that has been ontologised.

In *Of Spirit*, Derrida traces the term *Geist*, and its affiliates, *geistlich* and *geistig*, from *Being and Time* through Heidegger's later works, paying specific attention to his political writings.[25] Derrida takes on the most problematic of associations, acknowledging the connection between *geistig* and mission. He names four predicates of the spiritual mission, auspiciously four themes *gathered* into one: (1) question as will to knowledge or essence (*Wissenschaft, Wesenwille, Fragen*), (2) the spiritual world of a people (*geistige Welt*), (3) being nourished by earth and blood, and (4) resolve or resolute openness (*Entschlossenheit* – retained in *Gelassenheit*). *Geist* serves as the nodal centre for the conjunction of essence, the question, animality and epochality. Derrida's question is whether *Geist* merely ties these difficult themes together in an even more convoluted knot or whether their knotting is somehow indicative of what spirit is as a gathering together of the essential, entreating us to question how

216

they belong together, to think them together. The resonance between the polyvalence of thought identified by Derrida in thinking *Geist* and Heidegger's insistence on the dynamic chiasmus of thought are unmistakable: 'Through them [thoughts] everything, because it is separated (*auseinandergesetz*), belongs together. Spirit is unifying unity. This unity lets the being-together of everything real appear in its gathering' (GA4, 60/82). The crucial issue this raises is that of the relation between identity and difference in Heidegger's philosophy, a question that animates every stage of his thinking. From the existential analytic of *Dasein* in *Being and Time* to the thinking of the intimate relation of the fourfold, Heidegger is constantly interrogating the manner in which things belong together. The concepts of gathering, belonging and multiplicity are all ways of articulating the difficult *polemos* between unity and difference within being, a gathering of multiple senses that are not lost when unified under one concept. In *Origin*, Heidegger insists on thinking the conjoined strife of earth and world; in *What is Called Thinking?* the essence of thinking is this holding together and unification of the multiple. Language is also characterised as a gathering, one that speaks to the co-belonging of being, word, *logos* and *Dasein*. Additionally, words themselves are gathering places, vessels of meaning that open up to reveal multiple senses and histories. In all these cases, the very act of holding the multiplicity together, in thought, enhances them all. Thus enters the transformative potential of the work of art. The artwork provides a place in which gathering, first, can be seen, but, equally, can be preserved in order that the thinking of difference can occur. It is a place that establishes an opening for the gathering together of those decisions that would establish a people, an origin and a homeland, and thus the work answers the needs of a people-to-come.

This is what occupies Heidegger in *Identity and Difference*, which, Stambaugh claims in her introduction of the translated text, Heidegger considered his most important contribution since *Being and Time*. Its question is how to think the difference in identity. Deleuze refers to this work in *Difference and Repetition* in defence of Heidegger's struggle to wrest difference from representative models: 'Difference cannot, therefore, be subordinated to the Identical or the Equal, but must be thought as the Same, in the Same' (DR, 90/65). Through the Same, Heidegger is trying to think a gathering that is not reducible to empty indifferent oneness. Elsewhere, we have claimed that Deleuze intends to show how certain readings of the later Heidegger are really misunderstandings. In particular, Deleuze aims to outline a more accurate reading of the Heideggerian 'not', wherein 'the Heideggerian NOT refers not to the negative in being, but to being as difference; it refers not to negation but to the question' (DR, 91/66). Yet, Deleuze ends this section with a series of questions, which serve to cast doubt on the notion that speaking of the Same (gathering), rather than Identity, is really enough to think original difference (see also DR, 154/117), ending with the definitive claim that 'It seems not, given [Heidegger's] interpretation of Nietzsche's eternal return' (DR, 91/66), which Deleuze thinks is a view of the eternal return as a founded repetition, which would predetermine all the answers to the question. In contrast, what Deleuze sees in the eternal return doctrine is a very specific kind of repetition, one that, as he says, 'makes a difference' (DR, 85/60). The concept of Sameness still presupposes a homology between Being and beings that Deleuze is not willing to grant.[26]

This may seem tangential to the question of a people, but it is actually paradigmatic. The notion of a people involves the same need to delineate the relation between identity and difference.

Derrida's analysis in 'Geschlecht I' is illuminative of the stakes in Heidegger's understanding of the relation between the existential neutrality (identity) of the Dasein of Being and Time and the difference insinuated by the term Geschlecht.[27] Geschlecht is a term which Heidegger charges with a multiplicity of meanings: sex, genre, family, stock, race, lineage, generation,[28] a place or site (Ort) of this gathering, similar, in fact, to the polis as 'the whirl in which and around which everything revolves (GA53, 100). First, it must be noted that the diverse definitions of Geschlecht, as community, race, sex, group, reveal the hesitancy with which one must proceed on this subject. Each of these terms for Geschlecht has been exclusionary, as each has been based on certain criteria of similarity. No matter how open the criteria, there is always the possibility, and, in fact, inevitability, of exclusion. Derrida's query happens in the context of interrogating Heidegger's conception of Dasein with respect to its neutrality in terms of a particular kind of difference, sexual difference. Heidegger refers to Geschlecht as containing a multiplicity of senses simultaneously, which seems like difference, but the one difference that he is hesitant to assign Geschlecht to is the numerical two of sexual difference. We can therefore have nominal difference in referring to Geschlecht, which is the kind of nodal gathering that Heidegger encourages, but we cannot define Geschlecht as difference, which is to say, use it to name the difference of sex. In terms of *sexual difference*, *Geschlecht* is neutral, supposedly out of necessary consideration of the ontological. *Dasein* is the not yet of dispersion, and speaking of *Dasein*, rather than *Mensch*, marks its neutrality with regard to sex – it is neither male nor female. In fact, *Geschlecht* with respect to the ontological condition of *Dasein* is the mere possibility of sex, while sexual difference is dispersion in flesh, the ontic. *Dasein*'s neutrality is positive, a full positivity of origin, and from this grand original simplicity, dispersion or dissemination unfolds.[29] Derrida does claim that this implies an original dispersion within *Dasein*,[30] which must be the case in order that between birth and death all of *Dasein*'s possibilities unfold, but now, *Dasein* is itself an origin.

Why is this important? For Derrida, gathering does not have the unquestioned positive value that it does for Heidegger. Instead, it implies the prioritisation of identity and sameness over multiplicity and difference, and Derrida reveals this priority to be central to Heidegger's understanding of *Dasein* by referencing Heidegger's treatment, or refusal, of sexual difference. It is central to the elaboration of *Dasein*'s existential condition that difference be understood as a secondary factor – in other words, difference comes from or unfolds from an original oneness. As Derrida shows, sexual difference is actually the first difference that Heidegger neutralises – which at once suggests that difference is a potential in *Dasein*, but cannot be considered at the ontological level, only once *Dasein* is dispersed at the ontic level. Difference always refers back to *Dasein* understood in terms of wholeness and plenitude – an origin immanent to itself and with ontological priority given over to unity and the one. Derrida's worry speaks directly to our question of a people and the problem of thinking identity on the basis of unity. When applied to the notion of a people, it could imply a form of metaphysical racism, an immanence that disallows the real possibility of divergence or difference.

When one situates gathering alongside all of Heidegger's main concepts (i.e. being, destiny, origin, the proper), it is clear that his philosophy accentuates the unity of difference. In as much as Heidegger attends to difference and attempts to install it at the heart of any unity, he always reverts to unification, with difference immanent to origin. In the final analysis, his emphasis on return places his thought on the side of gathering. The spiritual mission, as endowed to thought and philosophy, unfolds as this prerogative, leading us to the decisive question: even if spirit can include otherness and heterogeneity, does it go far enough? Once we have identified this priority of unity, the nature of gathering and belonging present themselves in light of this priority. Belonging to being is central to Heidegger's formulation of *Ereignis*, which implies an assumed proximity between the human and being, an affinity which returns the spectre of humanism to Heidegger's work. Though the human is presented as shepherd of being rather than its master, the human still enjoys a relation of proximity that represents a metaphysical privilege.[31] Thus the privilege that we were worried about in Heidegger's notions of spirit and *Volk* return at this meta-level between the human and being.

This assumption of the propriety of the human and being is one that contemporary French thinkers identify as the core of phenomenological thinking, which they interrogate rigorously. After the Second World War and in the wake of the multiple upheavals of the mid-twentieth century, the ungrounding of phenomenology, philosophy and politics were inevitably 'in the air', requiring a response and a renewal of thought either along some other grounds or, as the case may be, outside of philosophically tainted grounds altogether. Though Deleuze and Derrida chose different paths in thinking through the ungrounding of philosophy, they share this *milieu*. For both, phenomenology presupposes an affinity between thought and being that is untenable, and it becomes important to reinterpret this relation in terms of dissymmetry, which translates for Deleuze in several ways: the nonrepresentational nature of thought, the nonsense within sense, the paradoxical immanence of the Outside (*Dehors*), and difference in itself. The difference between Derrida and Deleuze is itself intriguing, often characterised in terms of a tendency toward negativity on the one side and affirmation on the other. Derrida interprets the outside as the transcendence of the other that remains excessive to the self, while Deleuze interprets the outside as a limit of pure immanence that dissolves the self.[32] Put differently, Deleuze's philosophy offers the possibility of breaking through to the beyond of representation rather than focusing on the impossibility of representing.

As we have seen in the case of art, for Deleuze, phenomenology only reaches the surface of things. Although Merleau-Ponty's flesh as the final avatar of phenomenology does distance phenomenology from the thinking of the subject, it still does not reach the being of sensation, which is to say, the beyond of representation. Just as Bacon's paintings depict the flesh melting from the frames of his figures, we must move beyond flesh. The flesh is only a sign of becoming, 'only the thermometer of a becoming' (QP, 169/179). In other words, there

220

is something outside of our thought that impinges upon it and leaves traces of which we do not *make sense* but with which we engage to produce new thoughts that are incommensurate and do not resemble their sources. Deleuze rejects philosophy's implicit assumption that there is any affinity between thought and being. He is not concerned with the lack of self-transparency of the subject to itself or the correspondence of thought to the lived. Truth is no longer the goal of philosophy, even the reconceived truth of Heidegger's philosophy. In the next chapter, we present precisely how Deleuze envisions a post-Heideggerian change of terrain. From Deleuze's perspective, the dispersion of difference rather than its gathering is that which is truly innovative. Though Deleuze is sympathetic to Heidegger's attempts to think difference, he understands that Heidegger fails due to the circumscription of this project by reverence for the belonging of being and *Dasein*. For this reason Deleuze claims that, however close Heidegger comes to it, he cannot detach himself from the priority of the same, the re-inscribing of thought's dispersion within being.

## Rimbaud Plateau: Car il arrive à l'inconnu?

In this plateau, we situate Heidegger and Deleuze with respect to modernism, some of the indices of which are the shift away from a classical understanding of representation, the increasing emphasis on and fervour over technology and machines, the escalation of urbanisation, extreme political upheaval, and an explosion of artistic creativity. The status of modern art is at issue, as Heidegger dismisses it as rootless, self-referential and subjective, hence, incapable of uniting and grounding a people, or revealing their historical destiny, thereby establishing a homeland.

One can surmise that Heidegger had experienced a sense of urgency with respect to the onslaught of technology and machination, given that the progressive spirit in the post-war Weimar Period was typified by a genuine enthrallment with and remarkable turn toward technological potential. Exemplified by Fernand Léger, the acknowledged artist of the machinic age, in *La Ville* (1919), Le Corbusier's international review *L'Esprit Nouveau* (1920), the Futurist obsession with technological advancement, the Constructivist fascination with economy, efficiency and order, and the Bauhaus slogan 'Art and Technology – a New Unity' (1923), the art world embraced new scientific interpretations, new engineering, new possibilities provided through radio and electric music, and internationalism.[33] The well-accepted fact that Heidegger was not interested in this modern turn in art only serves to underscore his reactive stance toward it. Often, Heidegger's thought is characterised as a retreat from the negative impact of modernism, indicated by his caustic indictment of the globalising tendencies of technology.

By contrast, it is no secret that Deleuze's affinity lies predominantly with those artists of modernity seeking to break with tradition and the past, whose art practices move beyond representation and for whom the devastation and destruction of an epoch are an animating horizon. What is the connection between these artists and Deleuze's own sensibility? What we know is that Deleuze directed himself toward an understanding of 'the times', claiming 'we ought to establish the basic sociotechnological principles of control mechanisms as their age dawns . . . the key thing is that we are beginning something new' (N, 182). Remember that Deleuze approvingly acknowledges Axelos' recognition of the need to philosophise through the technological, within the destruction of value and philosophical foundation, to think within the abyss rather than beyond it. Therefore, it is non-controversial to suggest that Deleuze views these changes quite differently than Heidegger.

In light of the pivotal issue of the technological, which we may also understand in terms of the historical cusp of modernity, we propose another encounter between Heidegger and Deleuze, through the indirect (poetic) voices they invoke, appropriate to our preceding discussion given its focus on the import of Hölderlin for Heidegger's thinking. For Heidegger, the impending danger is announced through Hölderlin's untimely, or prescient, poetry. Clearly, Heidegger sees Hölderlin as a resource for understanding the tumultuousness of the *fin de siècle* and the early 1900s. Yet, Hölderlin is not the only voice of the *fin de siècle*. Arthur Rimbaud, born some ten years after the death of Hölderlin (1843 and 1854 respectively), also stands as a precursor to modernism, and poeticises the changing times from the hitherside of Romanticism, which was to be sure Hölderlin's milieu. Their respective poeticising of breakdown, the 'saying' of the moment as historical event, is decisive. We present Rimbaud as the filmic negative of Heidegger's Hölderlin, a Deleuzian precursor, or inspiration. In contrast with Hölderlin's nostalgia, we understand Rimbaud's poeticising as, however cynical, a forward attentiveness, as a matter of directionality or orientation to *topos* – looking forwards rather than backwards. This may be too simple. We desire to further orient Heidegger and Deleuze's differences through the comparison of Hölderlin and Rimbaud via these categories: pastorality versus urbanity; romantic return versus pure wandering; and the pure and proper versus the bastard and other.

Rimbaud, *le poet maudite*, records the urbanisation of the rural subject, poeticises the revolutionary indices of modernity, the violence of urban decay and the corruption of modernism, his illustrious depictions verging upon the apocalyptic. Yet, the crucial point is that, though professing a biting cynicism with regard to the promise of a utopian future brought about through progress, Rimbaud's poetry is far from nostalgic, or expressive of a yearning for the return of a lost era or origin. There is only going forward, and, though his poetry is paved with blood and destruction, Rimbaud poeticises this moment with strange exaltation:

*What does it matter to us, my heart . . .*

What does it matter to us, my heart, the sheets of blood
And of red-hot coals, and a thousand murders, and long howls
Of rage; sobbings from every inferno destroying
Every (kind of) order; and still the North wind across the wreckage

And all the vengeance? Nothing! . . . – But still, yes
We desire it! Industrialists, princes, senates,
Perish! Power, justice, history: down!
It is our due. Blood! blood! the golden flame!

All to war, to vengeance, to terror,
My soul! Let us turn in the wound: Ah! away with you,
Republics of this world! Of Emperors,
Regiments, colonists, peoples, enough!

Who should stir the vortices of furious flames
But we and those whom we imagine brothers?
It's our turn, romantic friends: we are
Going to enjoy it. Never shall we labour, O fiery waves

Europe, Asia, America – vanish!
Our march of vengeance has occupied every place,
Cities and countrysides! – We shall be smashed!
The volcanoes will explode! And the Ocean, smitten . . .[34]

Rimbaud embraces the destruction and excesses of city life as the symbol of modernity and the possibility of the future, devising an explicit plan of debauchery under the auspices of creative journeying and enlightenment. Nothing could be farther from Heidegger's sensibility, for whom modernism's fascination with technology was indicative of a growing rootlessness of art and humanity and the erosion of any possibility of a groundedness in being.

Yet, one of the main questions that occupies Rimbaud, '*How to make the unknown arrive?*' could pass from the lips of either Deleuze

or Heidegger. This task of bringing forth the unknown has deep resonance with the thought of both philosophers, for whom the unthought
remains a guiding theme. As we have claimed, how each understands
the unthought is of central import for unravelling their philosophic
resonances and dissonances. Both theorise at the limits of thought, and
envision philosophy's task in terms of moving beyond its self-imposed
limitations, and, for both, we clearly have not yet even begun to think.
But their responses to this desire for thought's movement lead us toward
something like opposite affective states: Heidegger's calm sway of
meditative thinking, patiently awaiting the bestowal of *Ereignis*, versus
Deleuze's embrace of Nietzschean dangerous living and adventurous
experimentation on the borders between reason and unreason, or, as
we have said, an inversion of the priority of *Grund* and *Ab-Grund* in
which Deleuze deepens *Ab-Grund* with respect to immanence and difference in itself.

Rimbaud's life is a testament to a self-conscious awareness of the
necessity of catastrophe for attaining the unknown, or by creative extension, the unthought. Rimbaud's self-described aim was to invent the
unknown, and his prescription for how to do this is documented in the
his famous *lettre du voyant*, written to his friend Paul Demeny:

> The Poet makes himself a *seer* by a long, gigantic and rational *derangement
> of all the senses*. All forms of love, suffering, and madness. He searches
> himself. He exhausts all poisons in himself and keeps only their quintessences.
> Unspeakable torture where he needs all his faith, all his super-human strength,
> where he becomes among all men the great patient, the great criminal,
> the one accursed – and the supreme Scholar! – Because he reaches the
> *unknown*![35]

Here, Rimbaud claims a seers' path for poetry, to invent the unknown
(*inventions d'inconnu*), a path which requires the disruption of all sense
as well as the sufferance of all manner of debauchery and excess. In
Rimbaud's world, this possibility must fall to 'the great patient, the great
criminal, the one accursed – and the supreme Scholar! – Because he
reaches the *unknown*!' (*Car il arrive à l'inconnu!*). The necessity of
the derangement of the senses suggests a method of becoming and
a response to modernity. Rimbaud channels death and destruction
through his persona into an unbearable suffering that explodes into a
creative outpouring of the unthought. In other words, Rimbaud enacts
a Nietzschean double affirmation – first, embracing the harbingers of
modernity, a cracked and burning reality, as he exuberantly claims in
*What does it matter to us, my heart . . .*, 'It's our turn, romantic friends:

we are going to enjoy it . . . We shall be smashed! The volcanoes will explode! And the Ocean, smitten . . .'[36] Rimbaud's response is to intensify this milieu, to drive full throttle into the maelstrom, *amor fati* and affirmation! If Deleuze invokes Rimbaud, as Heidegger invokes Hölderlin, this may offer some insight into Deleuze's understanding of the revelations of modernity. Rather than negating or denying the power of technology and the violence and destruction associated with the period, these must be embraced and suffered to render a double affirmation that transforms the reactive into the active in order that the unknown can arrive. And, in fact, this is what modern artists transmute through their art. Modern art is not rootless, it is rooted in the dissolution of an age and thus what it unconceals is not another earth, but the ungrounding of both the earth and world schema, but because of this, modern art moves beyond the hermeneutic circle of being in order to reveal pure difference at the heart of a cosmic becoming that subtends and envelopes these.

Our further claim is that Rimbaud is a poetic avatar of Deleuze's thought of becoming through the deterritorialisation of self. Indeed, Olkowski links Deleuze's advocacy of the unregulated exercise of all the faculties, the creative and disjunctive moment of the third synthesis found in *Difference and Repetition*, to Rimbaud's poetic formula of derangement.[37] Our caveat concerns the *how* of this derangement. Deleuze's is a philosophical derangement of the senses, and though he follows the intent of Rimbaud's method, he does not endorse it to the letter. In *A Thousand Plateaus*, Deleuze claims that there are many ways to make oneself a body without organs, but he specifically derides the kind of absolute deterritorialisation brought about through drugs or alcohol (MP, 187/150). He does not, though, associate Rimbaud purely with this kind of voiding debauchery. Rimbaud's poetic path is also informed by the need to confront alterity in a more intimate form, the alterity that informs the self. In another letter, to which Deleuze makes specific reference, Rimbaud formulates this schism within the self: 'For I is an other. If the tiger awakens . . . I witness the hatching of my thought, I watch it, I study it.'[38] For Rimbaud the derangement of the senses is the loosening of self-identity which would allow the other, the unknown, space to arise. Thus Deleuze identifies Rimbaud as attempting to conceive alienation as an interior limit indicating the fracture of self, which is then interpreted as the impossibility of closure or wholeness of thought to itself, and thus the awareness of thought's constitution from its outside. Deleuze goes on to say that what Rimbaud understands poetically, Kant thinks philosophically as the determination of indeterminate existence, or the arrival of thought, and this within the overall context of the re-conceptualisation of time as linear rather than cyclical, or time out of joint: 'with Kant something absolutely new begins: the other within thought'. Intriguingly, Deleuze has earlier referenced Hölderlin in this same lecture with regard to his Kantian-inspired re-conceptualisation of time as an unfurled line in which a moment of caesura simultaneously distributes a non-symmetrical before and after and which marks the birth of consciousness but also refers back to an indeterminate an-archism: 'So on time as a pure line the caesura of degree zero is marked, which will mean that before and after will no longer rhyme together.' The caesura which constitutes thought's arrival is itself no thought; it is the birth of interiority and the moment of dissipation simultaneously, and this modern consciousness of time also changes the relation to the limit: 'When time becomes a straight line, it no longer limits the world, it traverses it, it is no longer a limit in the sense of limitation, it is limit in this sense: it's at the extremity (bout), it never ceases to be at the extremity, it's the sense of a passage to the limit.' Here and elsewhere, Deleuze is interested in conceptualising a new sensibility brought on by the disorganisation of the senses, which appears under the titles of dramatisation, deterritorialisation and the body without organs (BwO). In dramatisation,[39] one of Deleuze's first attempts to articulate the processes involved in actualising events, the imperative is to affirm the intensive differences that populate any event, to go back in, as it were, and explicate the myriad potentialities that insist, a dramatic counter-actualisation that opens and intensifies the event. The discussion of limit is crucial for making sense of this movement, later associated with the passage to the BwO, which Deleuze calls a limit that can never be reached, corresponding to the sense of limit involved when time is out of joint. Making oneself a BwO is to reach toward degree zero, which then allows intensity to pass through the body, like the move from striated to smooth space.

Some are troubled by deterritorialisation, seeing see no political efficacy in Deleuze, because of what they deem as the absolute nature of the limit; these readings are predicated upon reservations concerning the idea of destruction, which we are here attempting to nuance. There is a double sense of destruction that maps on to our discussion of modernity and Rimbaud: the destruction of our representative models of thinking and the concomitant illusions concerning the wholeness and truth of being, and destruction of the self, which Deleuze, invoking Blanchot, distinguishes from literal bodily demise. The destruction of self indicates the evisceration of the intensive relations that attach it to the body, the disorganisation of our thoughts, and the flooding in of the impersonal and indeterminate: 'The other death, however, the other face or aspect of death, refers to the state of free differences when they are no longer subject to the form imposed upon them by an I or an ego, when they assume a shape which excludes my own coherence' (DR, 149/113). In our analysis of Tournier's novel in Chapter 4, we argued that Deleuze's imaginative projection therein dramatises an intensive dissolution into cosmic elementality, which is present in the preceding quotation. The question that is put forward here, anew, is how to accomplish a derangement of the senses without losing one's mind or destroying the body. How to do this not with drugs and alcohol, which would be the literal voiding of the body without organs, but to create a space of becoming which aligns that sensibility with a philosophical rigour and intensification of thought? Deleuze addresses what it means to go to the limit, to reach toward the zero point, as a kind of dramatisation that requires the specific attunement of affirmation and the activity of experimentation. Our bodies are spaces of potentiality, intensities implicated (literally folded in), which can be explicated (see DR, 305/237). To explicate, or actualise, these potentials is to cancel them, thus to reach a zero point, the intensive must be released through affirmation (DR, 314/243). Yet, Deleuze is also careful to counter this exuberant rush to zero with the admonition not to explicate oneself too much (DR, 314/244); there is an art to what will come to be understood under the heading of deterritorialisation, a careful balancing act that requires a strong spirit, or, perhaps, an artist's sensibility.

In 'How to Make Oneself a Body Without Organs' (MP, chapter 6), Deleuze is interested in the freeing of intensities, which is initiated through the fracture of self and reason, but just as important is the sewing up and cooling down of these intensities, which he describes as the establishment of plateaus, little pieces of immanence (MP, 196/158). Deleuze describes plateaus as continuous regions of intensity which are not interrupted by external termination but neither do they allow themselves to build toward a climax; which reminds us of the proximity of Deleuze's thought to Nietzsche's Great Health, which is to say the intense suffering of the return of everything for all time. One must remember that, on Deleuze's reading, the eternal return is a creative repetition, the paradoxical return of perpetual renewal. The greatest health is like an open wound – living on the surface of a sheer exposure to the outside and suffering the intensification of this moment: 'Robinson, through much suffering, discovers and conquers a Great Health – liberates an image without resemblance' (LS, 370/319). Moreover, for Deleuze, 'Thought is, rather, one of those terrible movements which can be sustained only under the conditions of a larval subject' (DR, 156/118), which also suggests a bare, vulnerable sensitivity to the outside. Thinking is to remain within intensity, to sustain the plateau wherein one experiences oneself as perpetually fractured. In terms of thought, there must be a kind of hyperconceptualisation, layerings upon layerings of ideas forming an intensive matrix that is almost too much to bear: 'drawing together a maximum of disparate series (ultimately, all the divergent series constitutive of the cosmos)' (DR, 159/121).

In characterising the movement of thought, which is also to say the arrival of the unknown, we cannot forget the importance of the being of the sensible for Deleuze, as it is always a dark precursor and a shock from the outside. Deleuze characterises it as an epiphany in which 'cosmic extension coincides with the amplitude of a forced movement which sweeps aside and overruns the series' (DR, 157/120), marking the arrival of the *imprévisible* unknown. Thought is not its own author. We do not construct or control, but, what we can do is cultivate vulnerability with respect to sheer immanence and affectivity. Without the development of this raw sensibility, we may remain unequal to the event. Rimbaud embodies a keen awareness of the need for such a sensibility, channelling the all-encompassing and overwhelming burden of the present in order to transpose it, through torturous double affirmation, into something new, to invent the unknown.

The question is then, what is to be invented? One commentator writes of Rimbaud, '*Inventions d'inconnu* is a remarkable phrase, implying as it does that the unknown is not something pre-existing that poetry might "discover," but an outcome, something that can exist only as a consequence of its having been poetically "invented."'[40] Invention, the arrival of the unknown, relies upon a dual process of defamiliarisation and laying bare of the device, an open fraudulence rendered through trope and figurality. Invention of the unknown is the unconcealment of deception, such as Deleuzian fabulations and simulacra, which are not predicated on a return to origins or a concept of truth. Which brings us to the final aspect of Rimbaud's significance for Deleuze: the nature of Rimbaud's inventing as inspiration for theorising a people-to-come. Rimbaud expresses the recurring theme of 'the search for a missing person who never existed'[41] which bleeds into the intense sense of futurity of his poetic task: 'to make his inventions felt, palpable to listen to'. Thus, he was occupied with inventing himself. Rimbaud's journey to find and even invent himself is an invocation of missingness, which we have claimed, already with Klee, as an essential component of Deleuze's people-to-come.

It is what Rimbaud desires, the persona that he yearns to invent, which is of particular importance. His influence is particularly crucial for understanding the elevation of the mixed and bastard as the banner for a people-to-come, as he constructs a persona castigating the purity of origin and the propriety of his birth. From the first lines of 'Bad Blood',[42] Rimbaud leaves no doubt that he detests his European origins: 'From my Gallic ancestors I have blue-white eyes, a narrow skull, and clumsiness in battle.' He then laments 'the inferiority of his race', 'that never rose up except to loot', and is exhilarated by the thought of an imaginary ancestry: 'I have never belonged to this race', 'The pagan blood comes back!' And finally, oft-quoted by Deleuze and Guattari, 'I am of a race inferior from all eternity . . . I am a beast, a *Negro*.'[43] Deleuze and Guattari recognise Rimbaud's rejection of European whiteness as an affirmation of the racial in all of its impurity and oppression. They invoke this phrase in service of the revolutionary consciousness which 'cuts across the interests of the dominated, exploited classes, and causes flows . . . flows capable of hallucinating history, of reanimating the races in delirium, of setting continents ablaze' (AO, 125/105). In fact, it is this very affirmation of the aleatory and inferior which designates the *minor* as that which opposes fascist and racist thought with all of its incumbent oppression, segregation and exclusion.[44]

Rimbaud's embrace of the inferior, an always differing racial fluidity, provides a model of that which cannot be avowed but must always be invented. The purposeful adoption of this identity suggests Rimbaud as a forerunner of a people-to-come as perpetually minor, eternally incomplete — the potentiality of missingness. Once again referencing Rimbaud, though now in the context of the becoming minor of the artist, Deleuze writes: 'a bastard people, inferior, dominated, always in becoming, always incomplete. Bastard no longer designates a familial state, but the process or drift of the races. I am at best, a Negro of an inferior race for all eternity. This is the becoming of the writer.'[45] Hence, Rimbaud is linked to two methods of becoming: the derangement of the senses and the embrace of the underlying fluidity of all identity, as a model for inventiveness and an example of an active fabulation of self. Rimbaud's path offers a stark contrast to Heidegger's reverence for the majesty of Hölderlin's wanderings, which underscores Deleuze's emphasis on the bastard and mixed as opposed to autochthonous purity. In *Anti-Oedipus*, Deleuze and Guattari deploy a critique of homogeneity and discourses of the proper at a geopolitical level, revealing the contradictions in fascist and nationalist visions, based as they are on mythical grounds of purity and necessary expulsion or oppression, and laying bare the deep-seated racial intensities involved in globalisation and the necessity of a politics of becoming.[46] Deleuze's philosophy names and accelerates bastard and mixed-blood realities, envisioning a people-to-come replete with materially differentiated bodies which resist a homogenising logic of representation that persistently erases otherness as the condition of identity. In the final chapter, we undertake the difficult task of developing the markers of a people-to-come which would maintain its heterogeneity, fluidity and missingness.

## Notes

1. 'These Heideggerian "topics for thought" are not merely elegiac variations on the innocent myth of Arcadia now transplanted into the Alemannic soil of the Black Forest. On the contrary, they constitute the subterranean or chthonic depth-dimension of a National Socialist metaphysics of racial exclusion and superiority that will be dislodged from the biological sphere of Eugenia, blood, and consanguinity even as it is reconfigured rhetorically in the pastoral language of autochthony. Such a maneuver is political to the core.' Bambach, *Heidegger's Roots*, p. 211. See also Victor Farias, *Heidegger and Nazism* (Philadelphia: Temple University Press, 1989).
2. See Beistegui, *Heidegger and the Political*, pp. 19–23.
3. 'It would be a mistake to suppose that Heidegger's insistence on the German people was simply the product of the nationalism of his time. The story according to which the Germans were the privileged heirs of the Greeks and shared a unique relation with them was not original to the twentieth century, although – as Heidegger himself pointed out (GA 53, 98/80) – it took a particularly distorted form among the National Socialists.' Bernasconi, 'Poet of Poets', p. 146.
4. Bourdieu, *Political Ontology of Martin Heidegger*, pp. 7–39. See also Hans Sluga, *Heidegger's Crisis: Philosophy and Politics in Nazi Germany* (Cambridge, MA: Harvard University Press, 1993).
5. Bourdieu, *Political Ontology of Martin Heidegger*, p. 34.
6. Ibid.
7. Beistegui, *Heidegger and the Political*, p. 19.
8. Ibid., p. 51.
9. Ibid., p. 88.
10. Haar, *The Song of the Earth*, p. 62.
11. Ibid.
12. Ibid., p. 63.
13. From 1933 to 1935 Heidegger includes poets, philosophers and state founders as 'authentic creators', but by the late 1930s his scepticism of Hitler is increasingly evident as he no longer includes statesmen. See Michael Zimmerman, *Heidegger's Confrontation with Modernity:*

*Technology, Politics, Art* (Bloomington: Indiana University Press, 1991), p. 114.

14. See Section 9 of Heidegger's *Hölderlin's Hymn 'The Ister'* (GA53).

15. Zimmerman, *Heidegger's Confrontation*, p. 114.

16. This interpretation is substantiated through Hölderlin's first letter to Böhlendorf (1801), which Heidegger takes seriously and incorporates into his philosophic understanding of the destiny of the German people. Heidegger explains this relationship in detail in 'Remembrance' (GA4, 88/112–13).

17. For a discussion of tendencies toward exclusion of heterogeneity from the social body and the concomitant exertion of violent fascist power, as a sovereign form of heterogeneity used to maintain qualities of homogeneity such as duty, discipline, and obedience in the face of the critical disintegration of homogeneous society, see Georges Bataille, 'The Psychological Structure of Fascism', in *Visions of Excess: Selected Writings, 1927–1939*, ed. Allan Stoekl (Minneapolis: University of Minnesota Press, 1985).

18. Bernasconi, 'Poet of Poets', p. 146.

19. See GA65, section 15: 'Philosophy as "philosophy of a people"'.

20. 'Does Heidegger frame history in such a way that it appears as essentially Greco-German? . . . Or are Greece and Germany here names for an asymmetrical relation, where Greece stands for the model of a relation to the foreign or the alien, a model that remains actual only in that respect, that is as an ability to relate to otherness, and where Germany stands as an historical task, as something to be achieved, and thus not as something that is quite yet historical?' Beistegui, *Heidegger and the Political*, p. 110.

21. A 1960 seminar prospectus on *Bild und Image* included Klee's 'On Modern Art', a quote from Heraclitus, a passage from Augustine's *Confessions*, and a passage from Chuang-tzu. Petzet, *Encounters and Dialogues*, p. 59. Most famously, Heidegger's *On the Way to Language* begins with 'A Dialogue on Language (between a Japanese and an Inquirer)', which is most often cited for Heidegger's positive disposition toward Taoist ideas.

22. Heidegger purportedly said, 'if I understand this man correctly, this is what I have been trying to say in all of my writings'. See W. Barrett, 'Zen of the West', in *Zen Buddhism: Selected Writings of D.T. Suzuki* (Garden City: Doubleday Anchor Books, 1956), p. xi.

23. Notably, Graham Parkes, ed., *Heidegger and Asian Thought* (Hawaii: University of Hawaii Press, 1990); Reinhard May, *Heidegger's Hidden Sources: East-Asian Influences on his Work*, trans. Graham Parkes (New York: Routledge, 1996).

24. See Lin Ma, *Heidegger on East-West Dialogue: Anticipating the Event* (New York: Routledge, 2008).

25. Jacques Derrida, *Of Spirit: Heidegger and the Question*, trans. Geoffrey Bennington and Rachel Bowlby (Chicago: University of Chicago Press, 1991 [1988]).
26. For an extended version of this analysis, see Lawlor and Sholtz, 'Heidegger and Deleuze'.
27. Jacques Derrida, '*Geschlecht* I: Sexual Difference, Ontological Difference', *Research in Phenomenology* 5:13 (1983), pp. 65–83.
28. Ibid., p. 69.
29. Ibid., pp. 74–5.
30. Ibid., p. 76.
31. See Jacques Derrida, 'The Ends of Man', *Philosophical and Phenomenological Research* 30:1 (1969), pp. 31–57.
32. See Leonard Lawlor, 'The Beginnings of Thought: The Fundamental Experience in Derrida and Deleuze', in Paul Patton and John Protevi, eds, *Deleuze and Derrida* (London: Continuum Press, 2003).
33. See John Willett, *The New Sobriety: Art and Politics in the Weimar Period 1917–33* (New York: De Capo Press, 1978).
34. Arthur Rimbaud, *Collected Poems*, trans. Oliver Bernard (London: Penguin Books, 1962), pp. 202–3.
35. Arthur Rimbaud, 'Letter to Paul Demeny, 15 May 1871', in *Complete Works, Selected Letters*, trans. Wallace Fowlie (Chicago: University of Chicago Press, 2005), p. 377.
36. Rimbaud, *Collected Poems*, pp. 202–3.
37. Olkowski, *Ruin of Representation*, p. 180. In her excellent reading of Deleuze's 'On Four Poetic Formulas which might Summarize the Kantian Philosophy', which was published as the preface to *Kant's Critical Philosophy: The Doctrine of the Faculties*, trans. Hugh Tomlinson and Barbara Habberjam (Minneapolis: University of Minnesota Press, 1984), Olkowski also refers to Rimbaud as a conceptual persona used by Deleuze to cultivate or enhance our awareness of the innovations of Kantian philosophy, particularly as emblematic of fracturing of the self, that the I is an Other, which becomes apparent as a consequence of Kant's rethinking of time. See Olkowski, 'Beside Us, In Memory', pp. 283–92.
38. All the following references to Deleuze's lecture are from DELEUZE/ KANT, Cours Vincennes 21/03/1978; available at <http://www.webdel euze.com/php/texte.php?cle=67&groupe=Kant&langue=2> (accessed 17 July 2014).
39. See 'The Method of Dramatization' in DI; also chapters 4 and 5 of DR.
40. Rose Chambers, 'On Inventing Unknownness: The Poetry of Disenchanted Reenchantment (Leopardi, Baudelaire, Rimbaud, Justice)', *French Forum* 33:1–2 (2006), pp. 15–36.
41. Referring specifically to *Une saison en enfer* and *Illuminations*. Graham

Robb, *Rimbaud: A Biography* (New York: W.W. Norton, 2001), p. 291.

42. Arthur Rimbaud, 'A Season in Hell', in *Complete Works,* pp. 264–75. Original published as *Une saison en enfer,* 1873. Citation refers to all subsequent lines quoted in this section.

43. Italics indicate a change in the translation. In the original French, the line reads '*je suis une bête, un negre*', which has been translated in this edition as 'I am a beast, a savage.' We have changed the translation in this case, to the more literal translation, which is consistent with Deleuze scholarship and reflects the fuller intensity of the line.

44. Unsurprisingly, Rimbaud was also a resource for the revolutionary spirit of May 1968 in its demise. In the aftermath of May 1968, the research collective, *Les Révoltes Logiques,* took their name from a line in Rimbaud's '*Democritie*'. *LRL* was critical of the role of the intellectual and activist left in speaking for the working class and sought to retrieve a thought from below (*la pensée d'en bas*), acknowledging complexity and plurality of the history of voices comprising the working class. '*Democritie*' evokes the 'wrenching emotional aftermath of the repression of revolution, the lived experience of political possibilities shutting down, the dismantling or dimming of utopian conceptions of change,' a disillusionment shared by *LRL*. See Kristin Ross, *The Emergence of Social Space: Rimbaud and the Paris Commune* (Minneapolis: University of Minnesota Press, 1987) and Ross, *May '68 and Its Afterlives* (Chicago: University of Chicago Press, 2002). Also see Anthony Iles and Tom Roberts, 'From the Cult of the People to the Cult of Rancière', *Mute,* 3:3 (2012), accessed from http://www. metamute.org/editorial/articles/cult-people-to-cult-ranci%C3%A8re (accessed 5 August 2014).

45. Gilles Deleuze, 'Literature and Life', trans. Daniel Smith, *Critical Inquiry,* 23:2 (1997), p. 228.

46. See Arun Saldanha, 'Introduction: Bastard and Mixed Blood are the True Names of Race' and Suzana Milevska and Arun Saldanha, 'The Eternal Return of Race', both in Arun Saldanha and Jason Michael Adams, eds, *Deleuze and Race* (Edinburgh: Edinburgh University Press, 2013).

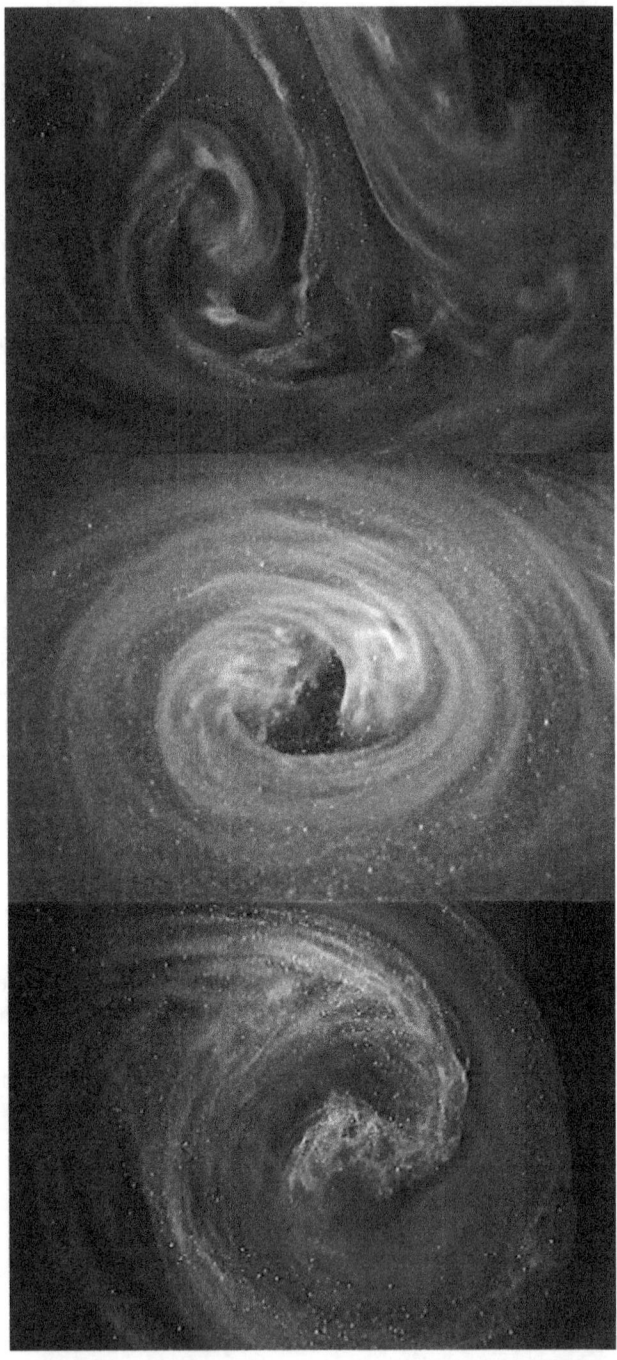

*Figure 6.1* Three stills from Brian Fridge's *Vault Sequence no. 10*, 2000, black and white silent video, 4 minutes.

6

# Deleuze and the Political

*Fridge Plateau: Being True to the Earth, or Cosmic Artisantry*

In 'The Ends of Man', Derrida presents a post-humanist, post-Heideg-gerian Nietzschean Overman, who will not be concerned with the meaning of being, but will instead 'dance outside the house', outside of being-at-home or homecoming, and from whose perspective the question of the truth of being would be the 'last sleeping shudder of the superior man'.[1] What we gather from this is that the question of the 'we' does not go away, but it does necessitate that the terrain of its conception must change. For Deleuze, who claims 'thinking takes place in the relationship of territory and the earth' (QP, 82/85), we can say that this endeavour to rethink the we means re-conceiving our relation to the earth. The question is 'how is earth transformed in Deleuze's philosophy?' and, then, 'what does it mean to be true to it?' We have given preliminary answers, developing a common refrain of the cosmic in Axelos and Klee. Here, we return to this matter in light of the untimely question of the we, drawing primarily from the fertile resources of Deleuze and Guattari's developed account of geophilosophy in *What is Philosophy?* and of a cosmic people in *A Thousand Plateaus* and invit-ing readers to imaginatively project themselves into the cosmic, artisanal space of Brian Fridge's *Vault Sequence n. 10*.

*What is Philosophy?* is remarkable in its clarity and directness, nowhere more evident than in its confrontation with Heidegger. In a stunning passage from the chapter devoted to geophilosophy, Deleuze claims that 'however close he got to it, Heidegger betrays the movement of deterritorialisation because he fixes it once and for all between being and beings, between the Greek territory and the Western earth that the Greeks would have called Being' (QP, 91/95). Deleuze makes two claims here, first with regard to ontological difference and, second, with regard to the philosophic history. In that Heidegger does not go farther than the Greeks, his questioning remains bound to the issue of ontological difference as developed from thinking the origin of philoso-phy as Greek. In other words, Heidegger is impeded by the parameters of his own question, remaining bound to a certain assumption about how being has been thought and, therefore, about what remains to be thought. What is missing is moving beyond the question of philosophy's and our *relationship* to being, beyond the question of ontological difference. We have seen that Heidegger's ontology is marked by its emphasis on the unity of being and that this represents a refusal to move beyond certain predilections for the proper relationship between being and *Dasein* that guarantees the priority of man and consistency of being.

What would it mean to unfix the movement of deterritorialisation from between being and beings? Once ontological difference is recognised, what is the next order of business? Deleuze's criticism of Heidegger implies that to unfix the movement of deterritorialisation would be to see this movement in the very composite nature of beings themselves – a move toward greater immanence. It would be to rid philosophy and thinking of its obsession with truth and authenticity. The difference between beings and being is only one issue, an issue of a particular time, and to remain within its framework is to fail to fully address the issue of the infinite movement of being that underlies it. What is more interesting is this movement and how the process of deterritorialisation works. This is the matter for thought. 'Deleuze's thought is not played out in being-in-the-world, but in the effectuation of a universe, or of several.'[2]

The plateau in *A Thousand Plateaus* entitled 'The Geology of Morals (Who Does the Earth Think It Is)' is instructive on the distinction Deleuze is making here, as the slippage from Nietzsche's genealogy to geology refers us to a history of immanence, rather than historicism. Literally, immanence transforms the scene of history, wresting history from the cult of necessity and reinstituting the priority of contingency (QP, 92/96). Deleuze associates Heidegger and Hegel as similarly committed to the idea of the internal progression of history, by which 'the unforeseeable creation of concepts is thus poorly understood' (QP, 91/95). In other words, there are aspects of being that go undefined within the existing framework of Heidegger's thought. Contingency and the real nature of becoming, as well as what the infinite movement of being entails, are obscured, or rather are undetectable when one assumes the relative stability of this movement between only two poles. Deleuze recognises that the movement of deterritorialisation is not one specific relation, between a certain people and their origin or a certain type of being and its genetic elements, but is a characteristic of every form of becoming, and every moment of development in philosophy, art and science reflects this: 'They do not need the No as beginning, or as the end in which they would be called upon to disappear by being realized, but at every moment of their becoming or their development' (QP, 206/218).

In Heidegger, there is no proliferation of infinite movements but only one instance of infinite movement: 'In Heidegger it is not a question of going farther than the Greeks; it is enough to resume their movement in an initiating, recommencing repetition' (QP, 91/95). Heidegger's thought is marked and impeded by its refusal to relinquish its particular emphasis on origin, on its Greek beginnings. Though Deleuze credits Heidegger with drawing together earth and territory, it is the desire to maintain an analytic and necessary principle linking philosophy to Greece that he opposes (see example 7 in QP, 90/94). Heidegger's refusal to relinquish the notion of origin, however transformed, translates into a specific way of approaching history. If one presupposes an origin, there is a point of departure for history that one may repeat. Thus, the fact that Heidegger's philosophy seems to be a repetition that never gets beyond being, as understood or implicit in its Greek beginnings, is the outcome of his initial starting point and reliance on the cult of origins. That Heidegger remains with this thought is a consequence of the structure of being itself, as Deleuze acknowledges. Heidegger does draw out the basic character of the infinite movement that comprises the earth and the turning away of being leads him to repeat the question, yet go no farther. For Deleuze, it is not that the conjunction of the Greek territory and Western earth is wrong, but that to continue to return to this origin is reductive. Yes, philosophy was something Greek, but this was a fortuitous conjunction of events that produced the encounter between the Greek milieu and the plane of immanence of thought: 'What we deny is that there is any internal necessity to philosophy' (QP, 89/93).

What Deleuze is interested in is the creation of new future earths, not focusing on a particular instance of the deterritorialisation/reterritoriali-sation relationship that has a particular originating point in the Greeks as a project of historical excavation. Territorialising on the Greeks closes off possibilities of the earth as the informal element. Thus, Deleuze presents another view of the earth in immanence, which issues in a geophilosophy and takes the concept of thought's relation to the earth to entirely different levels, or, one might say, strata. Earth can become reterritorialised in multiple ways and according to multiple temporalities; Deleuze re-envisions the untimeliness of history, and the contingency of the event, where the event puts the idea of history into crisis:[3]

Whether physical, psychological, or social, deterritorialisation is relative insofar as it concerns the historical relationship of the earth with the territories that take shape and pass away on it . . . Thinking consists in stretching out a plane of immanence that absorbs the earth (or rather, 'adsorbs' it). Deterritorialisation of such a plane does not preclude reterritorialisation but posits it as the creation of a future new earth. (QP, 85/88)

The upshot is that geophilosophy does not have to translate to a nationalistic metaphysics of the earth, or an underlying metaphysics that privileges one earth over another based on an implicit notion of authenticity. What if the earth itself is moving, changing and becoming? Deleuze describes it thus: 'the earth constantly carries out a movement of deterritorialisation on the spot, by which it goes beyond any territory: it is deterritorialising and deterritorialised' (QP, 82/85). To keep moving, to keep challenging the formations and the dominance of any peoples that do arise is a strategy that acknowledges our human tendencies to overlay reality with our own constructions. It is a more honest way of confronting the underlying chaotic ebbs and flows of the earth, and it yields a very different notion of a people-to-come as that which is always on the periphery, mutating and shooting off into a new direction so that we can barely keep up and must constantly say: the people is missing.

Deleuze acknowledges the element of invention as necessary, and even inevitable, but he is also aware of the egregious errors that can occur. One of the most intense dangers, which Deleuze warns against constantly, is the potential of fascism. He cites Heidegger's own experience as a failed attempt to invent, thus creating a new, possible future and people: 'He got the wrong people, earth, and blood. For the race summoned forth by art or philosophy is not one that claims to be pure but rather an oppressed, bastard, lower, anarchical, nomadic and irremediably minor race' (QP, 104–5/109). As we have argued, it is decisive that Deleuze agrees with Heidegger's overall intuition concerning the conjunction of these elements, and yet so clearly denies his results.

Defining a people will always involve drawing together territory and earth, yet, because of the prevailing of contingency, these contours are bound, in one instant, by that which is uncontrollably beyond and, in another, artifice. Two ways that one can think of the invention of a people in relation to artifice are myth and fabulation, which we link to Heidegger and Deleuze respectively. We can begin to understand the difference between fabulation and myth in terms of our discussion of Rimbaud. Rimbaud's inventing of the unknown relies on laying bare the device – akin to the acceptance of the powers of the false, which Deleuze undertakes to uphold both in *Difference and Repetition* and in terms of the simulacrum, while myth seeks to create an origin that, though invented, harkens back to an immemorial past in order to found and give the community a holistic view of itself.[4] Nancy critiques the genre of myth along just these lines. For Nancy, the interruption of myth is a positive strategy for escaping the violence of the logic of exclusion, by making it impossible to represent our common origin. Linking back to Lyotard's criticism of grand narratives, he replaces myth with the interminability and plurality of literature, *le petit récits*. Deleuze's concept of fabulation is akin to this move, yet, as Bogue points out, fabulation represents a highly specific approach to literature including the demands of becoming other, experimentation, legending, inventing and the deterritorialisation of language – indices of that which Deleuze refers to as the minor.[5] Deleuze takes the concept of fabulation from Bergson's *The Two Sources of Morality and Religion*, in which Bergson represents fabulation as an ominous power to create fictive visions so vivid and haunting that they may regulate behaviour.[6] Deleuze foregoes this restrictive view, by transferring registers from the religious to the free development of fabulatory fictions through art and literature (QP, 162/230n8). One of the clearest differences between Heideggerian mythologising of a people and Deleuzian fabulation pertains to time. For Heidegger, becoming a people is to become historical, to take up the past which was never present: and thus to be to be 'transposed into our endowment', which is to become thoroughly *Unheimlich*, as wanderers through what is strange to return to what is ownmost. 'From our human experience and history, at least as far as I am informed, I know that everything essential and great has only emerged when human beings had a home and were rooted in a tradition. Today's literature is, for instance, largely destructive.'[7] Deleuze, by contrast, explicitly claims that 'fabulation has nothing in the least to do with memory', reminding us once again of Rimbaud: the fabulating artist is 'a seer (*voyant*), a becomer (*devenant*)' (QP, 161/171), who embraces another kind of wandering, one with no return. In other words, we must not forget the timeliness in their thinking, its particular orientation. Deleuze experiences modernity and the technological from a different vantage than Heidegger, for whom, at least until his later years, there was a possibility of retreat or thought's retrieval. Deleuze approvingly claims that Axelos has converted Heidegger's terminology from the 'country to the city' (ID, 218–19/157–8). Our entry into this conversation will be in the form of a question: Given the unchallenged diagnoses of the planetary era (the technological age), is there the same sense of destitution for Deleuze as for Heidegger, and, if not, why not? With the onslaught of the planetary, Heidegger increasingly sees no way out (i.e. only a god can save us now). On the other hand, Deleuze conceives thinking from out of destruction and immanent to the technological, channelling the disillusionment of a generation, wrestling with a shattered world, and subject to the deterritorialising effects unleashed by atomic and capitalist forces. With this in mind, let us return to the issue of art.

Deleuze has the backdrop of modernity from which to draw, whereas Heidegger was only just recognising the potential of someone like Klee for rethinking philosophy. The affects of modern art which clearly fascinate and occupy Deleuze have this in common – they are grappling with a milieu forged in discontinuities, discordances and disseminations. Citing Klee specifically, Deleuze claims, 'If there is a modern age, it is, of course, the age of the cosmic' (MP, 422/342). In a remarkable passage from 'Of the Refrain' in A Thousand Plateaus, Deleuze provides an analysis of modernity, which speaks directly to a potential people-to-come and has stood in the background of our thinking of the cosmic from the beginning of this project:

> Finally, it is clear that the relation to the earth and the people has changed, and is no longer of the romantic type. The earth is now at its most deterritorialized: not only a point in a galaxy, but one galaxy among others. The people is now at its most molecularized: a molecular population, a people of oscillators as so many forces of interaction. The artist discards romantic figures, relinquishes both the forces of the earth and those of the people. The combat, if combat there is, has moved. The established powers have occupied the earth, they have built people's organizations. The mass media, the great people's organizations of the party or union type, are machines for reproduction, fuzzification machines that effectively scramble all the terrestrial forces of the people. The established powers have placed us in the situation of a combat at once atomic and cosmic, galactic . . . The question then became whether molecular or atomic 'populations' of all natures (mass media, monitoring procedures, computers, space weapons) would continue to bombard the existing people in order to train it or control it or annihilate it – or if other molecular populations were possible, could slip into the first and give rise to a people yet to come (people à venir) . . .
> Never has the artist been more in need of a people, while stating most firmly that the people is lacking – the people is what is most lacking. We are not referring to popular or populist artists. Mallarmé said that the Book needed a people. Kafka said that literature is the affair of the people. Klee said that the people is essential yet lacking. Thus the problem of the artist is that the modern depopulation of the people results in an open earth, and by means of art, or by means to which art contributes. Instead of being bombarded from all sides in a limiting cosmos, the people and the earth must be like the vectors of a cosmos that carries them off; then the cosmos itself will

be art. From depopulation, make a cosmic people; from deterritorialization, a cosmic earth – that is the wish of the artisan-artist, here, there, locally. (MP, 426–8/345–6)

Heidegger awakened the trembling ground with his questioning about the relation of earth and people, yet we can see that Deleuze acknowledges and embraces the subterranean rumbling of the ground that makes Nietzsche dance, taking the trembling to another level and asking in all literalness: what about this trembling ground, this trembling, rumbling underneath every edifice, every being and all Being? The human does not disappear from his analysis, but it must become that which understands itself from a conception of earth and Being of pure and radical immanence, that cuts through the values that we have imposed and smashes the boundaries between the human and the nonhuman. What characterises the modern age is a different relation to matter, looking beyond the matter-form relation to the direct relation of material-forces, molecularised matter which issues in a molecularised people. The Earth is envisioned here as a plane of rhythmic, intensive vibration which displaces the question of the origin of a people toward questions of pure relations, chance encounters, and perpetual motion (oscillators). The modern figure responsive to this terrain is not founder (and, of course, we think of Heidegger here), not creator, not even artist, but a cosmic artisan (MP, 426/345), working from within the scrambling of terrestrial forces – machines, mass media, computers, weapons. Deleuze and Guattari define the artisan as 'one who is determined in such a way as to follow a flow of matter, a machinic phylum. The artisan is the itinerant, the ambulant. To follow the flow of matter is to itinerate, to ambulate' (MP, 509/409). Therefore, a cosmic artisan would be one who follows the flow of cosmic forces and intensities. The cosmic artisan intensifies and enlivens the event, connecting flows and traversing genres, in order that the bombardment of the miniscule, the mundane, or the machinic is transmuted into a vision of excessive beauty and invention.

Brian Fridge's *Vault Sequence* is a stunning example of the possibilities of cosmic artisanal production. *Vault Sequence No. 10*, a silent four-minute black-and-white video, can be seen at the Modern Art Museum of Fort Worth. The work is an assemblage of the technological and the natural, capturing the mundane processes of suspended ice formation, which issues in a spectacular cosmic scene, one that elicits comparison with entire galaxies and challenges the imagination with possible worlds. Utilising a camcorder to capture ice and vapour moved by condensation in a freezer, Fridge's piece accomplishes a double deterritorialisation of expectation and forces, of our impression of nebulous and far away universes, and the mundane functions of appliance and water. The installation is a destabilised artistic space in which the viewer is enveloped by the installation which plays across the entire wall, surrounded by the projection of these micrological processes writ large. Rather than understanding the cosmic as a matter of otherworldliness, and lines of flight as literally flying off from the earth into the universe, Fridge's work brings us a vision of inter-worldly cosmic intensity – of immanence. The cosmic is inside us, it is us, molecular movement and the coursing of spatio-temporal dynamisms operating on the plane of immanence. Accordingly, Fridge's work illustrates the possibilities within the terrestrial, technologically saturated world, to harness these forces and put them to minor uses that open us to experiences of the extra-ordinary, the unexpected and the imperceptible. The work arrests us in its perpetual motion, made possible only through the intervention of technology,[8] in a way that overwhelms us by the affect of the cosmic, directly rather than intellectually (the immediate rather than the mediated).

Since everything exists on the same plane of immanence, it is not a matter of dispensing with or changing the conditions of the cosmic age, our milieu, but of what we do with it. This is why art is so important for Deleuze: the potential exists for the technological to be dominated by mechanical reproduction, overcome by the masses, characterised by the lack of thinking, or we become cosmic artisans – capable of fabulating – and, by tapping into the self-organising and emergent capacities of molecularised material, 'loose molecular populations in hopes that this will sow the seeds of, or even engender, the people to come, that these populations will pass into a people to come, open a cosmos' (MP, 427/345). Cosmic artisans exist at the limit, are fabulators in the sense that they actualise lines of flight, potentials that exist immanently, virtually, intensively. For Deleuze, it has always been the case that we are dealing with forces to be harnessed; it has only become the case that we are in a situation to respond to this, to perceive it, as Deleuze says. Thus, rather than destitution, there is hope?

As opposed to the kind of exclusionary myths that create a people based on a common origin, blood or race, or even language, in which art speaks to a particular earth of a particular people, the kind of people that arise from this earth would have to be brought together out of their common dispersion, from the very fact that they are engaged in or produced by the deterritorialisations of dominant (molar) apparatuses, and from the artisan's liberation of these mired forces and products. So the question of what it means to be a people in this world is a very different question, but one that we must still ask, even after this notion has been uprooted. We do not abandon the idea of peoples completely, but our idea of what it means to be on this earth must correspond to the real conditions of the world. This is the task for humanity — to become a people that parallels the ebbs and flows of the earth, but the earth reconfigured not as homeland or as proper to us or as 'ours' in any way, but as one that includes forces that may well overwhelm and swallow us.

If for Heidegger a people is defined by its relation to the earth, for Deleuze a people goes beyond grounding altogether. The cosmic also relates to the un-grounding of worldly meaning and human referentiality, because 'the great refrain arises as we distance ourselves from the house' (QP, 181/191). The great refrain is the Deterritorialised, the Cosmos or pure plane of immanence, while the house refers to the grounding of these forces. In going beyond the earth, we also change what it means to be human: 'even if this is in order to return, since no one will recognize us any more when we come back' (QP, 181/191). That 'no one will recognize us anymore' implies that we move beyond our generic ideals of the human. By engaging on levels of affect rather than at the level of subjects, becoming happens on imperceptible levels that eventually change us. 'The affect certainly does not undertake a return to origins . . . it is a question only of ourselves, here and now; but what is animal, vegetal, mineral, or human in us is now indistinct' (QP, 164/174). We are part of machinic assemblages that include all of these. We artificially limit ourselves, our humanity, by thinking of these things as other than us. According to Deleuze, becoming imperceptible is what we are rushing toward in order that we may more authentically join in the unending intensive flow of cosmic being, to 'better make audible the truth that all becomings are molecular' (MP, 379/308).

Having distinguished Heidegger and Deleuze's orientation toward invention (historical founder or cosmic artisan), we proceed to ask, 'What kinds of invention does Deleuze's art imply?', and, in the interest of diligence, 'what justifies Deleuze's view over any other?' How can one make the claim that one perspective on invention is more adequate than another, if there is no truth to any and we take his claims of immanence seriously? Is it merely the value of inclusion that guides Deleuze's judgement that Heidegger got the wrong earth, the wrong people? One could defer to pragmatism at this point, i.e. his system is better because it does not yield fascism, while the other obviously did.

Yet, Deleuze is not making a claim to a better interpretation of a people but to a new model for thinking of a people as such, one which would be able to account for an infinite number of fabulations while allowing that there is something beyond our fabulations, beyond our humanity that engages us. Can we begin to give an outline of how this cosmic people might be composed? Deleuze provides the conceptual figures to do so, and we propose to draw these lines of thought together to provide a sketch, an outline or diagram, of this people – because to do more would be to mar the intensely fragile mobility that it requires. In what follows, we explore the various parameters of art and territory in order to provide an outline of a cosmic people and then address how art is integral to inventing fabulations that support such a vertiginous model.

## A Model-less Model of a People-to-come: Missing, Minor, Cosmic

The problem of the model-less:

> A good group does not take itself to be unique, immortal, and significant, unlike a defense ministry or homeland security office, unlike war veterans, but instead plugs into an outside that confronts the group with its own possibilities of nonsense, death, and dispersal 'precisely as a result of its opening up to other groups.' (DI, 270–1/193)

In *A Thousand Plateaus*, Deleuze presents a model of group formation that draws upon the elements of the aesthetics of territory formation that we have previously described. The good group, as opposed to the mass characterised by homogeneity and indistinctiveness, follows the model of the pack, characterised by heterogeneous parts and the anomalous as a bounding yet fluid ordering structure. This conception of group interaction addresses the problem of inclusivity and exclusivity and represents the politics of becoming by conceiving of a collectivity as a multiplicity-assemblage, emphasising the fringe (minoritarian), contagion (change), and the between (relations), which affirms the absolutely contingent as a positive and necessary condition (MP, 305–6/249–50).

For the purpose of the analogy with art, we begin with the role of the anomalous. Notably, Deleuze emphasises its priority as well: 'All that counts is the borderline – the anomalous' (MP, 300/245). As a porous, mutable borderline that defines the pack, the anomalous is 'neither individual nor species; it has only affects' (MP, 299/244), suggesting that it operates at the level of the sensible and pre-personal. Rather than representing a category (of individuals or species) that the pack then identifies with, the anomalous connects with its interior group by means of partial objects and affects. Just as its name suggests, the anomalous is atypical, even deviant.[9] It is not related to the pack through recognition or resemblance, and just as the artwork destroys clichés of prior representation and creates new orderings, the anomalous creatively retraces its boundaries and is a catalyst for group mutation by selecting affects from its composite, sometimes drawing from its centre and sometimes introducing new affects that it encounters from the outside. It is the act of drawing a dynamic line which members of the group attain and then re-group from.

Emphasising the anomalous allows Deleuze to question the fierce duality and separation between the inside and the outside. As a phenomenon of bordering, the anomalous calls attention to the reciprocal relation between the exterior and interior just as the framing does for the artwork. It represents the encounter of new singularities from the outside that can be swept up by those internal to it. The point is that the borderline is a mechanism of transformation by which the group can enter into becomings, yet it is also a thin membrane to ward off total dissipation, a continuance of the dual imperative of deterritorialisation: explicate but not too much! Each group is a multiplicity, composed of heterogeneous forces and affects that are continually transforming. Defined by externality, it is a system that remains open to the outside, rather than a unity or totality that opposes itself to objects that remain other.

In what follows, we link this model of group formation to the criteria of missingness and the minor, which traffic positively in the nebulous and provide new methods of approach to infinite variation. Related to the first of these criteria, Paul Klee prophetically pronounced: 'For we still lack the ultimate power, for: the people are not with us. But we seek a people.'[10] Deleuze understands this as the expression of a need. He thus adopts the theme of a missing people, *le peuple qui manqué* (who are lacking), as a way of enjoining us to think of a people-to-come and the role of art in its invention. In *Cinema II* Deleuze, bequeathing to art its political space, concludes: 'if there were a modern political cinema, it would be on this basis: the people no longer exist, or not yet'.[11] Rather than a lament, Deleuze views a missing people as a positive criterion for the creative act and vision. He says, 'this acknowledgement of a people who are missing is not a renunciation of political cinema, but on the contrary a new basis on which it is founded' (CII, 217). The element of missingness is thus indicative of Deleuze's political vision. Rather than the

Romantic utopian vision of a people, who come together on the basis of a shared history, rootedness and return to origins, or a vision of an idyllic future, the people of which Deleuze has need are culled from the process of fabulation,[12] as a self-aware process of invention drawn from the powers of the false. Deleuze could not be clearer on this matter: 'art must take part in this task . . . of contributing to the invention of a people' (CII, 217). If we grant 'missingness' as a positive criteria, we can say that a people-to-come is not true, it is not whole, it is not pure; instead, a people-to-come is lacking, or one might say, in process of becoming and thus never complete.

Klee suggests that art must be conceived as an enactment of genesis and that this 'gives birth to new possibilities', but also requires a people adequate to it. Deleuze sees in Klee a counterpart to his own thoughts about a people. Focusing on genesis in itself, Klee taps into the world of forces and intensities that Deleuze is attempting to reveal. Klee laments that the people is lacking yet essential. A missing people corresponds to Klee's call for a people adequate to modern art. The missing people will resonate with the responsibilities formerly enumerated. It will be one that is adequate to the conditions of immanence, and thus it will always have the quality of missingness, because creative becoming is the condition of living. As we have seen, Deleuze was also inspired by Rimbaud's inventions, his fabulating of a minor identity. Rimbaud's cognisance of the racial inadequacy of his own white Anglo background and constant denigration of cultural homogeneity fills out the picture, hence the qualification of the people-to-come as bastard, anarchical, mixed.

The second of our criteria, Deleuze's concept of the minor, stands as an important intermediary between the visceral and visionary discussion of the cosmic and Deleuze's minoritarian politics, or nomadology. Deleuze develops the theme of minority in *Kafka: Towards a Minor Literature*, which in turn is related to the summoning forth of a minor people. The criteria of the minor are: (1) it is affected by a high degree of deterritorialisation; thus the minor must always happen from within the larger molar structures that it must or does deterritorialise; (2) that everything to do with a minor literature is political, connecting with the social milieu; in other words, it uses the same elements as the major and is composed within the major political system, producing a movement from 'inside' the major; (3) that everything takes on a collective value, and as such involves a collective enunciation and a calling forth of new kinds of collectivities. This last criterion should be linked to the image of group formation presented earlier.

Above all, minor practice involves resistance, resistance to the territorialisations of the present, to coded social flows and to the overcodings of the state. To become minor is to connect the elements of the major (these codings) differently; for instance, to make a major language stammer through new idioms and the arresting of its sense, or to take from one register and connect with another. For example, when I had taken up residence in Paris, some young Parisians had a phrase which caught my attention: *Tu as un probleme* became *t'as'bleme*. It seemed to me that they were flouting the infamous national pride in the beauty of the French language as well as the tendency to socially demarcate individuals according to that language. This was more than slang, it was political, addressed to a generation who were disenfranchised, under-educated, unemployable by the standards of the mainstream. Spoken with a deep, guttural affect, the shortened phrase was unrecognisable to those who were 'well-spoken', but to those who used the phrase, it connoted a forceful challenge: 'Do you have a problem?'

The inventiveness of the minorisation of language takes many forms according to Deleuze and Guattari. In *Kafka*, Deleuze espouses the ability of minor literature to reveal a revolutionary potential, one which takes the idea of the minor to a more radical extreme than in our example. The minor can follow the sober path of syntactical invention, can operate through mixture and the slidings of portmanteaus, or it can involve the release of language from sense altogether, such as the cries and gasps of Artaud's theatre and the animal warbles of Kafka's Gregor (K, 48–9/26). Yet, this always happens by the minor working from within the major, as is the case with our example of the manipulation of the French language. There is something stirring within this example, the promise or inevitability of a constant variation that may be released. The French language is connected in a new and deviant way. This practice is a collective enunciation, one that gathers together those dissatisfied with the social hierarchy and exclusionary nationalism in France. Minor practices like this have the potential to draw a people together. These practices are always localised, specific and transitory, because otherwise they risk becoming rigidified and absorbed back into the major. In other words, one of the characteristics of the minor is that it is always in process and becoming. This is something that we must incorporate into our notion of a people-to-come. A Deleuzian people-to-come will have this in common: their exclusion from dominant systems, their excessiveness to any model, perhaps their 'failure to live up to any model'.[13] This is a politics of the dispossessed, the divergent and anomalous, on the fringes of society, as opposed to the major State politics or a dominant politics of homogeneity. The minor is deviant with respect to the majoritarian regime and always connotes a disruption of the dominant system, but a productive, creative disruption. To use the language of deterritorialisation, lines of flight must never just be about escape; they must also be creative. Combining resistance and the cosmic, one recognises that a minor people is a people that breaks free of habitual modes of representation, a people engaged in the processes of becoming and taking up the molecular side of being, imagining and inventing new subjectivities, connecting in new and creative ways, capturing new forms of life.

Of course, the minor is a concept developed specifically in relation to art. Art, in its a-signifying capacity, operates to disrupt sense and meaning and dominant systems of thought. Therefore, art is a catalyst for becoming minor, for the transformation of politics: 'Creation is always a controversial deviance with regard to the dominant values which define a normal society. Art follows life and the same process which drives privileging the body without organs over constituted organisation drives posing the minoritarizing of cultural norms as veritable creation.'[14] Moreover, in the disruption of sense that art produces, the being of the artwork, the sensible aspect or affective quality, rises to the fore. It is the creative aspect of the artwork that allows for the creation of new peoples rather than just a critique of old regimes.

In 'From Stuttering and Stammering to the Diagram: Deleuze, Bacon and Contemporary Art Practice', Simon O'Sullivan extends the idea of the minor by combining the criteria for a minor literature with those of art practices, thus linking the political imperative of a minor people with the deterritorialising features of art which Deleuze develops primarily in *Logic of Sensation*. O'Sullivan develops the figural as a key feature of art indicative of its propensity toward the minor. The figural is used by Deleuze to distinguish the non-representative tendencies, or potential, inherent in artworks from the traditional understanding of the representative function of art. The figural deforms the figurative, through isolation (minimalism). This isolation serves to open the figural to new series.[15] Sullivan also emphasises probe-heads, using Bacon's paintings as exemplars of this element of the artwork. Probe-heads function against the processes of faciality (i.e. significance and subjectification), these are lines of escape from determined and recognisable representations. We can interpret these probes as liberations of sensual materials or potentialities within the various art forms – music: sonority; painting: figure and colour.

The final element indicating how art is minor is the diagram, which, as we have seen, always has a deterritorialising function, meant to reveal the heterogeneity of expressive materials. The essential point of the diagram is contingency. Thus, 'random occurrences are ontologically constitutive of art'.[16] This opens up possibilities of multiplicity or proliferation. Philosophically, the diagram is the *in between*, marking the event of becoming. These elements – the figural, isolation, probe-heads (or liberation of elements), and the diagram – serve to open the canvas or framework onto its outside, to dissolve the clichés of representation and habituation. These elements amount to the equivalent (for minor art) of Deleuze's stammering of language (for minor literature), what O'Sullivan refers to as 'the glitch'.[17] The glitch is what one might call the power of art to counteract signifying regimes as a rupturing event.

These models of precariousness which connect philosophy to the creative impetus of art can help us understand a people-to-come, which is always minor and thus in process. Indeed, Deleuze's vision includes an incessant process of reorganisation, an infinite and continuous movement that eschews the death of fixed form and invariability. A missing people is equal to the untimeliness of the event. A cosmic people is a people that understands itself and connects through affects and forces, enframed yet constantly negotiating itself via these connections and exchanges. Just as the anomalous is not a matter of the exceptional individual, a people is not determined at the individual level, as separate ego-entities. Instead, a people is individualised 'according to the affects it experiences' (MP, 421/341) at the level of the pre-personal, and molecular.

The logic of defining and providing criteria for a people-to-come illuminates one more risk which always remains implicit in such an endeavour or remains a possibility within such practices: the risk of becoming reterritorialised as a method of fascistic control. Logically, as soon as a people is defined, it can be stratified and absorbed into regimes of dominance or state apparatuses – this is always a possibility, especially so in what Deleuze refers to as our contemporary 'control societies'. Moreover, this must be the case if one remains committed to a thoroughgoing immanence. In order to address this, Deleuze links the invective of deterritorisation to a political stance which corresponds to a particular topology and movement, which productively de-centres the *polis* by countering it with *nomos* in order to open a new space of conceptualisation and concept of space. In what follows, we correlate the hypothetical model suggested above to nomadological traversing of smooth space found in *A Thousand Plateaus*.

## Nomadic Wandering, or Against the Sedentary as Minoritarian Politics

In *A Thousand Plateaus*, Deleuze and Guattari develop the concept of the nomadological war machine as a model for minoritarian political and social assemblages. Nomadology operates according to the principles of the war machine and can be understood, noologically, as a critical consciousness of constantly questioning and resisting socially coded or rote paradigms, and, topologically, by a constantly shifting borderline reminiscent of the anomalous and continuous variation, always in tension with the existing dominant social order (see MP, esp. 434–81/351–87). Deleuze and Guattari outline three distinct aspects of the nomadological war machine: (1) spatiogeographical; (2) arithmetic or algebraic; (3) affective. Most pertinent to our discussion is that nomadology requires a specific relation to the earth and locality. Deleuze and Guattari oppose the closed space and sedentary living of the *polis*, understood as bounded and limited spaces of the state (striated), to the deterritorialised, open space and fuzzy aggregation of the *nomos* (smooth). Thus, this discussion of nomadology is integrally connected to its non-dialectical relation to the state apparatus.

In terms of the spatiogeographic aspect, Deleuze and Guattari offer several clarifying interventions. First, they differentiate between nomads and migrants. While migrants move from point to point, the nomad exists in the intermezzo, the between of two points. What this suggests is that the process of what happens in between is what is important rather than the goal of reaching another point; moving from point to point is only a consequence: 'There exists a nomadic absolute, as a local integration moving from part to part and constituting smooth space in an infinite succession of linkages and changes in direction. It is an absolute that is one with becoming itself, *with process*' (MP, 617/494, emphasis added). Nomads distribute themselves in a constantly renegotiated open space, rather than a closed space to be filled. This means that the *nomos* is experimental and fluid. In other words, nomadism suggests 'the kind of

subjects who relinquish all ideas, desire, or nostalgia for fixity'.[18]
Second, the *nomos* does not parcel out space to people (as would the
State), but instead distributes people in space (upsetting the value of
property as a war machine decoding). Deleuze and Guattari liken
this handling of space to the constitution of a fuzzy aggregate, which
recalls our understanding of the amorphous pack and our discussion
of the spatial dynamism of the territorial milieu. Boundaries are in
flux, permeable. Finally, the overall paradigm for the relation of the
nomad to the earth is the deterritorialised, because there is precisely
no reterritorialisation but instead a constant forwardness, what we
have called a wandering without return. Summarily, the nomad is
defined by no points, paths or lands (MP, 473/381), a poignant counterpoint to the Heideggerian language of destiny, paths and earth.

Yet, counterintuitively, Deleuze and Guattari are not advocating that everyone literally uproot themselves, become nomads and
roam the earth, though they are suggesting that nomadology reveals
a different way of being in relation to space and others that can be
incorporated and mobilised for political activity and change. It offers
a way of living outside the model of the state apparatus, which preserves itself vociferously through domination and control of spaces
to make social order and rule intractably sedentary. The wandering
or movement that happens via nomadology happens in place. Indeed
the most definitive attribute of the nomad is that it *occupies* smooth
space, thus the nomad does not move as in the traditional or literal
understanding. Rather, the movements happen in places and signify
a different relation to those places:

> Voyage in place: that is the name of all intensities, even if they also
> develop in extension. To think is to voyage; earlier we tried to establish
> a theo-noological model of smooth and striated spaces. In short, what
> distinguishes the two kinds of voyages is neither a measurable quantity of
> movement, nor something that would be only in the mind, but the mode
> of spatialization, the manner of being in space, of being for space. Voyage
> smoothly or in striation, and think the same way ... (MP, 602/482)

In order to understand this, nomadic thought and practices have to
be linked to the discussion of the two kinds of multiplicity provided
at the beginning of Chapter 4. Rather than a segmented multiplicity
that divides according to the equal, it is a matter of a multiplicity
that changes in kind, or, vis-à-vis the nomad, that changes the space.
This is why no one will recognise us when we return, because we do
not return. This is why we have suggested nomadology as a critical

consciousness; there is a change in relation to place that occurs immanent to that space.

As a matter of delineation, if the definitive characteristic of the nomad is that it occupies and holds smooth space, the war machine invents the nomad because it is constitutive of smooth space. The war machine, in a non-dialectical relation to the state apparatus, is characterised by the tendency or sheer function of decoding, and as such is always exterior and irreducible to the state apparatus. While the state reproduces itself and is constituted by its interiority, the war machine 'exists only in its metamorphoses' (MP, 446/360) as a perpetual field of interaction which emphasises process rather than end.

The other particularly salient aspect of the war machine is that it operates at the level of affects, which perpetuate relays, unforeseeable connections, and transversal lines that disrupt territories and burst out upon exterior smooth space. Here one finds Deleuze and Guattari's fiercest language concerning the power of affect, as they likenthem to projectiles or weapons (see Proposition VII, MP, 491/395). Distinguishing affect, as an active discharge of emotion, from feeling, as always displaced, retarded, resisting emotion, allows Deleuze and Guattari to make another distinction that gives us an insight into the specific way they conceive of a war machine: Affects are projectiles just like weapons; feelings are introceptive like tools (MP, 497–8/400). Whereas the semiotisation of the sign-tool makes it immobile, interior, the activity of capture by state-apparatus, the a-signifying quality of the affect, makes it essentially disruptive, an event of decoding.

Thus a nomadological consciousness would be one that is prepared by the sensibility we have advocated in the previous chapters – a sensitivity to the affect, the imperceptible, the being of sensation – in order that connections, flows and relations, are made through affect, rather than through identification between constituent members, and can be the inspiration for drawing creative intersections and new lines of development. This is a political theatre elaborated in assemblages that are neither those of family, religion, nor State but conceived rather in terms of territorial aesthetics and functions, ultimately yielding a people concerned with forces and engendering new connections rather than remaining bound by particular territories and identities.

Deleuze and Guattari say that nomadology everywhere approaches the totalising, universalising effects of State stratification as a war machine which undoes them. This undoing of things raises the difficult issue of political violence as constitutive of nomadology and the dilemma of creative destruction: 'Lines of flight . . . are very dangerous for societies' (MP, 250/204), yet they are also instrumental in producing a milieu in which change is possible. There are, of course, several worries. The first of which is that there is always the possibility, and in many respects an inevitability, that the war machine will be appropriated for the state apparatus, thus immobilising its affects and rendering a method of control *tout court*. The second is the totalisation of the war machine, which would amount to another kind of fascism. If the model of the war machine were extended to the entire earth, even to constitute smooth space, it would signify a totalising and debilitating process of enclosure.[19] Recognising these inherent dangers, Deleuze and Guattari insist that war machines must remain local and singular, and nomadology must remain minoritarian, a powerful fringe that exists *between* the territories of the state apparatus. In both instances, what has ceased to exist is the fundamental aspect of movement, or constant variation as that which connects the war machine to the deterritorialised earth and constitutes the essential value of nomadology in the first place.

As a final caveat to these types of worries, it must be noted that disruption is not necessarily violence. In Proposition IX, Deleuze and Guattari begin by claiming that the war machine does not have war as its object, though battle may be its necessary result (MP, 518/416). The Occupy Wall Street movement provides an example of how the war machine decodes, but through non-violent methods. As Ian Buchanan aptly observes, 'Occupy Wall Street and the corresponding Occupy Movement that sprang up in its wake was premised on the idea that change is not achieved by violence or extortion, but rather by presence and permanence.'[20] Occupy Wall Street, in its first iteration, brought the *nomos* and its war machine to the city, turning a public park into a land, creating a fluid open space within the heart of the New York City grid. Their main intent was to be a persistent presence, *to occupy*, in order to challenge the phantasmic image of American democracy and draw attention to how it has become infiltrated by a political and economic despotism.

Occupy's refusal to stake out a boundary for their discourse or assign leadership indicates the desire for a new kind of political organisation and invites easy parallels to the nomadological, with the anomalous nature of its make-up and borders. Occupy had the effect of confounding mainstream media, an outlet that can certainly be aligned with the paradigm of the state apparatus, because the

occupiers refused to speak in the language of demands and plat-
forms; they demanded nothing except to be noticed.[21] Their silence
spoke volumes, as Ian Buchanan aptly identifies: 'it made the point
that there is no democratic agency in the US that their concerns could
be addressed to because all of them are in some way or another
beholden to the corporate world'.[22] This was pure interruption, and
it unleashed a plethora of affects, arousing the ire and spite of the
media and politicians, revealing an ugly willingness of individuals to
castigate and disparage – perhaps as the result of opening a wound in
American consciousness concerning the frailty of its ideal. Yet, also
endemic to the event is that it has generated a new discourse and new
concepts which have indelibly left a mark and changed the linguistic
landscape. Occupy Wall Street is not a political party, nor a group
with an existing membership; it is a constantly variegating, rhizomatic assemblage that connects heterogeneous elements of discontent
(affect), political critique, physical bodies, and the multiplicitous
Idea. In so doing, it is a form of minoritarian politics, existing in the
interstices of our own hostile and controlling state apparatus.

Of course, the literature and scholarship surrounding nomadology
and the war machine, as well as applications of these to other revolutionary political movements, far exceed our schematic interjection
here. But our intent is not to parse out the various political interventions and potential revolutionary movements to which the concepts
give rise. Though crucially important, that is the subject of another
book, one which exceeds the parameters of our endeavour to develop
the connection between political ontology and art. Nonetheless, in
order to make these connections, some brief interlude in this arena
was necessary, if for no other reason than to broach the subject of
the implicitness of destruction requisite for the creative proposition as such and the possibility for the transmutation of violence
through art, as positive rupture. These themes return us to the value
of revolutionary practices of art: writing as a process of undoing the
stability of meaning, art as a means of de-centring the priority of the
human, music as a method of engaging us in the cosmic refrain. If
war machines are a matter of affect, then can engaging the sphere
of affect creation be a way of transmuting constitutive political violence? Artaud once said, with respect to Van Gogh, that his paintings
were like atomic bombs.[23] What this means to us is that art is not a
choice, but a devastating projectile which engages and transforms us.

Granted, because of this power, art too can become despotic, as
for example in futurism's heralding of fascism or Hitler's galvanising

of classical art to advocate his grotesque form of political purity
and order. Yet, it is the potential of art, of a minor art, in which we
are interested. The affects of art, as we have outlined throughout,
prepare the sensibility necessary for the critical consciousness that
is nomadology. Furthermore, the notion of the war machine, as a
necessary disruption of striated space at the level of affect, parallels
that of the passage of the artist through catastrophe toward creation,
thus we find a parallel to artistic, creative *ethos*, which enhances our
outline of a particular model-less model of a people-to-come.

## Reflections on Ethos and Invention

> Art, and especially cinematographic art, must take part in this task: not
> that of addressing a people, which is presupposed already there, but of
> contributing to the invention of a people. (CII, 217)

The essential claim with which we have been working is that art is
tasked with inventing a people. Rather than representing an already
present audience, a people-to-come implies that the people is always
ahead of itself, thus *missing* in the particular present. Art is the
vehicle for such a conjuring because it is a fundamental power of
invention, which has the power to go beyond reality and hold open
the question of what could be and what kind of beings *we* could be.

There are three permutations of invention that we wish to develop.
First, art prepares the way for a people-to-come by opening up an
experience of immanence. This experience is critical for grasping that
the operations of territorialisation and deterritorialisation apply to
the earth, language, ideas, bodies and art. Deleuze reveals the human
practice of art as a practice with counterparts in the natural world
and as occupying a position on the same level of existence. One may
point to the musical refrain, understood in terms of the territorial. 'In
music Deleuze finds the key to an understanding of art's relation to
the natural world.'[24] The refrain belongs not to the human but to the
cosmic, the world. Understanding music in this way allows Deleuze
to draw the human and the animal worlds closer, and also to extend
the aesthetic to life itself. Art lives on zones of indetermination where
objects and strata pass into one another, going beyond their lived
counterparts. 'Life alone creates such zones where living beings whirl
around, and *only art* can reach and penetrate them in its enterprise
of co-creation' (QP, 164/173, emphasis added).

The last two permutations of invention are two different ways of fabulating. First, art contributes to the invention of a people by releasing new affects into the world. The affect is a passage of intensity on the body, and this passage is the dark precursor of thought. The immediate visceral experience actually creates changes on and through bodies, potentially engendering different perceptual fields and modes of thought. Encountering new affects, shocking affects, spurs thought to create new concepts, and thus to introduce new concepts into the social sphere. Ultimately, the work of art calls a new people (and a new earth) into being through the production of affects – or what we are calling *the adventure of the affect*.

As we have said, with the anomalous as the porous frame for a model-less model of a people-to-come, the affect is everything. The anomalous selects affects from its composite, sometimes drawing from its centre and sometimes introducing new affects that it encounters from the outside. Therefore, a people-to-come will be related at the level of affect and functionality, not identity. It is this final emphasis that cements the importance of art for the invention of a people, for art creates affects, blocks of sensation released into the world which adventure forth and participate in the invention of new assemblages, new possible modes of being.

On the second point, that of the imaginative creation of different worlds, we refer to Deleuze's utilisation of Leibniz's theory of incompossibility. When Deleuze speaks of the artwork's ability to create possible worlds, possible worlds refer both to the converging, extensive series of which any individual only has access to one and to the incompossible divergent series. In the first respect, art is involved in opening us to the worlds (i.e. perspectives) of others. Art allows us to take leave of our own perspective on the world. In fact, Deleuze will say that there is no other intersubjectivity other than the artistic. Aesthetic figures can express the experience of others, allowing us to access or experience a world other than our own, thereby creating an intersubjective space. But Deleuze is positing something more radical than this when he speaks of creating new earths and new peoples. Imagining different, non-actual worlds is more than a matter of perspective, it is a matter of creating new arrangements of the virtual. Art is unique in its ability to produce other worlds, incompossible worlds.[25] Artworks can express fields of potentiality, universes which go beyond anything present in the world, the ethical consequences of which we take up in the following paragraph. These affects are otherworldly, specifically non-representative and irreducible to sameness or likeness. They are fabulations of other worlds, which provoke us to imagine the world differently. The artwork, then, is a relay for the gathering of collectivities that exemplify new ways of being and new sensibilities as portals to incorporeal universes, affects which actually can have the effect of changing the potentialities that we then take up and live.

One finds theoretical support for this second understanding of possible worlds in Guattari's monographic work, *Chaosmosis*, in which he speaks of an aesthetic paradigm attesting to the power of emergence that brings incorporeal Universes into being.[26] His point is that an incorporeal universe is an *ethos*, a certain refrain of the social, comprised of abstract perceptions of form, intensity and movement that connect us to the existential territories in which we exist. They are fields of virtuality that contain the incorporeal structures of the potential future and the traces of the past. Drawing upon Bergson's understanding of duration, Deleuze proposes an alternative to linear temporality, where past and future are virtual structures inhering in every moment of the present. These potentials are not pre-existing in the sense of being ready-at-hand options, but are selected according to situations and ostensibly created as an event of becoming. These structures are genetic, providing potentialities that may then become actualised.

Deleuze and Guattari emphasise the blindness of philosophical innovation and the ambiguous nature of the future, contingency. But they affirm this blindness and transmute contingency into a positive category of resistance. In order to resist the present, thinking must incorporate and counter-actualise the virtual elements of the present, a paradoxical imperative, unless perhaps for the spaces opened by and through aesthetic creation. For some this imperative to resist is not sufficient. Those who would not accept that resistance is itself something to be achieved, striven for, and that movement as opposed to the sedentary at least provides a possibility for a different future, may well accuse Deleuze of a brand of Romanticism, predicated on a utopianism or impossible politics which offers no conceivable programme for real world situations. Yet, unless one wants to claim satisfaction with what we have, or to claim that no other forms of social organisation are possible, there is a place and a need for such forms of resistance. Deleuze has a discourse of utopia, and it is a far cry from the Romantics. A Deleuzian utopia engages the negation of *topos*, the limits of our imagined spaces, and the untimely present. Not merely a vision of progress and perfection, utopia joins the ranks of the impossible and the unworkable, presenting virtual cartographies which provide a reflective pool showing us ourselves at the limit of destruction seeded from the present. With respect to the inventions of art, incompossible worlds that may be actualised in the work of art can provide a vision of the incompatibilities and the intolerable immanently awaiting us. As Buchanan suggests, 'the most deeply utopian texts are not those that propose or depict a better society, but those that carry out the most thoroughgoing destruction of the present society',[27] calling for what he calls total critique. We cannot help but think of the unrelenting, apocalyptic vision of Cormac McCarthy's *The Road*, which essentially shows us what we are becoming, and, in essence, what insists in the world that has already been created, perhaps providing the necessity for inventing a new future, one that does not lead to ash and cannibalism.

In 'Disposable Futures',[28] Evans and Giroux's claim that the present is thoroughly dystopian, where dystopia has become a control mechanism of neoliberal discourse. Dystopian politics means that it has become acceptable and commonplace to regard certain segments of society as excess, consigned to zones of abandonment, surveillance and incarceration – disposable. That dystopian reality has become a norm indicates that we, as a global community, no longer have a political vision, just resignation. That they link this situation to the paucity of imagination serves to strengthen our position concerning the need for art, for invention, and the cultivation of a sensibility to the affect as forms of resistance to the present. Indeed this is just what Evans and Giroux advocate, claiming that 'an act of resistance is a creative act'. What we need are new forms of thought, or the invention of the unthought. If the dystopian future has arrived, the utopia of the untimely present would demand the indictment of the intolerable and the exposure of limits and absurdities. Even on this reading, McCarthy's work is a powerful vision in that one cannot ghettoise the devastation or treat it as excess; it is quite simply everywhere, thus intensively registering the need for total critique and resistance rather than quiet acceptance.[29] Three consequences issue from this view of art which are imperatives for a kind of living: (1) Art opens us to immanence and our complicity with the world around us. As a passage through catastrophe, art discloses the world of molecular becoming, making visible the invisible of forces. 'It is only after matter has been sufficiently deterritorialised that it itself emerges as molecular and brings forth pure forces attributable to the Cosmos' (MP, 428/347). (2) Art opens up new worlds through the production of new affects. First, the extraction of new affects in art creates mutant subjectivities, literally and viscerally transforming bodies and adding to the possibilities for experimental ways of living, which must then be taken up and conceptualised; this is philosophy's role. Artworks are by their nature new varieties of compounds, new rhythms that re-order our bodily rhythms and cadences. (3) Art opens an untimely present. Its affects necessarily have no counterpart in our world, and yet are of this world and therefore speak to the virtuality of future worlds. These worlds have not been imaginable because they have not been incorporated. 'Patently, art does not have a monopoly on creation but it takes its capacity to invent mutant coordinates to extremes; it engenders unprecedented, unforeseen and unthinkable qualities of being.'[30]

Our responsibility is thus threefold: (1) a responsibility to others, the nonhuman as well as the nonorganic, that form and in-form us; (2) the freeing of the molecular – becoming imperceptible (a new kind of subjectivity) and thus developing a sensitivity to the affect; (3) responsibility for the worlds that are engendered. Therefore, a people-to-come, foremost, is an ethics, an ethics of aesthetic creation, which is characterised by a sensibility for force and disruption, issuing in questioning and creativity, that is able to engage in new alliances and welcome change. A Deleuzian *ethos* is a practice of living that is more adequate to the conditions of living, the genesis of beings, which celebrates the fabulatory artifice of living, but even more so instantiates the aesthetic in the heart of becoming. If a thing, body or soul, is defined by a certain power of being affected, then how or by what that thing is affected will be extremely important to its existence. Encounters with art offer a paradigm of aesthetic living, engaging with and creating affects that literally transform one's world and being. Given the saturation of philosophy with linguistic and semiotic privilege, the possibility of thinking otherwise comes from the exteriority of the non-discursive. The path to this escape is the pathic, as anterior to discursivity, though in constant complication with encodings, identifications, territorialisations. The aesthetic then exceeds art and becomes a practice of living. The encountering of artworks is experimentation. It is to enter into other worlds and, as Deleuze says, the artwork is the only way to enter into the world of the other. Engaging the artwork may not be enough, but it is a beginning, another beginning.

Deleuze's philosophy offers an open, dynamic concept of group interaction which can be marshalled for thinking what it means to be a people beyond borders, nations, or race, corresponding to the continuously transforming plane of immanence. A minor people cannot think of itself on the basis of inclusion and exclusion or a common heritage. These are models of the past. In fact, what a minor people must have in common is their not belonging. Their exclusion from dominant systems is an occasion for collective, albeit passing, mobilisation. Also, since a people-to-come will be related at the level of affect and functionality, not identity, its members need not resemble each other. A people-to-come may have complimentary affects, or enter into productive relations according to functionality. Humanity must become that which understands itself from a new conception of earth, to become a people that parallels the ebbs and flows of the earth reconfigured through pure immanence, as an open, dynamic system of intensities, forces and multiplicities. Deleuze's imperative is to 'make of us a cosmic people', but as continuous wanderers who have no place to which to return. This is not to become inhuman, but to think about the human, or being human, differently, as an open possibility constantly bombarded by and in tandem with myriad forces and affective relations to other beings, human and otherwise. It is to inhere, to dwell even, in the same space, yet differently and with an alternate relation to these potential connections and minor voices. Cultivating a sensibility, as open vulnerability, directed toward this is a matter of inspiration, the needful inspiring of philosophy through non-philosophy and the developing of a new sensitivity to this outside, for which art prepares the way – which brings us to the question of how art actually contributes to the invention of a people. In what follows, we experiment with this line of thought by focusing on how art contributes to the invention of communities or 'peoples' through the lens of the practice of art itself.

## Notes

1. Derrida, 'The Ends of Man', p. 136.
2. Jean-Luc Nancy, 'The Deleuzian Fold of Thought', in Paul Patton, ed., *Deleuze: A Critical Reader* (Oxford: Blackwell, 1996), p. 111.
3. Zourbichivili, *Deleuze: Une philosophie de l'événement*, p. 19.
4. See Jean-Luc Nancy's critique of myth in 'Myth Interrupted', in *The Inoperative Community*.
5. Ronald Bogue, *Deleuzian Fabulation and the Scars of History* (Edinburgh: Edinburgh University Press, 2010), p. 9.
6. Henri Bergson, *The Two Sources of Morality and Religion*, trans. R. Ashley Audra and Cloudsley Brereton (New York: Doubleday Anchor,

1954 [1932]), p. 109. Also see Bogue's excellent analysis in chapter 1 of *Deleuzian Fabulation*.

7. Interview (23 September 1966), published posthumously in *Der Spiegel*, 31 May 1976, trans. Maria P. Alter and John D. Caputo in Wolin, ed., *The Heidegger Controversy*.

8. By this we mean the appliance and the camera. The artist would like to emphasise that no computer software was used to alter or render the imagery.

9. 'The deviant becomes a decisive concept for describing multiplicities: a multiplicity is defined neither by its extended elements nor by known characters, but by its anomalous border, or line of variation.' François Zourabichvili, Anne Sauvagnargues and Paola Marrati, *La philosophie de Deleuze* (Paris: Presses Universitaires de France, 2004), p. 153.

10. Klee, *On Modern Art*, p. 55.

11. Deleuze specifically refers to the fact that the truly revolutionary potential of cinema to make the masses a true subject has been thwarted, by the misuse and abuse of the art form in the service of Hitler's propaganda, Stalinism, the break-up or radical individualism of the American neo-Western. These are all associated with a cinema that suggests the presence of a people: the people already there. The idea of a people-to-come is a critical rejoinder to these, one that relies upon the voices of the minor (CII, 216–17).

12. From a 1990 interview with Toni Negri: 'We ought to take up Bergson's notion of fabulation and give it a political meaning' (N, 173). Fabulation is described by Deleuze as a kind of legending: 'To catch someone in the act of legending (*Prendre les gens en flagrant délit de légender*) is to catch the movement of constitution of a people. A people isn't something already there. A people, in a way, is what's missing, as Paul Klee used to say' (N, 125–6).

13. Simon O'Sullivan, *Art Encounters Deleuze and Guattari* (Basingstoke: Palgrave Macmillan, 2006), p. 78.

14. Zourabichvili et al., *La philosophie de Deleuze*, p. 154.

15. Simon O'Sullivan, 'From Stuttering and Stammering to the Diagram: Deleuze, Bacon and Contemporary Art Practice', *Deleuze Studies* 3:2 (2009), p. 253.

16. Ibid., p. 225.

17. Ibid., p. 250.

18. Rosi Braidotti, *Nomadic Subjects* (New York: Columbia University Press, 1994), p. 22.

19. This point about the double-edge of the war machine is made by Eugene Holland in 'Schizoanalysis, Nomadology, Fascism', in Ian Buchanan and Nicholas Thoburn, eds, *Deleuze and Politics* (Edinburgh: Edinburgh University Press, 2008), pp. 82–3. See also Paul

Patton, 'Politics and the War-Machine in "*Mille Plateaux*"', *SubStance* 13:3/4 (1984), pp. 61–80.

20. Thanks to Ian Buchanan for providing me privately his essay, 'September 17, 2011: Occupy without Counting.'

21. There was a kind of manifesto, *The Declaration of the Occupation of New York City*, as well as a kind of newspaper, *The Occupied Wall Street Journal*, yet, as Buchanan notes, these were less important in terms of their readership than in terms of laying bare the process of the movement to itself, a chronicle or mapping of the events transpiring.

22. Buchanan, 'September 17, 2011: Occupy without Counting.'

23. 'No, Van Gogh was not mad, but his paintings were Greek torches, atomic bombs whose angle of vision ... would have been capable of seriously upsetting the grub-like conformity of the Second Empire bourgeoisie.' Antonin Artaud, *Van Gogh, Le suicidé de la société* (Paris: Gallimard, 2001), p. 27.

24. Bogue, *Deleuze on Music, Painting, and the Arts*, p. 2.

25. This distinction is made in QP, where Deleuze and Guattari address the possible world invoked by the other person, the face, and the difference from the virtuality of the Leibnizian model, positing the possible becoming of a more nuanced and singularised concept of the Other Person as the expression of a possible world in a perceptual field that has been fundamentally renegotiated, such as in Tournier's *Friday*. See QP, 22–5/17–19.

26. Guattari, *Chaosmosis*, p. 102.

27. Buchanan, *Deleuzism*, p. 94.

28. Brad Evans and Henry Giroux, 'Disposable Futures', Op-Ed, *Truthout*, 1 June 2014, available at http://www.truth-out.org/opinion/item/23998-disposable-futures (accessed 6 August 2014); see also Brad Evans and Henry Giroux, *Disposable Futures: Violence in the Age of the Spectacle* (San Francisco: City Lights, 2015).

29. For an extended yet complementary account of McCarthy's *The Road* see Brad Evans and Julian Reid's *Resilient Life: The Art of Living Dangerously* (Cambridge: Polity Press, 2014), pp. 156–7.

30. Guattari, *Chaosmosis*, p. 107.

# Concluding Event

## Fluxus Plateau: From Ontology to Fluxology

*It was as if it started in the middle of the situation, rather than at the beginning.*[1]

In light of these considerations, we share Deleuze's question, 'Who are our nomads today, our real Nietzscheans?', those who are able to wander without return and be true to the cosmic (earth) as a matter of 'constant flux and the disruption of that flux'.[2] This last plateau continues the theme of imaginative projection, linking to particular figures as conceptual personae. Yet, this plateau seeks to do more, transforming the notion of conceptual personae into an embodied multiplicity, *a conceptual collectivity*. Indeed, even the desired effect of this plateau is multiple: (1) to find an example in art that actually contributes to the invention of a people, containing the Deleuzian elements that make it resistant, or revolutionary, and (2) to show how art and art practices can be a model for community based on the criteria we have developed for a people-to-come.

The problem is, 'how does one speak of that which is always to come, which abides in the paradigm of missingness?' Traditional ways of speaking of concepts, of group identities, of definitions fail us. 'The minor is thus marked by a certain "impossibility". Every movement presents a boundary or an impasse to movement rather than a simple possibility or option.'[3] Deleuze's endeavour to speak of the fluidity of concepts, to capture (in words) the movement of matter, of becoming, is at issue here. What this necessitates is a sketch that can never be filled in completely – *a diagram, perhaps?* We are not interested, then, in offering a new political programme or ideology, but in constructing a diagram of the features of openness that will allow the kind of movement and becoming that must be indicative of any future peoples, especially if they are not going to fall foul of the kind of processes of totalisation and stagnation that lead to the worst types of exclusion, and even eliminatory practices.

In order to do this, we examine the rise of the 1960s avant-garde art collective Fluxus, whose purpose and origin uncannily cohere with many of the elements of Deleuze's thought. First, there are clear connections between the art collective as a practice and Deleuzian prerogatives: the emphasis on heterogeneity, collective enunciation, the firm entrenchment in practices of resistance, and the imperative of experimentation. Fluxus is an art collective whose only consistency lies in basically arguing against all fixed notions about everything, hence its suitability for elaborating a minor art that might summon a people-to-come. As Hannah Higgins, historiographer of Fluxus claims, 'The elasticity and diversity of Fluxus gives us, I think, some idea of how this structural openendness might play itself out as a modus operandi of a group.'[4] Fluxus invented new methods (lines of flight) of presentation and challenged the proper place of art, eschewing museums in favour of street performances and conscientiously avoiding the commodification of its output; thus it existed as a minor art within the major art industry. The collaborative, collective enunciations of this group, its composition of international and minority members, and its anti-establishment imperative provide a real example of the features of a people-to-come, a cosmic people which may also aptly be spoken of as a people in-between, the nomadic intermezzo.

We understand Fluxus as an ever-renewing singularity which exemplifies a perpetual and processive 'in between' in the following ways: (1) temporally, as event, with no distinct beginning or origin, and no end; (2) in terms of its composition – Fluxus is heterogeneous and hybrid, it resists determination; it is never possible to specify its full meaning nor its membership, which parallels the events that comprise it; (3) in terms of genre – Fluxus liberates affects from traditional modes of expression; it is anti-art; (4) in terms of its aesthetic – it is in between art and life, committed to merging the two rather than separating art as a cultural achievement; (5) topologically – it is based upon a paradigm of de-centring, indicative of Deleuze's privileging of milieu over origin, and offers us a way of envisioning a mobile and permeable group or community; and finally (6) for its overall paradigm – it bears the mark of indeterminacy, which is born through the consciously orchestrated and incorporated presence of contingency. Fluxus performances cannot be known in advance; they play with variability, contradiction, shifting processes, and the insurgence of chance.

# Concluding Event

*Fluxus* In Between

| Temporality | Event |
|---|---|
| Compositionality | Hybrid Multiplicity |
| Genre | Anti-Art |
| Aesthetic | Merging Art and Life |
| Topography | De-Centered and In-Between |
| Paradigm | Indeterminancy |

## I. EVENT

As a way of interpreting Klee's 'the people are missing' and its emphasis on the future, Ronald Bogue argues that the future is now – the now of untimely becoming in the present,[5] an aporetic temporality that suggests that a people-to-come is constitutively determined by absence – the people is not present, so it has not happened, and is only possible in a future that has not arrived.[6] The most we can warrant is that it is, or could be, happening. This is similar to Lawlor's characterisation of the 'fragility of the event', where the event is unlimited (*'il ne cesse pas'*), it is perpetually bidirectional, a temporal paradox that has always already occurred (never begun) and yes can never fully occur (never ending) – 'an infinite movement' (QP, 148/157), leaving us with the perpetual question, 'is it happening?'[7] To illuminate the temporal paradox of Fluxus and its affinity with the Deleuzian event, we refer to Fluxus artists themselves. Some abide by the idea that 'Fluxus has fluxed', while others insist that 'Fluxus hasn't ever taken place yet.'[8] Both are right – what characterised Fluxus from the beginning, which itself is a matter of multiple beginnings, is that Fluxus was and is always be-coming. In a sense, it started after it had already started and its endings stretch far into the future, and there is no present Fluxus, because there is no one 'Fluxus'. The most one could say is that 'Flux-events' happen with no possibility of saying what will happen in them – each event is constructed upon contingency, an open system. Each event holds several futures, incorporeal variations, and Fluxus, like Deleuze's event, is never exhausted in its fluxing: it never was and so never is.[9]

Historically, Fluxus is seen as part of a larger conceptual development of the Western avant-garde, Marcel Duchamp and John Cage in particular, and heir to defining principles of modernism such as artistic

267

activism and the integration of art-making with socio-political criticism, community-building, and release from formalism. Socio-politically, Fluxus is a post-Second World War development coming out of influences that largely span from 1940 to 1960. This was a period of significant social and political change: post-war disillusionment, the Vietnam War and the civil rights movement provide the horizon for Fluxus activities, reflecting the entwinement with the political and the witness to suffering that is necessary for a minor art.

Paul Klee wrote that 'the more horrible this world . . . the more abstract our art, whereas a happy world brings forth an art of the here and now'.[10] What is needed to 'resist the present', according to Deleuze, is an art born out of need. Fluxus, in responding to its present, is such an art – reflecting the need to address the radical narrowing of human perspective, the rigidification of political space, and the heightening of human aggression and repression. Of course, it is difficult to claim a definitive connection between the rising tide of counter-cultural sentiment and Fluxus' actions; this is the problem that a minor politics or minor art must have, because it would not and could not operate through the molar structures of legislation or policy. Minor art channels flows and energies, undercurrents, which exist but as somewhat virtual intensities. Fluxus has been called the most radical and experimental art movement of the 1960s:[11]

> More than an art movement: *Fluxus* was a gigantic release of creative energy into human culture, along came this small band of *Fluxus* folks around the world who used radical art, strange activities, objects and performances in upside down creativity to reverse this narrowing down restrictive tendency in the evolution of human culture. They were huge cultural tricksters . . . by expanding and in some cases obliterating what we considered to be normal, interesting and human behavior to be. *These guys brought on the 60s . . .* expanded the potential and possibilities in human culture.[12]

Fluxus arose from a web of interconnected activities, a volatile artistic primordial soup. Often the group is associated with George Maciunas, yet, though an organising force for Fluxus, he was never considered its leader. One could say that he occupies the position of the anomalous because of his role with respect to selection, publication and promotion of Fluxus works.

The actual name Fluxus began as an idea for a magazine for experimental artists in 1961, but its official performance beginning was in 1962 with the Fluxfest concert of experimental music in Weisbaden Germany. But the Fluxus assemblage also applies to what have been called proto-Fluxus events. John Cage's lectures at the New School for Social Research, which emphasised the deconstruction of sound and the primacy of chance, helped galvanise several future members of Fluxus. There were loose associations of artists holding performances in New York lofts, outside of and in opposition to the gallery scene, such as the Chamber Street Performance series curated by Yoko Ono and La Monte Young in 1961, Allan Kaprow's Happenings, and the Audio Visual Group – these are where Fluxus is said to have been born, at least in spirit. Thus, Fluxus is 'in between', and can be described as *beginning in the middle*.

## II. COMPOSITION

Fluxus resists determination through its heterogeneity and hybridity. Its composition and activities were international, not located in one space or identified with a consistent membership; it exists as an 'interface' in and out of which artists flowed. As emphasised by Fluxist artists themselves, Fluxus should not be considered a movement.[13] With no ideology, manifestos, no common cause or theme,[14] it was described by Ken Friedman as a 'laboratory of ideas, a virtual colloquium', and by another as 'nebulous'.[15] Friedman's point to the contrary, Maciunas himself wrote several versions of a 'manifesto', yet, as with the Occupy Movement, these have never been viewed as offering a set of consistent or affirmed prerogatives. Maciunas' manifestos are so many suggestions. The first of these began with Maciunas consulting a dictionary and finding a total of 17 meanings for the word 'flux'. In 1963, he selected three particular senses of the word – purge, tide and fuse – and amplified each with his own comments, which oriented the definitions toward a quasi-political intent. The outcome is a three-part manifesto consisting of photostats of eight of the dictionary definitions inserted between handwritten sections.[16] The second 1965 *Manifesto on Art / Fluxus Art Amusement* reflects the general anti-art-establishment stance of Fluxus, setting up the elite status of the professionalised art world against the unpretentious inclusivity of Fluxus art-amusement intended to bring art and life closer.[17]

Paralleling the lack of conceptual coherence, there is no coherence of genre or practice, the hallmarks of traditional art and historical categories. Fluxus' activities constitute a rhizomatic web of musical performance, publications and anthologies, street performance, poetry, mailings, theatre events, and often a combination of these which marks the origin of intermedia phenomena. There was no common aesthetic or common genre to unite the artists of Fluxus; this was the coming together of experimental artists; their commonality resulted from paradoxical characteristic of resisting characterisation. Thus its identity lies in its multiplicity, as an ever changing, in-flux entity: 'the Fluxus attitude replaces the traditional master codes (static points of conceptual reference or grounding such as a single type or style of performance) with a constantly shifting code of situational reference, particularly in the idea of open-ended play of difference'.[18] Its hybrid nature is fitting for a philosophy that suggests that the people called forth through art 'is not one that claims to be pure but rather an oppressed, bastard, lower, anarchical, nomadic and irremediably minor race' (QP, 104–5/109). Therefore, to get a sense of Fluxus, we must engage it in its moments of singularity. Thus, in what follows, we propose to engage with Fluxus by identifying several trends that Fluxus artists gravitate toward, which correspond to the four remaining modes of being in-between: anti-art and the liberation of the affect; merging art and life; de-centring; and indeterminacy, accompanying them with examples of particular Fluxus works.

## III. Anti-art

Originally, there was a development of a new performative sensibility among proto-Fluxist artists, linking to what was called new music, or anti-music. Maciunas understood the major thrust of Fluxus musical innovation under the term concretism, which indicates a departure from the abstraction of formalist conceptions of pure pitch and controlled tones by breaking open material sound 'with all its inherent polychromy and pitchlessness and "incidentalness"'[19] through indeterminacy and improvisation. As Maciunas explains, each composition is a kind of framework, an '"automatic machine" within which or by which nature (either in the form of an independent performer or indeterminate-chance compositional methods) can complete the art-form, effectively and independently of the artist-composer'.[20] This description, in relation to music, resembles one of the main elements of the artwork that Deleuze emphasises in the diagram. In order to escape clichés and mere representation, the work must contain the seeds of chance from which arises a new ordering of sensible components, and it is the diagram that accomplishes this, constituting the space of passage from chaos to order.

The transfer of the diagram to music is consistent in that Deleuze always privileges music as that art which gives access to the processes of creation and chaos. When speaking of the minor quality of Kafka's language, Deleuze and Guattari's focus turns to the affective quality of

270

language – to Gregor, whose sounds are not just animalist but musical warbles, or the sister's violin. There Deleuze identifies the informal element of sound as that which 'leads to active disorganization of expression' (K, 51/28). The minor is the liberation of language, but it is evident that what is liberated is not words per se, but sound, the elementality of language as the unformed matter of expression (K, 13/6). This is the stammering of language. It is sound, itself, that will be deterritorialised, absolutely (K, 38/21), and, in this sense, it no longer belongs to a language of sense.

Our point is to draw attention toward the process that is involved in minor literature and to what becomes liberated in and through it. Minor literature liberates expressive material for non-paradigmatic, transgressive uses. It is this connection with affectivity, conceptualised in *Logic of Sensation* as the creation and release of new blocs of sensation, which allows us to begin to think of the minor in terms of art in general. This liberation is only one stage; it must be reconnected in order to produce new contents and new expressions. The minor only becomes revolutionary if it affects the language in which it was effected. Transposing this phenomenon of the minor to art, and more specifically, Fluxus, a revolutionary art will be one that affects the art or culture in which it was effected.

A paradigmatic example of this kind of revolutionary affect is Philip Corner's iconic *Piano Activities*, performed at the International Festival of the Newest Music in Wiesbaden, Germany, in 1962, significant in that it was the first public event described as Fluxus. The impact of this performance was profound; it was met with shock from the community, outrage, and even riots.[21] Corner provided a score with minimum of notation and instructions, and the performers radically interpreted it to include a methodical yet random destruction. Corner's piece is iconic in that it represents the first ever effective realisation of the anti-art intentions of Fluxus. Nam Jun Paik played the piano while several other members of the ensemble set to work destroying it. Given that Corner's score is not traditionally directive, a set of instructions to be followed fastidiously, it introduces the element of contingency associated with a diagram. Like Deleuze's diagram, 'the score that Corner wrote was intended to shape something coherent out of the chaotic reservoir of sounds that he saw in the instrument and to broaden the field of possibilities for freedom in performance'.[22] This was not mere destruction for destruction's sake, but improvisation in which the artists responded to each other, carefully loosening a string, hammering the legs of the piano, in order to give 'an opening to the previously unheard-of'.[23] This performance illustrates the

271

passage through catastrophe, the liberation of affect, and the creation of a new sensible being, in this case 'collective noise landscapes', which art undergoes.

What makes *Piano Activities* so significantly different from the kind of instrument destruction prevalent in the rock music genre[24] is that rather than being an addendum to a performance, in Corner's piece, the destruction was the performance. This is creative destruction, to make music from the destruction of the musical form and instrument. Moreover, this example is indicative of one of the main criteria for a minor art – the breaking open of the art form (in this case, musical) from within. Fluxus music or anti-music is a musical stammering, the intent of which is to release or liberate the sound within music – beyond expression or toward the heterogeneity of expression.

Corner's piece is also an instance of the deformation of the traditional score format. There are also transversal lines connecting Corner's experimentation with other experimental phenomena of new music. Notably, Sylvano Bussotti, an Italian composer who often performed at Flux events and is undoubtedly identified as a Fluxus artist, experimented with graphic scores which represent music through the use of visual symbols rather than traditional notation. Significantly, the opening image of *A Thousand Plateaus*, which inaugurates Deleuze and Guattari's introductory chapter, is the final page of Bussotti's composition, *XIV Piano Piece for David Tudor*. It is a visual/musical evocation of their key figure, the rhizome.[25] Bussotti's presence in their thought helps us weave Ariadne's thread between Fluxus and Deleuze and Guattari.

## IV. ART TO LIFE

Fluxus focuses on the process of creation itself. In many cases the artist is a merely a conduit, letting events unfold in the moment. 'Central to Fluxus is the idea that art is part of life, as opposed to culture, and should therefore imitate the universal processes of flux and change.'[26] The idea of merging art and life is one that resonates with Deleuze's ontology, as we have discussed it in terms of the connection of framing and territory. As Thoburn puts it, 'Deleuze's task is to develop a politics adequate to the complexity of life, a politics that can make the human worthy of the material universe of infinite interaction.'[27] Deleuze insists that art can reach into the deep recesses of the generative movements of life: 'Life alone creates such zones where living beings whirl around, and only art can reach and penetrate them in its enterprise of co-creation' (QP, 164/173). Fluxus realises this merging by tying art to everyday experience, making the mundane uncanny and strange. George Brecht sought to locate art in the minutia of the everyday, 'the smallest unit of the situation', claiming that this was to ensure 'that the details of everyday life, the random constellations of objects that surround us, stop going unnoticed'.[28] Allison Knowles' infamous 'Make a Salad', which literally involves making a salad on stage, exemplifies connecting art with daily life.

## V. DE-CENTRING

We understand de-centring as a transformative function. It unhinges expectation, shocks sensibility, causing a 'glitch' that provokes new ways of thinking through 'loosening' the parameters of inclusivity with respect to the artist, the art world and work, and the viewer. In terms of art forms, Fluxus was known for irreverently crossing genre boundaries, creating assemblages that incorporated musical compositions, concrete poetry, visual art and writing, giving rise to what Dick Higgins called *intermedia*, a dialogue between two or more media to create a third, entirely new fused art form. 'With intermedia there is a conceptual fusion, and you can't really separate out the different media in an integral way.'[29] This fusion of art paradigms reflects the sense of becoming proposed by Deleuze, wherein the becoming is always a double becoming. Describing Kafka's paradigmatic examples of becoming-animal, Deleuze and Guattari relate the process to flux: 'there is no longer man or animal, since each deterritorializes the other, in a conjunction of flux' (K, 40/22). This refusal to maintain the purity of art forms is also a de-centring, in effect, creating a zone of indeterminacy between art forms.

Maciunas also insisted on the anonymity of Fluxus productions, which had a de-centring effect on the sanctity of the artist and is another example of its minor status, through the promotion of the collective.[30] Multiples, usually boxes that contained small objects, games, or instructional cards, were composed from the offerings of several artists, yet these Fluxboxes would bear only the title of the collective. Fluxus is thus a collective enunciation, individualised through its affects rather than its individuals, or, as Deleuze advocates, according to the affects it experiences. Reflecting the de-centring of the artist as well as de-centring of art as object, many Fluxus works are a fusion of the horizons between performer and audience, collaborations which transform both through their interaction. 'Event-Scores' are such an example, wherein the distance or even distinction between artist and audience is eliminated.[31] An Event-Score provides instructions that either involve the audience at some level or challenge the prerogative of artistic genius. Simple instructions – such as for Brecht's 'Three Lamp Event', whose bullet-pointed instructions read: (1) off.on; (2) on.off; (3) lamp – provide that they can be performed anywhere and by anyone. They require no elaborate costumes, no intricate stage design, no professional training, and no expensive materials. The simplicity of the score is intended as a commentary on the elitism of the professional art industry. Often, they also include elements of the absurd, in a kind of self-referential critique of the aggrandisement of art.

Though many were actually used in live performance as flexible road maps with purposively unforeseeable consequences, frequently these 'scores' were printed on cards and then packaged into plastic boxes and sold as inexpensive multiples. 'In the Event, an instruction may be realized in the mind of the reader as an idea or, conversely, as live performance with or without an audience.'[32] As these scores can be performed by anyone at any time, they remind us of Deleuze's anyone and anyplace whatsoever, wherein the anonymity is a means of disrupting signification and disengaging subjectification.

Fluxus is also associated with minimalist performance art known for its untraditional narrative matrix and absence of theatrical technique.[33] There are myriad examples of Fluxus performance pieces, such as Yoko Ono's iconic 'Cut Piece: First Version for single Performer' which was performed in 1964 at the Yamaichi Concert Hall in Kyoto, Japan. The performance requires active audience participation for its realisation. The instructions are:

> Performer sits on stage with a pair of scissors in front of him. It is announced that members of the audience may come on stage – one at a time – to cut a small piece of the performer's clothing to take with them. Performer remains motionless throughout the piece. Piece ends at the performer's option.

Ono's piece has been repeated on several occasions, to different effect. The original performance had a particular disruptive value, and it was this affect of disruption that Fluxus strove to produce as a way of calling individuals back to their roles and presence in the world around them. In other words, though seemingly absurd or whimsical vignettes, Fluxus was plugged into a larger social critique. These minor disruptions were meant to expose something of the rapidity and monotony of cultural practice.

Performance-based art de-centres the understanding of art as object-oriented, while also de-centring the expectations of traditional performance or theatre, by breaking with expectations of completeness and linear narrative through the contingency of audience interaction. It also illustrates the importance of chance and contingency, which are hallmarks of Fluxus events. One never knows what the response of the audience will be, who will come to the stage, what they will cut, or when the performance will be over. Ono was one of many Fluxus artists who used open-endedness and minimalism in terms of instructions to amplify the element of chance.

## VI. INDETERMINACY

We have offered several examples of how Flux events privilege the element of chance. They are assemblages that emphasise spontaneity and contingency, 'ultimately predicated on an affirmation of indeterminate structures and shifting situational constructs'.[34] Fluxus did mean to shock, but, as opposed to Dada, which was a reaction to the destruction and the perceived senselessness of the era, Fluxus events were meant to 'jolt the audience and break open the established structures of reception'.[35] In other words, Fluxus lines of flight were not just means of escape or reactive to the present, they were meant to create new modes of being and perceiving.

In keeping with the paradigm of merging art and life, there is a 'recognition of indeterminacy as a prevailing principle of nature, a conception of the world based on ambiguities, ruptures, and incongruities',[36] reminiscent of Axelos' epiphenomena and Deleuze's dark precursors. Indeterminacy was a form of resistance for Fluxus,[37] resistance to a prevailing arts culture based on commodification, resistance to prevailing art forms, resistance to social normalisation, resistance to perceptual habitualisation, in essence, *resistance to its present*.

An artwork that we believe captures the spirit of Fluxus, its commitment to open-endedness and indeterminacy, is Dick Higgins' *A Thousand Symphonies*. This performance embodies the force of rupture, the untimely temporality of the event, the affect of contingency and the minorisation of art and the political. In 1962 Higgins composed a series of events called *Danger Music*, in which his intent was to alternately put the body of the performer, the composer, or an audience member at risk. *A Thousand Symphonies* is inspired by this series, quite literally in fact, since one of the Danger Music series, #12 (March 1962), is a score whose sole directive is to 'write a thousand symphonies'. In 1968, Danger Music #12 is realised by Higgins' enlisting a New Jersey Police office to fire a 9mm MP40 Schmeisser submachine gun at sheets of orchestral music paper. Higgins explains:

> In the spring of 1968 Geoffrey Hendricks and Robert Watts told me of a project that was afoot at Douglass College to organize a show around guns. At that time the USA police seemed to have nothing better to do than to chase down teenagers for possessing minuscule amounts of marijuana and throwing them in jail, thus ruining their lives . . . I decided it would be more worthy if one could set all the policemen in the USA to composing symphonies themselves. So I proposed that the beautiful music paper be machine gunned and that symphonies be derived from the result.

As Higgins describes it, his intent is to cause the state apparatus to enter into an aesthetic becoming. 'An act of simultaneous destruction and creation, the gesture [is also an act of resistance], emphasising the use of guns for a purpose other than killing Viet Cong and scattering protestors.'[38] A Thousand Symphonies catalyses the political and social arena, as an example of the transmutation of violence and the material triggers of violence into an affective logos about violence, for which we posed a question earlier in the chapter.

So, what happens? The orchestral sheets are placed in a metal waste basket, which is fired upon by the police officer. Bullets rip through the pages, producing random holes and marring them with heat scars, which will later be stencilled onto upshot paper using paints and inks. The actual papers themselves were also used as notation for the creation of several symphonies, which were then played by an orchestra at a later date. From a Deleuzian perspective, this is an event of becoming: an absolute deterritorialisation of the score as well as a deterritorialisation of the artist/composer. The fact that the music is composed by automatic weapons suggests a deterritorialisation of the very principles of musical arrangement, with no principle of order or rational decision. The scores are a dis-arrangement, a compositional body without organs. This also means that, strangely, the composer of this symphony, Higgins, is not the composer of the symphony, yet is the creator of this symphony-producing event. The score and artist/composer have entered into a double becoming, where each has changed in kind, by way of the machine gun.

The importance of both the virtual and actual aspects of A Thousand Symphonies embodies the doubled-sidedness of the event, as well as exemplifying the paradox of actualising a model-less model. The performance reveals that there are a thousand scores implicit in the pages. No possibility has been eliminated by selection, by consideration of form, musical methodology, or harmony. Everything that makes a score musical is missing, and the score is a virtual plenitude because of this quality of missingness. The artist is the composer of the *event*, an assemblage waiting to be actualised, rather than the score itself, which is the affect produced through the actualisation of the event. The actualisation of the event happens as an assemblage of the force, speed and heat of the bullets, the aim of the police officer, as well as the intent of the artist and the materiality of the paper. Finally, the initial differentiation that occurs in the moment undergoes a further process of selection, as the symphonies are finalised through the applications and tracings of the artist. These processes engender another performance, which may be considered a line of flight to an orchestral assemblage. A volunteer orchestra, conducted by Philip Corner, performed nine of the resulting symphonies at Douglass College, the event's musical realisation, a counter-actualisation releasing the virtual sound-affects implicit in the score. There are also temporal lines of flight to consider. One of the fascinating things about performance is that it is always a creative repetition, as Deleuze notes in his discussions of theatre. *A Thousand Symphonies* has generated numerous lines of flight in this regard. Most recently, Dennis Rosenthal, the director of Higgins' estate, arranged with the City of Chicago to have four Chicago Police officers shoot new notation paper, commemorating the fiftieth anniversary of the event – Fluxus keeps fluxing.

The score is a material record of the fusion of performance, the artist's actions, and its production as visual art, as such it is a exemplary intermedia assemblage. What *A Thousand Symphonies* accomplishes, or releases, is the affect of indeterminacy, monumentalised in the bullet-riddled paper of the score, a visible sign of indeterminacy resonant with and amplificatory of the untimeliness of the Deleuzian event.

The assiduous incorporation of chance and indeterminacy into event-scores and performance, culminating in our final example, evidences the commitment of Fluxus to a contingent, unknowable future.[39] Fluxus' challenge to conventional thinking on art and culture is connected to, maybe even speaks for, a people, the rise of a counter-culture community. Appreciably, Fluxus was indicative of the rise of one of the most visible counter-cultures in contemporary history. It also had a central role in the birth of such key contemporary art forms as conceptual art, installation and performance art, pop-ups, intermedia and video art. The modern collective, taking its cue from Fluxus, has undergone multiple iterations, taking on more diverse hues of political engagement and remaining always outside or against mainstream societal norms. This,

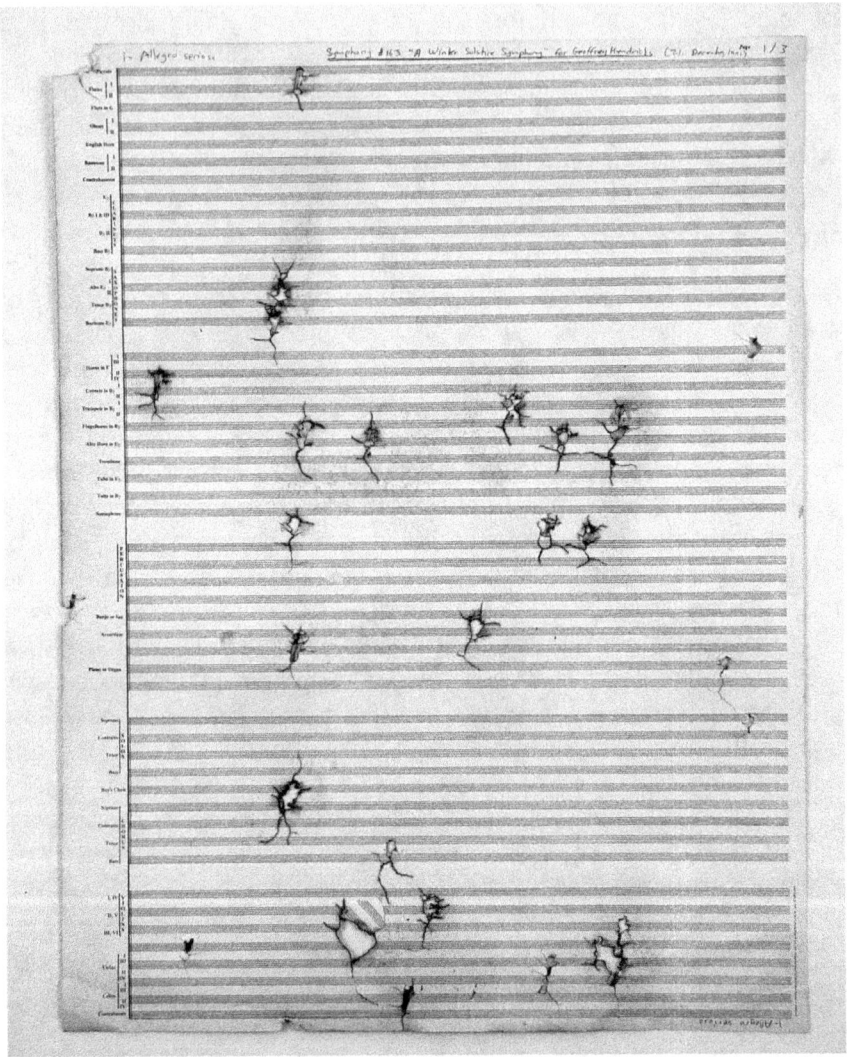

*Figure 6.2* Dick Higgins, *A Thousand Symphonies*, 1968, orchestral paper, bullet holes © The Estate of Dick Higgins. All rights reserved. DACS, London / ARS, NY 2014. *Photo courtesy of Geoffrey Hendricks.*

This is the first page from 'Winter Symphony', one of the symphonies composed from the performance of *A Thousand Symphonies* in 1968. *A Thousand Symphonies* is the realisation of Fluxus artist Dick Higgins' *Danger Music #12*, which included the sole instruction to 'write a thousand symphonies'. In 1968, Higgins had a New Jersey police officer fire an automatic weapon at hundreds of sheets of orchestral paper, the results of which were random patterns of bullet holes of which the above is an example. Shortly after, the musical scores were played by an ensemble.

in itself, is the perpetuation of a people-to-come that speaks to the paradoxical features of coherence and openness to which we have referred and illustrates the lines of flight that connect different assemblages to one another.

Fluxus is always to come, becoming or fluxing by embracing uncertainty and risking randomness. As such, it is a model for the model-less, a diagram filled with chance marks, scratches, or random brush strokes, which provides just enough of a framework to ward off chaos and enough openness to allow movements to proliferate. By layering these conceptual elements and coupling them with art-affects, we have offered the Fluxus paradigm as a model for speaking about a minor people and a minor art. Whatever a people-to-come will be, it must be a moving concept, one that enjoins itself to the flux and flows of life, in order to be equal to the conditions of life, creation and immanence. Our culture has been shaped by this art. Fluxus' affects (and effects) are like the spray of bullets in *A Thousand Symphonies*, released, liberated lines of flight that have introduced new ways of doing art and new ways of being into our cultural landscape. It is an art that is necessarily going beyond itself, perpetually minoritarian. In order to be equal to *this* event,[40] ontology must become a *fluxology*.

## Notes

1. Dick Higgins on FLUXUS, interview by Carl Nørrested and Svend Thomsen in connection with 'Metadrama' performances at SMFK, Copenhagen 1986, Video: © TVF 1986/2005, available at https://www.youtube.com/watch?v=9feLztCuQ18.
2. Gilles Deleuze, 'Nomad Thought', in David Allison, ed., *The New Nietzsche: Contemporary Styles of Interpretation* (Cambridge, MA: MIT Press, 1985), pp. 149 and 146.
3. Nicholas Thoborn, *Deleuze, Marx and Politics* (New York: Routledge, 2003), p. 19.
4. Hannah Higgins, 'Fluxus Fortuna', in *The Fluxus Reader*, ed. Ken Friedman (London: Academy Editions, 1998), p. 32. Digital edition at http://researchbank.swinburne.edu.au/vital/access/manager/Repository/swin:9624 (accessed 6 August 2014).
5. Ronald Bogue, 'Deleuze and Guattari and the Future of Politics: Science Fiction, Protocols and a People-to-Come', *Deleuze Studies 5* (2011), Supplement, pp. 77–97.
6. Ibid., p. 79.
7. See Leonard Lawlor's excellent account of the event in 'Phenomenology and Metaphysics, and Chaos: On the Fragility of the Event in Deleuze',

in Smith and Somers-Hall, eds, *The Cambridge Companion to Deleuze*, pp. 103–25.

8. Tomas Schmit, Letter to Gil Silverman, 3 February 1981, in *Fluxus, Etc: The Gilbert and Lila Silverman Collection* (Cranbrook Academy of Art Museum, 1981), p. 49.

9. See Deleuze's discussion of the Event at QP, 147–51/156–9.

10. Paul Klee, Diary entry (1915), # 951, in *The Diaries of Paul Klee, 1898–1918* (Berkeley: University of California Press, 1968), p. 313.

11. See Harry Rue, *Fluxus: The Most Radical and Experimental Art Movement of the Sixties* (Amsterdam: 'A', 1979).

12. See Allen Burkoff's commentary, 'What is Fluxus?', available at http://www.youtube.com/watch?v=cGZ9OS1Oj14 (accessed 24 July 2014).

13. In a 1985 interview with Alison Knowles, Esteva Milman suggests that Fluxus is a conceptual community that grants short-term citizenship ('Fluxus History and Trans-History', *Fluxus Reader*, p. 156). Dick Higgins says that the idea of Fluxus as a 'collective' arose as a response or alternative to being called a movement, explaining that Fluxus had no stated programme or manifesto which it had to match or represent (Higgins, *Fluxus Reader*, p. 221).

14. Owen Smith, *Fluxus: The History of an Attitude* (San Diego: San Diego State University Press, 1998), p. 9.

15. Ibid., p. 227.

16. The three sections written by Maciunas to complement the senses of flux as purge, tide and fuse are as follows: (1) 'Purge the world of bourgeoisie sickness, "intellectual," professional and commercialized culture, purge the world of dead art, imitation, artificial art, abstract art, illusionistic art, mathematical art, – PURGE THE WORLD OF 'EUROPEANISM!' (2) 'PROMOTE A REVOLUTIONARY FLOOD AND TIDE IN ART, promote living art, anti-art, promote NON ART REALITY to be fully grasped by all peoples, not only critics, dilettantes and professionals.' (3) 'Fuse the cadres of cultural, social & political revolutionaries into a united front & action'. George Maciunas, 'Fluxus Manifesto', 1963. See Clive Phillpot, 'Fluxus: Magazines, Manifestos, Multum in Parvo', available at http://georgemaciunas.com/cv/manifesto-I (accessed 24 July 2014).

17. See http://www.artnotart.com/fluxus/gmaciunas-artartamusement.html (accessed 24 July 2014).

18. Smith, *Fluxus: The History of an Attitude*, p. 10.

19. George Maciunas, 'Neo-Dada in Music, Theater, Poetry, Art', in *Fluxus: Selections from the Gilbert and Lila Silverman Collection/Clive Phillpot and Jon Hendricks* (New York: The Museum of Modern Art, 1988), p. 26. This piece was read by Arthur C. Caspari, in German, at the Fluxus concert *Aprés Cage*, Wuppertal, West Germany, 9 June 1962.

20. George Maciunas, 'Neo-Dada in Music, Theater, Poetry, Art', p. 27.
21. According to Dick Higgins, the reaction of the public (to Weisbaden) ranged 'from explosive (we had two riots) to docile and indifferent to sympathetic'. See http://piano-activities.de/englindex.html#_edn14 (accessed 24 July 2014). According to Maciunas, 'Wiesbaden was shocked', KRAB Radio Broadcast, Seattle, Washington, September 1977, Clip 3, available at http://www.fluxus.org/FLUXLIST/maciunas (accessed 24 July 2014).
22. See http://www.a-musik.com/p/product/philip-corner-piano-activities-world-premiere-at-the-festum-fluxorum-wiesbaden-1962-lp-084065.html (accessed 24 July 2014).
23. Gunnar Schmidt, *Klavierzerstörungen in Kunst und Popkultur* (Berlin: Reimer 2012); translated by Philip Corner as 'FluxClang! Sensational Uncovered Source of Fluxus Movement History', available at http://piano-activities.de/englindex.html#_edn15 (accessed 24 July 2014).
24. When one thinks of iconic images of instrument destruction, it is the smashing and burning of electric guitars. Pete Townshend is known as the first guitar-smashing rock artist (at the Railway Hotel in 1964), and *The Who* became known for destroying their instruments during performances, such as at the 1967 Monterey Pop Festival, at the end of performing, appropriately, *My Generation*.
25. Ronald Bogue gave an excellent lecture on the significance of this score and graphic music at the International Deleuze Studies workshop in Lisbon, Portugal in 2013, and has since written an article on Bussotti to be published in the *Deleuze Studies* journal.
26. Smith, *Fluxus: The History of an Attitude*, p. 235.
27. Thoborn, *Deleuze, Marx and Politics*, p. 15.
28. See http://members.chello.nl/j.seegers1/flux_files/brecht.html (accessed 24 July 2014).
29. Nicholas Zurbrugg, *Art, Performance, Media* (Minneapolis: University of Minnesota Press, 2004), p. 201.
30. Duchamp's de-prioritisation of the artist with his ready-mades is helpful in understanding the Fluxus decentring, in terms of resistance (to the elitism of the art world) and as collective enunciation. See Smith, *Fluxus: The History of an Attitude*, p. 108.
31. For examples, see 'Selected Fluxus Event Scores', available at http://cuma.periplurban.org/wp-content/uploads/2008/06/fluxus.pdf (accessed 24 July 2014).
32. Hannah Higgins, 'Fluxus Fortuna', p. 32.
33. Dick Higgins, *Fluxus Reader*, p. 235.
34. Smith, *Fluxus: The History of an Attitude*, p. 227.
35. Dorothée Brill, *Shock and the Senseless in Dada and Fluxus* (Hanover: Dartmouth College Press, 2010), pp. 130–1.
36. Ibid., p. 234.

37. 'Protocols of experimentation can provide a certain scaffolding for resistance.' Bogue, 'Deleuze and Guattari and the Future of Politics', p. 82.
38. See http://grahamfoundation.org/public_events/4938-dick-higgins-the-thousand-symphonies (accessed 24 July 2014).
39. See George Brecht, *Chance Imagery* (New York: Something Else Press, 1966).
40. 'There is a dignity of the event that has always been inseparable from philosophy as *amor fati*: being equal to the event, or becoming the off-spring of one's own events' (QP, 151/159).

# Index

remembrance, 86, 112, 198, 213
repetition, 62, 65, 74, 83–4, 107, 116,
    160, 199, 218, 237
  creative, 34, 49–50, 59, 66, 74, 206,
    218, 227, 277
resistance, 43n2, 136, 247–8, 257–8,
    266, 275–6
  to the present, 157, 163, 247, 257,
    268, 275
resoluteness, 79, 195–6, 200
revaluation of values, 31, 37, 38
reversing Platonism, 49–54
rhizomatics, 126, 135
rhythm, 117, 128, 133, 143, 145,
    147–8, 152, 155, 157–66, 170,
    192, 241, 259; see also variation
Rimbaud, Arthur, 221–30, 233n44,
    238, 239, 246
*Riss* (rift, design), 77, 101–2, 104,
    115–16
Romanticism, 222, 257
rootedness (*Bodenstandigkeit*), 194–5,
    197, 199, 201, 204–5, 210, 215,
    246; see also autochthony

Sauvagnargues, Anne, 117, 129–30,
    136, 138
saving power, 26, 89, 91–2, 94, 106
semiotics
  of affect, 117
  of creativity, 130, 136
  critique of, 138–43
sensation, 147–50, 151, 153, 155–9,
    163–4, 168–70, 271
  logic of, 135, 142, 145, 155
  *see also* being of sensation
sensibility, 60–1, 65, 130, 148, 149,
    171, 174, 226, 260
sensitivity
  to affect, 167, 170–1, 228, 252, 259
  to immanence, 68, 174, 228, 246,
    260
  *see also* vulnerability
sentiendum, 150, 155
shock, 114, 130, 132, 134, 145, 147,
    150, 256, 271, 273
simulacrum, 50–4, 67, 117, 130–2,
    133, 134, 145, 228, 238

singularity, 143, 245, 266
  of the artwork, 104
spirit (*Geist*), 32, 210
  Derrida's critique of, 216–20
spiritual, 88, 194, 210, 211, 216
spiritual-historical mission, 88, 89,
    120n13, 211, 213, 216, 219; *see
    also* world-historical
state apparatus, 251–3, 276
strife, 39, 79, 96, 101, 106, 113, 115,
    157, 161, 205, 212, 217
style, 140, 150, 159, 162, 164, 167,
    175, 176–7
subjectivism, 30, 49, 65
suffering, 87, 224, 227, 268

*technē*, 27, 33–4, 37, 45n17, 77, 86–7,
    161, 196
technology, 84–93, 221–2, 225
  age of, 126–7, 239
  forces of, 116
  technological, 241–2
temporality, 39, 40, 49, 63, 92, 195,
    197, 210, 226, 257, 267, 275
thinking
  inceptive, 74, 93
  planetary, 21n29, 126–8
  technological, 12, 84, 87, 93, 105
*A Thousand Symphonies*, 275–9; *see
    also* Fluxus
totalitarianism, 6, 211
Tournier, Michel, 171–4, 175, 227,
    262n25
Trakl, Georg, 109, 111
transversal/transversality, 58, 131, 135,
    139, 153, 159, 174, 252, 272

*Unheimlich/Heimlich*, 76, 165–6,
    174, 192, 206, 214, 239; *see also*
    foreign
universe/s, 115, 125, 165–7, 236, 256
  incorporeal, 257
unknown (*l'inconnu*), 79, 86, 174–5,
    192
  invention of, 223–5, 228, 238, 258
unthought, the, 40, 42, 73–4, 77–9, 84,
    86, 103, 110, 127, 178, 191–2,
    206, 224, 258; *see also* earth

EU representative:
Easy Access System Europe
Mustamäe tee 50, 10621 Tallinn, Estonia
Gpsr.requests@easproject.com

www.ingramcontent.com/pod-product-compliance
Lightning Source LLC
Chambersburg PA
CBHW071711170526
45165CB00005B/1970